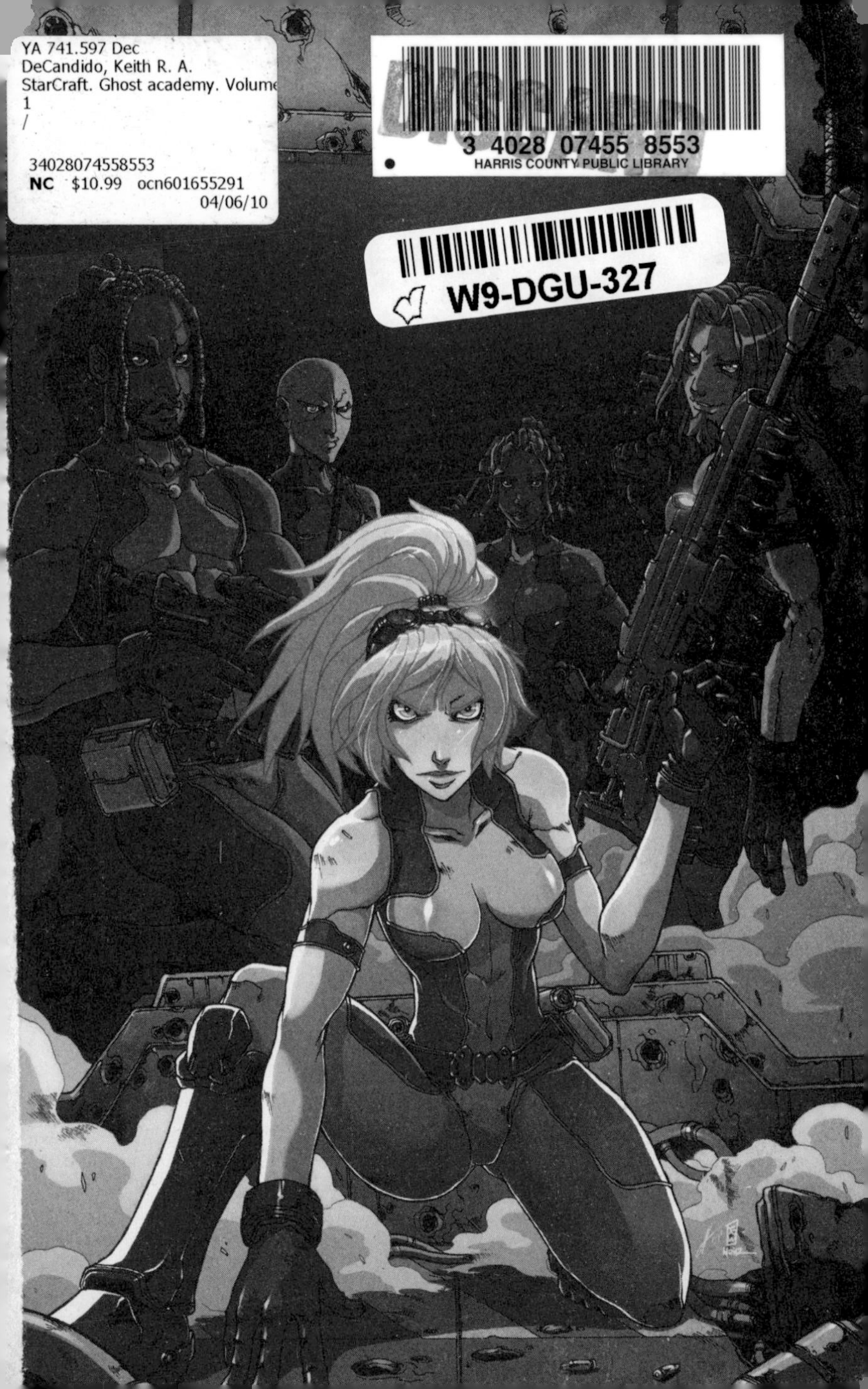

StarCraft: Ghost Academy Vol. 1
Story by: Keith R.A. DeCandido
Art by: Fernando Heinz Furukawa

Contributing Editor - Troy Lewter
Interior Design, Lettering & Retouch Artist - Michael Paolilli
Creative Consultant - Michael Paolilli
Cover Designer - Louis Csontos
Cover Artist - Fernando Heinz Furukawa

Editor - Hope Donovan
Print Production Manager - Lucas Rivera
Managing Editor - Vy Nguyen
Senior Designer - Louis Csontos
Art Director - Al-Insan Lashley
Director of Sales and Manufacturing - Allyson De Simone
Associate Publisher - Marco F. Pavia
President and C.O.O. - John Parker
C.E.O. and Chief Creative Officer - Stu Levy

BLIZZARD ENTERTAINMENT
Senior Vice President, Creative Development - Chris Metzen
Director, Creative Development - Jeff Donais
Lead Developer, Licensed Products - Mike Hummel
Publishing Lead, Creative Development - Rob Tokar
Senior Story Developer - Micky Neilson
Story Developer - James Waugh
Art Director - Glenn Rane
Director, Global Business
Development and Licensing - Cory Jones
Associate Licensing Manager - Jason Bischoff
Historian - Evelyn Fredericksen
Additional Development - Samwise Didier and Tommy Newcomer

A  Manga

TOKYOPOP and ⊙ are trademarks or registered trademarks of TOKYOPOP Inc.

TOKYOPOP Inc.
5900 Wilshire Blvd. Suite 2000
Los Angeles, CA 90036

E-mail: info@TOKYOPOP.com
Come visit us online at www.TOKYOPOP.com

ISBN: 978-1-4278-1612-2

First TOKYOPOP printing: January 2010

10 9 8 7 6 5 4 3 2 1

Printed in the USA

STARCRAFT
GHOST ACADEMY

VOLUME 1

STORY BY:

KEITH R.A. DECANDIDO

ART BY:

FERNANDO HEINZ FURUKAWA

TOKYOPOP

HAMBURG // LONDON // LOS ANGELES // TOKYO

StarCraft
Ghost Academy

CONTENTS

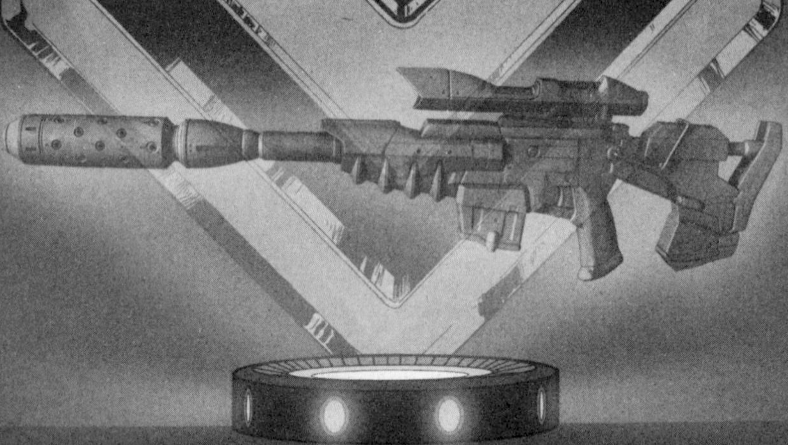

Psi-Ops Division of the Terran Dominion

Based on your son/daughter's exceptionally high test scores and aptitude with standardized psi-evaluations, he or she has been chosen to take part in specially sanctioned government trials to identify and develop their latent psionic potential. It is the duty of all similarly gifted Dominion citizens to apply their gifts for the betterment of mankind.

Thus we are proud to inform you that he/she has been selected as a candidate for our Dominion Ghost Program. They are ordered to report to their nearest Dominion military installation for processing and transfer to their new home away from home, at our newly re-designed Ghost Academy.

I can only imagine the pride you must feel knowing your son/daughter will become one of the top defenders of the Dominion.

Sincerely,

Arcturus Mengsk

Non-compliance with this letter will result in penalties, and Dominion officers will be dispatched to accompany your dependent to the Ghost Academy. This is for their own safety and the safety of all those around them, until they have been taught to control their incredible gifts.

UNN

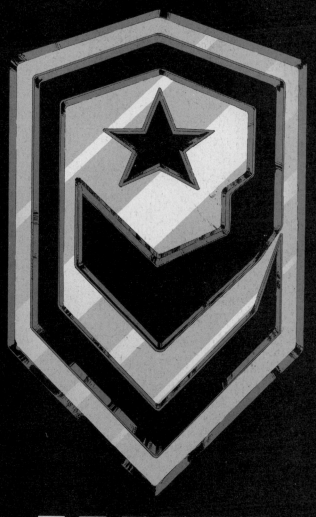

WE HAVE TO STOP THIS *INSANITY* BEFORE MORE CHILDREN LIKE MY SON COLIN ARE TAKEN AWAY!
THE GHOST ACADEMY *MUST* BE SHUT DOWN!
I HAVE NOTHING BUT RESPECT FOR EMPEROR MENGSK AND FOR THE DOMINION.
BUT TO TAKE OUR CHILDREN AWAY AND PUT THEM IN SOME SECRET INSTITUTION TO EXPERIMENT ON THEM?
THAT'S THE SORT OF THING THE *CONFEDERACY* WOULD HAVE DONE.
I URGE YOU ALL TO CONTACT YOUR SENATORS AND TELL THEM THAT YOU WANT THE GHOST ACADEMY TO *CLOSE ITS DOORS!*

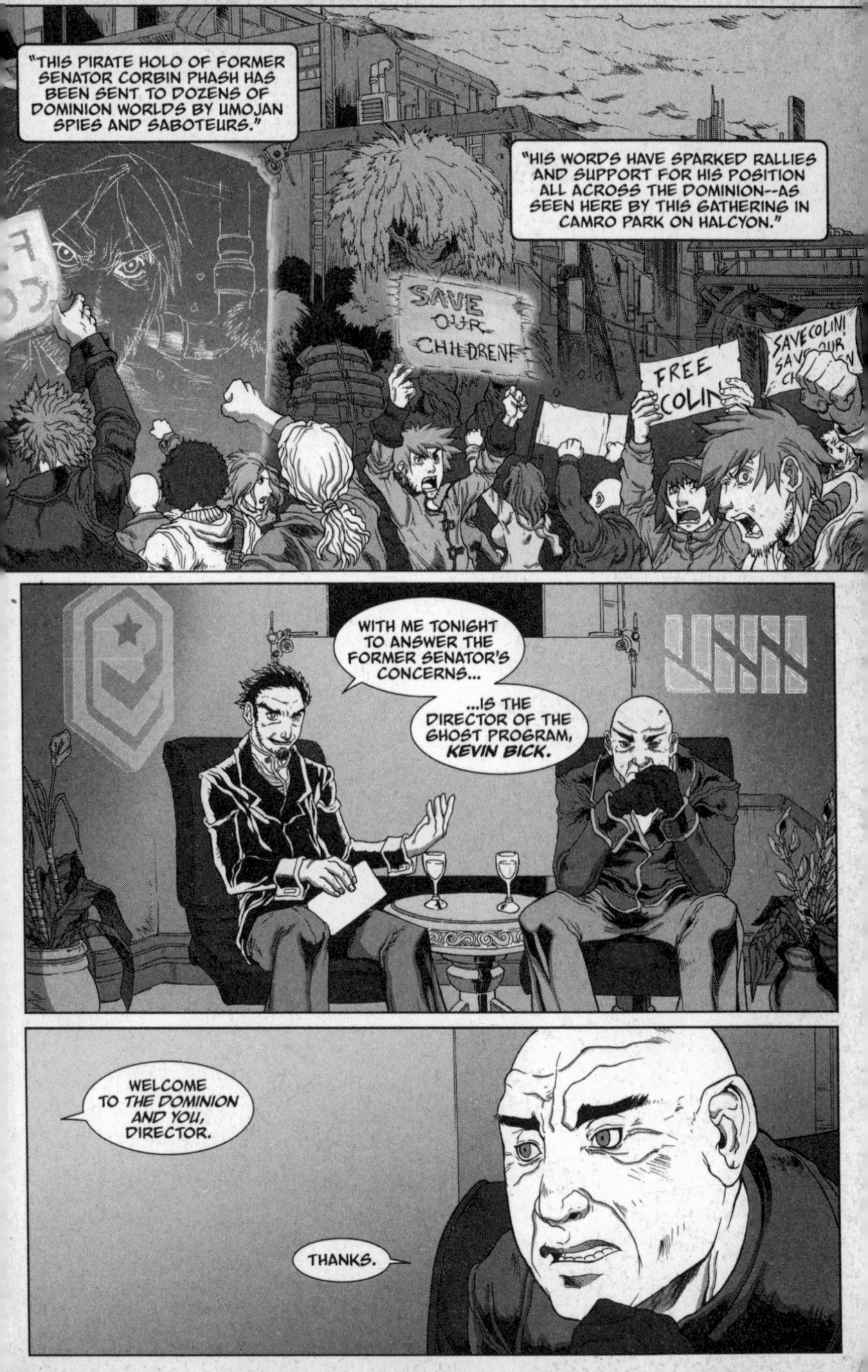
"THIS PIRATE HOLO OF FORMER SENATOR CORBIN PHASH HAS BEEN SENT TO DOZENS OF DOMINION WORLDS BY UMOJAN SPIES AND SABOTEURS."
"HIS WORDS HAVE SPARKED RALLIES AND SUPPORT FOR HIS POSITION ALL ACROSS THE DOMINION--AS SEEN HERE BY THIS GATHERING IN CAMRO PARK ON HALCYON."
SAVE OUR CHILDREN!
FREE COLIN
SAVE COLIN!
WITH ME TONIGHT TO ANSWER THE FORMER SENATOR'S CONCERNS...
...IS THE DIRECTOR OF THE GHOST PROGRAM, *KEVIN BICK.*
WELCOME TO *THE DOMINION AND YOU,* DIRECTOR.
THANKS.

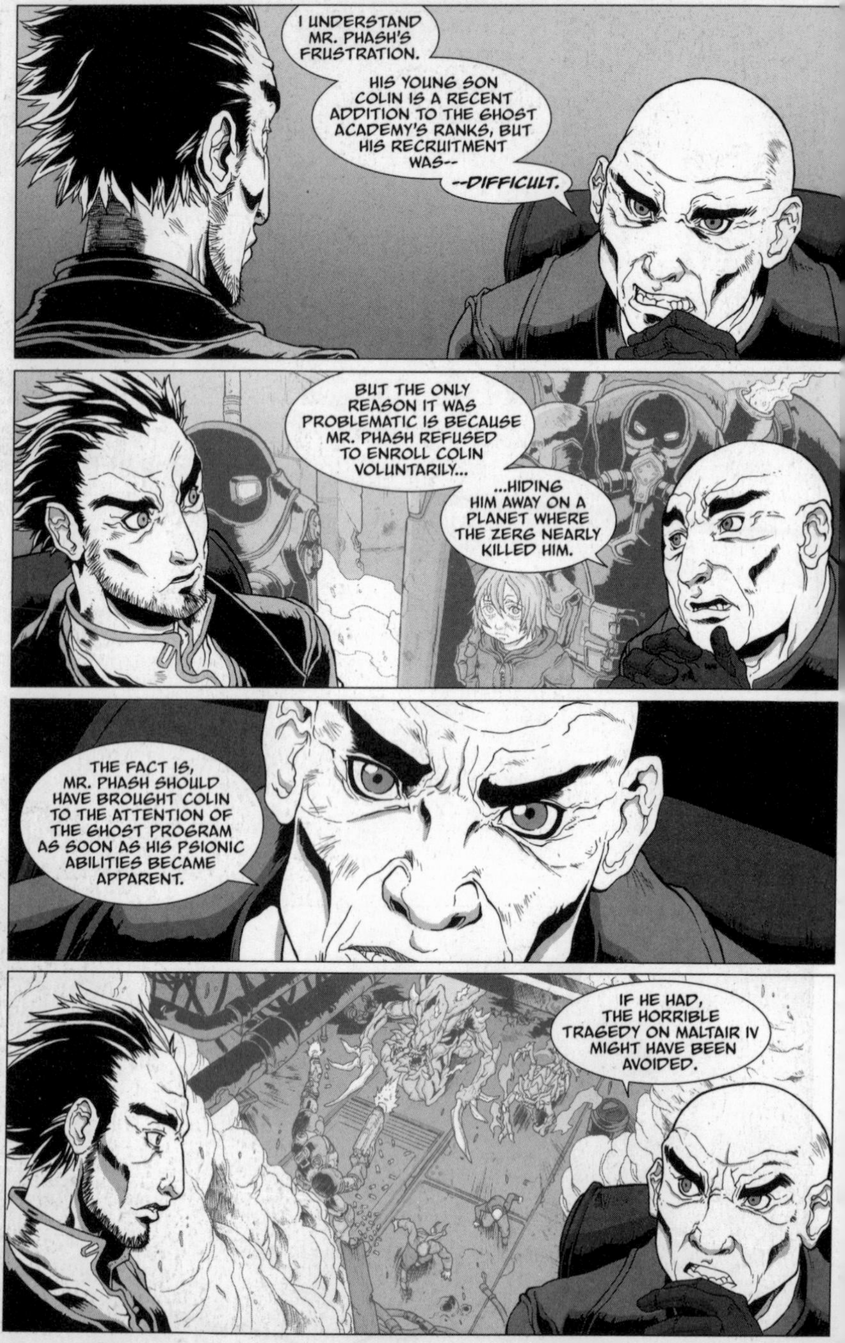
I UNDERSTAND MR. PHASH'S FRUSTRATION.
HIS YOUNG SON COLIN IS A RECENT ADDITION TO THE GHOST ACADEMY'S RANKS, BUT HIS RECRUITMENT WAS--
--DIFFICULT.
BUT THE ONLY REASON IT WAS PROBLEMATIC IS BECAUSE MR. PHASH REFUSED TO ENROLL COLIN VOLUNTARILY...
...HIDING HIM AWAY ON A PLANET WHERE THE ZERG NEARLY KILLED HIM.
THE FACT IS, MR. PHASH SHOULD HAVE BROUGHT COLIN TO THE ATTENTION OF THE GHOST PROGRAM AS SOON AS HIS PSIONIC ABILITIES BECAME APPARENT.
IF HE HAD, THE HORRIBLE TRAGEDY ON MALTAIR IV MIGHT HAVE BEEN AVOIDED.

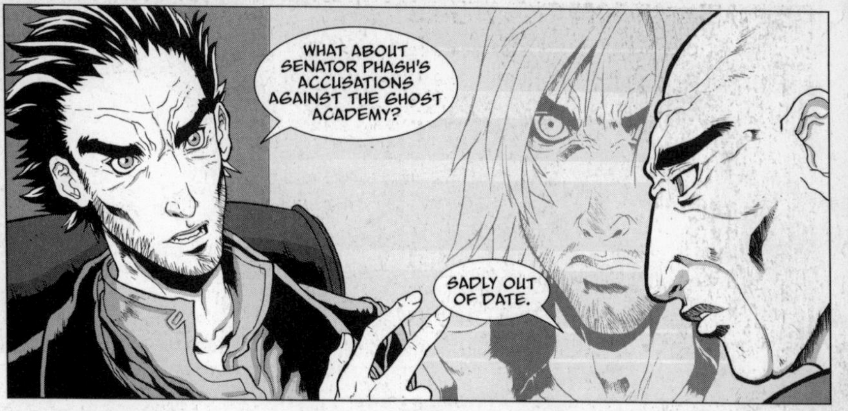
WHAT ABOUT SENATOR PHASH'S ACCUSATIONS AGAINST THE GHOST ACADEMY?
SADLY OUT OF DATE.

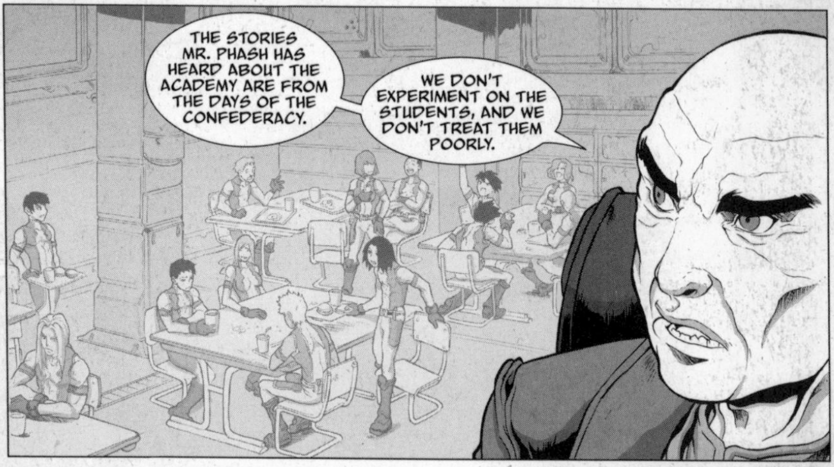
THE STORIES MR. PHASH HAS HEARD ABOUT THE ACADEMY ARE FROM THE DAYS OF THE CONFEDERACY.
WE DON'T EXPERIMENT ON THE STUDENTS, AND WE DON'T TREAT THEM POORLY.

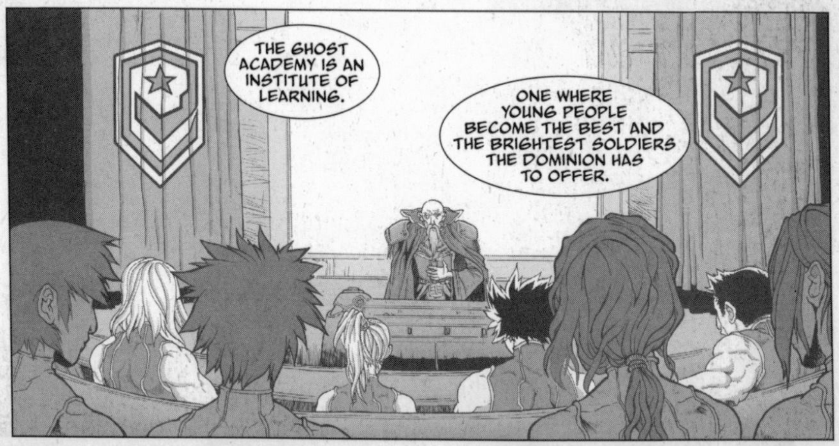
THE GHOST ACADEMY IS AN INSTITUTE OF LEARNING.
ONE WHERE YOUNG PEOPLE BECOME THE BEST AND THE BRIGHTEST SOLDIERS THE DOMINION HAS TO OFFER.

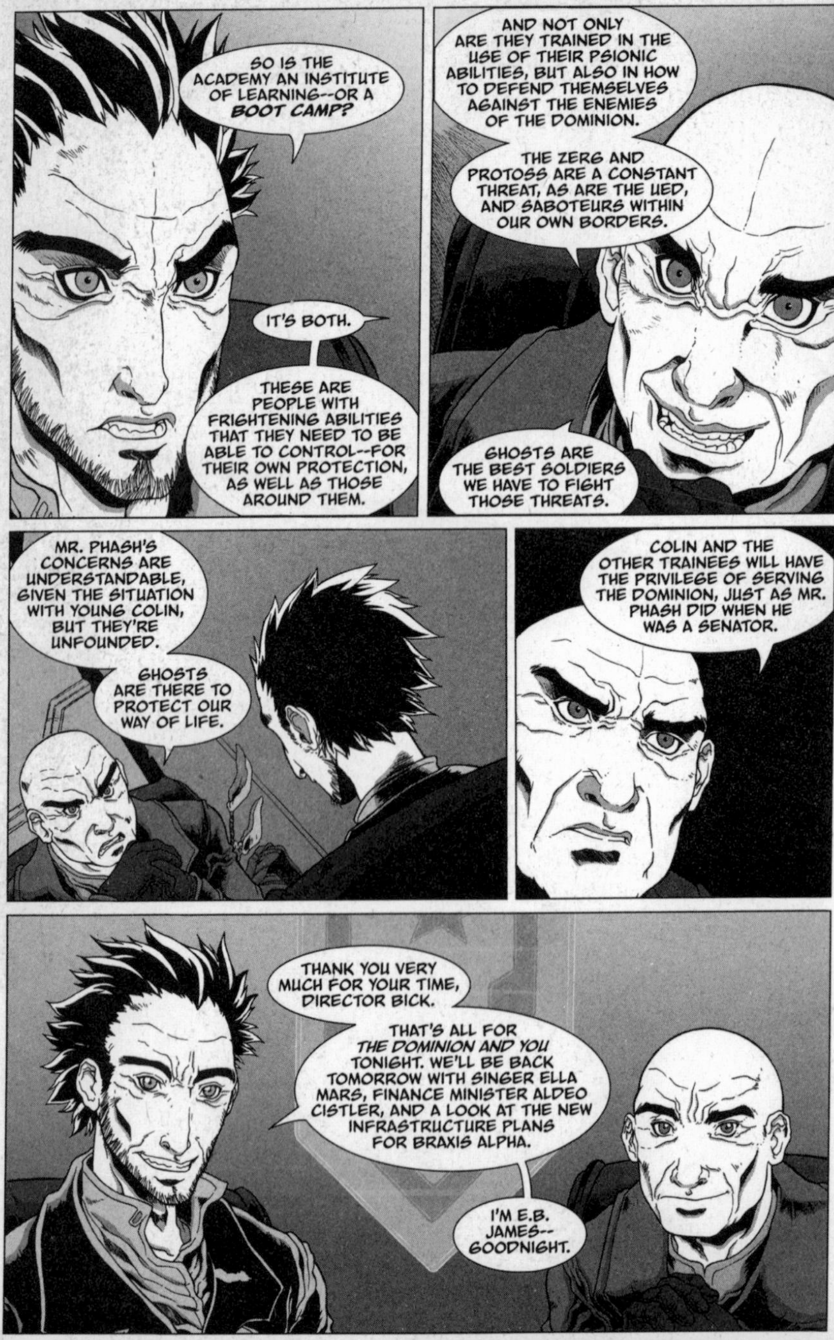
SO IS THE ACADEMY AN INSTITUTE OF LEARNING--OR A *BOOT CAMP?*
IT'S BOTH.
THESE ARE PEOPLE WITH FRIGHTENING ABILITIES THAT THEY NEED TO BE ABLE TO CONTROL--FOR THEIR OWN PROTECTION, AS WELL AS THOSE AROUND THEM.
AND NOT ONLY ARE THEY TRAINED IN THE USE OF THEIR PSIONIC ABILITIES, BUT ALSO IN HOW TO DEFEND THEMSELVES AGAINST THE ENEMIES OF THE DOMINION.
THE ZERG AND PROTOSS ARE A CONSTANT THREAT, AS ARE THE UED, AND SABOTEURS WITHIN OUR OWN BORDERS.
GHOSTS ARE THE BEST SOLDIERS WE HAVE TO FIGHT THOSE THREATS.
MR. PHASH'S CONCERNS ARE UNDERSTANDABLE, GIVEN THE SITUATION WITH YOUNG COLIN, BUT THEY'RE UNFOUNDED.
GHOSTS ARE THERE TO PROTECT OUR WAY OF LIFE.
COLIN AND THE OTHER TRAINEES WILL HAVE THE PRIVILEGE OF SERVING THE DOMINION, JUST AS MR. PHASH DID WHEN HE WAS A SENATOR.
THANK YOU VERY MUCH FOR YOUR TIME, DIRECTOR BICK.
THAT'S ALL FOR *THE DOMINION AND YOU* TONIGHT. WE'LL BE BACK TOMORROW WITH SINGER ELLA MARS, FINANCE MINISTER ALDEO CISTLER, AND A LOOK AT THE NEW INFRASTRUCTURE PLANS FOR BRAXIS ALPHA.
I'M E.B. JAMES--GOODNIGHT.

CHAPTER 1
IT'S ALL OVER NOW, TEAM BLUE

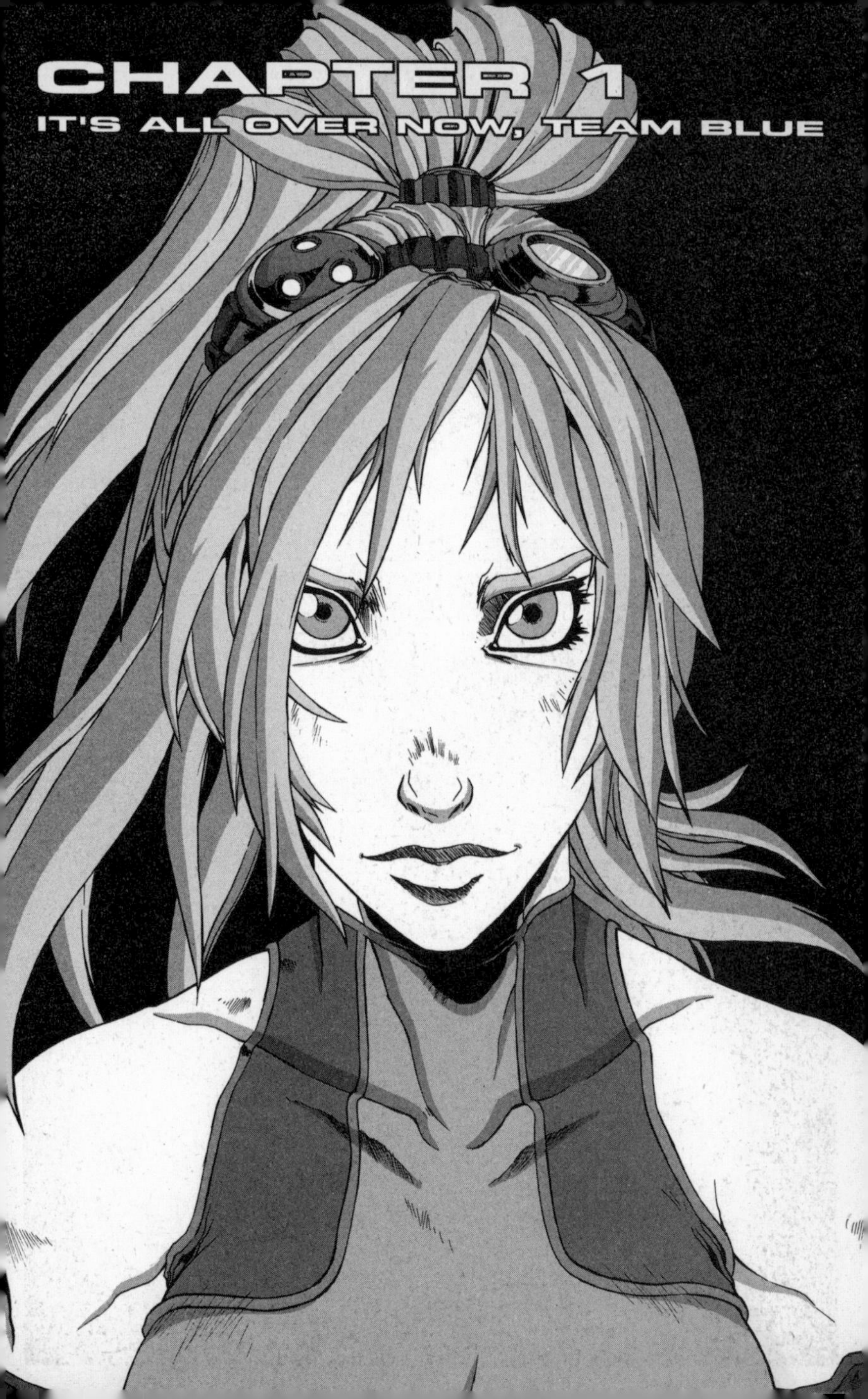

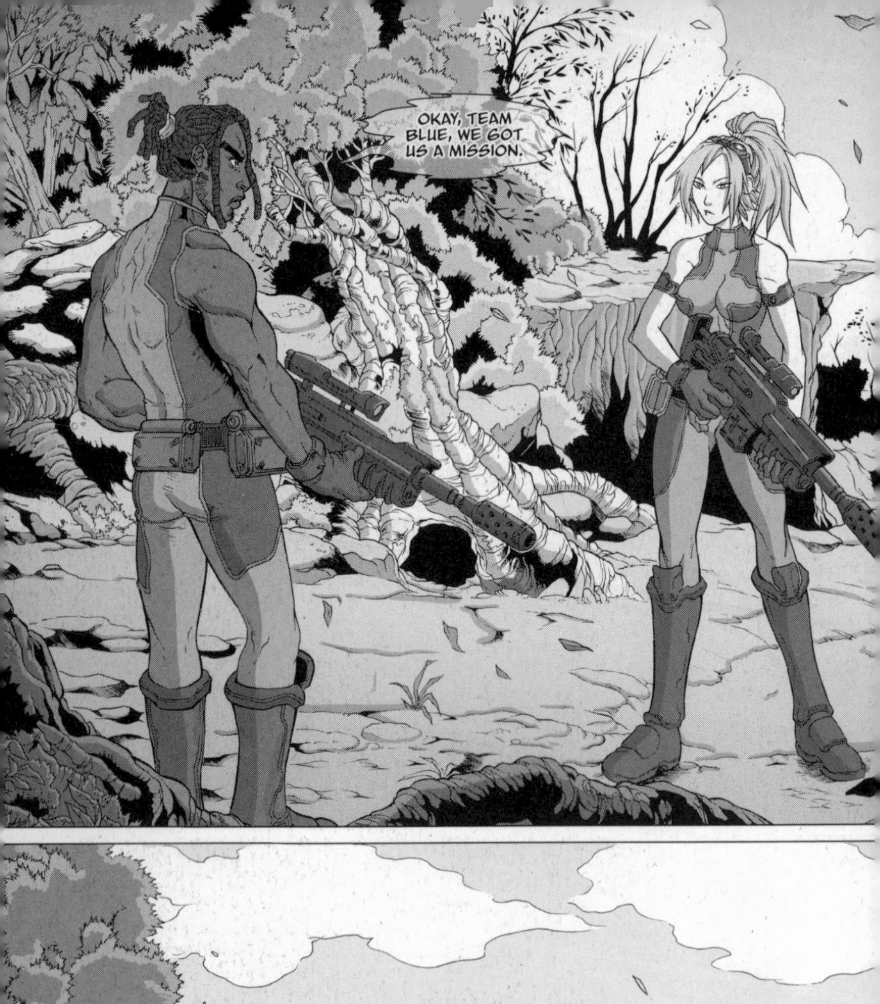
OKAY, TEAM BLUE, WE GOT US A MISSION.

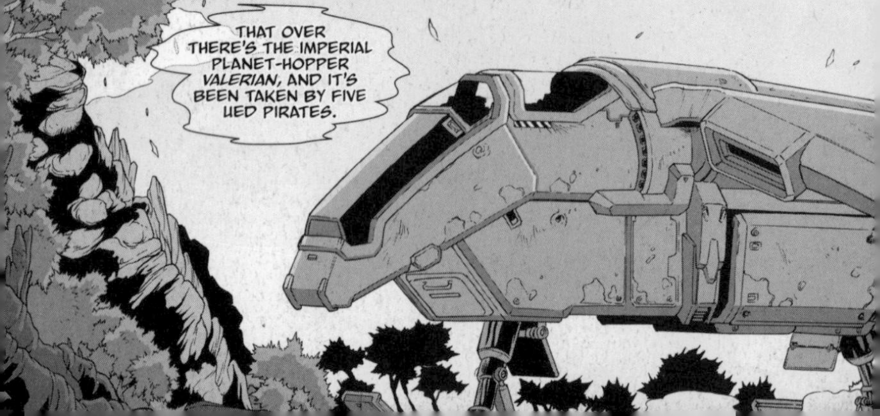
THAT OVER THERE'S THE IMPERIAL PLANET-HOPPER *VALERIAN*, AND IT'S BEEN TAKEN BY FIVE UED PIRATES.

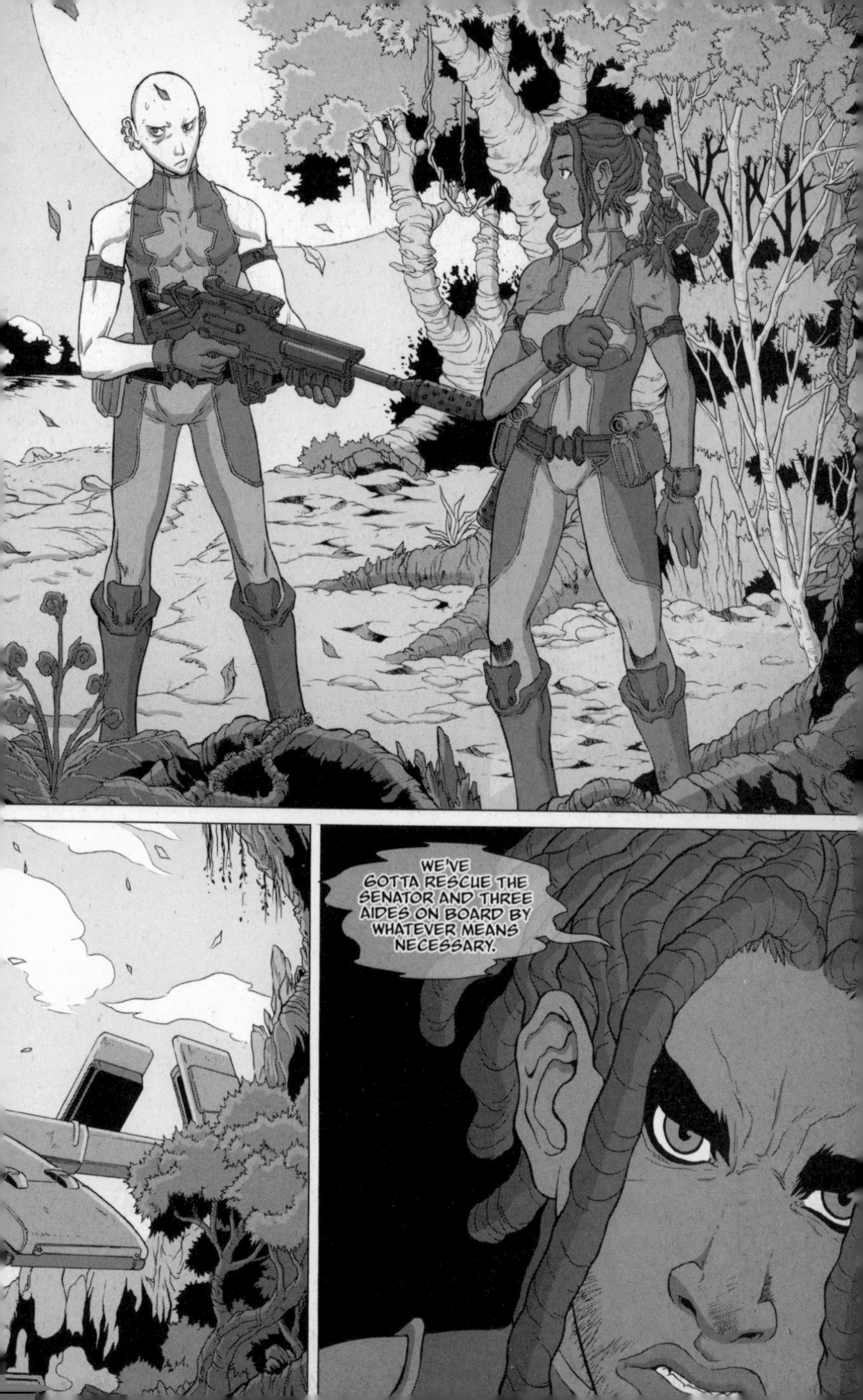
WE'VE GOTTA RESCUE THE SENATOR AND THREE AIDES ON BOARD BY WHATEVER MEANS NECESSARY.

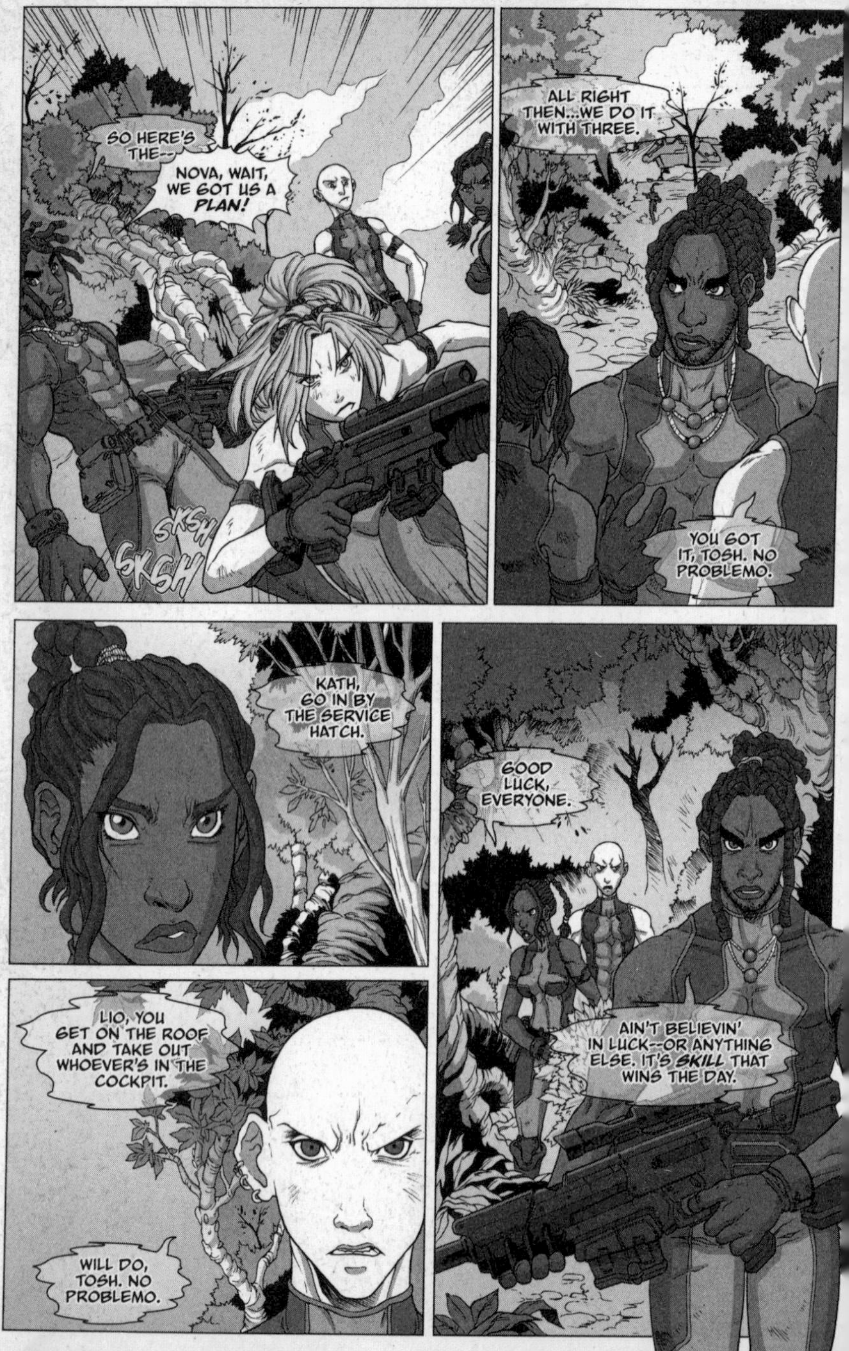
SO HERE'S THE--
NOVA, WAIT, WE GOT US A *PLAN!*
SKSH SKSH
ALL RIGHT THEN...WE DO IT WITH THREE.
YOU GOT IT, TOSH. NO PROBLEMO.
KATH, GO IN BY THE SERVICE HATCH.
LIO, YOU GET ON THE ROOF AND TAKE OUT WHOEVER'S IN THE COCKPIT.
WILL DO, TOSH. NO PROBLEMO.
GOOD LUCK, EVERYONE.
AIN'T BELIEVIN' IN LUCK--OR ANYTHING ELSE. IT'S *SKILL* THAT WINS THE DAY.

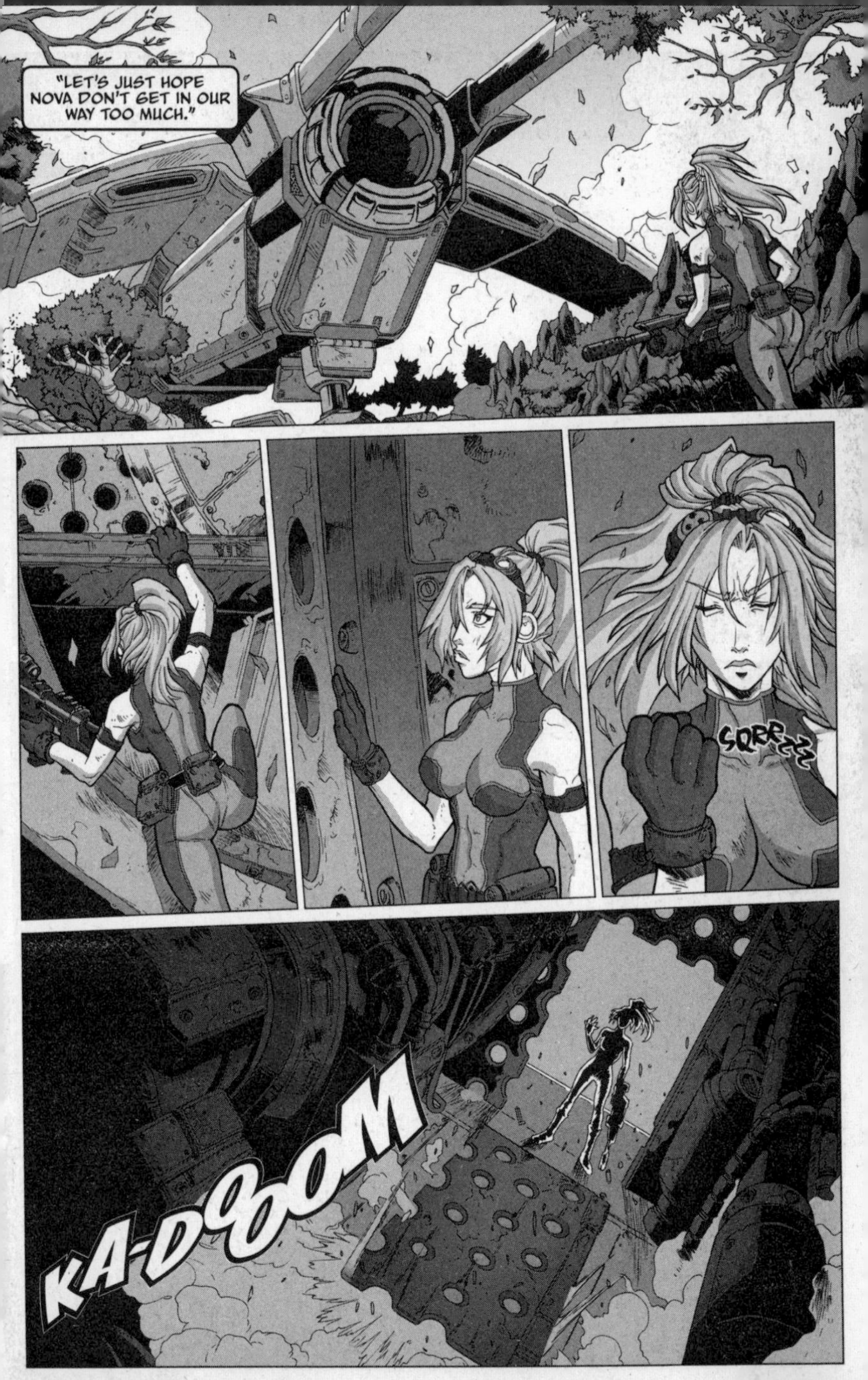
"LET'S JUST HOPE NOVA DON'T GET IN OUR WAY TOO MUCH."
SQRRZZZ
KA-DOOOOM

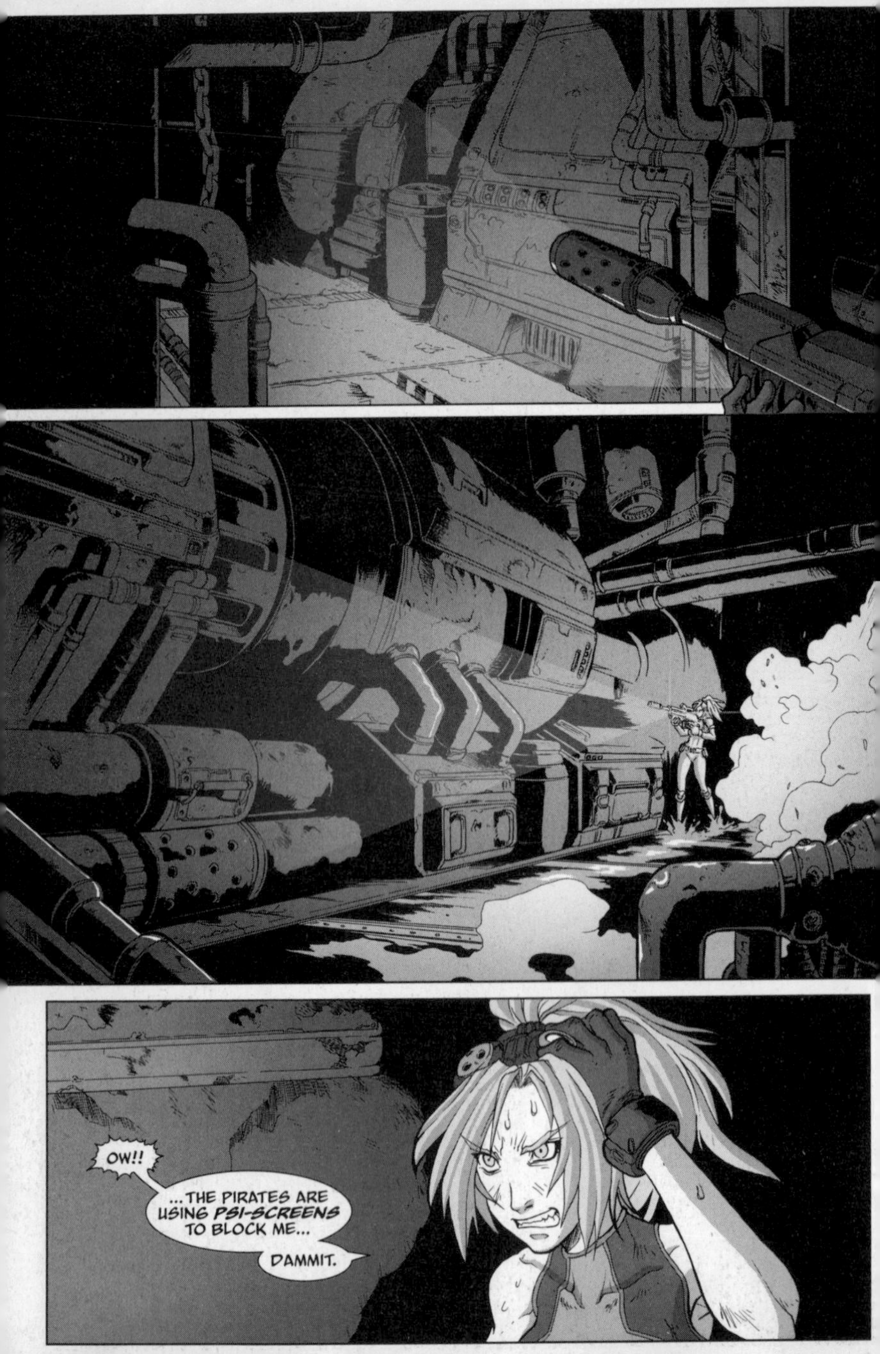
OW!!
...THE PIRATES ARE USING PSI-SCREENS TO BLOCK ME...
DAMMIT.

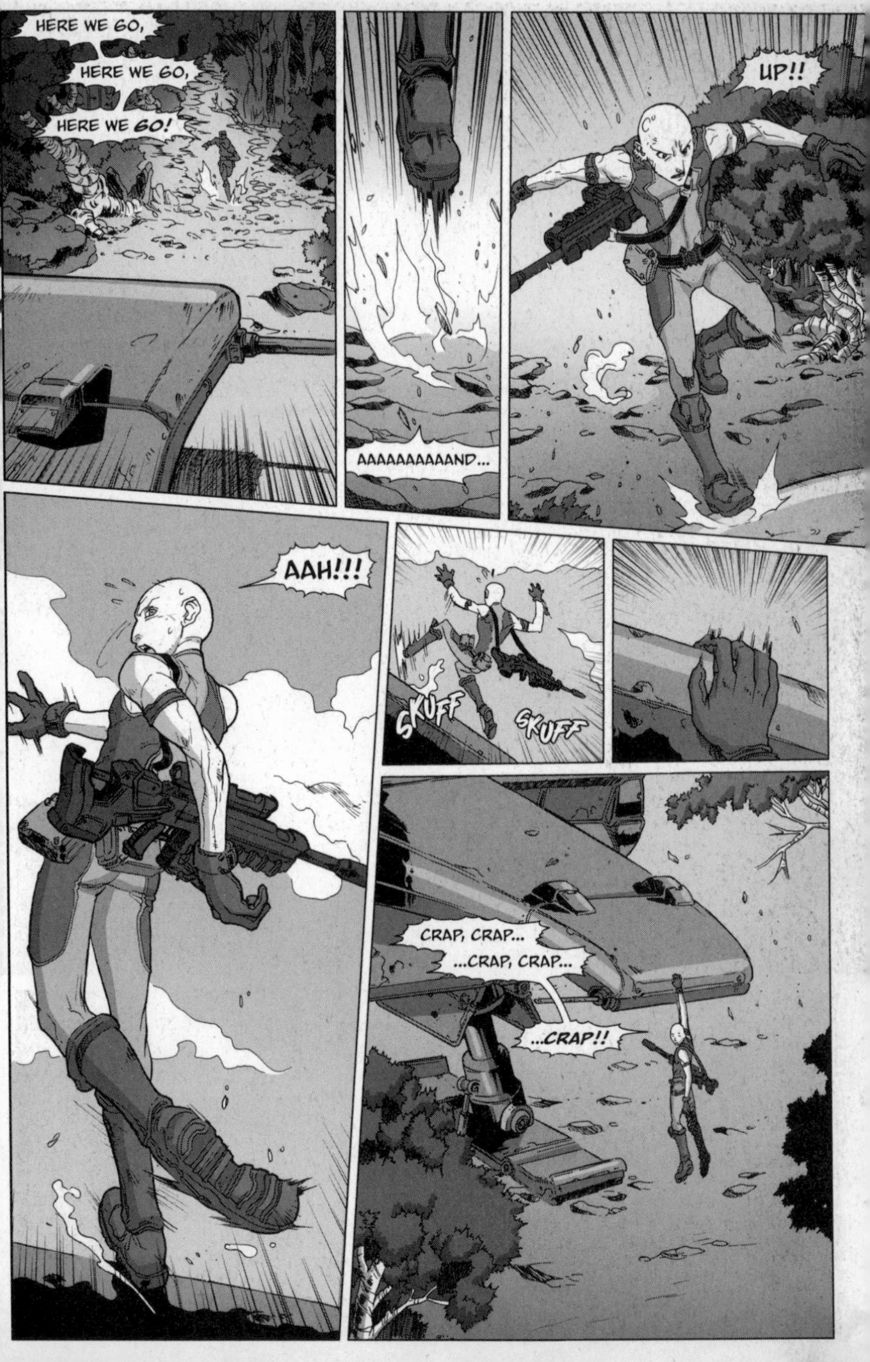
HERE WE GO,
HERE WE GO,
HERE WE GO!
AAAAAAAAAAND...
UP!!
AAH!!!
SKUFF
SKUFF
CRAP, CRAP...
...CRAP, CRAP...
...CRAP!!

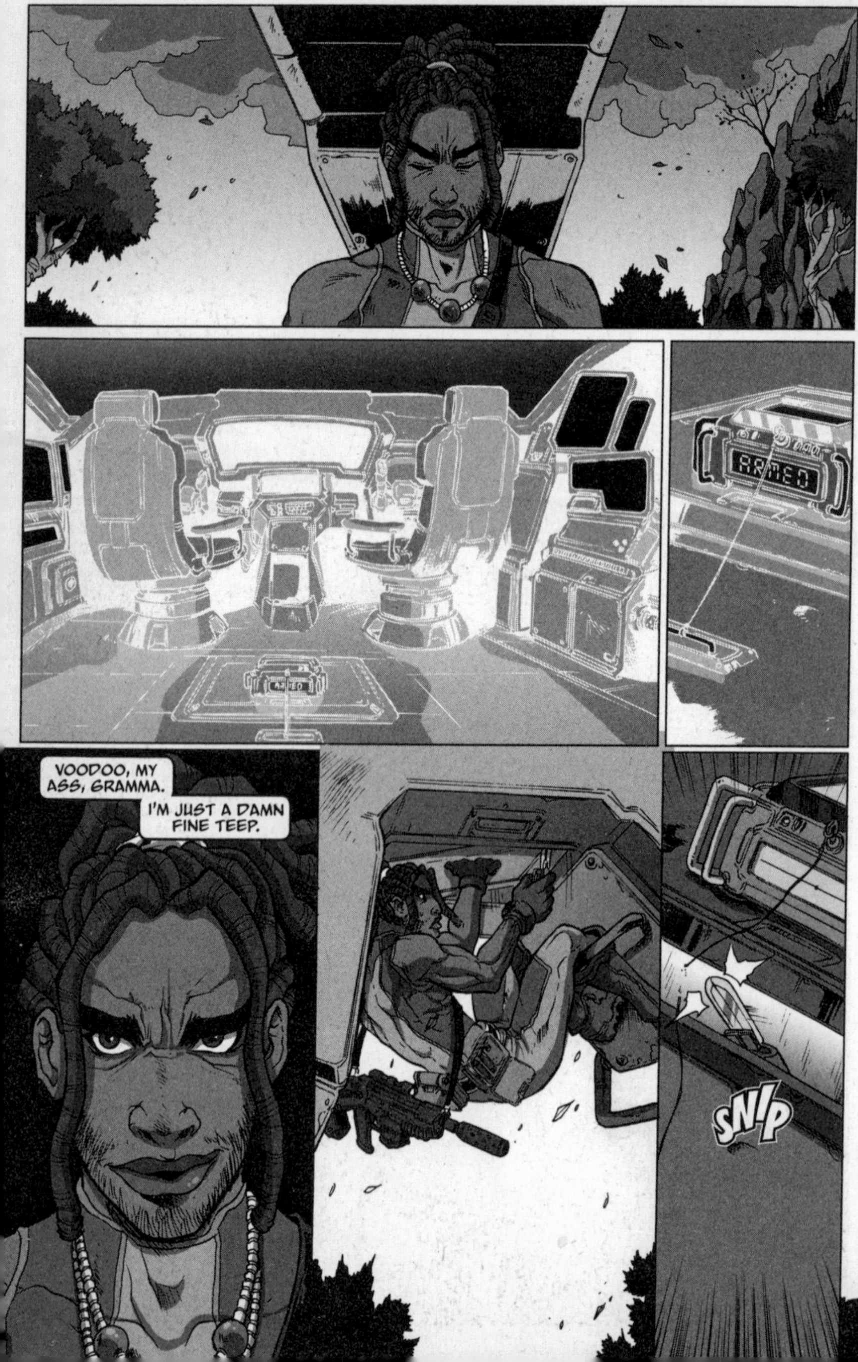
ARMED
ARMED
VOODOO, MY ASS, GRAMMA.
I'M JUST A DAMN FINE TEEP.
SNIP

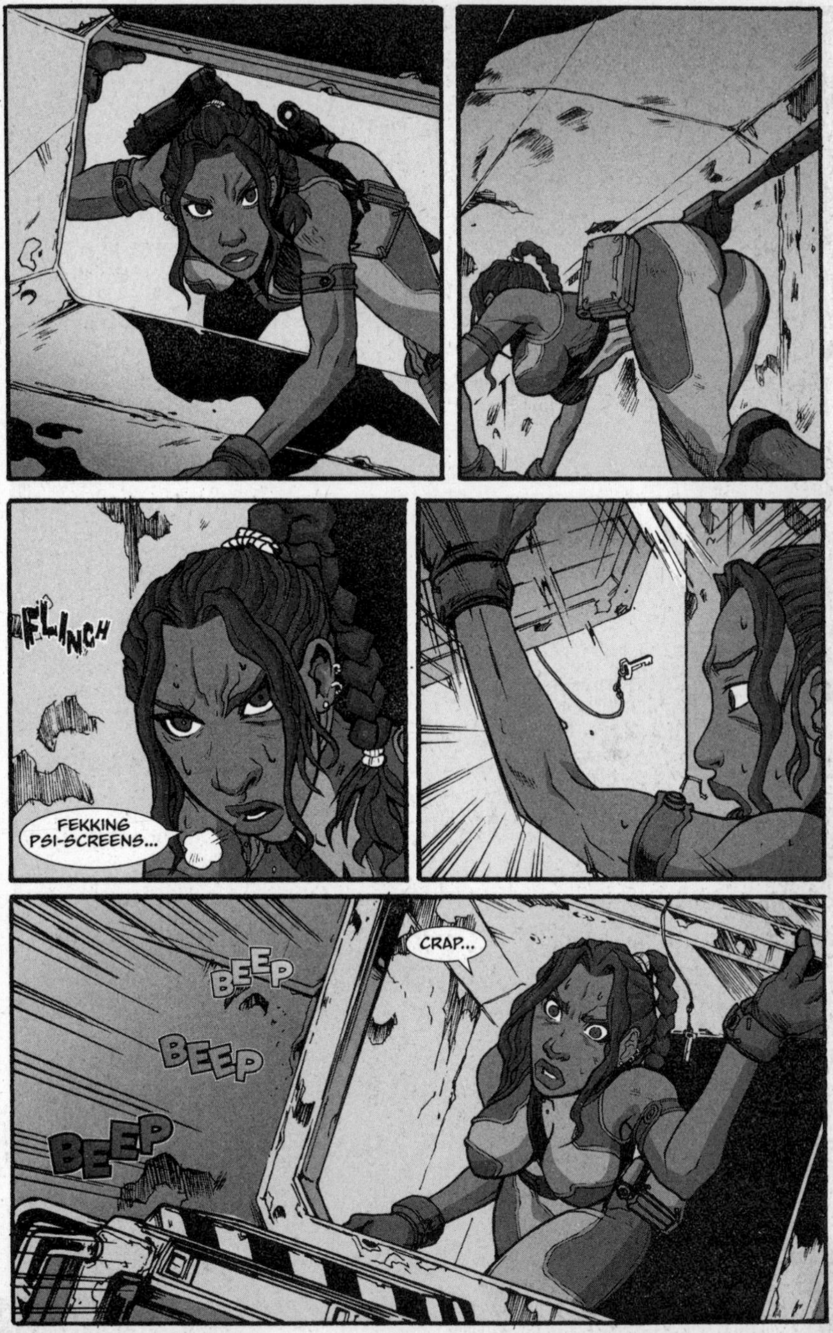
FLINCH
FEKKING PSI-SCREENS...
CRAP...
BEEP
BEEP
BEEP

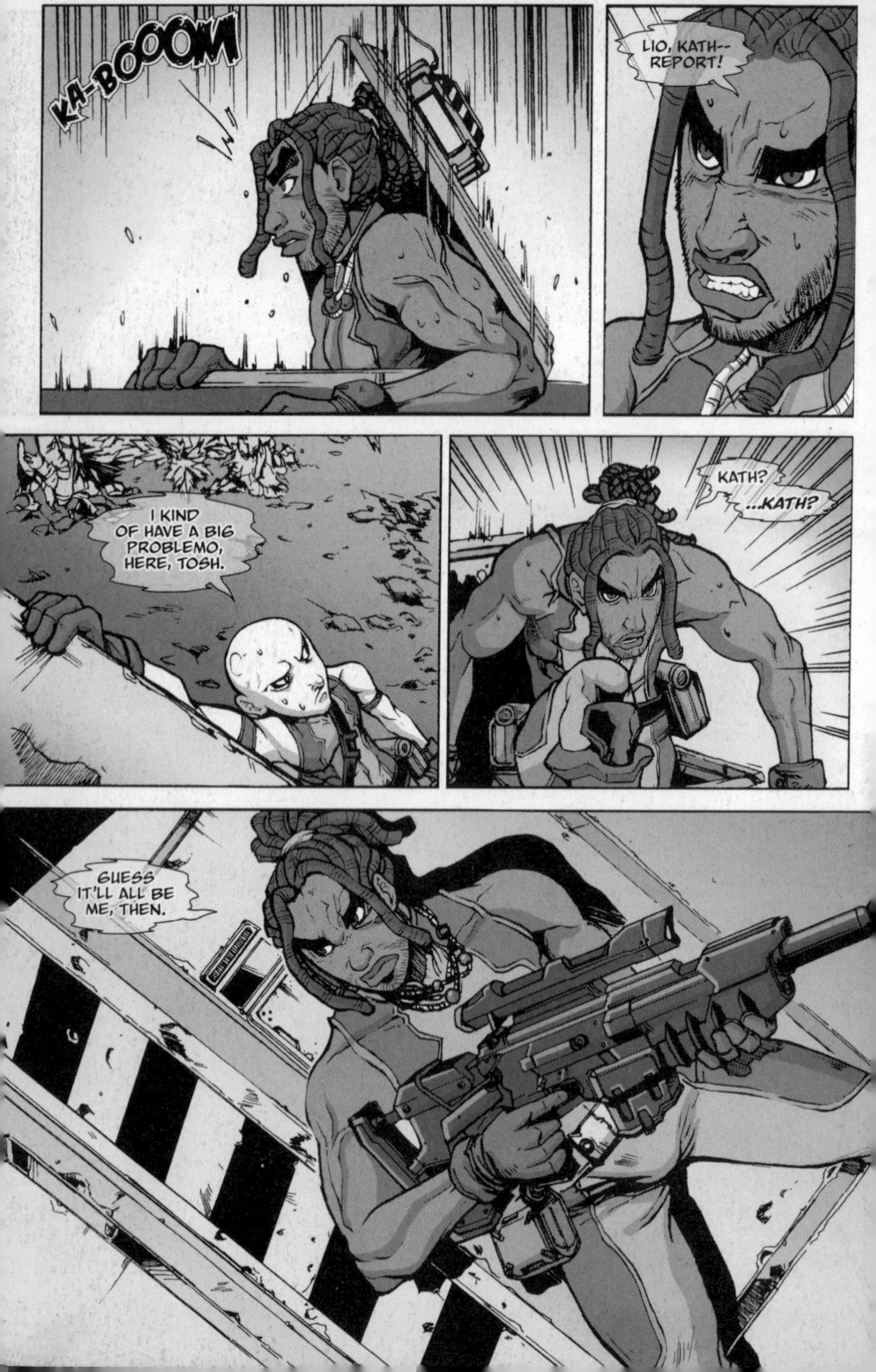
KA-BOOOM
LIO, KATH-- REPORT!
I KIND OF HAVE A BIG PROBLEMO, HERE, TOSH.
KATH?
...KATH?
GUESS IT'LL ALL BE ME, THEN.

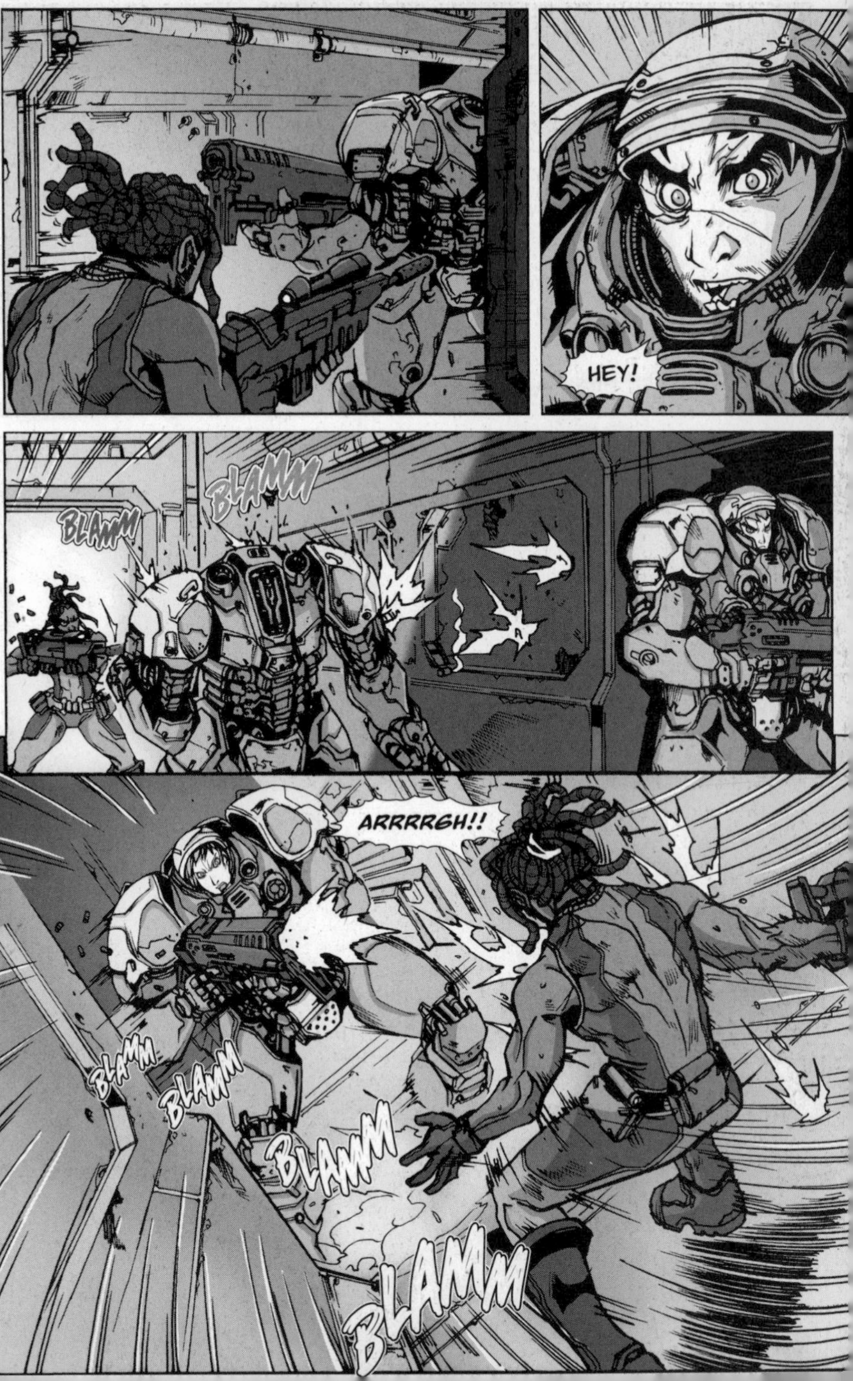
HEY!
BLAMM
BLAMM
ARRRRGH!!
BLAMM
BLAMM
BLAMM
BLAMM

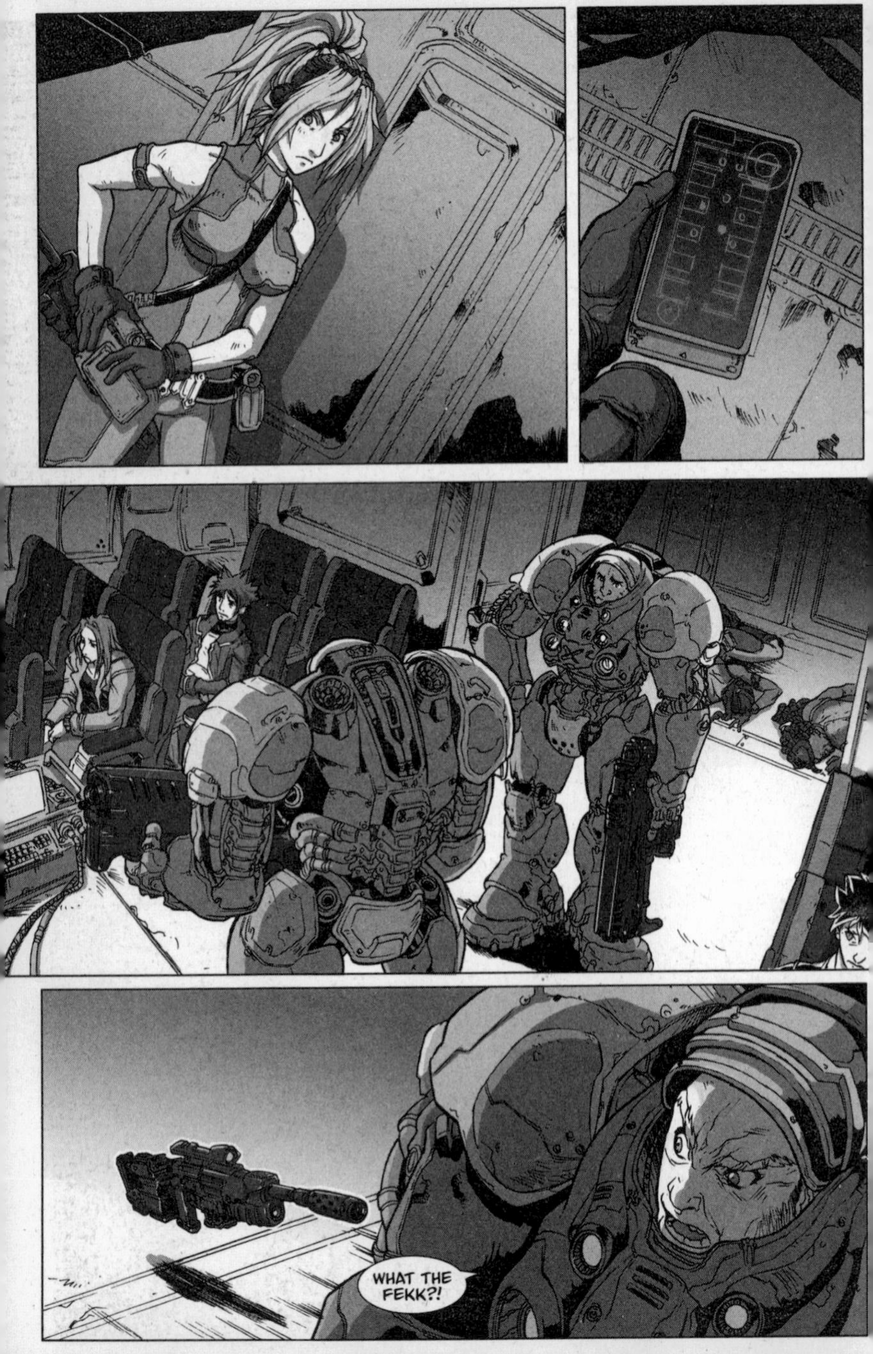
WHAT THE FEKK?!

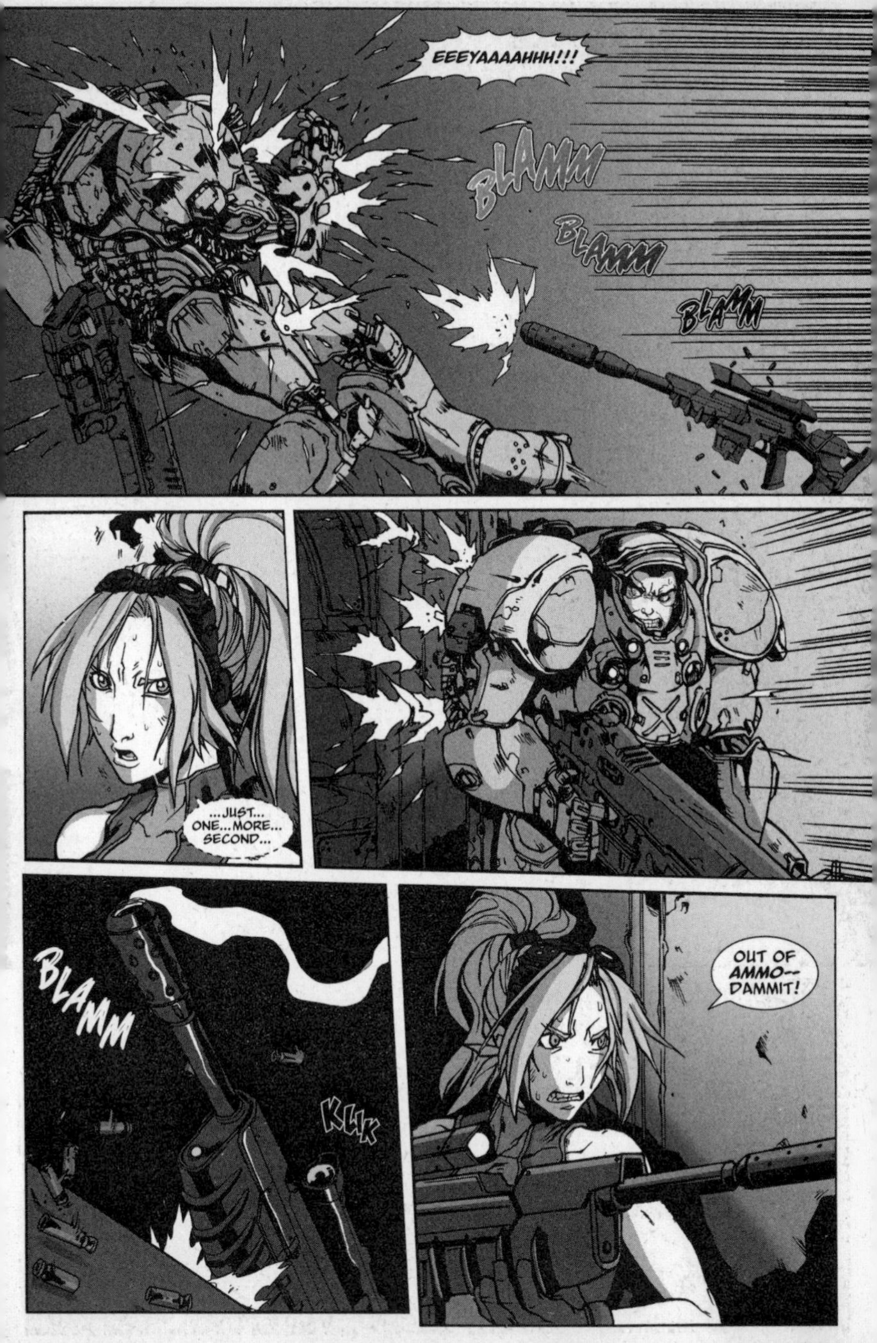
EEEYAAAAHHH!!!
BLAMM
BLAMM
BLAMM
...JUST... ONE...MORE... SECOND...
BLAMM
KLIK
OUT OF AMMO-- DAMMIT!

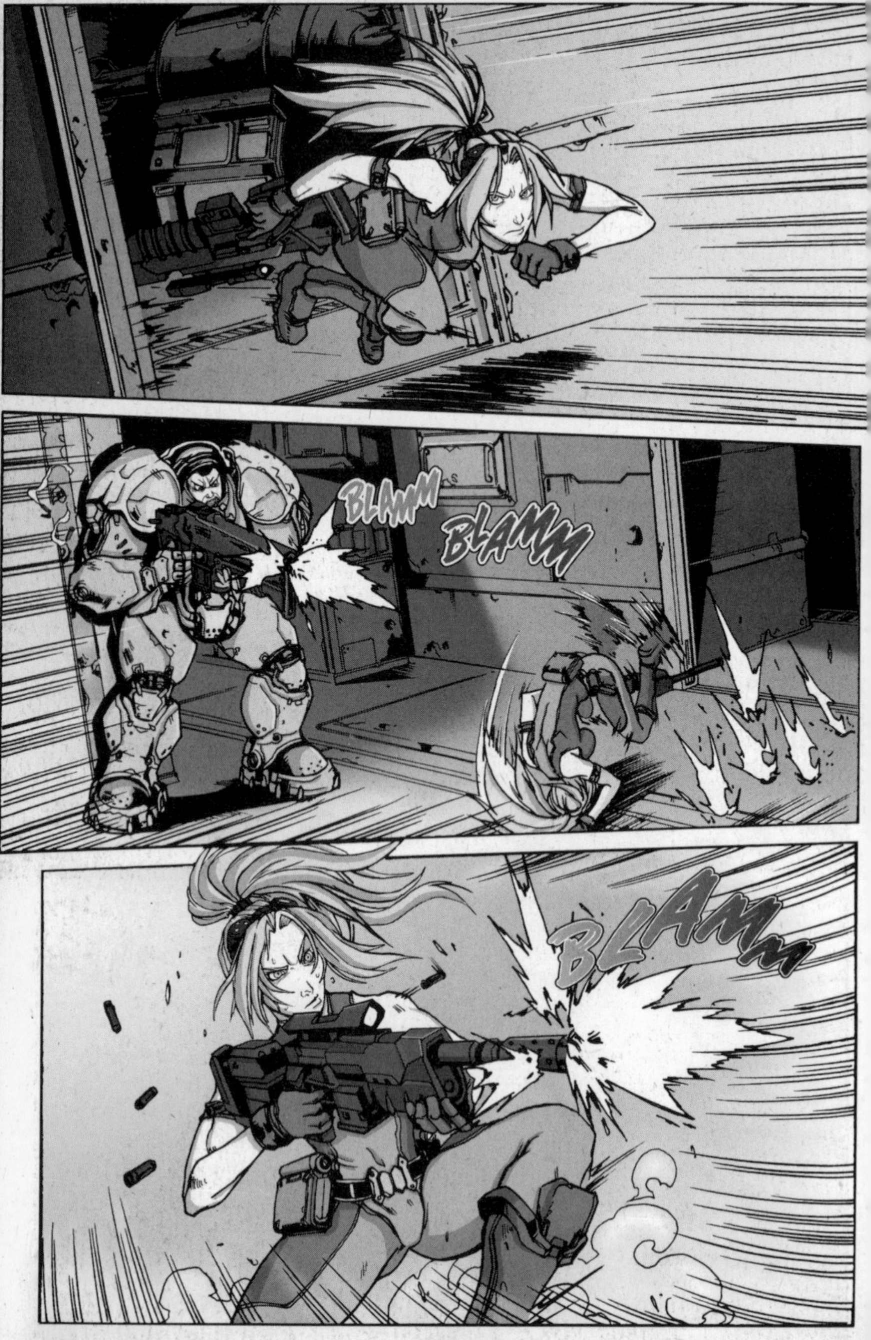
BLAMM
BLAMM
BLAMM

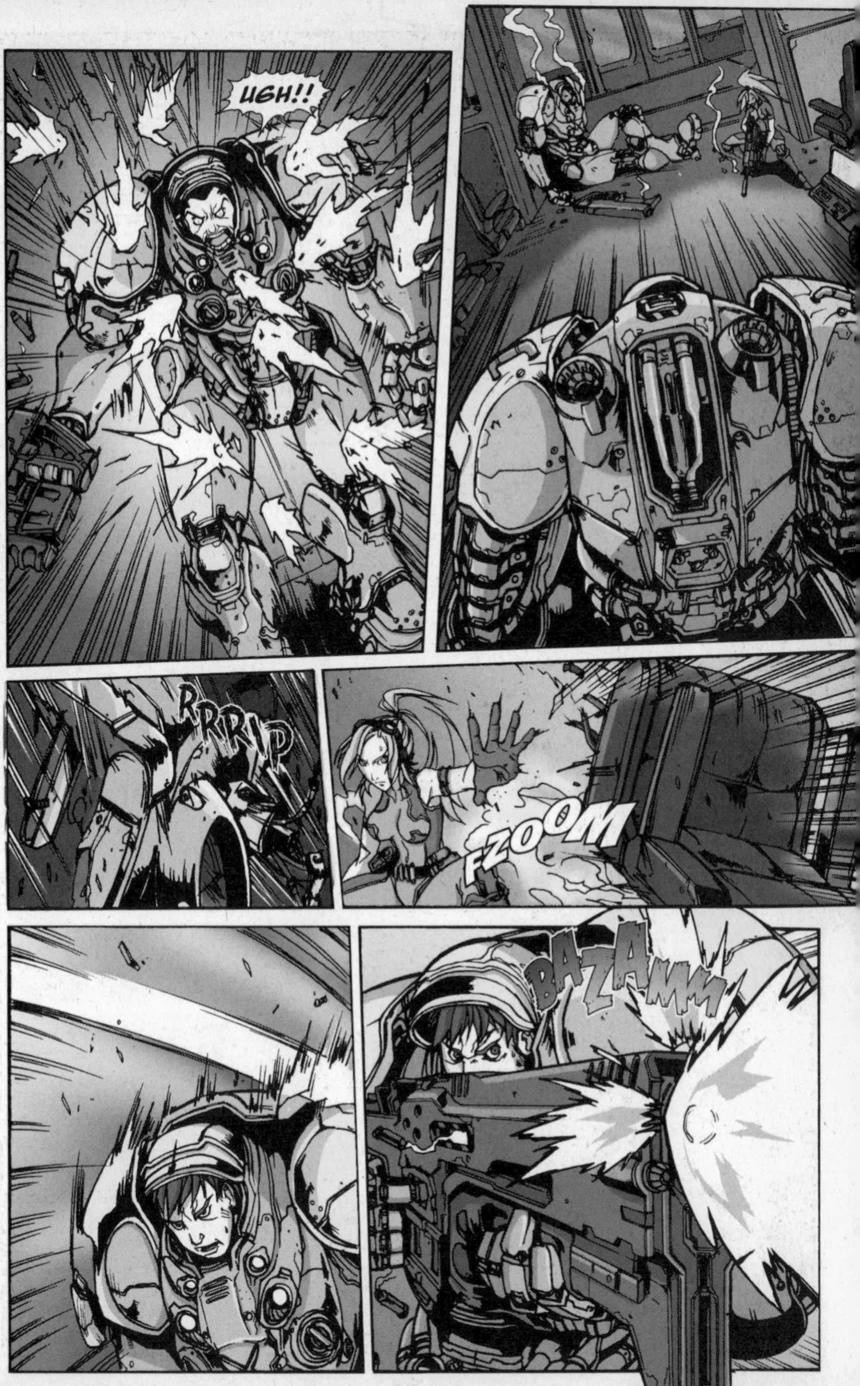
UGH!!
RRRIP
FZOOM
BAZAMM

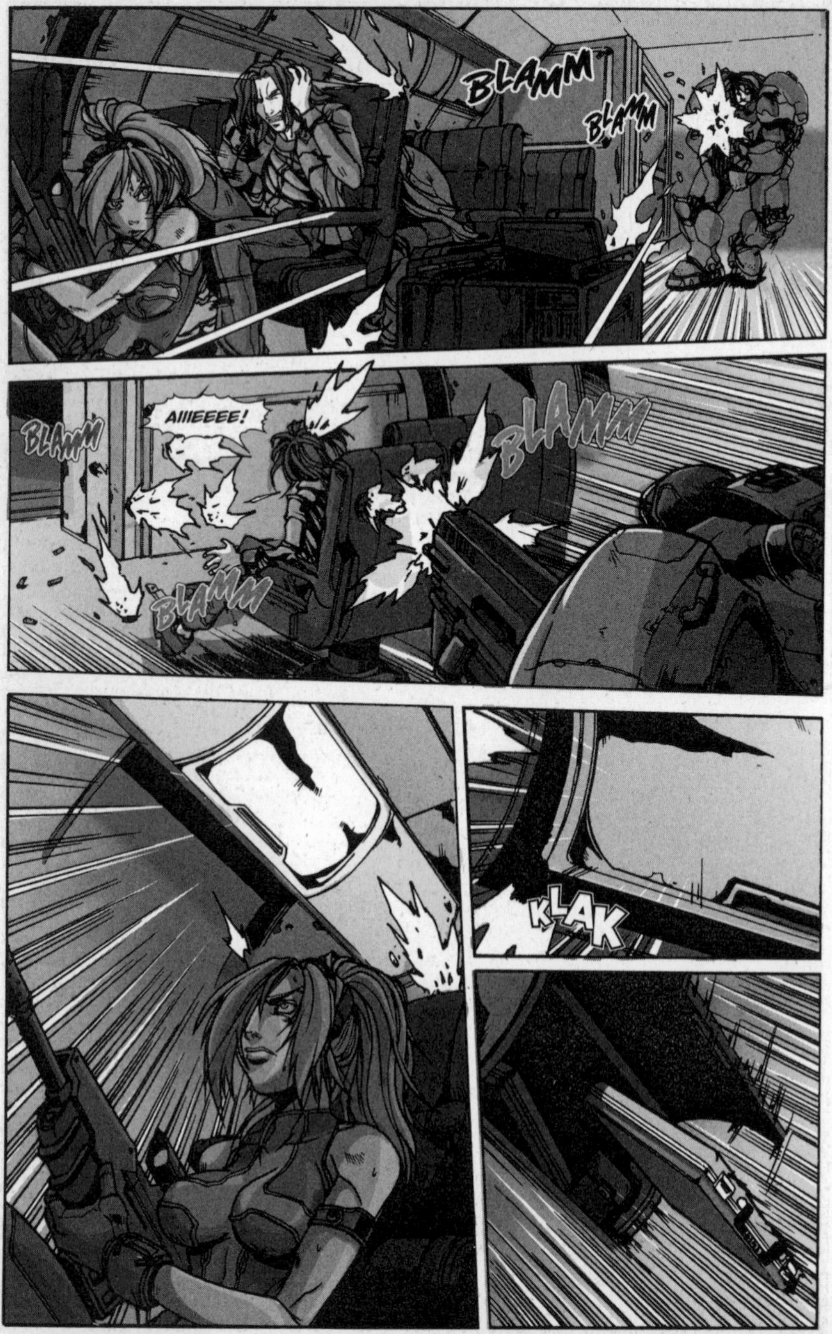
BLAMM
BLAMM
BLAMM
AIIIEEEE!
BLAMM
BLAMM
KLAK

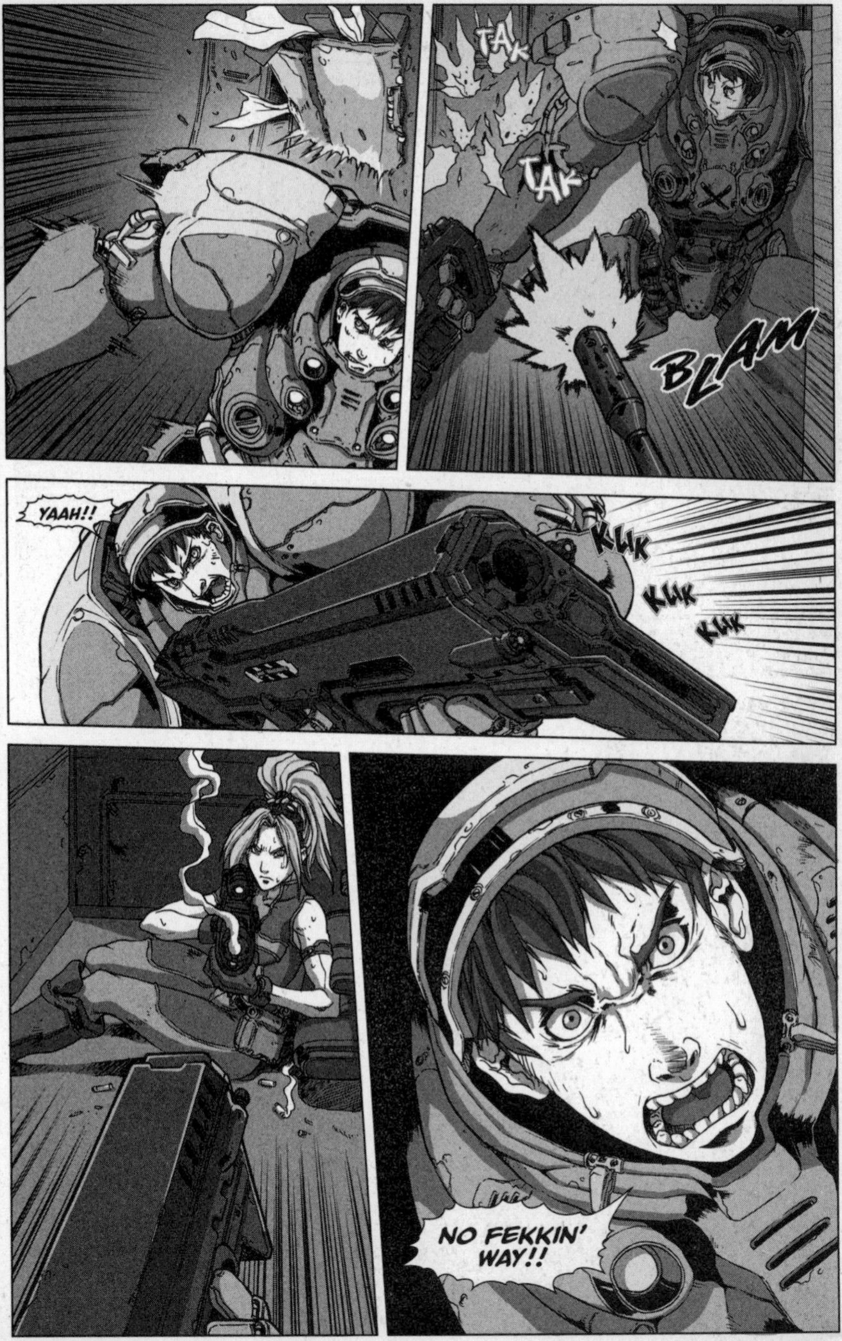
TAK
TAK
BLAM
YAAH!!
KLIK
KLIK
KLIK
NO FEKKIN' WAY!!

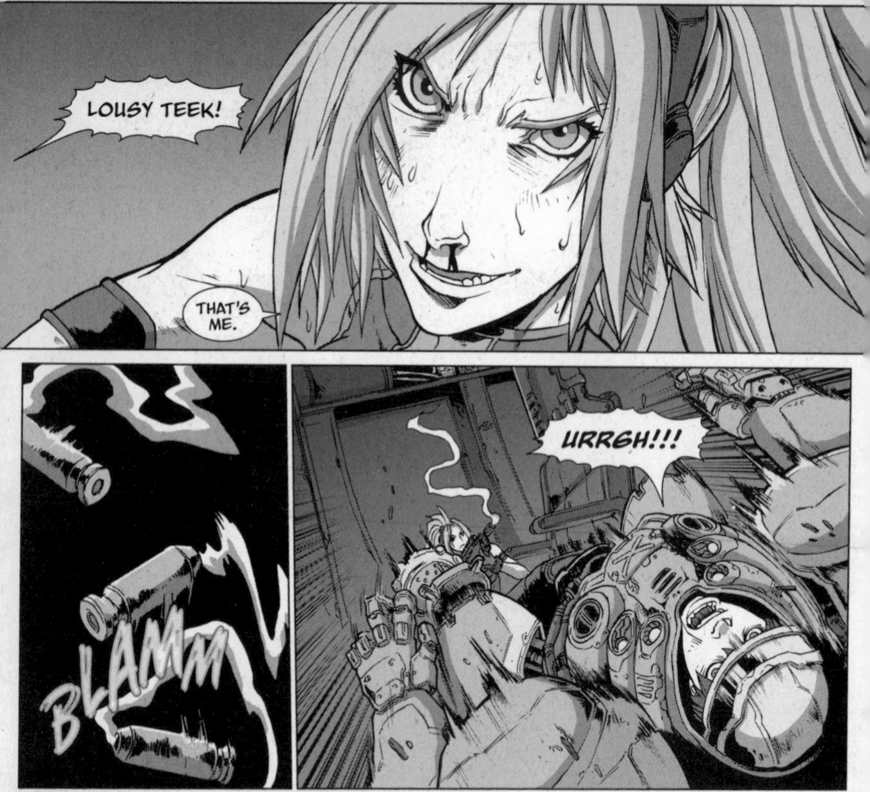
LOUSY TEEK!
THAT'S ME.
BLAMM
URRGH!!!

Teek: slang for telekinetic

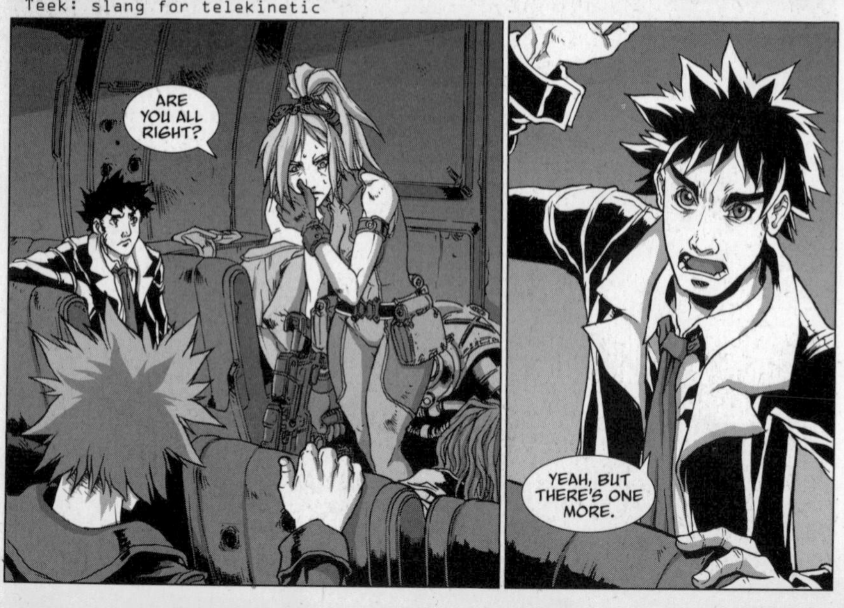
ARE YOU ALL RIGHT?
YEAH, BUT THERE'S ONE MORE.

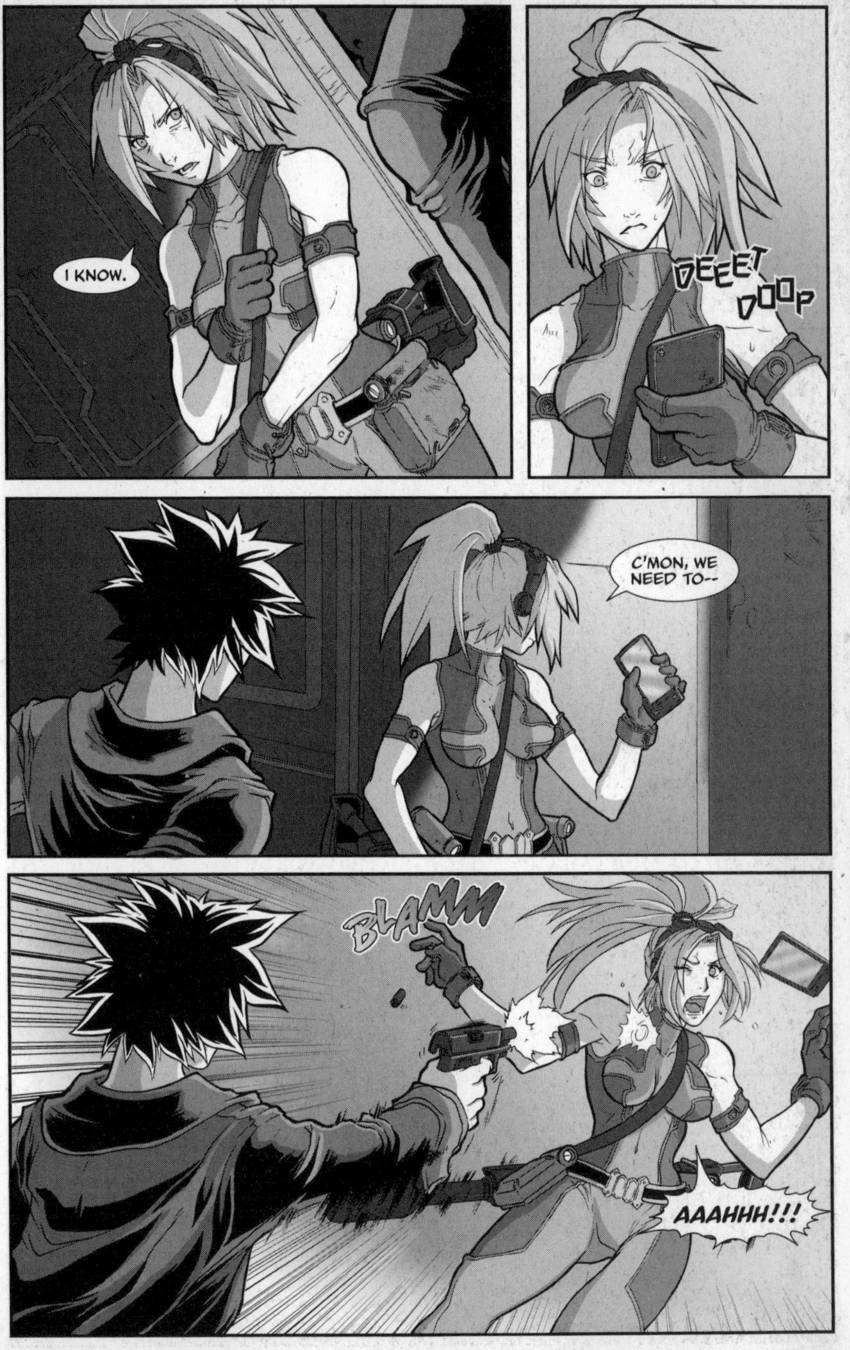
I KNOW.
DEEEET DOOP
C'MON, WE NEED TO--
BLAMM
AAAHHH!!!

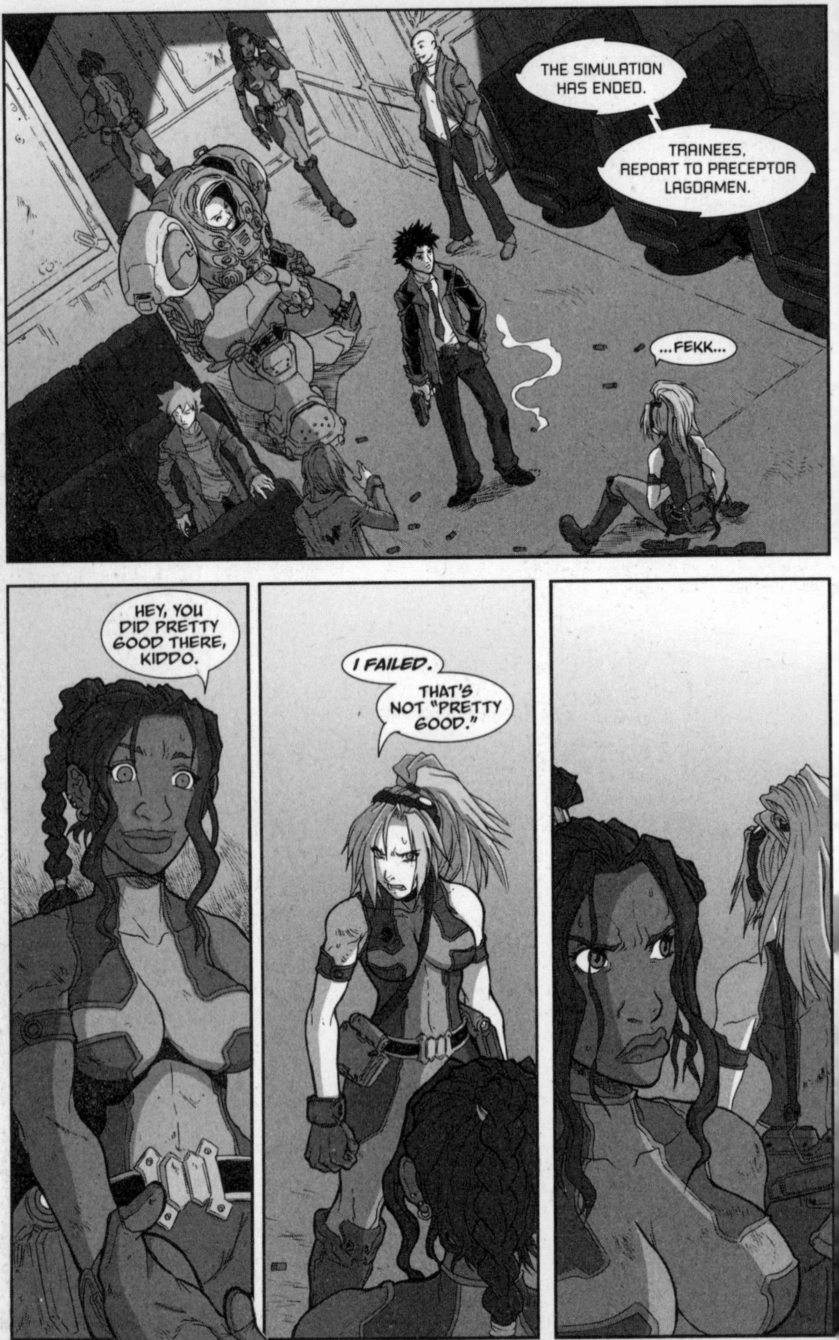

THE SIMULATION HAS ENDED.
TRAINEES, REPORT TO PRECEPTOR LAGDAMEN.
...FEKK...
HEY, YOU DID PRETTY GOOD THERE, KIDDO.
I FAILED.
THAT'S NOT "PRETTY GOOD."

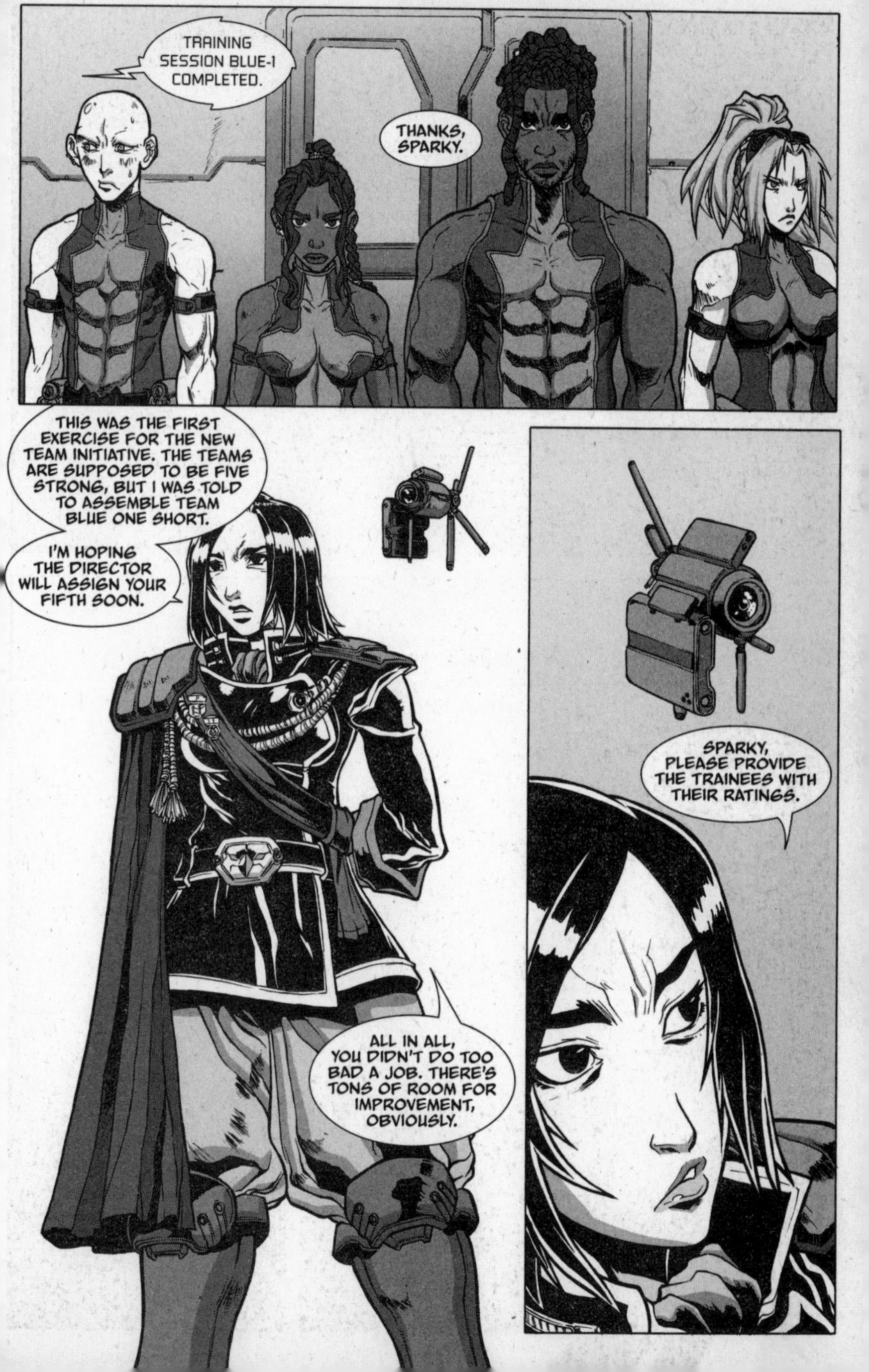
TRAINING SESSION BLUE-1 COMPLETED.
THANKS, SPARKY.
THIS WAS THE FIRST EXERCISE FOR THE NEW TEAM INITIATIVE. THE TEAMS ARE SUPPOSED TO BE FIVE STRONG, BUT I WAS TOLD TO ASSEMBLE TEAM BLUE ONE SHORT.
I'M HOPING THE DIRECTOR WILL ASSIGN YOUR FIFTH SOON.
ALL IN ALL, YOU DIDN'T DO TOO BAD A JOB. THERE'S TONS OF ROOM FOR IMPROVEMENT, OBVIOUSLY.
SPARKY, PLEASE PROVIDE THE TRAINEES WITH THEIR RATINGS.

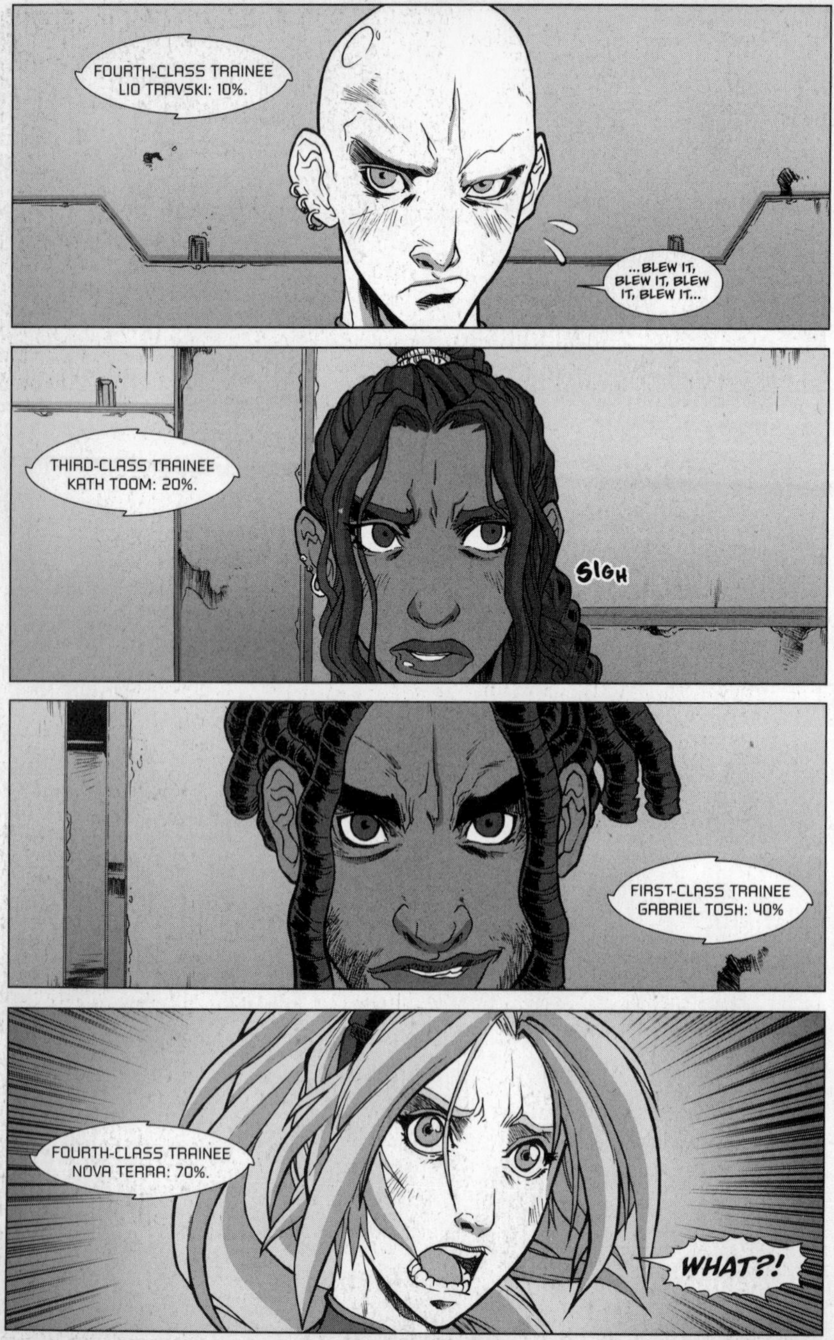

FOURTH-CLASS TRAINEE LIO TRAVSKI: 10%.
...BLEW IT, BLEW IT, BLEW IT, BLEW IT...
THIRD-CLASS TRAINEE KATH TOOM: 20%.
SIGH
FIRST-CLASS TRAINEE GABRIEL TOSH: 40%
FOURTH-CLASS TRAINEE NOVA TERRA: 70%.
WHAT?!

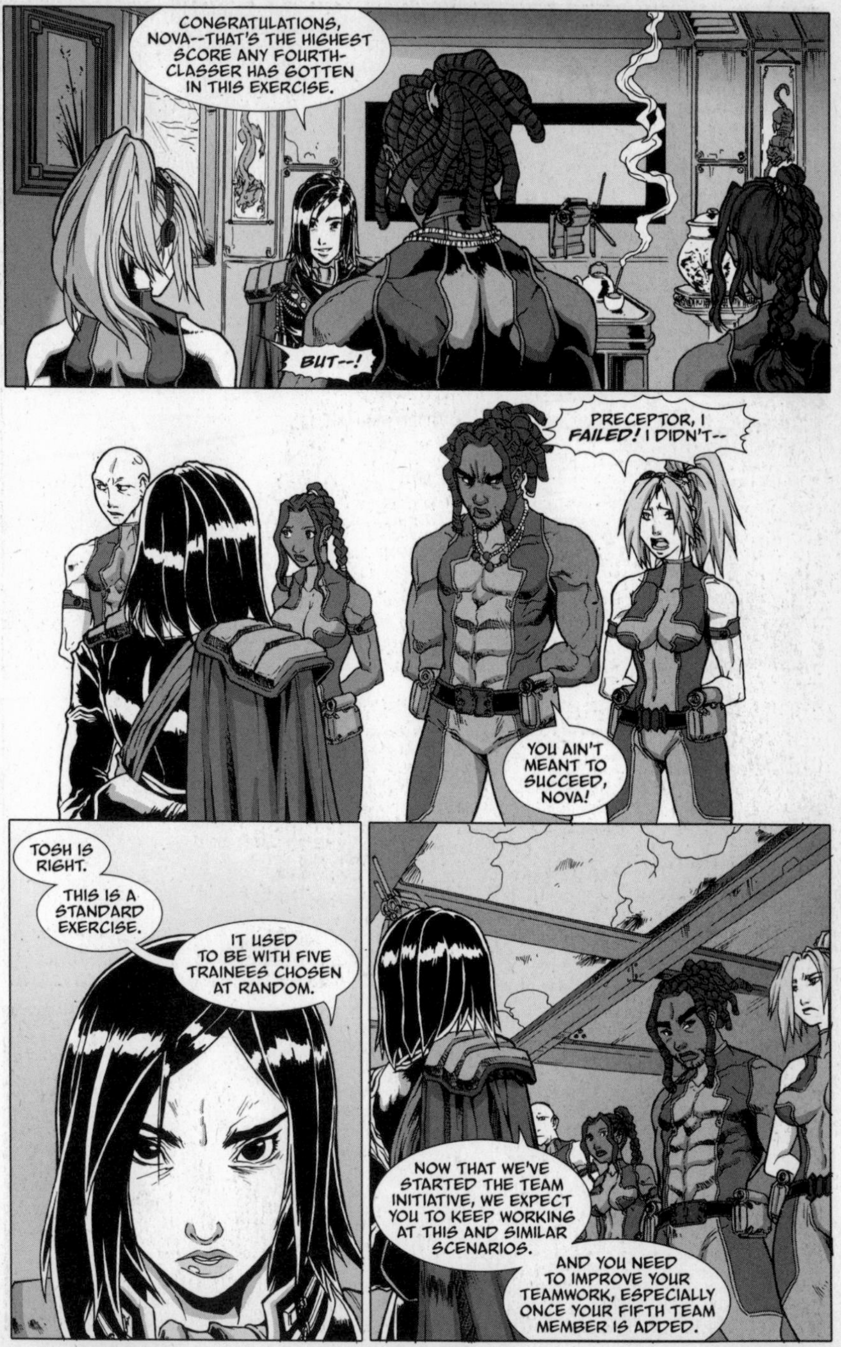
CONGRATULATIONS, NOVA--THAT'S THE HIGHEST SCORE ANY FOURTH-CLASSER HAS GOTTEN IN THIS EXERCISE.
BUT--!
PRECEPTOR, I FAILED! I DIDN'T--
YOU AIN'T MEANT TO SUCCEED, NOVA!
TOSH IS RIGHT.
THIS IS A STANDARD EXERCISE.
IT USED TO BE WITH FIVE TRAINEES CHOSEN AT RANDOM.
NOW THAT WE'VE STARTED THE TEAM INITIATIVE, WE EXPECT YOU TO KEEP WORKING AT THIS AND SIMILAR SCENARIOS.
AND YOU NEED TO IMPROVE YOUR TEAMWORK, ESPECIALLY ONCE YOUR FIFTH TEAM MEMBER IS ADDED.

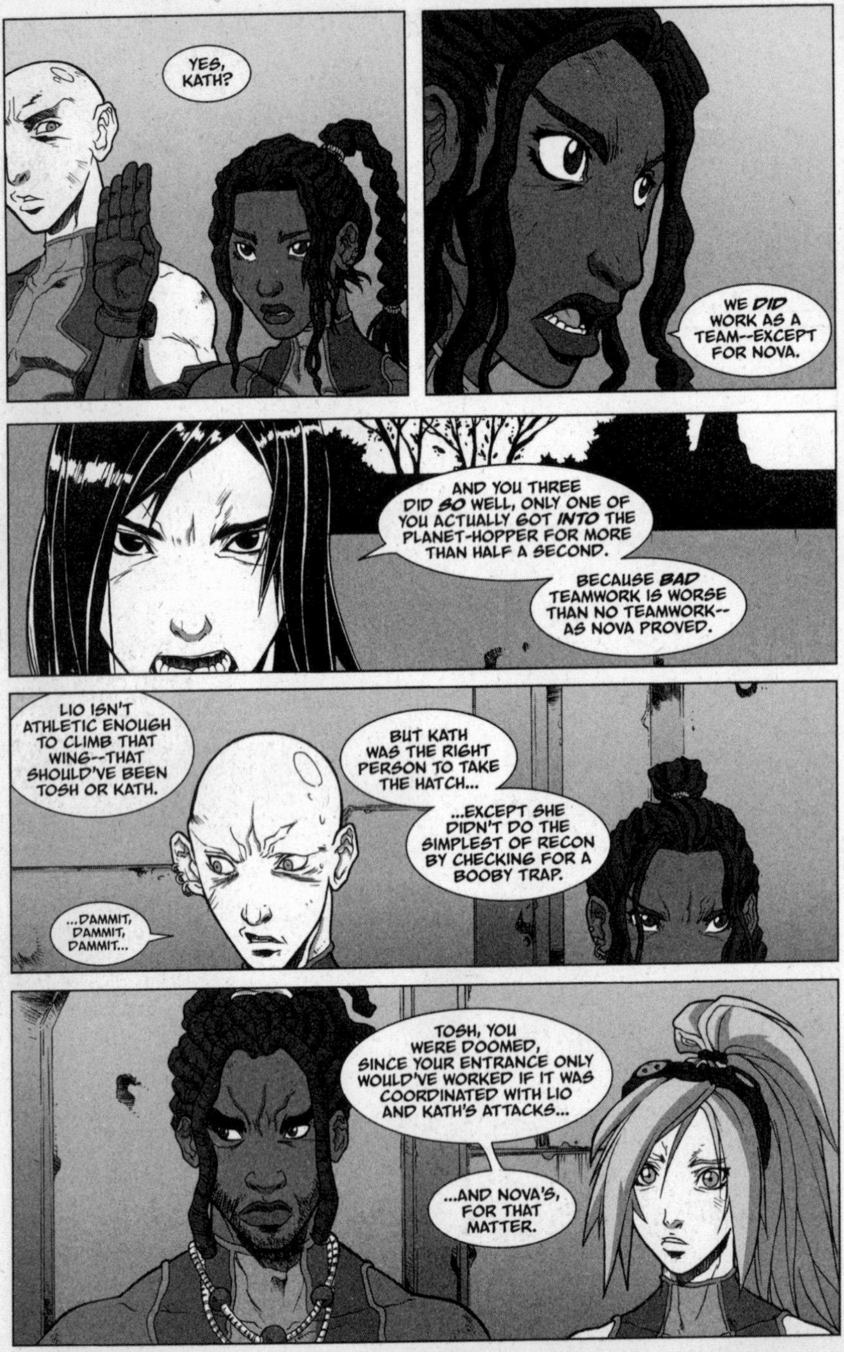
YES, KATH?
WE DID WORK AS A TEAM--EXCEPT FOR NOVA.
AND YOU THREE DID SO WELL, ONLY ONE OF YOU ACTUALLY GOT INTO THE PLANET-HOPPER FOR MORE THAN HALF A SECOND.
BECAUSE BAD TEAMWORK IS WORSE THAN NO TEAMWORK--AS NOVA PROVED.
LIO ISN'T ATHLETIC ENOUGH TO CLIMB THAT WING--THAT SHOULD'VE BEEN TOSH OR KATH.
BUT KATH WAS THE RIGHT PERSON TO TAKE THE HATCH...
...EXCEPT SHE DIDN'T DO THE SIMPLEST OF RECON BY CHECKING FOR A BOOBY TRAP.
...DAMMIT, DAMMIT, DAMMIT...
TOSH, YOU WERE DOOMED, SINCE YOUR ENTRANCE ONLY WOULD'VE WORKED IF IT WAS COORDINATED WITH LIO AND KATH'S ATTACKS...
...AND NOVA'S, FOR THAT MATTER.

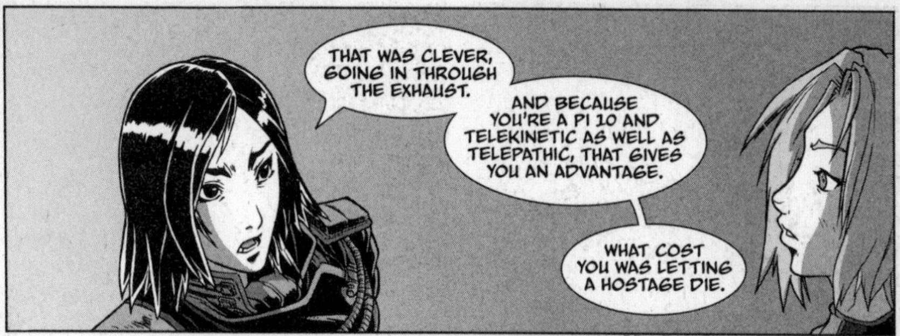
THAT WAS CLEVER, GOING IN THROUGH THE EXHAUST.
AND BECAUSE YOU'RE A PI 10 AND TELEKINETIC AS WELL AS TELEPATHIC, THAT GIVES YOU AN ADVANTAGE.
WHAT COST YOU WAS LETTING A HOSTAGE DIE.

PI= Psi Index

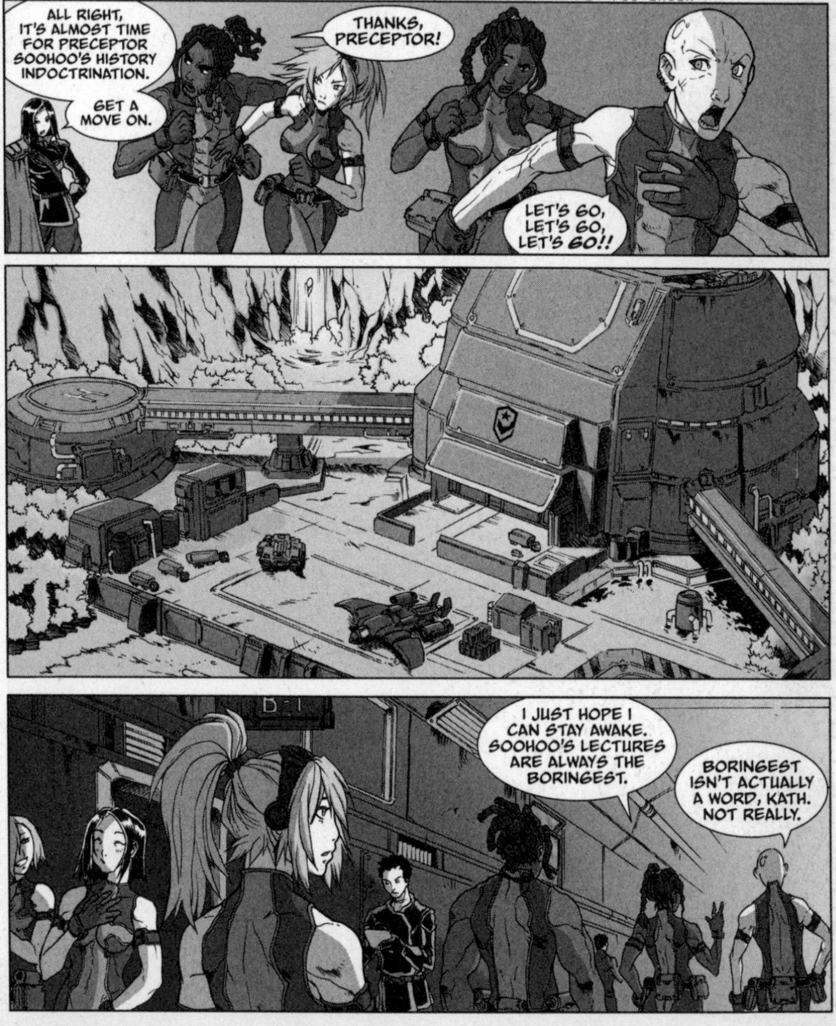
ALL RIGHT, IT'S ALMOST TIME FOR PRECEPTOR SOOHOO'S HISTORY INDOCTRINATION.
GET A MOVE ON.
THANKS, PRECEPTOR!
LET'S GO, LET'S GO, LET'S GO!!
B-1
I JUST HOPE I CAN STAY AWAKE. SOOHOO'S LECTURES ARE ALWAYS THE BORINGEST.
BORINGEST ISN'T ACTUALLY A WORD, KATH. NOT REALLY.

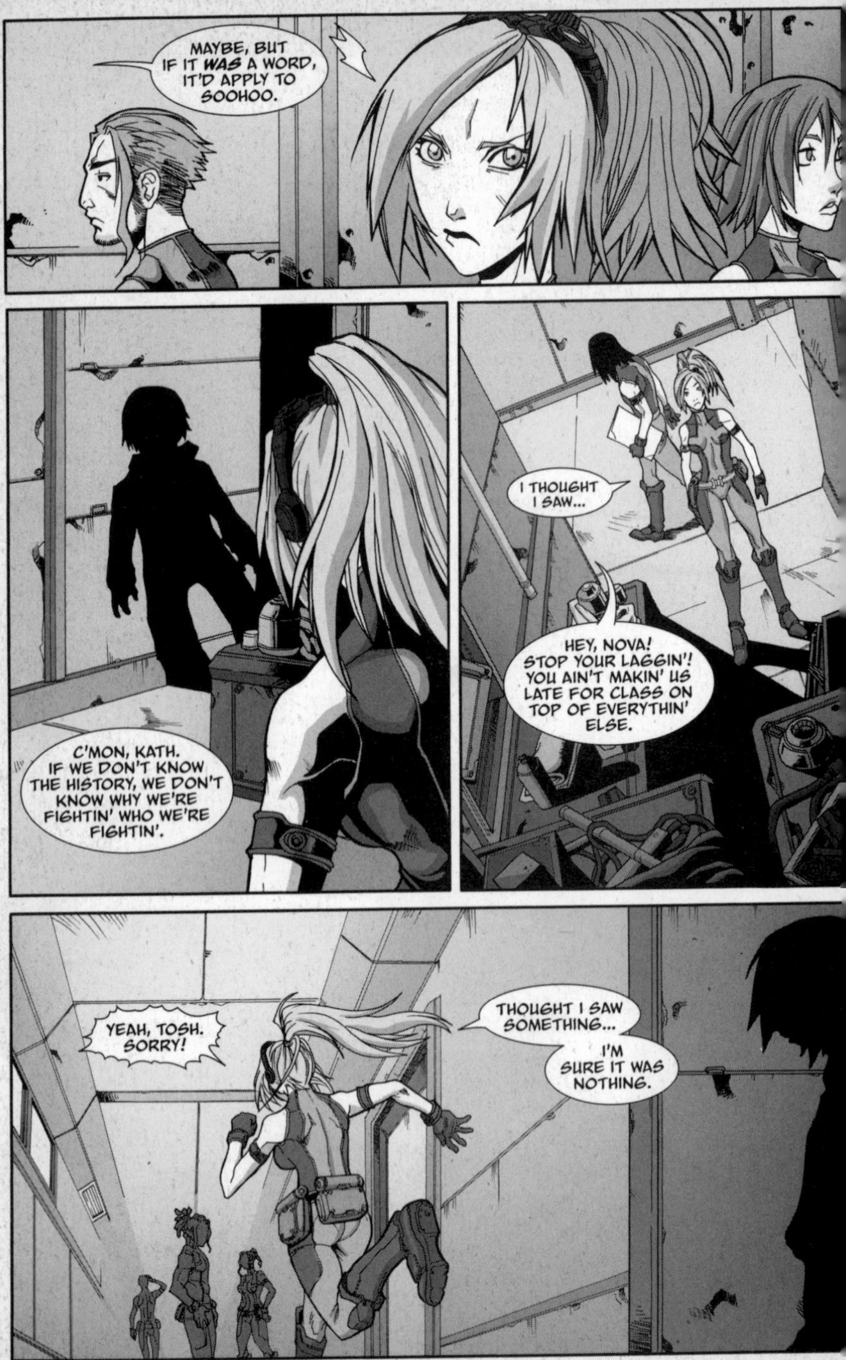
MAYBE, BUT IF IT WAS A WORD, IT'D APPLY TO SOOHOO.
C'MON, KATH. IF WE DON'T KNOW THE HISTORY, WE DON'T KNOW WHY WE'RE FIGHTIN' WHO WE'RE FIGHTIN'.
I THOUGHT I SAW...
HEY, NOVA! STOP YOUR LAGGIN'! YOU AIN'T MAKIN' US LATE FOR CLASS ON TOP OF EVERYTHIN' ELSE.
YEAH, TOSH. SORRY!
THOUGHT I SAW SOMETHING...
I'M SURE IT WAS NOTHING.

CHAPTER 2
TAKING CARE OF BUSINESS

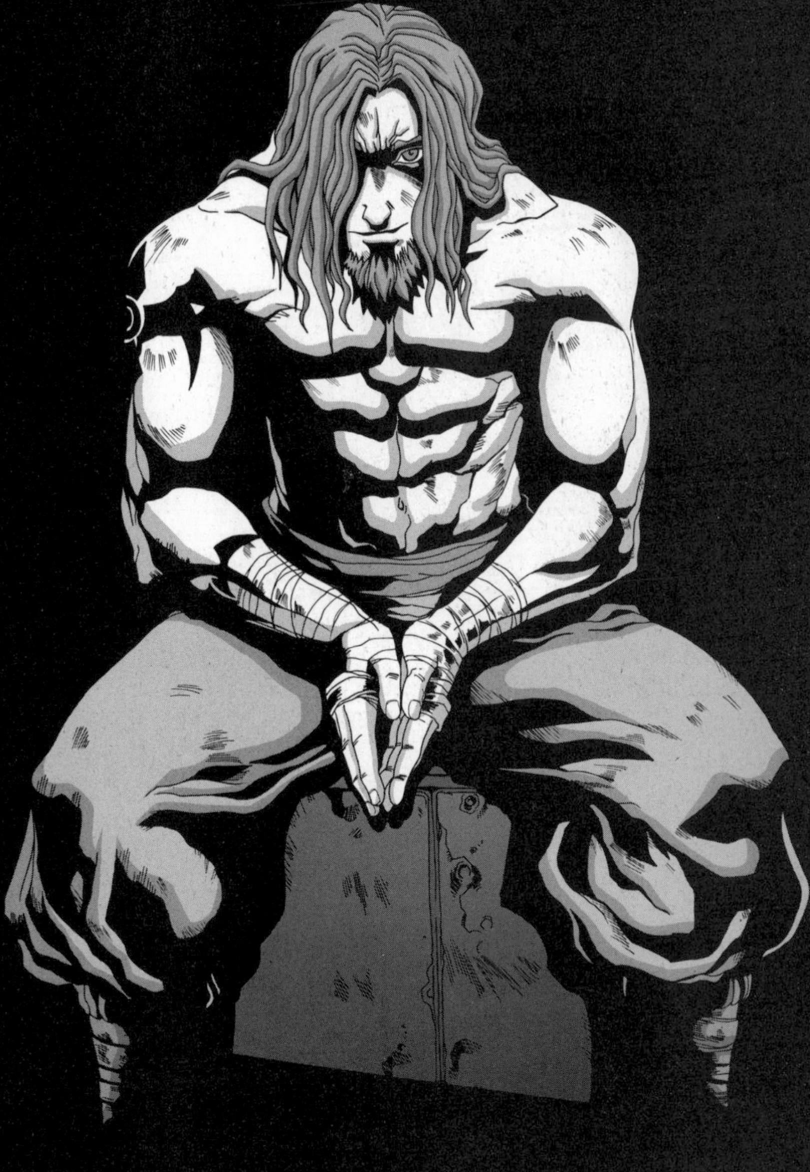

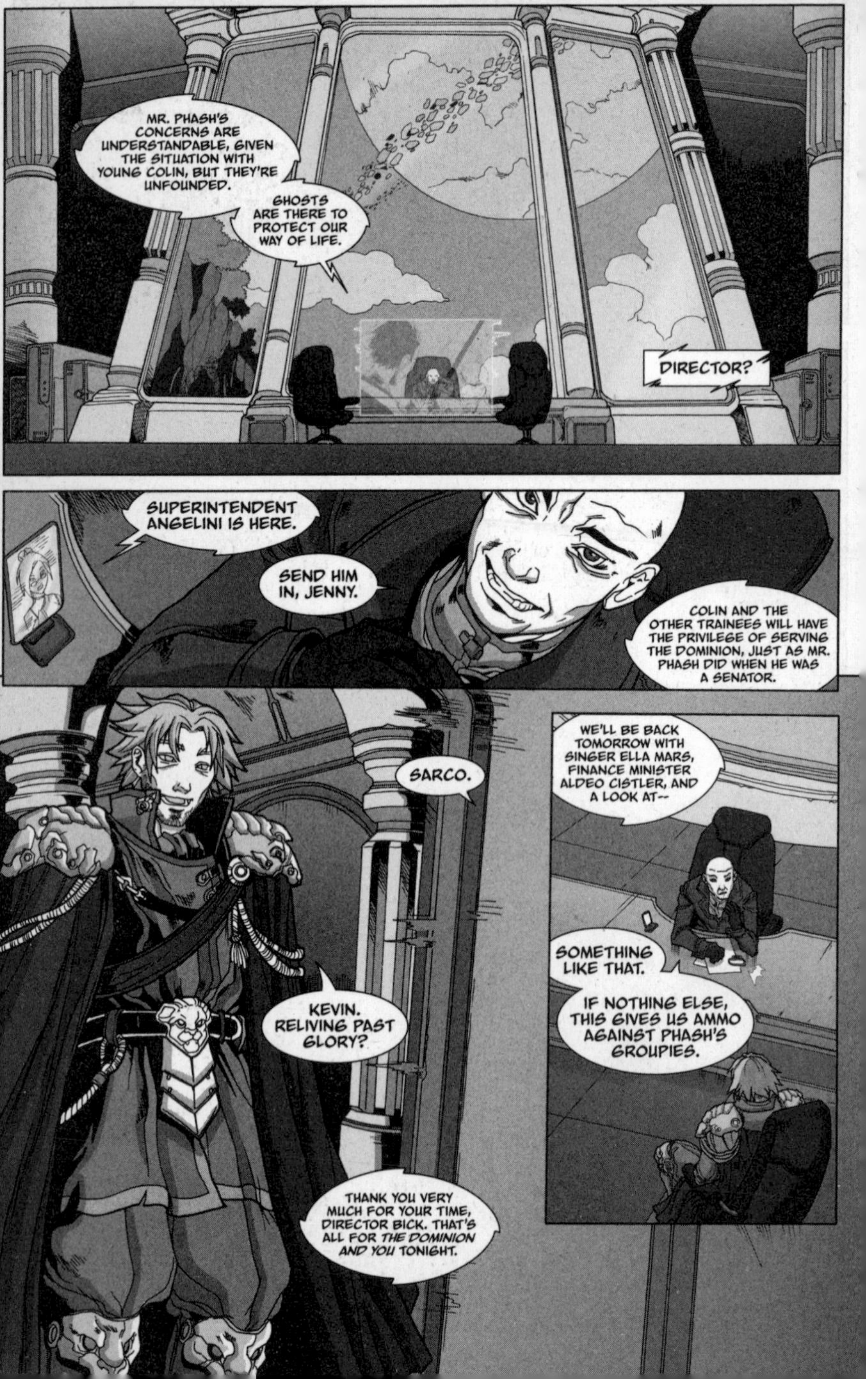
MR. PHASH'S CONCERNS ARE UNDERSTANDABLE, GIVEN THE SITUATION WITH YOUNG COLIN, BUT THEY'RE UNFOUNDED.
GHOSTS ARE THERE TO PROTECT OUR WAY OF LIFE.
DIRECTOR?
SUPERINTENDENT ANGELINI IS HERE.
SEND HIM IN, JENNY.
COLIN AND THE OTHER TRAINEES WILL HAVE THE PRIVILEGE OF SERVING THE DOMINION, JUST AS MR. PHASH DID WHEN HE WAS A SENATOR.
SARCO.
KEVIN. RELIVING PAST GLORY?
THANK YOU VERY MUCH FOR YOUR TIME, DIRECTOR BICK. THAT'S ALL FOR *THE DOMINION AND YOU* TONIGHT.
WE'LL BE BACK TOMORROW WITH SINGER ELLA MARS, FINANCE MINISTER ALDEO CISTLER, AND A LOOK AT--
SOMETHING LIKE THAT.
IF NOTHING ELSE, THIS GIVES US AMMO AGAINST PHASH'S GROUPIES.

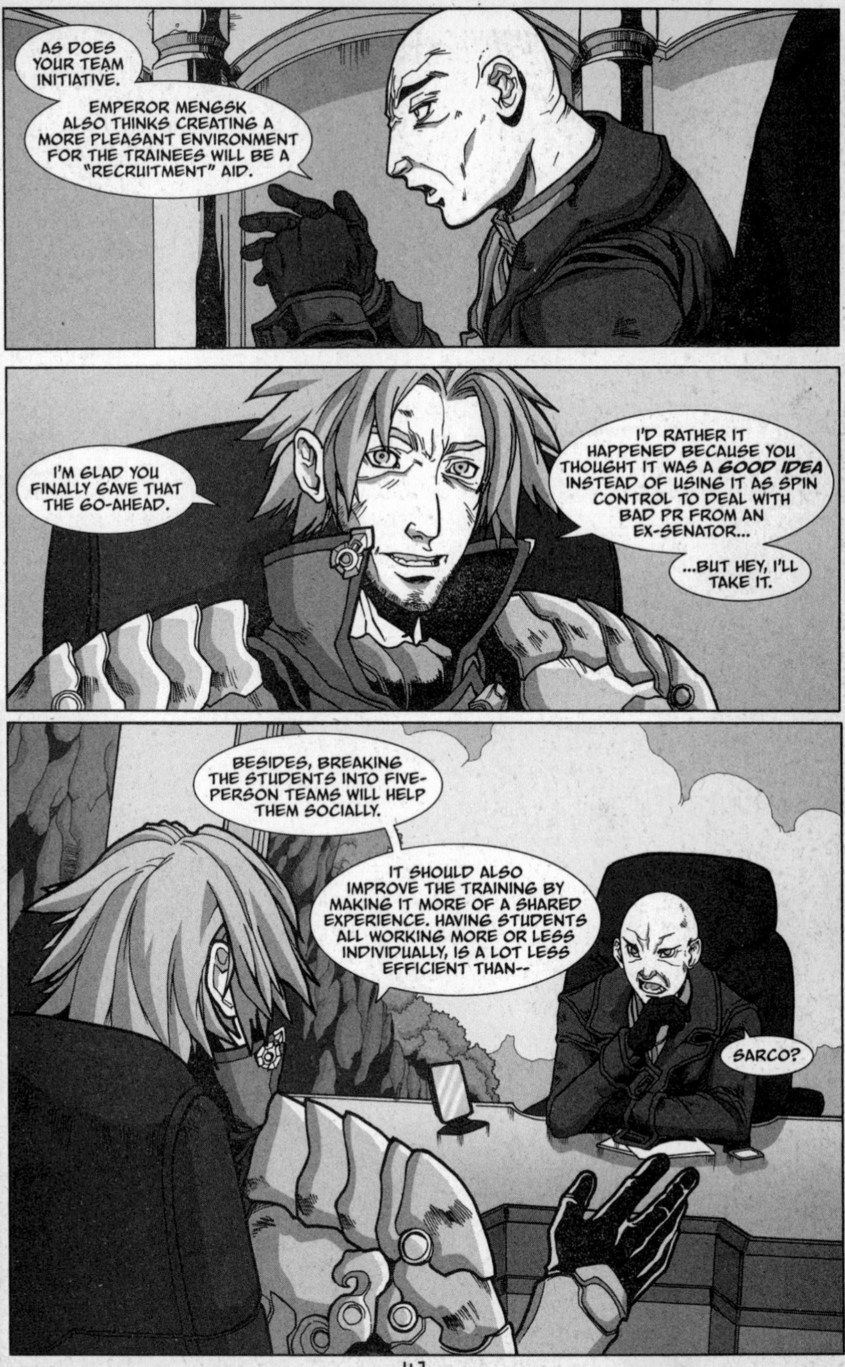
AS DOES YOUR TEAM INITIATIVE.
EMPEROR MENGSK ALSO THINKS CREATING A MORE PLEASANT ENVIRONMENT FOR THE TRAINEES WILL BE A "RECRUITMENT" AID.
I'M GLAD YOU FINALLY GAVE THAT THE GO-AHEAD.
I'D RATHER IT HAPPENED BECAUSE YOU THOUGHT IT WAS A GOOD IDEA INSTEAD OF USING IT AS SPIN CONTROL TO DEAL WITH BAD PR FROM AN EX-SENATOR...
...BUT HEY, I'LL TAKE IT.
BESIDES, BREAKING THE STUDENTS INTO FIVE-PERSON TEAMS WILL HELP THEM SOCIALLY.
IT SHOULD ALSO IMPROVE THE TRAINING BY MAKING IT MORE OF A SHARED EXPERIENCE. HAVING STUDENTS ALL WORKING MORE OR LESS INDIVIDUALLY, IS A LOT LESS EFFICIENT THAN--
SARCO?

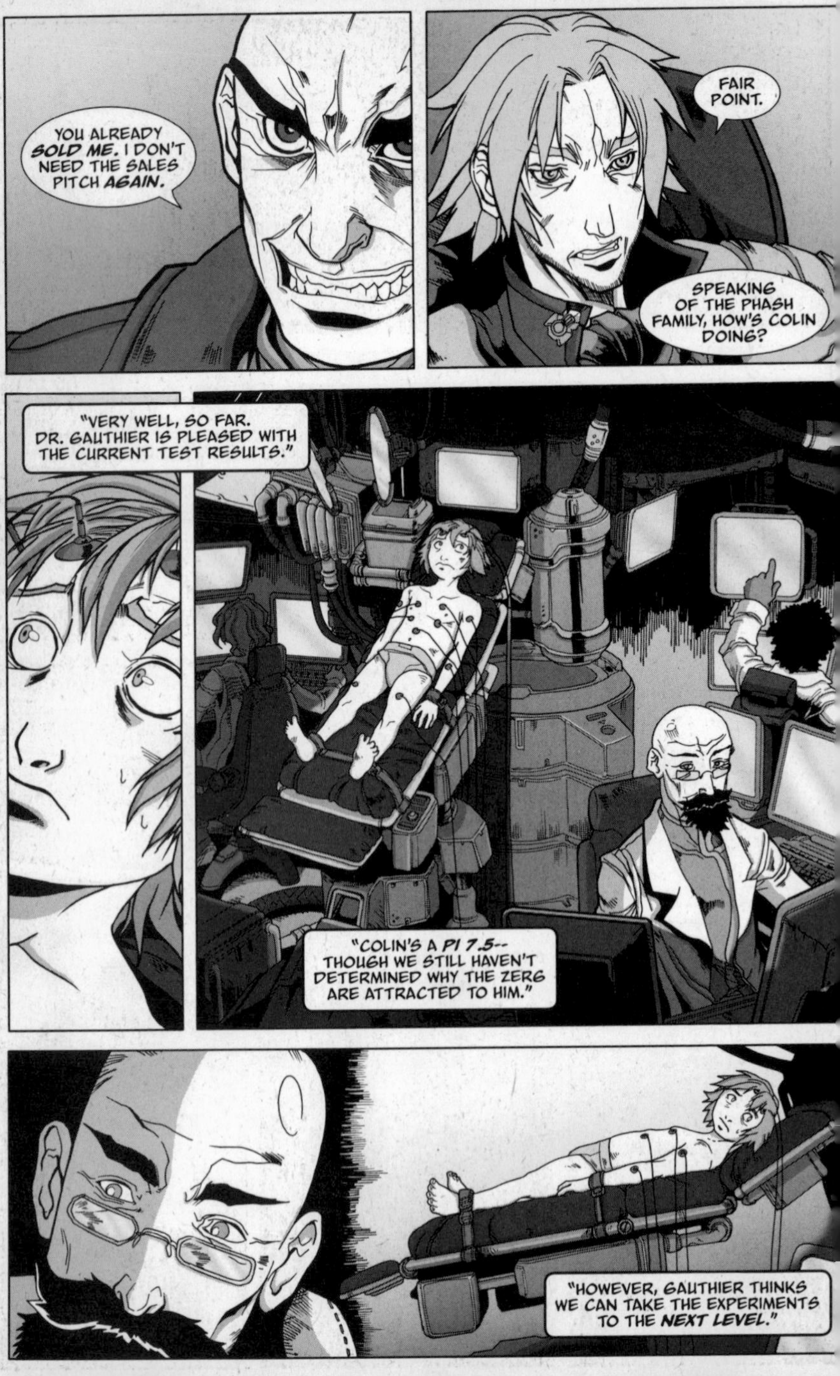
YOU ALREADY SOLD ME. I DON'T NEED THE SALES PITCH AGAIN.
FAIR POINT.
SPEAKING OF THE PHASH FAMILY, HOW'S COLIN DOING?
"VERY WELL, SO FAR. DR. GAUTHIER IS PLEASED WITH THE CURRENT TEST RESULTS."
"COLIN'S A PI 7.5-- THOUGH WE STILL HAVEN'T DETERMINED WHY THE ZERG ARE ATTRACTED TO HIM."
"HOWEVER, GAUTHIER THINKS WE CAN TAKE THE EXPERIMENTS TO THE NEXT LEVEL."

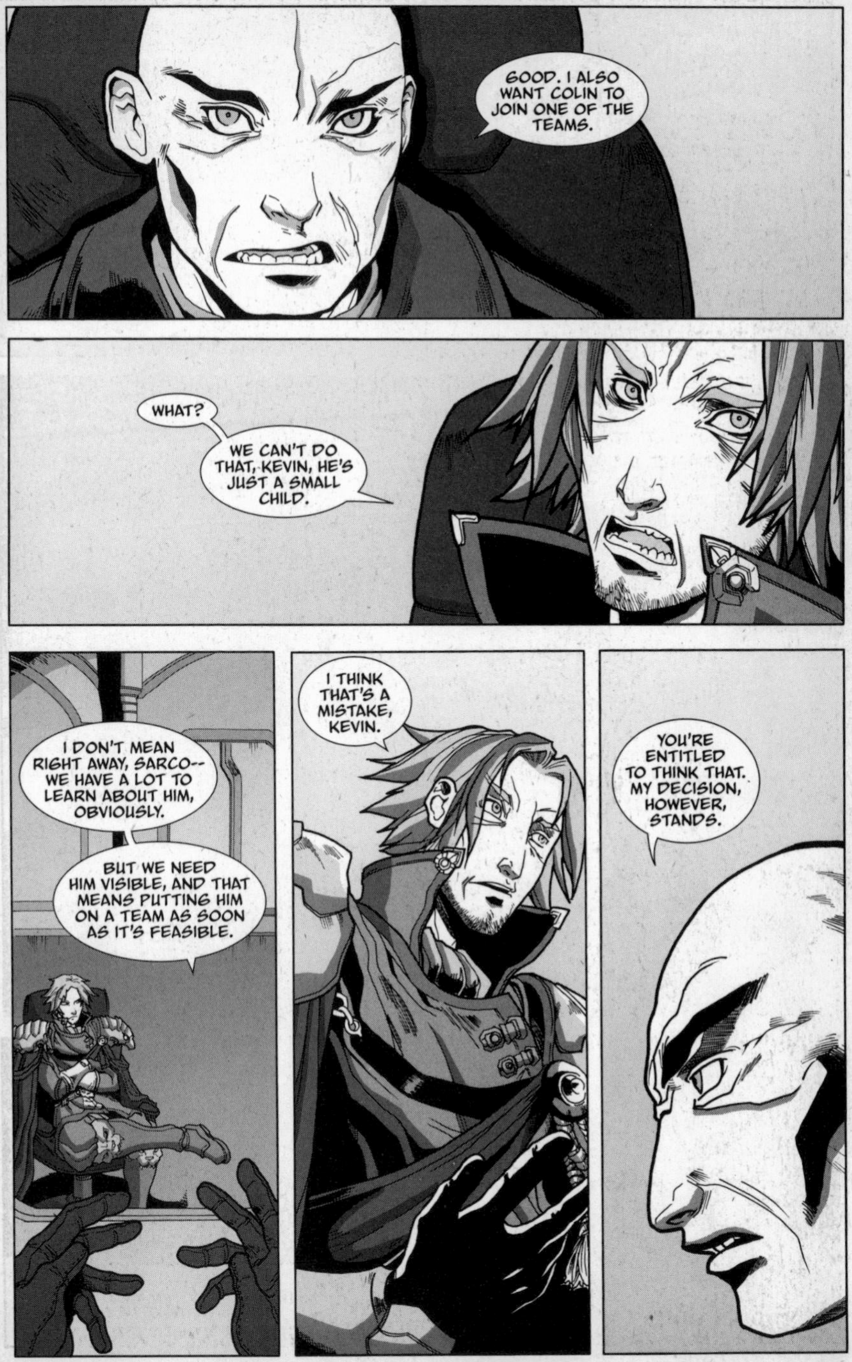
GOOD. I ALSO WANT COLIN TO JOIN ONE OF THE TEAMS.
WHAT?
WE CAN'T DO THAT, KEVIN, HE'S JUST A SMALL CHILD.
I DON'T MEAN RIGHT AWAY, SARCO-- WE HAVE A LOT TO LEARN ABOUT HIM, OBVIOUSLY.
BUT WE NEED HIM VISIBLE, AND THAT MEANS PUTTING HIM ON A TEAM AS SOON AS IT'S FEASIBLE.
I THINK THAT'S A MISTAKE, KEVIN.
YOU'RE ENTITLED TO THINK THAT. MY DECISION, HOWEVER, STANDS.

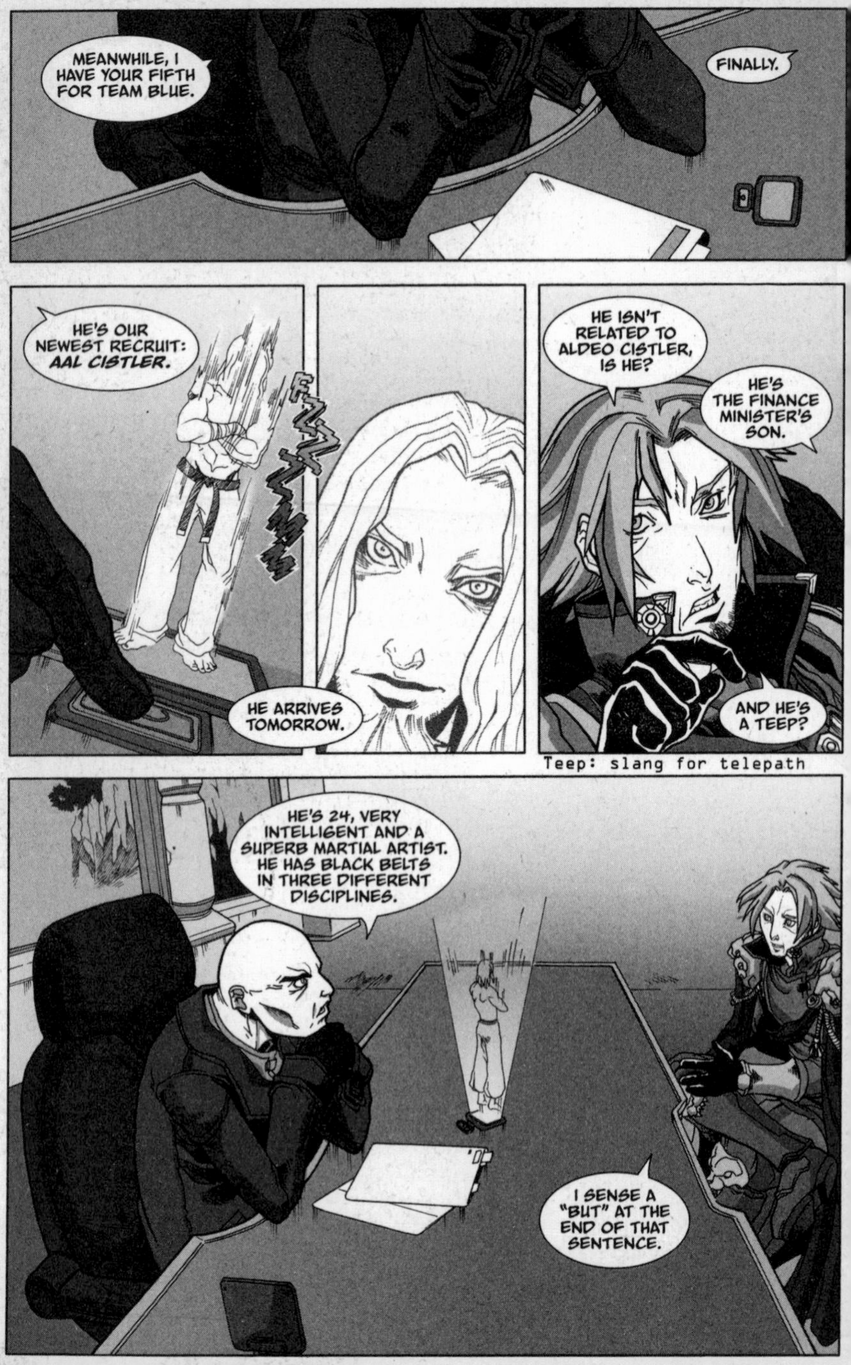
MEANWHILE, I HAVE YOUR FIFTH FOR TEAM BLUE.
FINALLY.
HE'S OUR NEWEST RECRUIT: *AAL CISTLER.*
FZZZZMMM
HE ARRIVES TOMORROW.
HE ISN'T RELATED TO ALDEO CISTLER, IS HE?
HE'S THE FINANCE MINISTER'S SON.
AND HE'S A TEEP?
Teep: slang for telepath
HE'S 24, VERY INTELLIGENT AND A SUPERB MARTIAL ARTIST. HE HAS BLACK BELTS IN THREE DIFFERENT DISCIPLINES.
I SENSE A "BUT" AT THE END OF THAT SENTENCE.

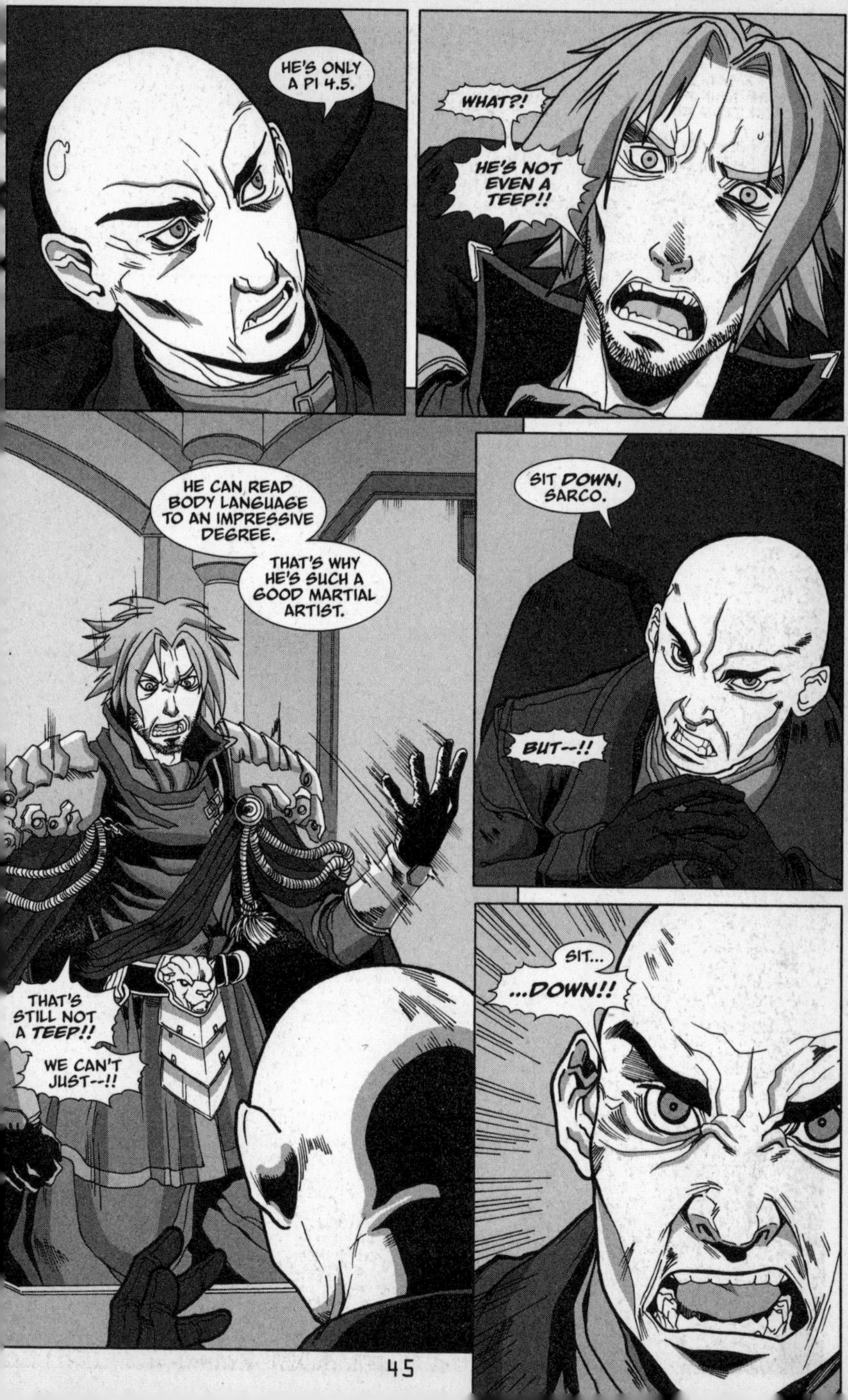
HE'S ONLY A PI 4.5.
WHAT?!
HE'S NOT EVEN A TEEP!!
HE CAN READ BODY LANGUAGE TO AN IMPRESSIVE DEGREE.
THAT'S WHY HE'S SUCH A GOOD MARTIAL ARTIST.
THAT'S STILL NOT A *TEEP!!*
WE CAN'T JUST--!!
SIT *DOWN,* SARCO.
BUT--!!
SIT...
...DOWN!!

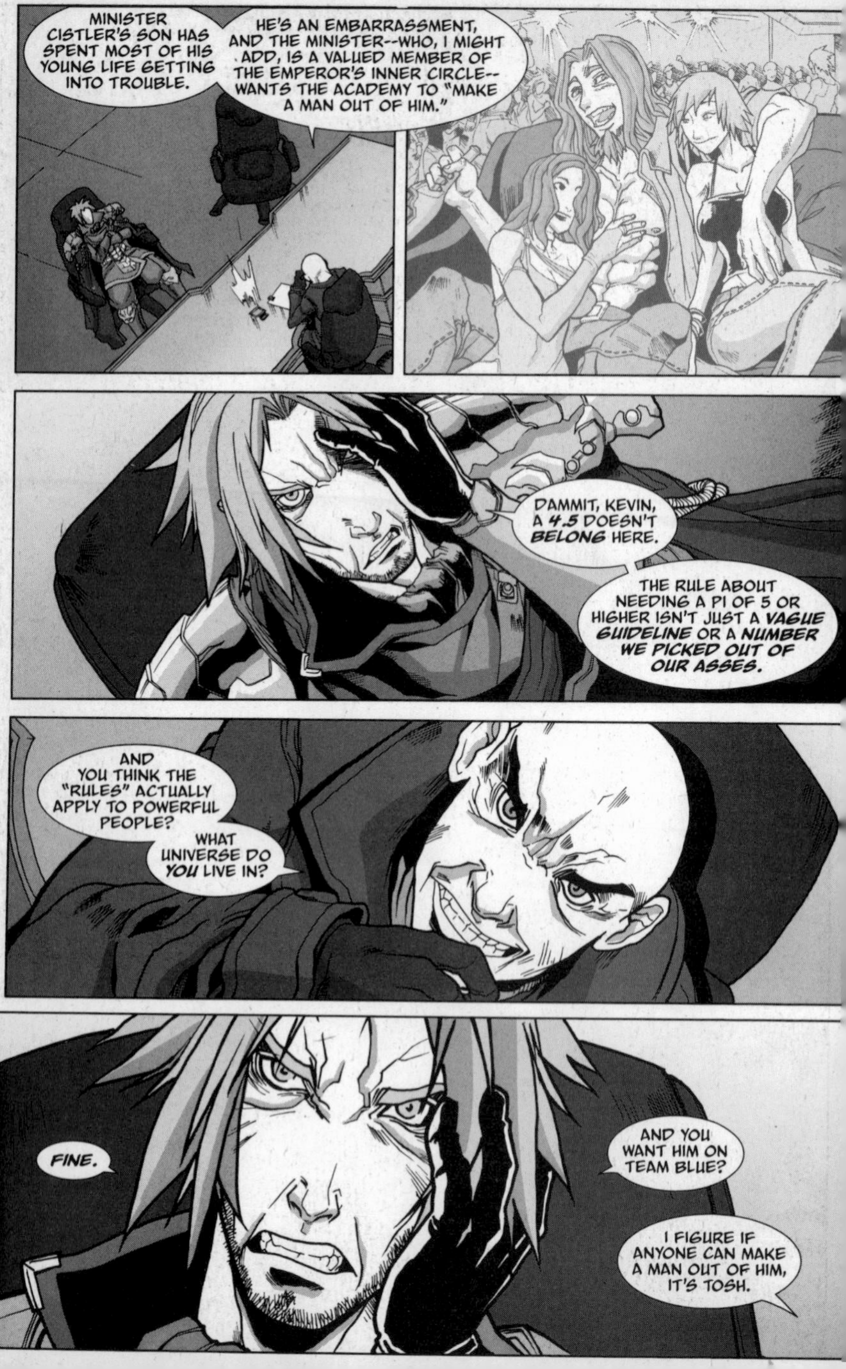
MINISTER CISTLER'S SON HAS SPENT MOST OF HIS YOUNG LIFE GETTING INTO TROUBLE.
HE'S AN EMBARRASSMENT, AND THE MINISTER--WHO, I MIGHT ADD, IS A VALUED MEMBER OF THE EMPEROR'S INNER CIRCLE--WANTS THE ACADEMY TO "MAKE A MAN OUT OF HIM."
DAMMIT, KEVIN, A 4.5 DOESN'T *BELONG* HERE.
THE RULE ABOUT NEEDING A PI OF 5 OR HIGHER ISN'T JUST A *VAGUE GUIDELINE* OR A *NUMBER WE PICKED OUT OF OUR ASSES.*
AND YOU THINK THE "RULES" ACTUALLY APPLY TO POWERFUL PEOPLE?
WHAT UNIVERSE DO *YOU* LIVE IN?
FINE.
AND YOU WANT HIM ON TEAM BLUE?
I FIGURE IF ANYONE CAN MAKE A MAN OUT OF HIM, IT'S TOSH.

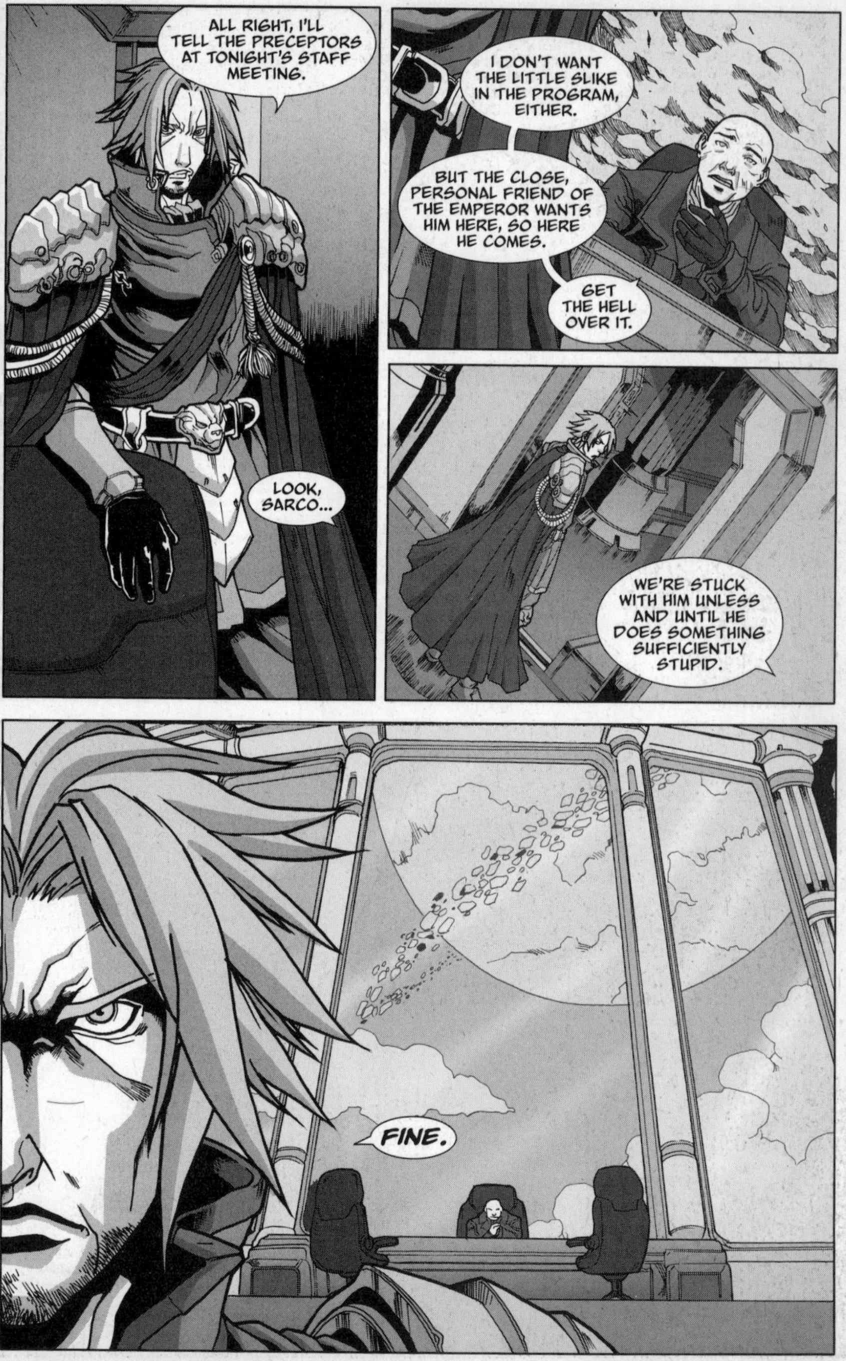
ALL RIGHT, I'LL TELL THE PRECEPTORS AT TONIGHT'S STAFF MEETING.
LOOK, SARCO...
I DON'T WANT THE LITTLE SLIKE IN THE PROGRAM, EITHER.
BUT THE CLOSE, PERSONAL FRIEND OF THE EMPEROR WANTS HIM HERE, SO HERE HE COMES.
GET THE HELL OVER IT.
WE'RE STUCK WITH HIM UNLESS AND UNTIL HE DOES SOMETHING SUFFICIENTLY STUPID.
FINE.

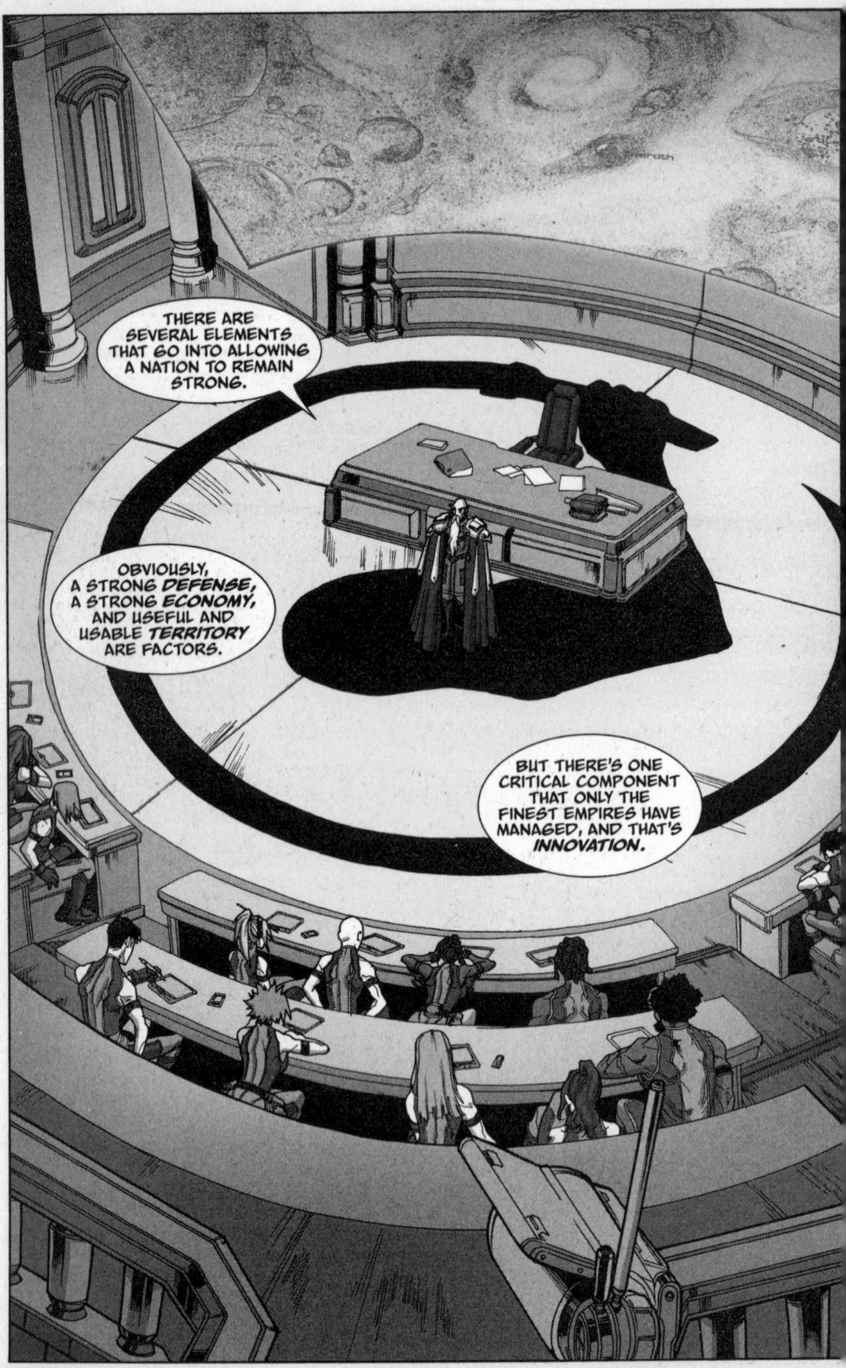
THERE ARE SEVERAL ELEMENTS THAT GO INTO ALLOWING A NATION TO REMAIN STRONG.
OBVIOUSLY, A STRONG *DEFENSE*, A STRONG *ECONOMY*, AND USEFUL AND USABLE *TERRITORY* ARE FACTORS.
BUT THERE'S ONE CRITICAL COMPONENT THAT ONLY THE FINEST EMPIRES HAVE MANAGED, AND THAT'S ***INNOVATION.***

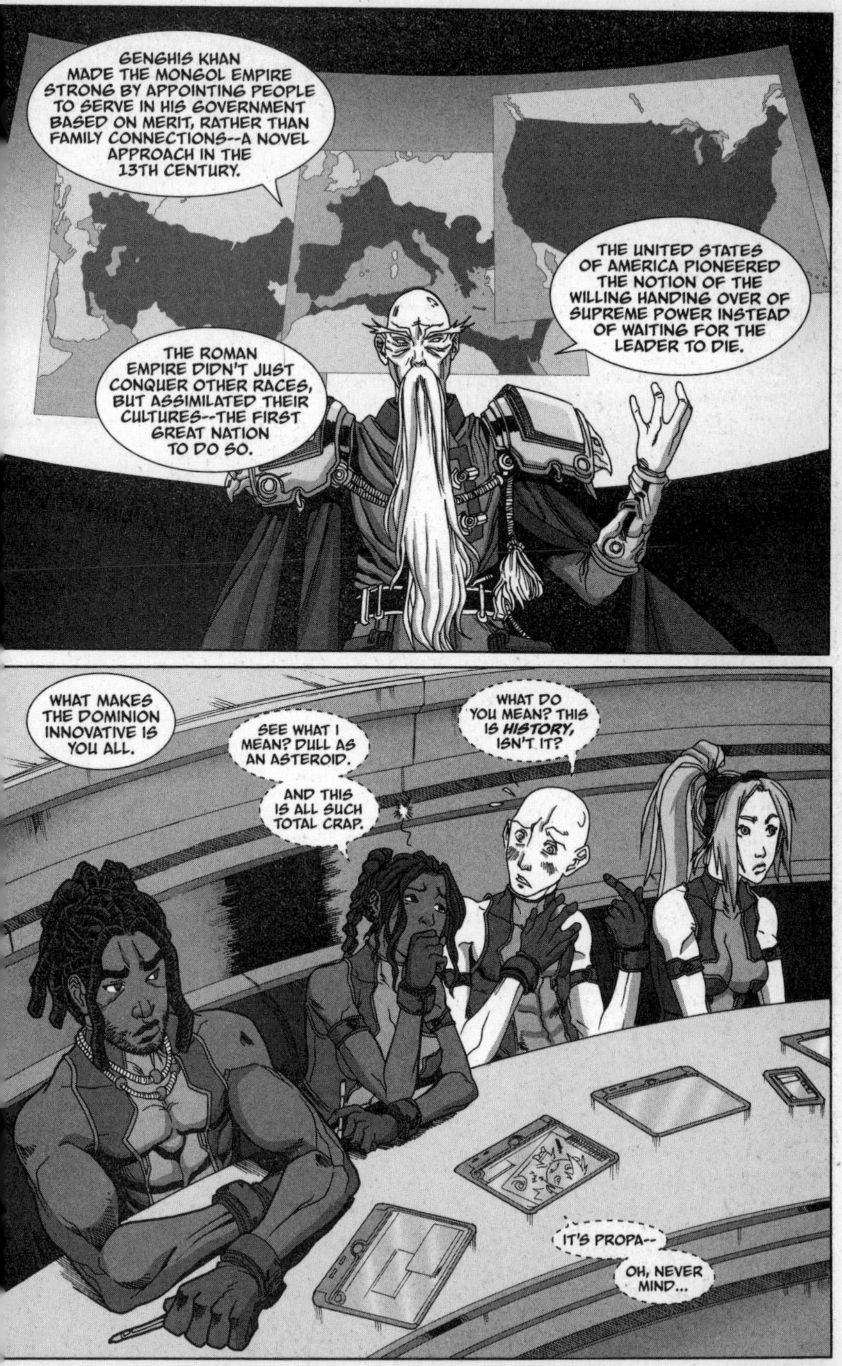
GENGHIS KHAN MADE THE MONGOL EMPIRE STRONG BY APPOINTING PEOPLE TO SERVE IN HIS GOVERNMENT BASED ON MERIT, RATHER THAN FAMILY CONNECTIONS--A NOVEL APPROACH IN THE 13TH CENTURY.
THE ROMAN EMPIRE DIDN'T JUST CONQUER OTHER RACES, BUT ASSIMILATED THEIR CULTURES--THE FIRST GREAT NATION TO DO SO.
THE UNITED STATES OF AMERICA PIONEERED THE NOTION OF THE WILLING HANDING OVER OF SUPREME POWER INSTEAD OF WAITING FOR THE LEADER TO DIE.
WHAT MAKES THE DOMINION INNOVATIVE IS YOU ALL.
SEE WHAT I MEAN? DULL AS AN ASTEROID.
AND THIS IS ALL SUCH TOTAL CRAP.
WHAT DO YOU MEAN? THIS IS *HISTORY,* ISN'T IT?
IT'S PROPA--
OH, NEVER MIND...

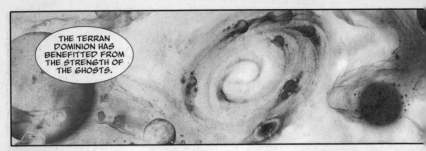

THE TERRAN DOMINION HAS BENEFITTED FROM THE STRENGTH OF THE GHOSTS.

TRAINING PEOPLE WITH PSIONIC TALENTS AND TURNING THEM INTO SOLDIERS...

...HAS BEEN THE SOURCE OF THE DOMINION'S POWER.

LIO?

WELL, I MEAN, WHAT ABOUT THE CONFEDERACY?

THEY HAD GHOSTS TOO, RIGHT?

RIGHT? RIGHT? RIGHT?

I'M GLAD YOU MENTIONED THAT, LIO.

STRICTLY SPEAKING, YES, THEY DID.

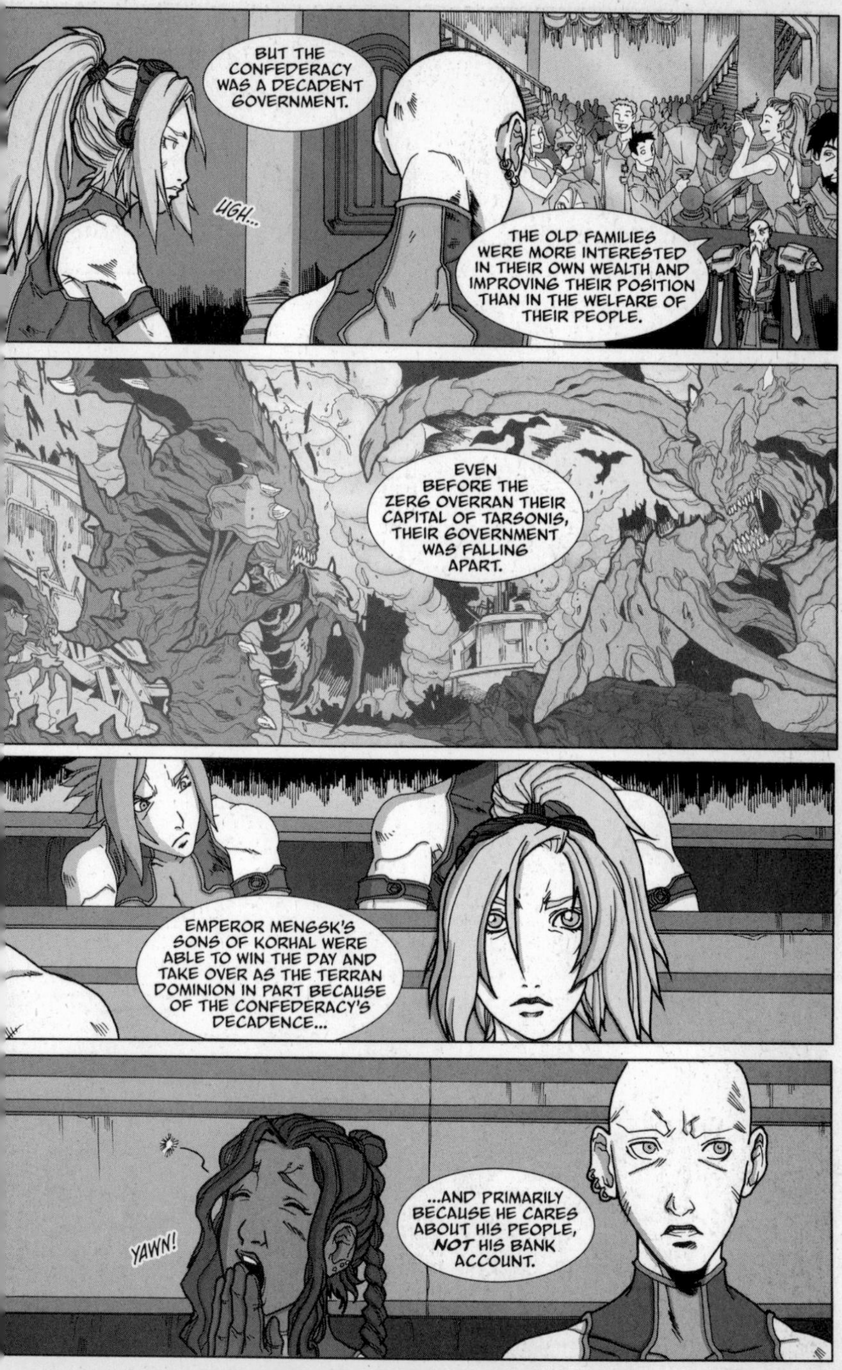
BUT THE CONFEDERACY WAS A DECADENT GOVERNMENT.
UGH...
THE OLD FAMILIES WERE MORE INTERESTED IN THEIR OWN WEALTH AND IMPROVING THEIR POSITION THAN IN THE WELFARE OF THEIR PEOPLE.
EVEN BEFORE THE ZERG OVERRAN THEIR CAPITAL OF TARSONIS, THEIR GOVERNMENT WAS FALLING APART.
EMPEROR MENGSK'S SONS OF KORHAL WERE ABLE TO WIN THE DAY AND TAKE OVER AS THE TERRAN DOMINION IN PART BECAUSE OF THE CONFEDERACY'S DECADENCE...
YAWN!
...AND PRIMARILY BECAUSE HE CARES ABOUT HIS PEOPLE, *NOT* HIS BANK ACCOUNT.

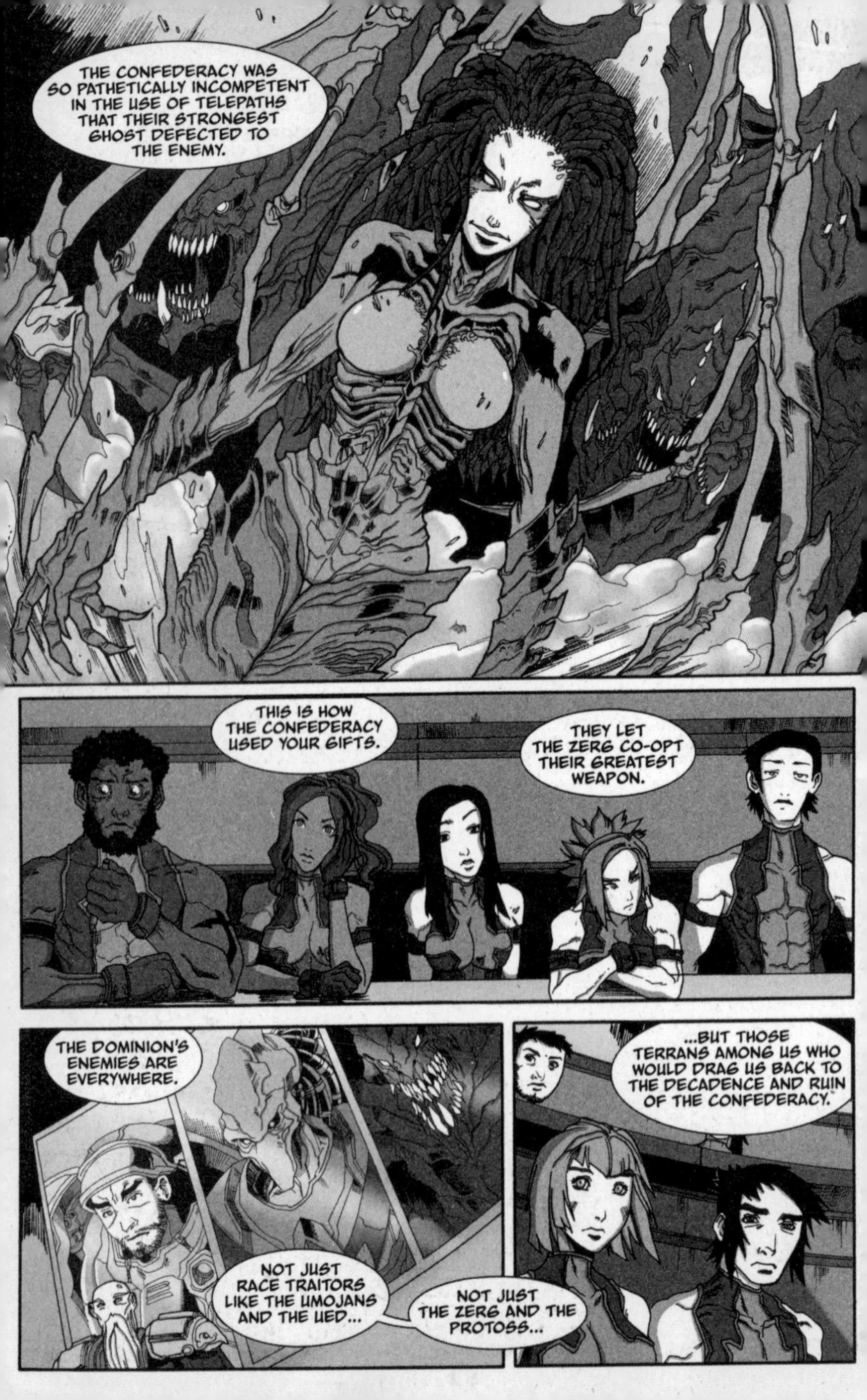
THE CONFEDERACY WAS SO PATHETICALLY INCOMPETENT IN THE USE OF TELEPATHS THAT THEIR STRONGEST GHOST DEFECTED TO THE ENEMY.
THIS IS HOW THE CONFEDERACY USED YOUR GIFTS.
THEY LET THE ZERG CO-OPT THEIR GREATEST WEAPON.
THE DOMINION'S ENEMIES ARE EVERYWHERE.
NOT JUST RACE TRAITORS LIKE THE UMOJANS AND THE UED...
NOT JUST THE ZERG AND THE PROTOSS...
...BUT THOSE TERRANS AMONG US WHO WOULD DRAG US BACK TO THE DECADENCE AND RUIN OF THE CONFEDERACY.

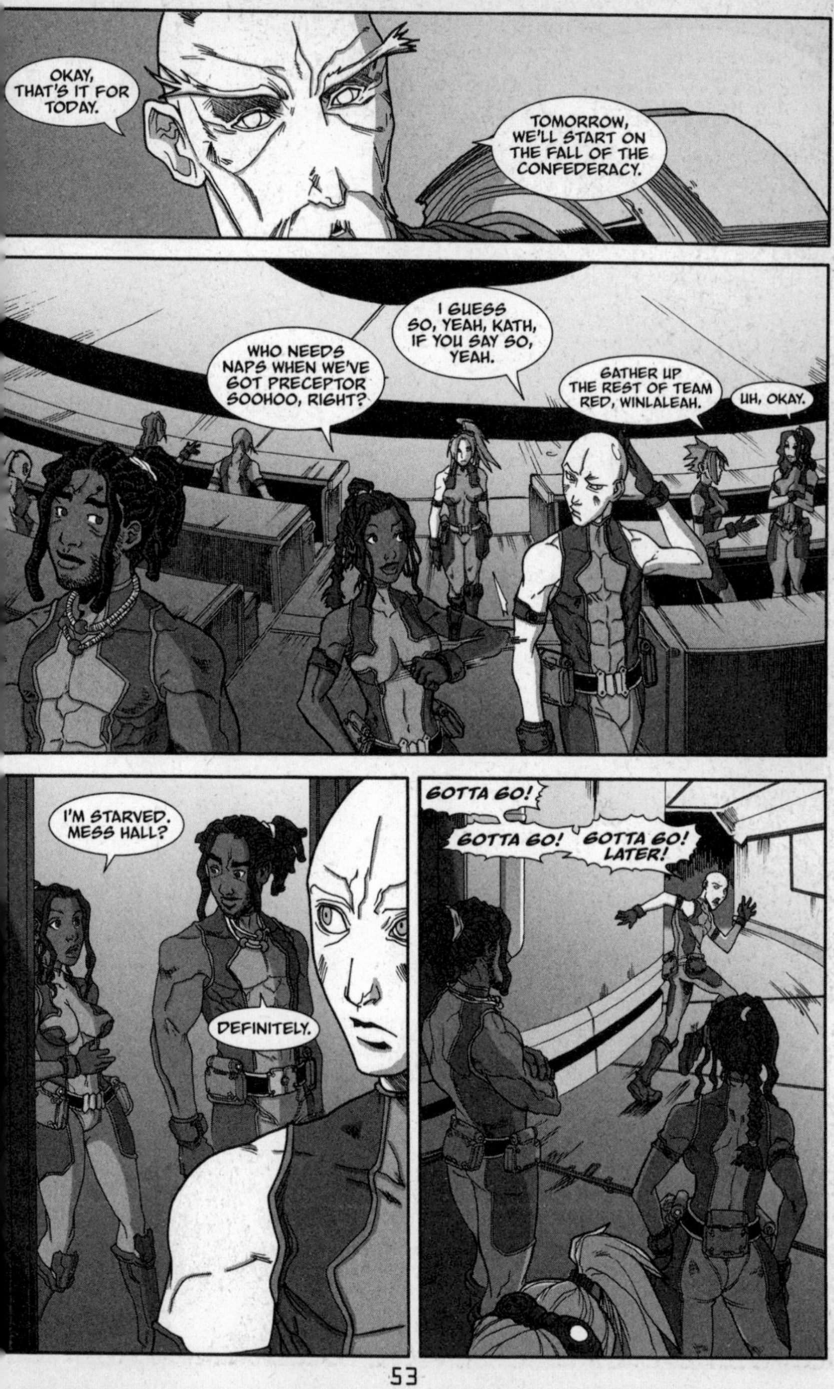
OKAY, THAT'S IT FOR TODAY.
TOMORROW, WE'LL START ON THE FALL OF THE CONFEDERACY.
WHO NEEDS NAPS WHEN WE'VE GOT PRECEPTOR SOOHOO, RIGHT?
I GUESS SO, YEAH, KATH, IF YOU SAY SO, YEAH.
GATHER UP THE REST OF TEAM RED, WINLALEAH.
UH, OKAY.
I'M STARVED. MESS HALL?
DEFINITELY.
GOTTA GO!
GOTTA GO!
GOTTA GO! LATER!

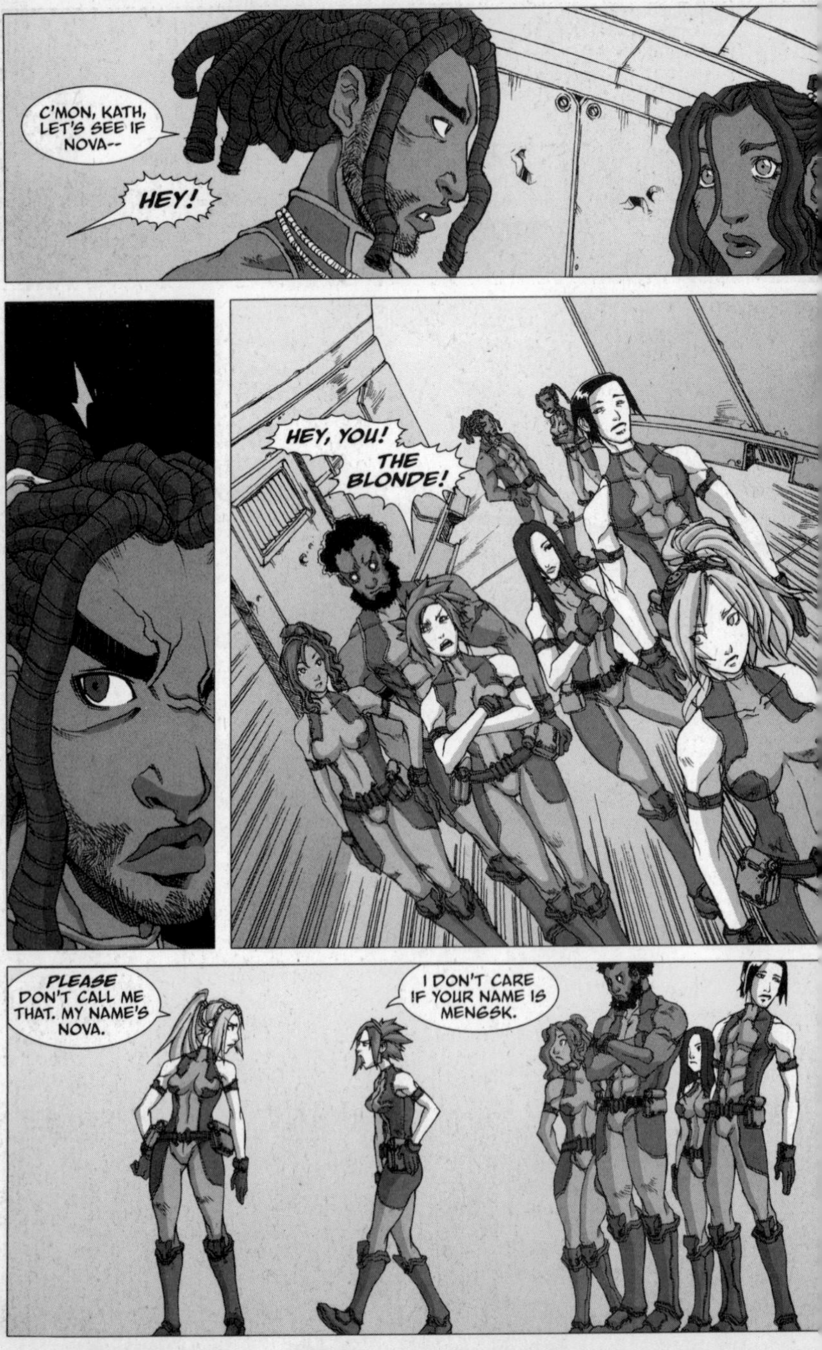
C'MON, KATH, LET'S SEE IF NOVA--
HEY!
HEY, YOU!
THE BLONDE!
PLEASE DON'T CALL ME THAT. MY NAME'S NOVA.
I DON'T CARE IF YOUR NAME IS MENGSK.

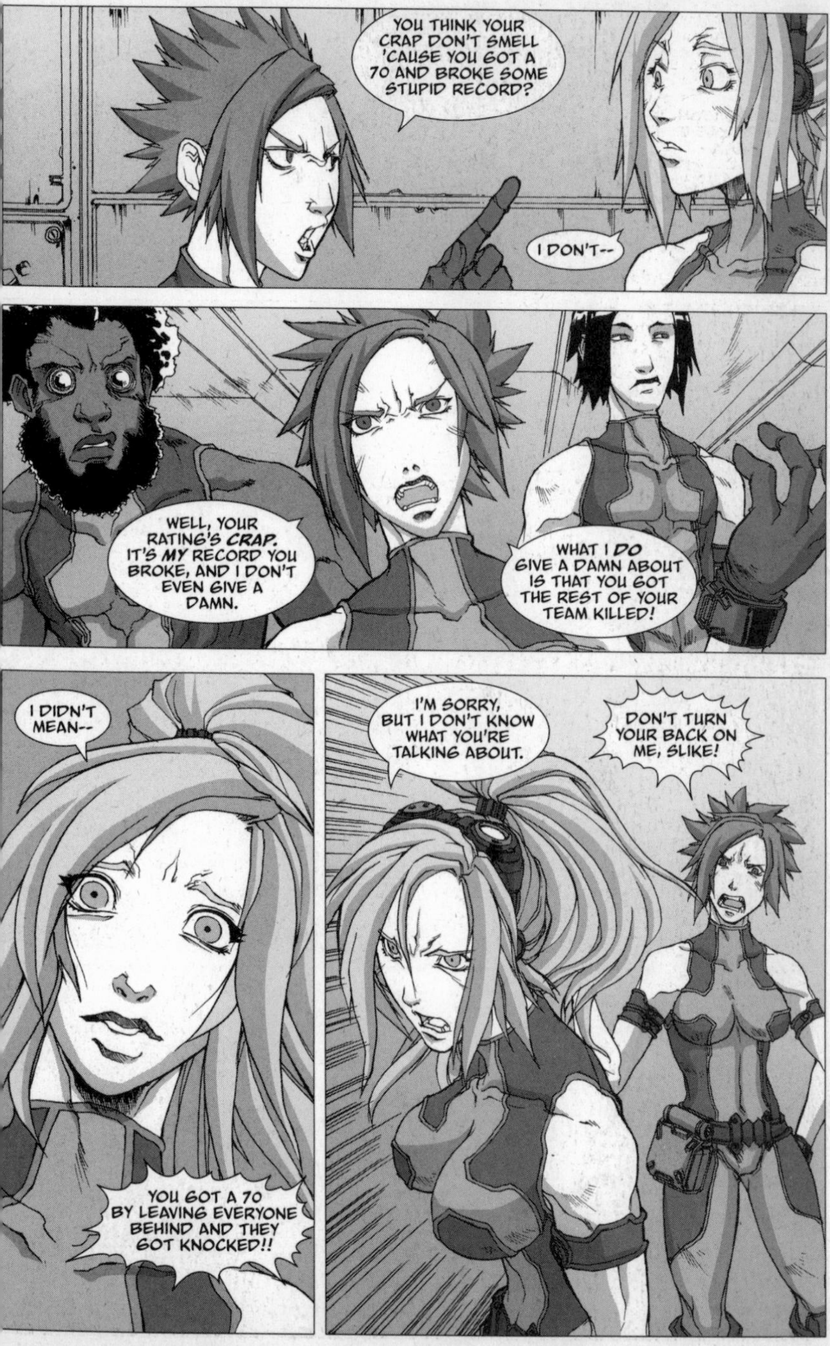
YOU THINK YOUR CRAP DON'T SMELL 'CAUSE YOU GOT A 70 AND BROKE SOME STUPID RECORD?
I DON'T--
WELL, YOUR RATING'S *CRAP.* IT'S *MY* RECORD YOU BROKE, AND I DON'T EVEN GIVE A DAMN.
WHAT I *DO* GIVE A DAMN ABOUT IS THAT YOU GOT THE REST OF YOUR TEAM KILLED!
I DIDN'T MEAN--
YOU GOT A 70 BY LEAVING EVERYONE BEHIND AND THEY GOT KNOCKED!!
I'M SORRY, BUT I DON'T KNOW WHAT YOU'RE TALKING ABOUT.
DON'T TURN YOUR BACK ON ME, SLIKE!

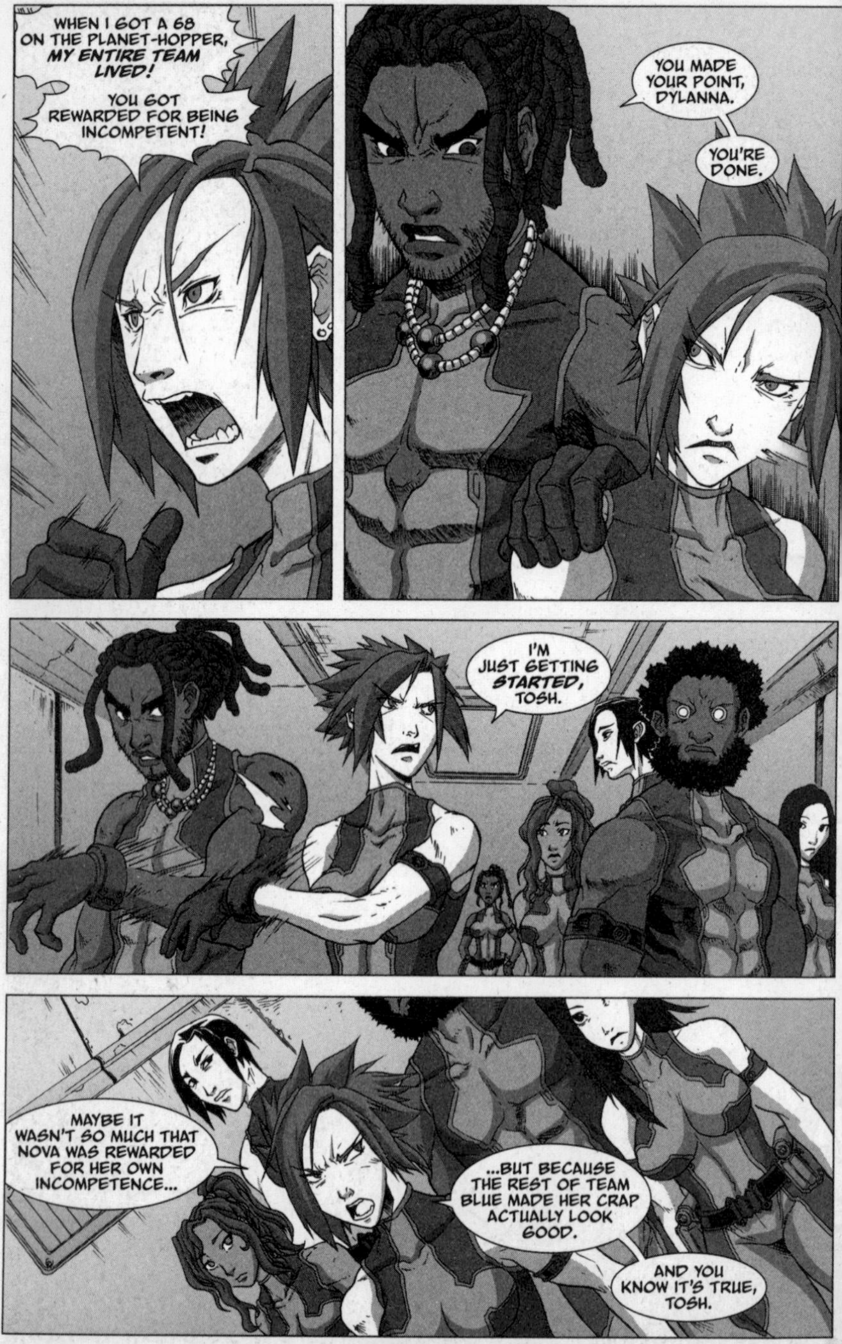
WHEN I GOT A 68 ON THE PLANET-HOPPER, ***MY ENTIRE TEAM LIVED!***
YOU GOT REWARDED FOR BEING INCOMPETENT!
YOU MADE YOUR POINT, DYLANNA.
YOU'RE DONE.
I'M JUST GETTING ***STARTED,*** TOSH.
MAYBE IT WASN'T SO MUCH THAT NOVA WAS REWARDED FOR HER OWN INCOMPETENCE...
...BUT BECAUSE THE REST OF TEAM BLUE MADE HER CRAP ACTUALLY LOOK GOOD.
AND YOU KNOW IT'S TRUE, TOSH.

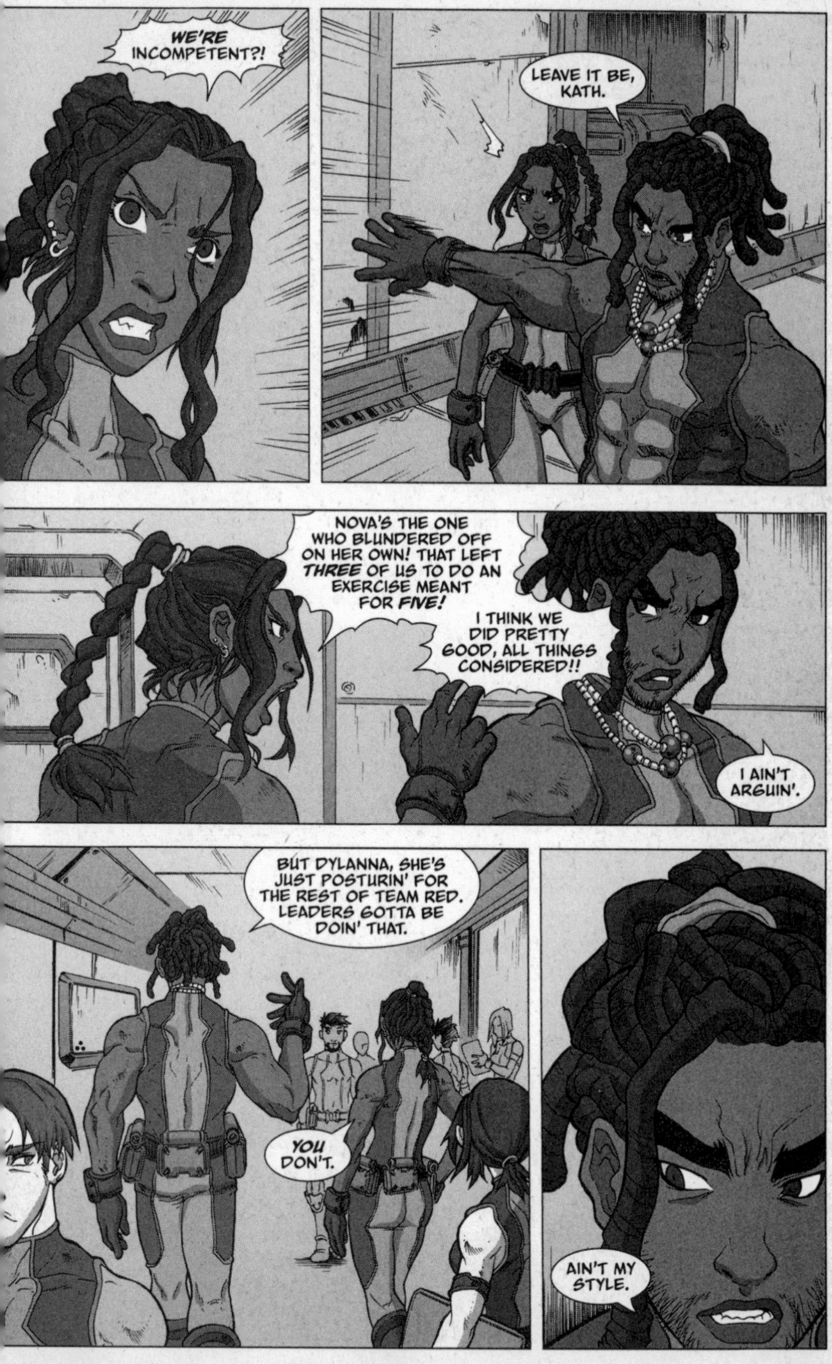
WE'RE INCOMPETENT?!
LEAVE IT BE, KATH.
NOVA'S THE ONE WHO BLUNDERED OFF ON HER OWN! THAT LEFT THREE OF US TO DO AN EXERCISE MEANT FOR FIVE!
I THINK WE DID PRETTY GOOD, ALL THINGS CONSIDERED!!
I AIN'T ARGUIN'.
BUT DYLANNA, SHE'S JUST POSTURIN' FOR THE REST OF TEAM RED. LEADERS GOTTA BE DOIN' THAT.
YOU DON'T.
AIN'T MY STYLE.

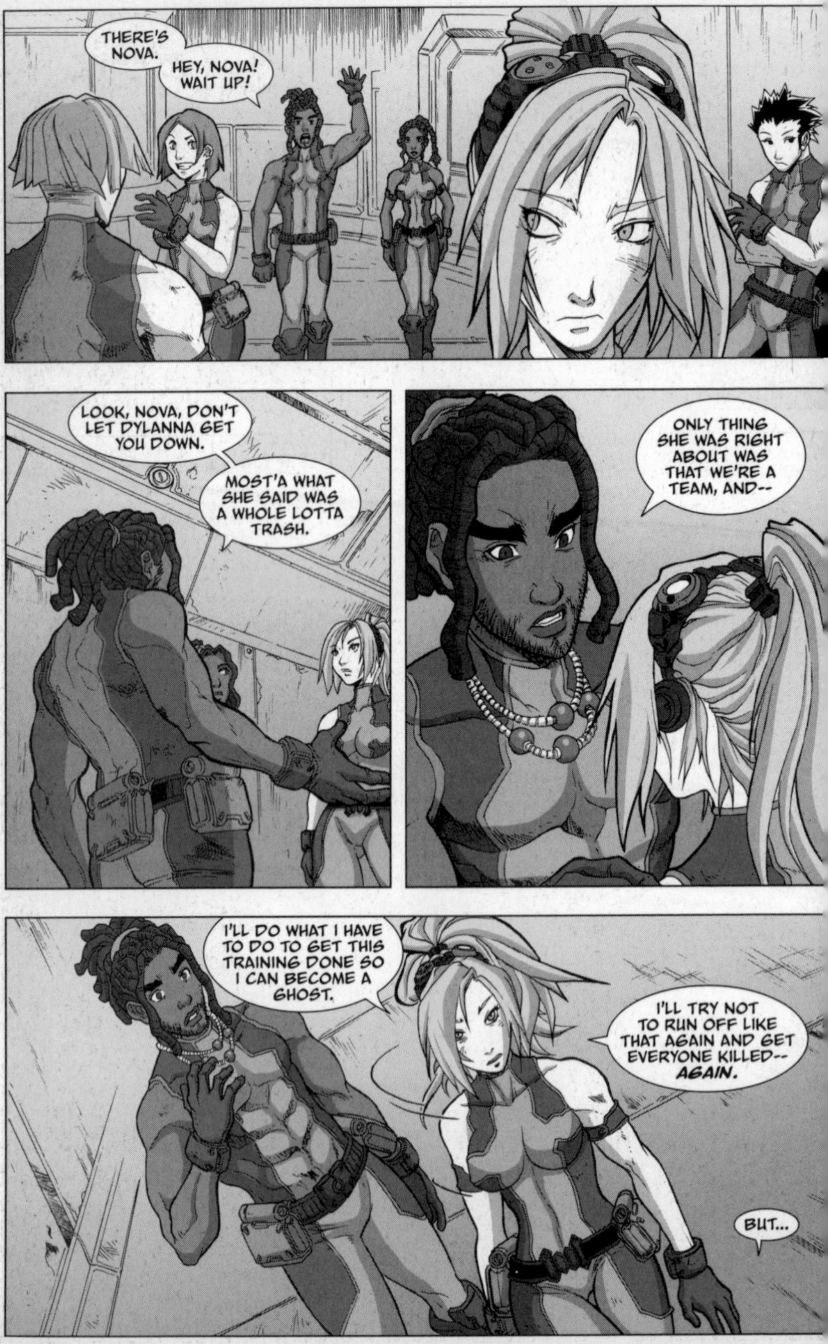
THERE'S NOVA.
HEY, NOVA! WAIT UP!
LOOK, NOVA, DON'T LET DYLANNA GET YOU DOWN.
MOST'A WHAT SHE SAID WAS A WHOLE LOTTA TRASH.
ONLY THING SHE WAS RIGHT ABOUT WAS THAT WE'RE A TEAM, AND--
I'LL DO WHAT I HAVE TO DO TO GET THIS TRAINING DONE SO I CAN BECOME A GHOST.
I'LL TRY NOT TO RUN OFF LIKE THAT AGAIN AND GET EVERYONE KILLED-- ***AGAIN.***
BUT...

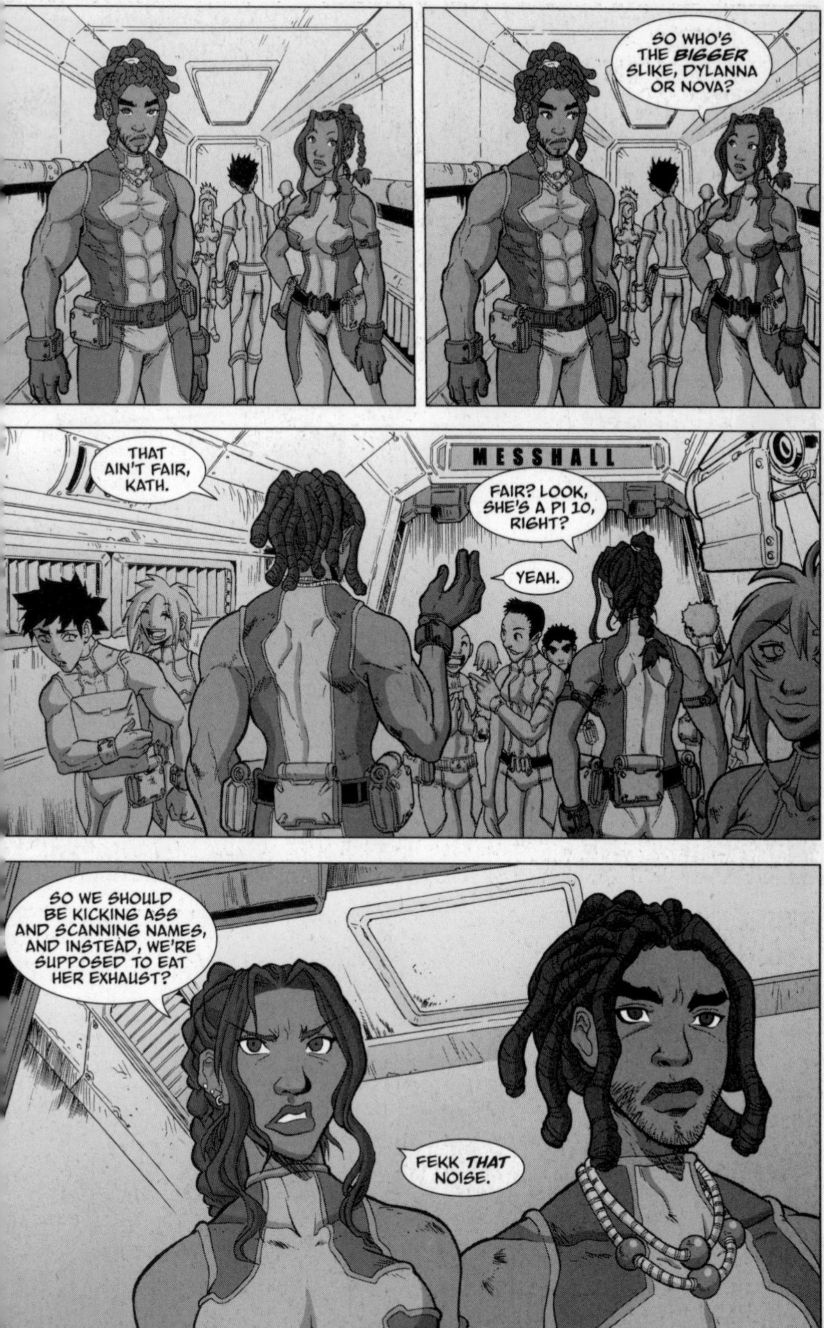
SO WHO'S THE *BIGGER* SLIKE, DYLANNA OR NOVA?
MESSHALL
THAT AIN'T FAIR, KATH.
FAIR? LOOK, SHE'S A PI 10, RIGHT?
YEAH.
SO WE SHOULD BE KICKING ASS AND SCANNING NAMES, AND INSTEAD, WE'RE SUPPOSED TO EAT HER EXHAUST?
FEKK *THAT* NOISE.

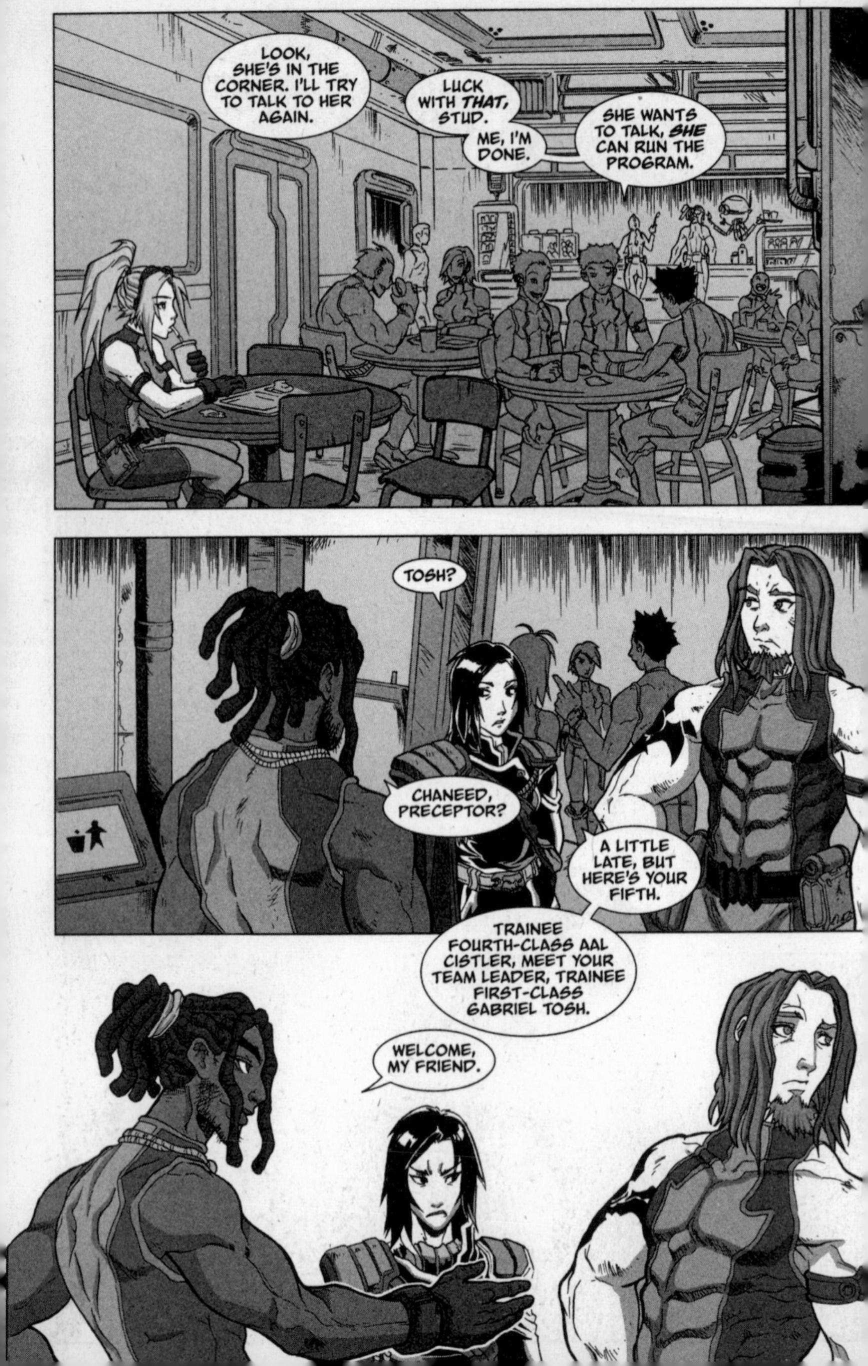
LOOK, SHE'S IN THE CORNER. I'LL TRY TO TALK TO HER AGAIN.
LUCK WITH THAT, STUD.
ME, I'M DONE.
SHE WANTS TO TALK, SHE CAN RUN THE PROGRAM.
TOSH?
CHANEED, PRECEPTOR?
A LITTLE LATE, BUT HERE'S YOUR FIFTH.
TRAINEE FOURTH-CLASS AAL CISTLER, MEET YOUR TEAM LEADER, TRAINEE FIRST-CLASS GABRIEL TOSH.
WELCOME, MY FRIEND.

I DON'T HAVE ANY FRIENDS HERE.

SORRY ABOUT THAT. HE'S A BIT...

I RECOGNIZE THE STUD.

HE'S THE FINANCE MINISTER'S BOY?

MHM. HERE ON THE MY-FATHER'S-IMPORTANT SCHOLARSHIP PLAN.

NO WORRIES, PRECEPTOR. I'LL BE TAKIN' CARE OF HIM.

HOPE SO. HE'S ONLY A PI 4.5.

A 4.5?

I KNOW, I KNOW--LOOK, THIS COMES STRAIGHT FROM BICK.

HEY, I ALWAYS SAY I LIKE A CHALLENGE.

GOOD THING, 'CAUSE YOU GOT ONE WITH THIS SLIKE.

BELIEVE ME.

DEAR UNCLE DESI:

DEAR UNCLE DESI:
HOPE ALL'S WELL ON
PRIDEWATER. YOU WERE LUCKY
TO GET OUT OF NIDHOGG.
SO WAS I, HONESTLY.

REALLY REALLY AWFUL.
I TOTALLY CRACKED UP IN
CLASS TODAY. GOT A 10%,
WHICH IS WHAT THEY GIVE
YOU FOR SHOWING UP.

YOU FOR SHOWING UP.
BUT THAT'S NOT THE
REALLY REALLY REALLY
REALLY AWFUL THING.

SO WAS I, HONESTLY.
SOMETHING REALLY
REALLY REALLY REALLY
AWFUL HAPPENED TODAY.

AWFUL HAPPENED TODAY.
ACTUALLY, TWO
SOMETHINGS AWFUL,
BUT ONE OF THEM WAS
JUST AWFUL, NOT REALLY
REALLY REALLY AWFUL.

HOW'S IT
GOIN', LIO?

GAAHHHH!!!

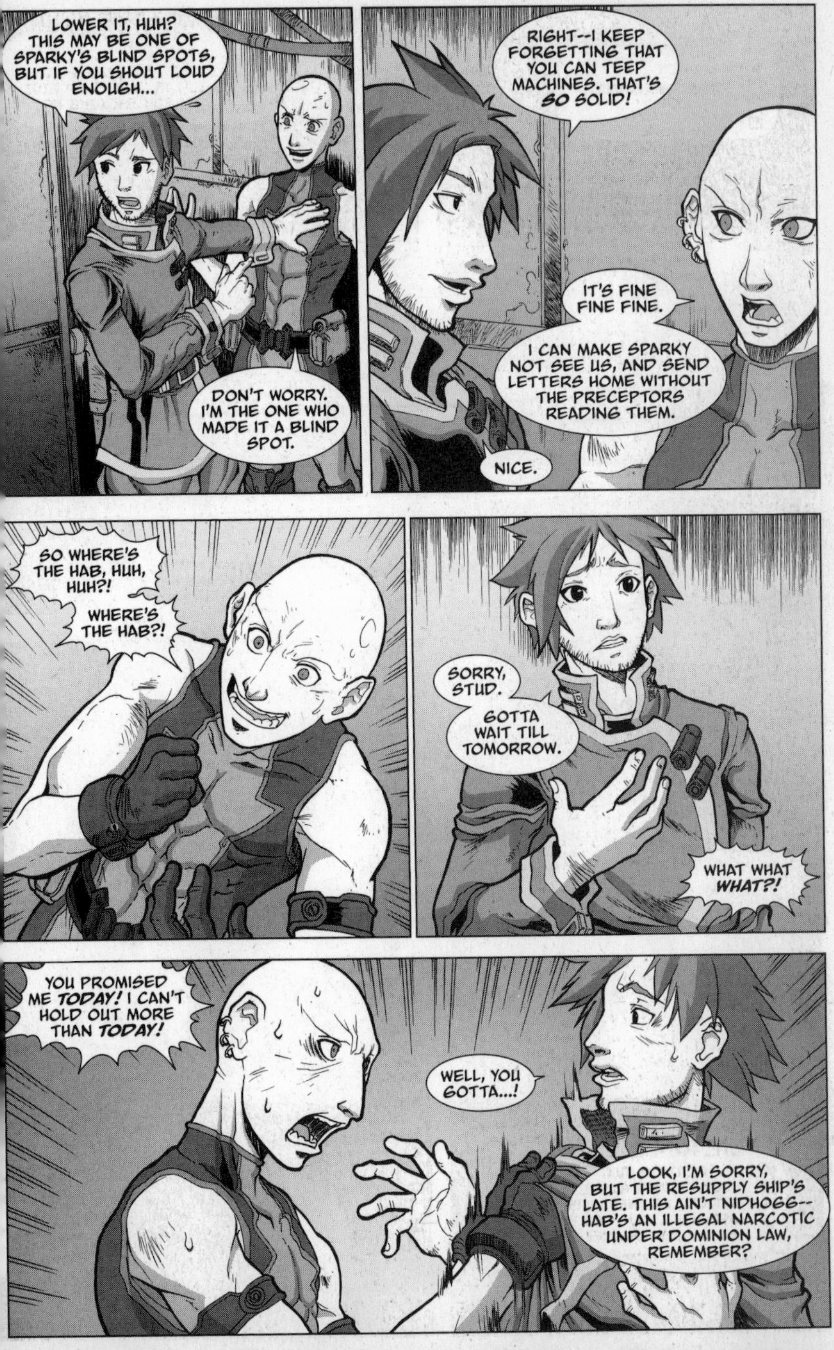
LOWER IT, HUH? THIS MAY BE ONE OF SPARKY'S BLIND SPOTS, BUT IF YOU SHOUT LOUD ENOUGH...
DON'T WORRY. I'M THE ONE WHO MADE IT A BLIND SPOT.
RIGHT--I KEEP FORGETTING THAT YOU CAN TEEP MACHINES. THAT'S *SO* SOLID!
IT'S FINE FINE FINE.
I CAN MAKE SPARKY NOT SEE US, AND SEND LETTERS HOME WITHOUT THE PRECEPTORS READING THEM.
NICE.
SO WHERE'S THE HAB, HUH, HUH?!
WHERE'S THE HAB?!
SORRY, STUD.
GOTTA WAIT TILL TOMORROW.
WHAT WHAT *WHAT?!*
YOU PROMISED ME *TODAY!* I CAN'T HOLD OUT MORE THAN *TODAY!*
WELL, YOU GOTTA...!
LOOK, I'M SORRY, BUT THE RESUPPLY SHIP'S LATE. THIS AIN'T NIDHOGG--HAB'S AN ILLEGAL NARCOTIC UNDER DOMINION LAW, REMEMBER?

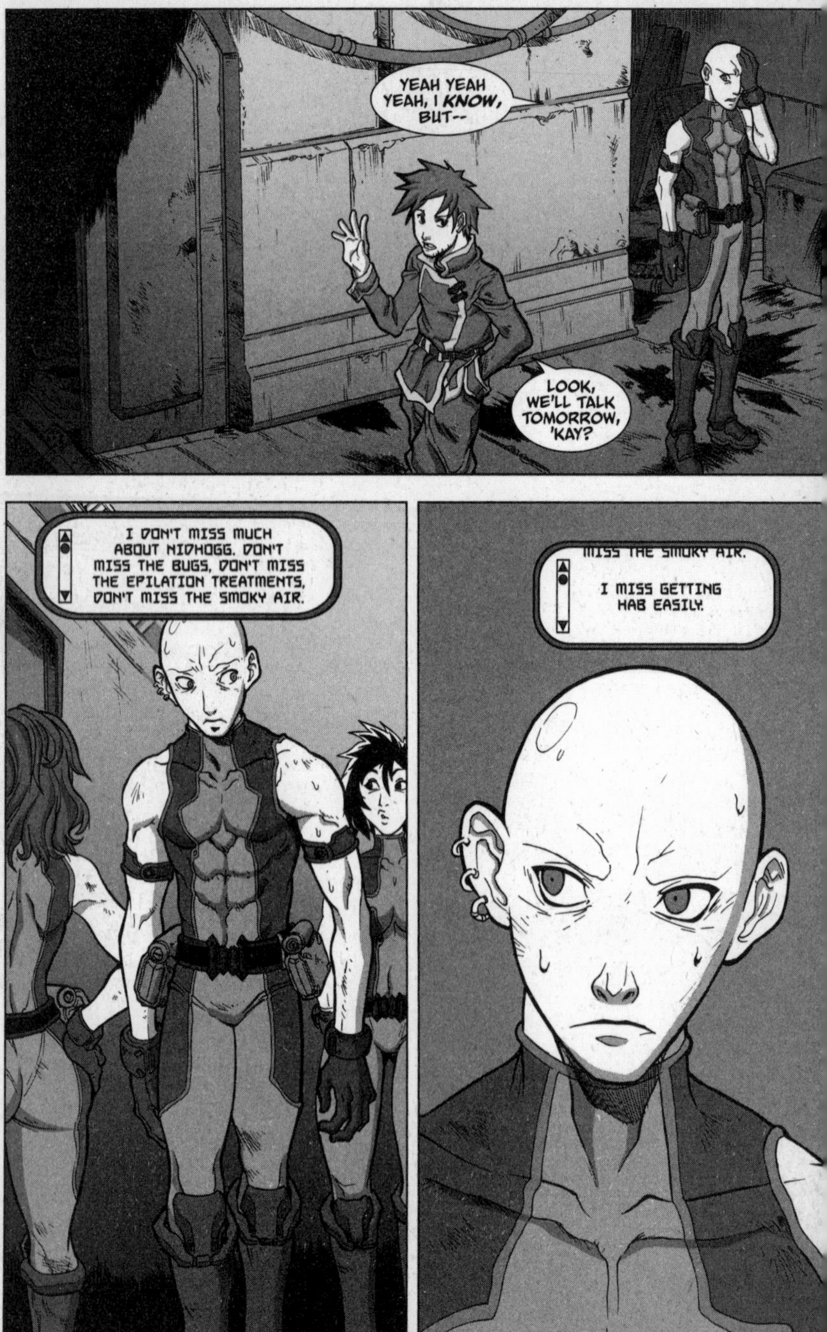
YEAH YEAH YEAH, I **KNOW**, BUT--
LOOK, WE'LL TALK TOMORROW, 'KAY?
I DON'T MISS MUCH ABOUT NIDHOGG. DON'T MISS THE BUGS, DON'T MISS THE EPILATION TREATMENTS, DON'T MISS THE SMOKY AIR.
I MISS GETTING HAB EASILY.

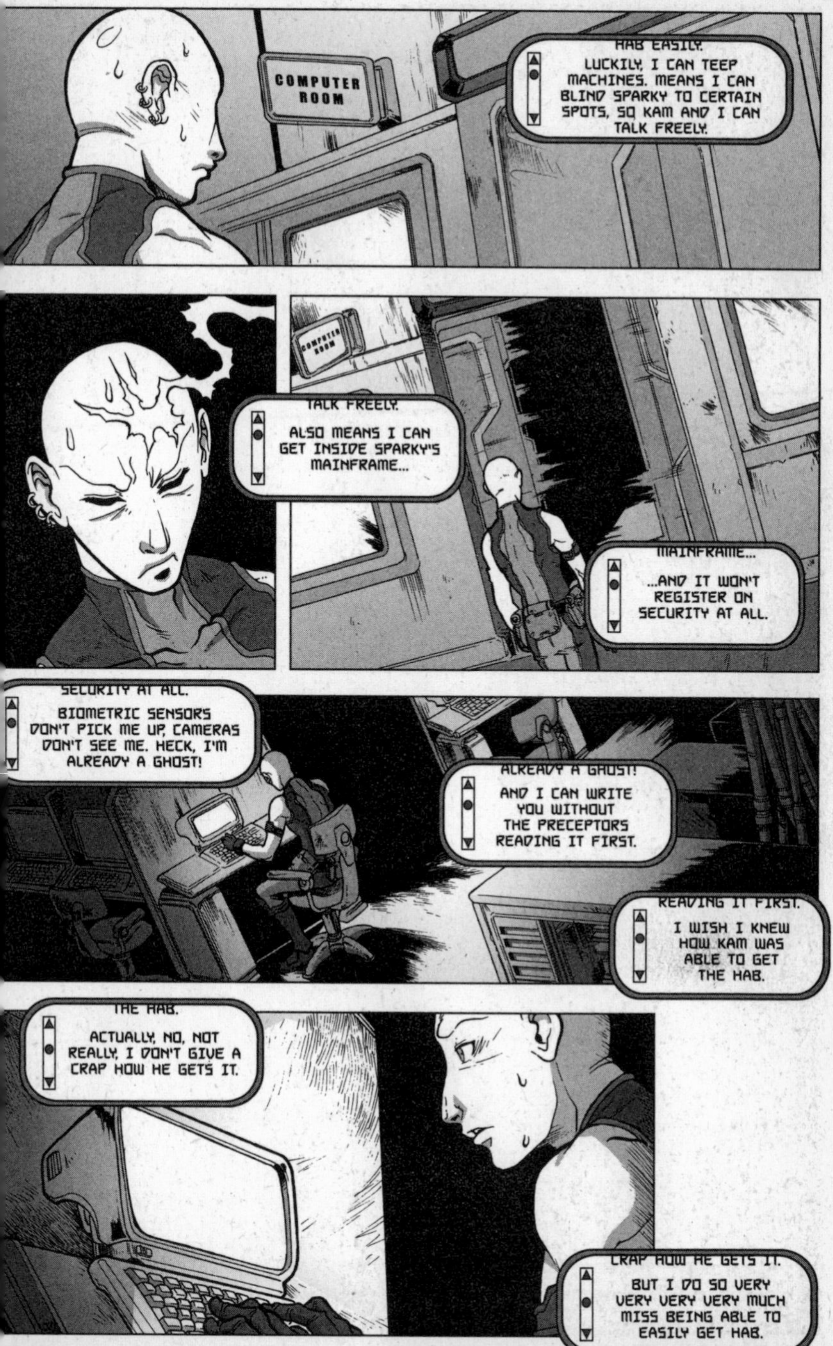
HAB EASILY.
LUCKILY, I CAN TEEP MACHINES. MEANS I CAN BLIND SPARKY TO CERTAIN SPOTS, SO KAM AND I CAN TALK FREELY.
COMPUTER ROOM
TALK FREELY.
ALSO MEANS I CAN GET INSIDE SPARKY'S MAINFRAME...
COMPUTER ROOM
MAINFRAME...
...AND IT WON'T REGISTER ON SECURITY AT ALL.
SECURITY AT ALL.
BIOMETRIC SENSORS DON'T PICK ME UP, CAMERAS DON'T SEE ME. HECK, I'M ALREADY A GHOST!
ALREADY A GHOST!
AND I CAN WRITE YOU WITHOUT THE PRECEPTORS READING IT FIRST.
READING IT FIRST.
I WISH I KNEW HOW KAM WAS ABLE TO GET THE HAB.
THE HAB.
ACTUALLY, NO, NOT REALLY, I DON'T GIVE A CRAP HOW HE GETS IT.
CRAP HOW HE GETS IT.
BUT I DO SO VERY VERY VERY VERY MUCH MISS BEING ABLE TO EASILY GET HAB.

EASILY GET HAB.

I WISH WISH WISH THAT THE REST OF THE DOMINION WOULD GET WHAT THE DOCS ON NIÐHOGG GET...

ON NIÐHOGG GET...

THAT HAB ISN'T *JUST A PARTY DRUG.*

JUST A PARTY DRUG.

WITHOUT IT, I'D BE SO COMPLETELY FOGGED.

FOGGED.

CAN'T FOCUS, CAN'T THINK STRAIGHT, CAN'T EVEN ALWAYS SEE STRAIGHT.

SEE STRAIGHT.

HOPE KAM CAN GET IT SOON.

060

GET IT SOON.

I ALSO HOPE SUPERINTENDENT ANGELINI NEVER FINDS OUT, OR HE'LL WASH ME OUT OR WORSE.

OUT OR WORSE.

WELL, I NEED TO GO, UNCLE DESI.

GO, UNCLE DESI.

I NEED TO SLEEP, SINCE I'M OUT OF HAB, AND I NEED TO BE FOCUSED TOMORROW AND WITHOUT HAB I HAVE TO SLEEP AT LEAST TEN HOURS TO GET THAT. IF KAM DOESN'T HAVE THE SUPPLY TOMORROW, I DON'T KNOW WHAT I'LL DO.

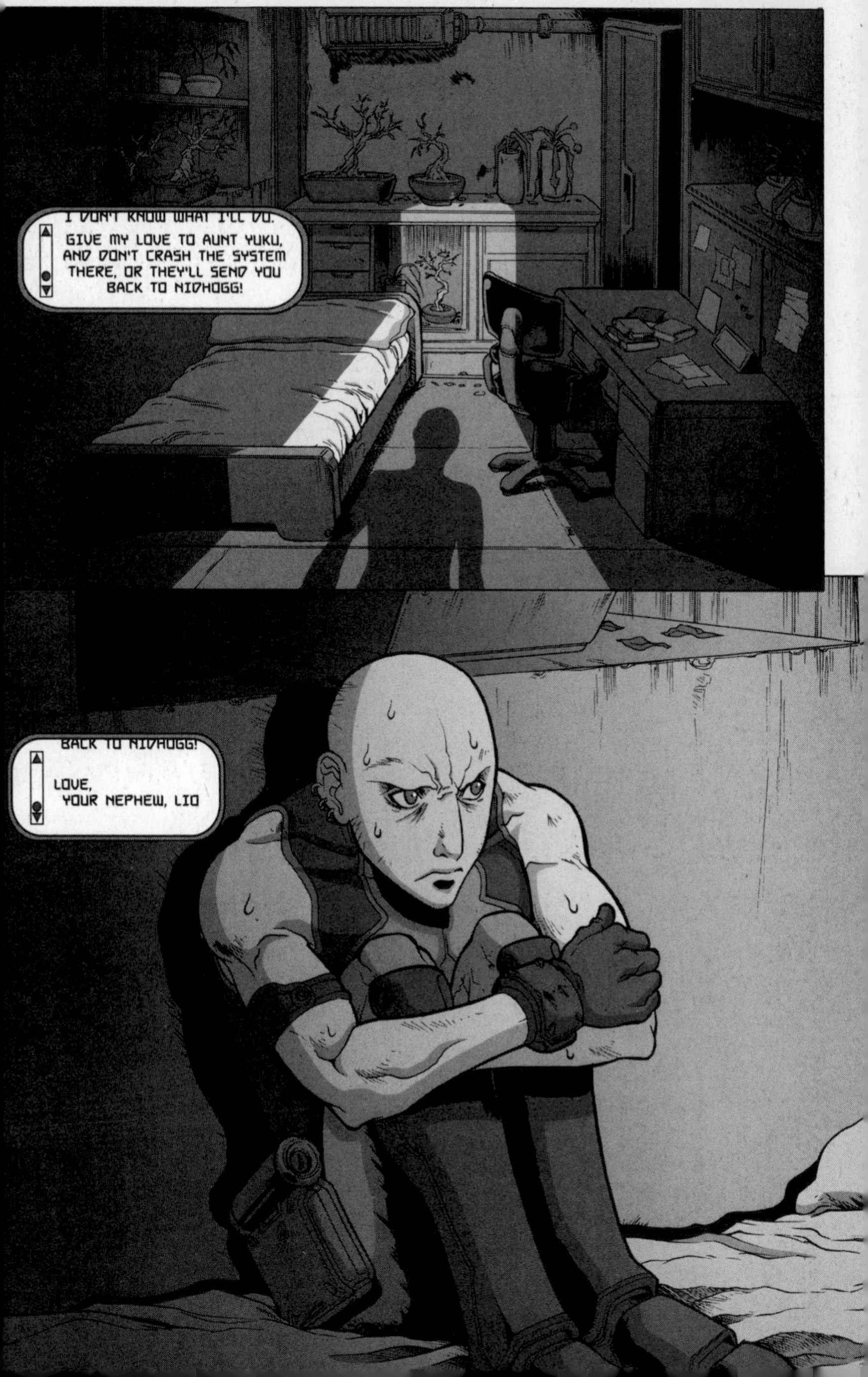
I DON'T KNOW WHAT I'LL DO.
GIVE MY LOVE TO AUNT YUKU, AND DON'T CRASH THE SYSTEM THERE, OR THEY'LL SEND YOU BACK TO NIDHOGG!
BACK TO NIDHOGG!
LOVE, YOUR NEPHEW, LIO

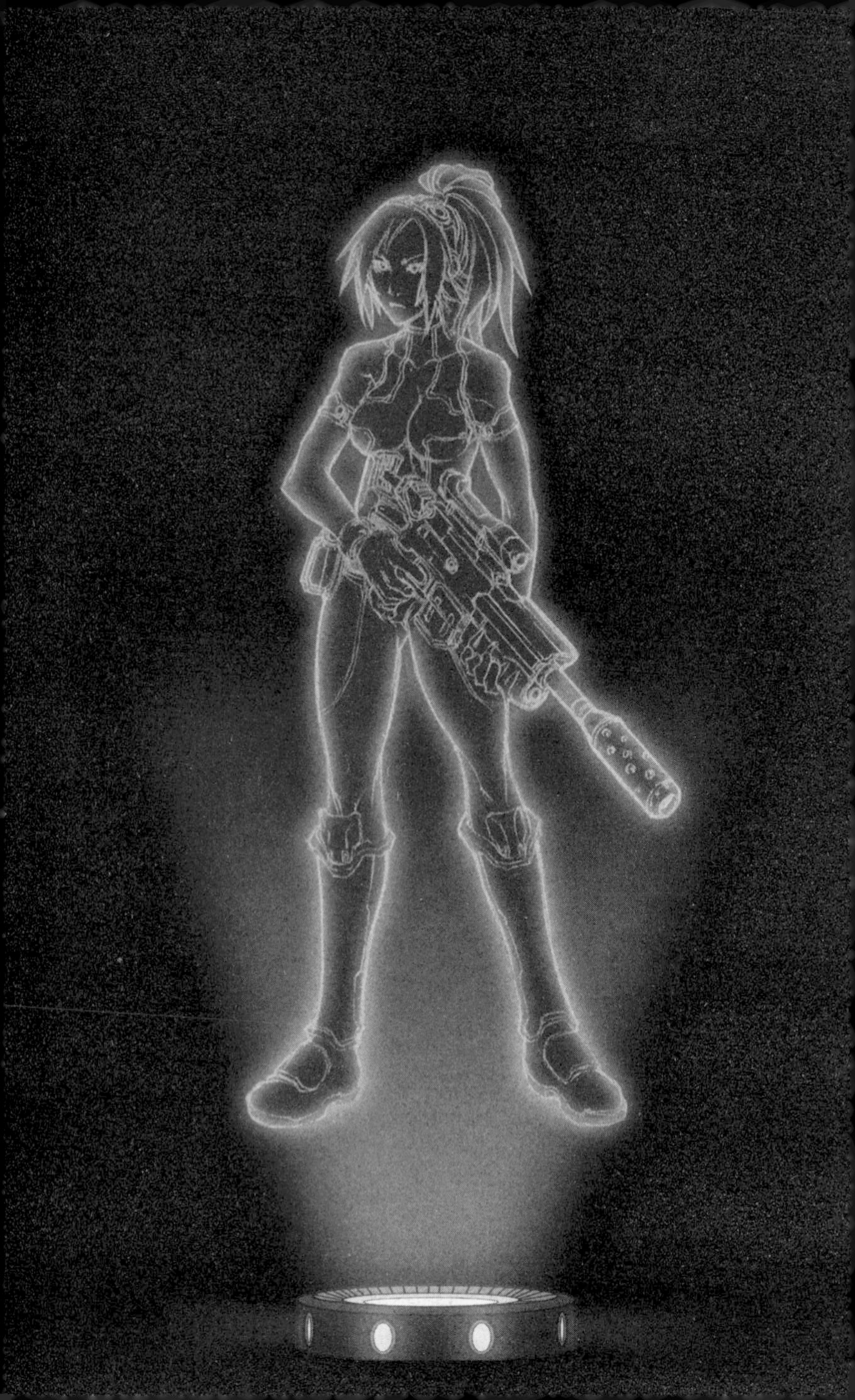

CHAPTER 3

SEVEN TIMES FALL DOWN, EIGHT TIMES GET UP

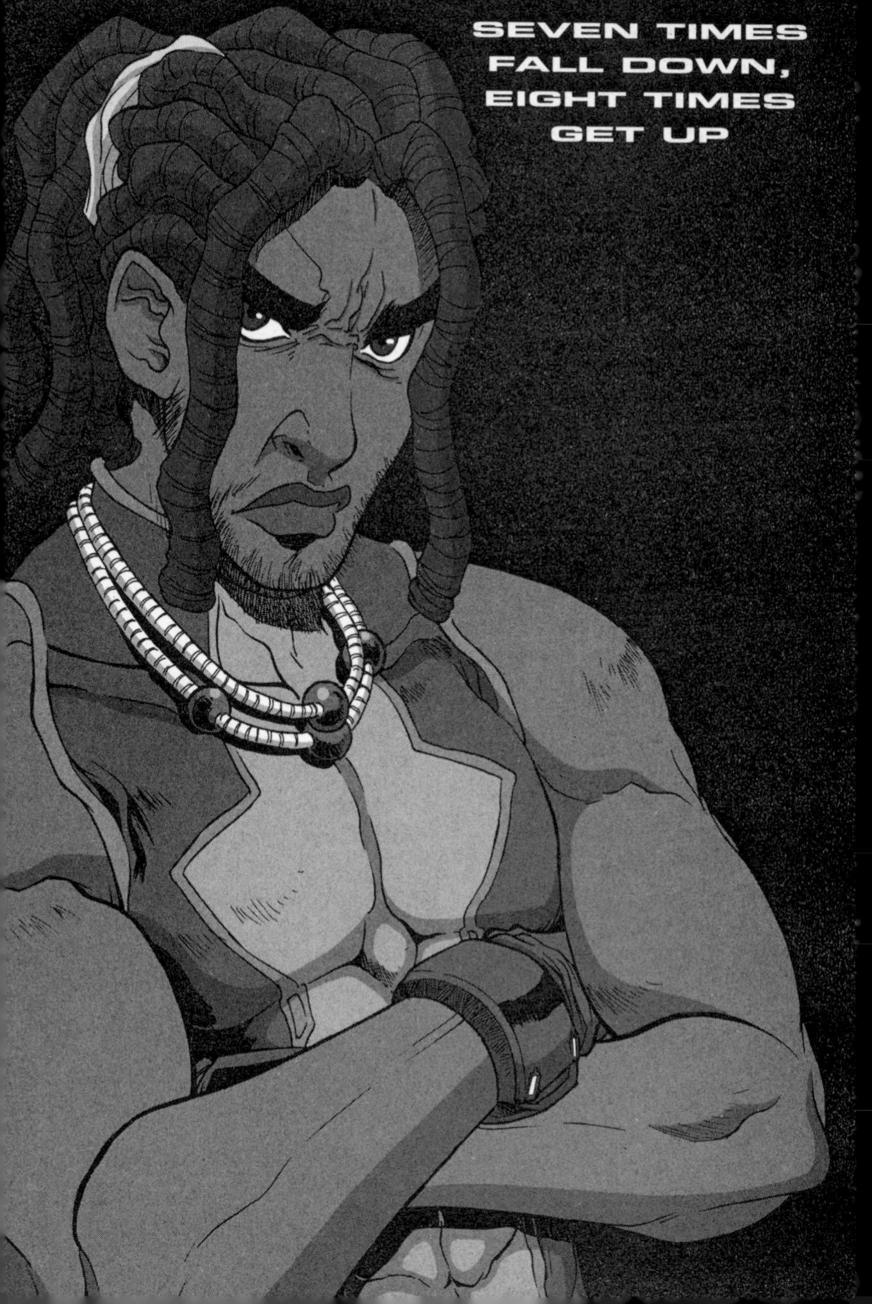

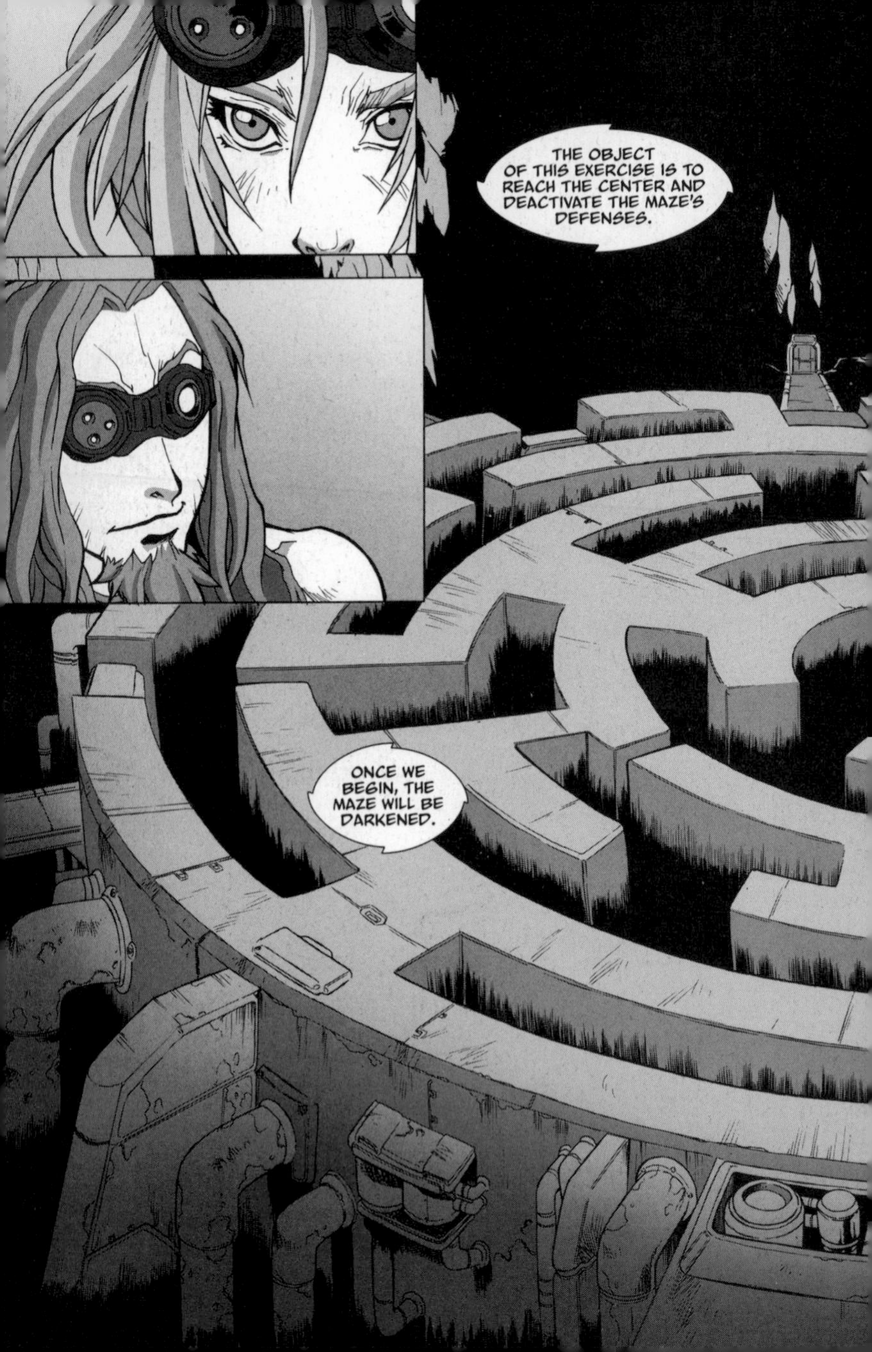
THE OBJECT OF THIS EXERCISE IS TO REACH THE CENTER AND DEACTIVATE THE MAZE'S DEFENSES.
ONCE WE BEGIN, THE MAZE WILL BE DARKENED.

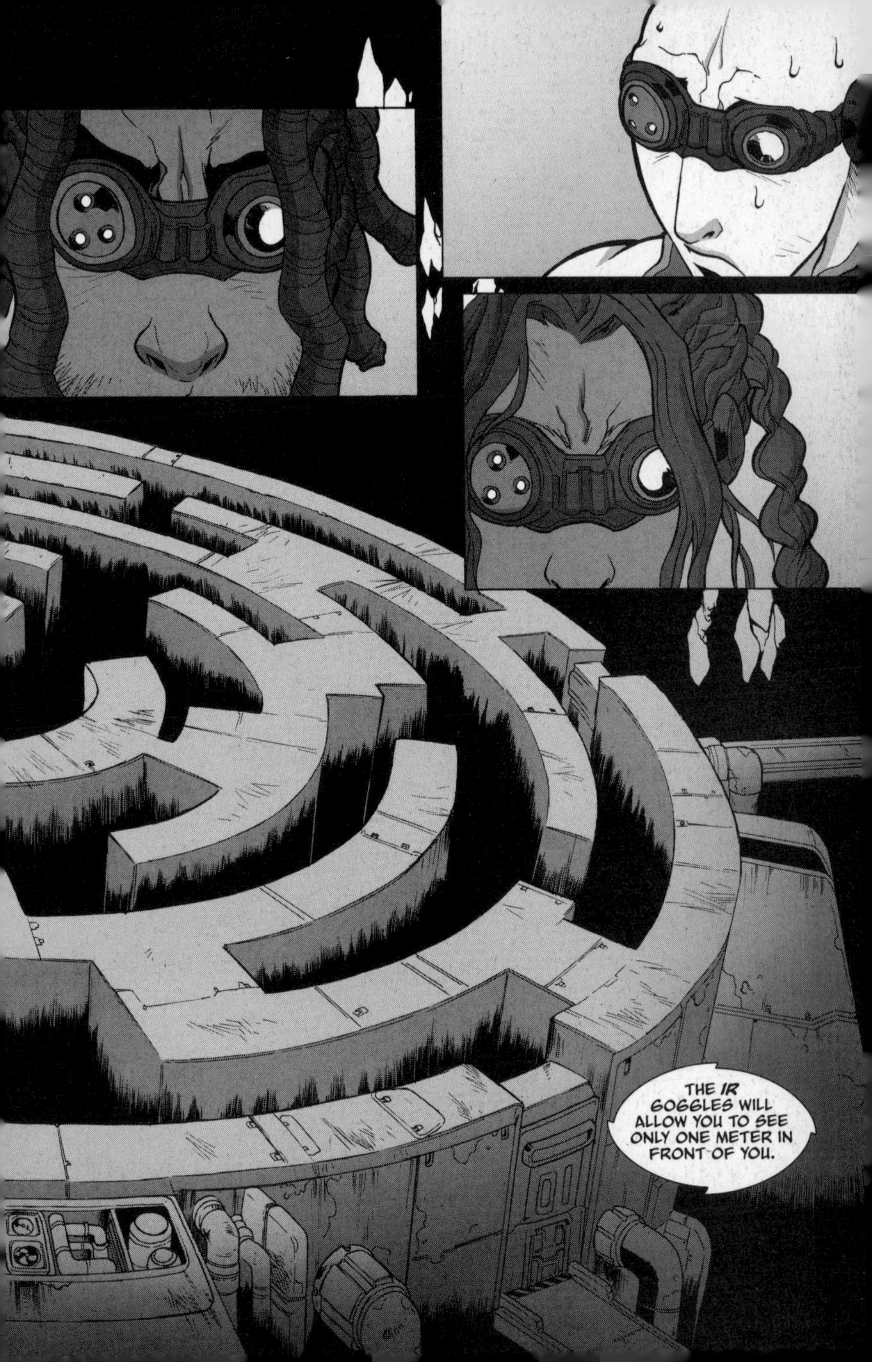
THE IR GOGGLES WILL ALLOW YOU TO SEE ONLY ONE METER IN FRONT OF YOU.

BEGINNING...

NOW!

OKAY, TEAM...

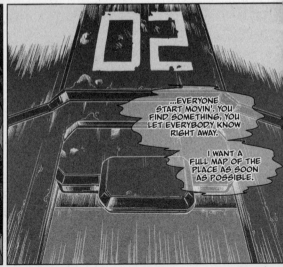

...EVERYONE START MOVIN'. YOU FIND SOMETHING, YOU LET EVERYBODY KNOW RIGHT AWAY.

I WANT A FULL MAP OF THE PLACE AS SOON AS POSSIBLE.

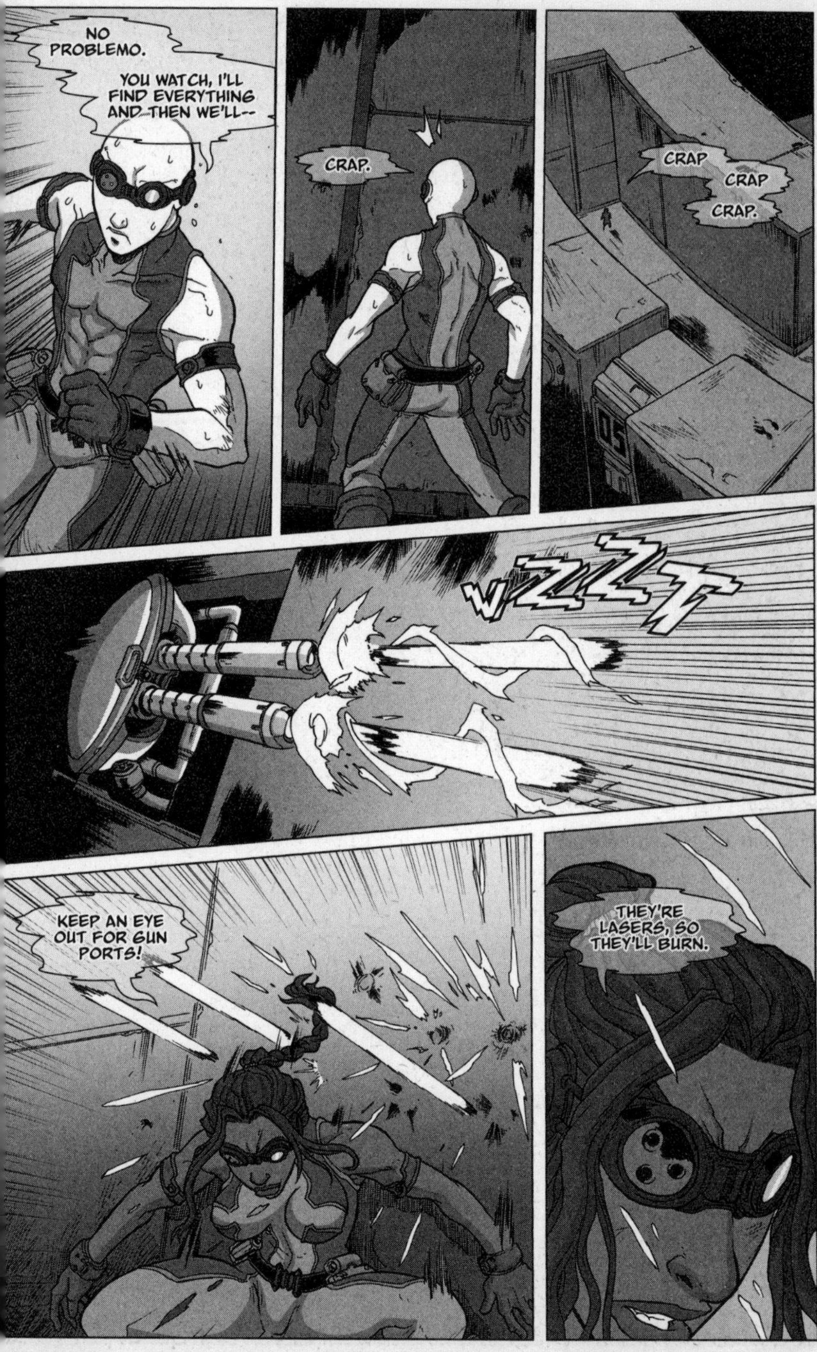
NO PROBLEMO.
YOU WATCH, I'LL FIND EVERYTHING AND THEN WE'LL--
CRAP.
CRAP
CRAP
CRAP.
05
VZZZT
KEEP AN EYE OUT FOR GUN PORTS!
THEY'RE LASERS, SO THEY'LL BURN.

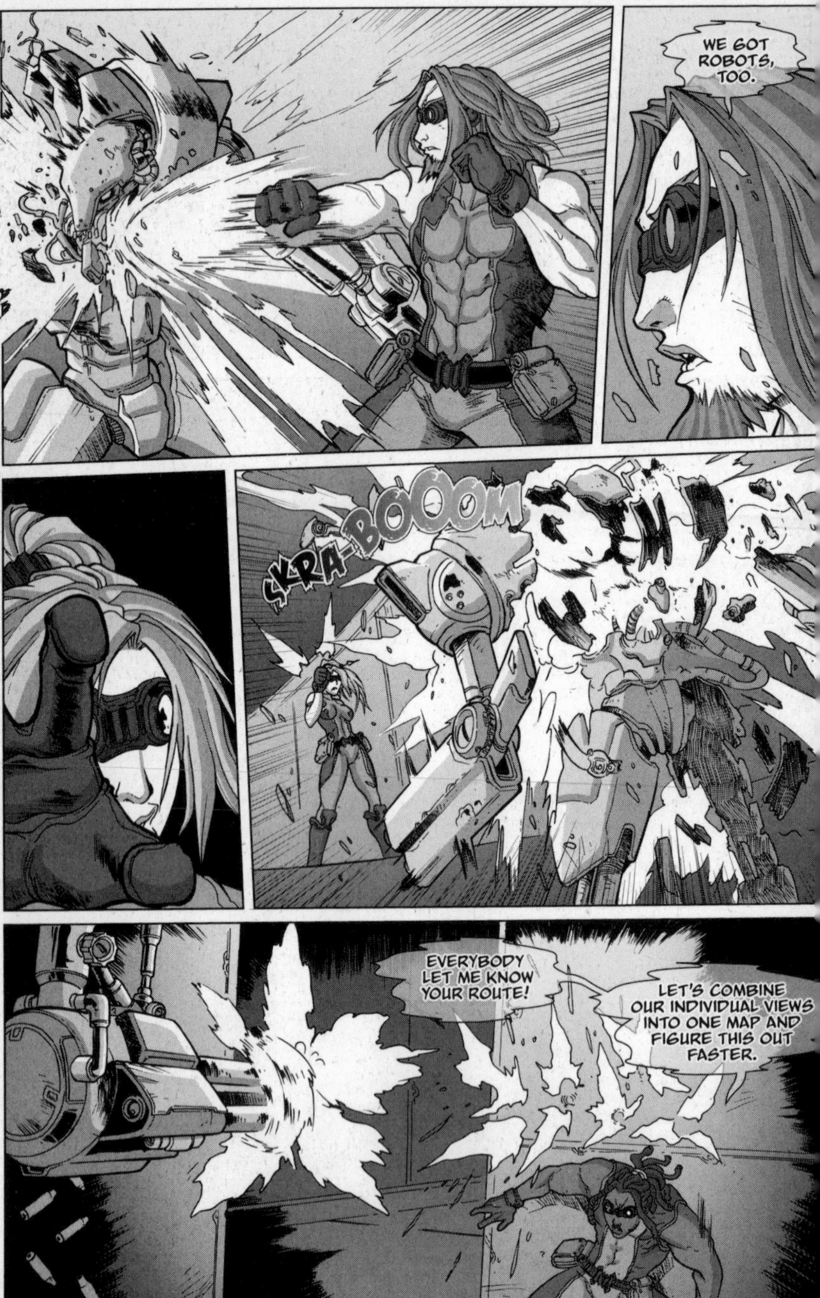
WE GOT ROBOTS, TOO.
SKRA-BOOOM
EVERYBODY LET ME KNOW YOUR ROUTE!
LET'S COMBINE OUR INDIVIDUAL VIEWS INTO ONE MAP AND FIGURE THIS OUT FASTER.

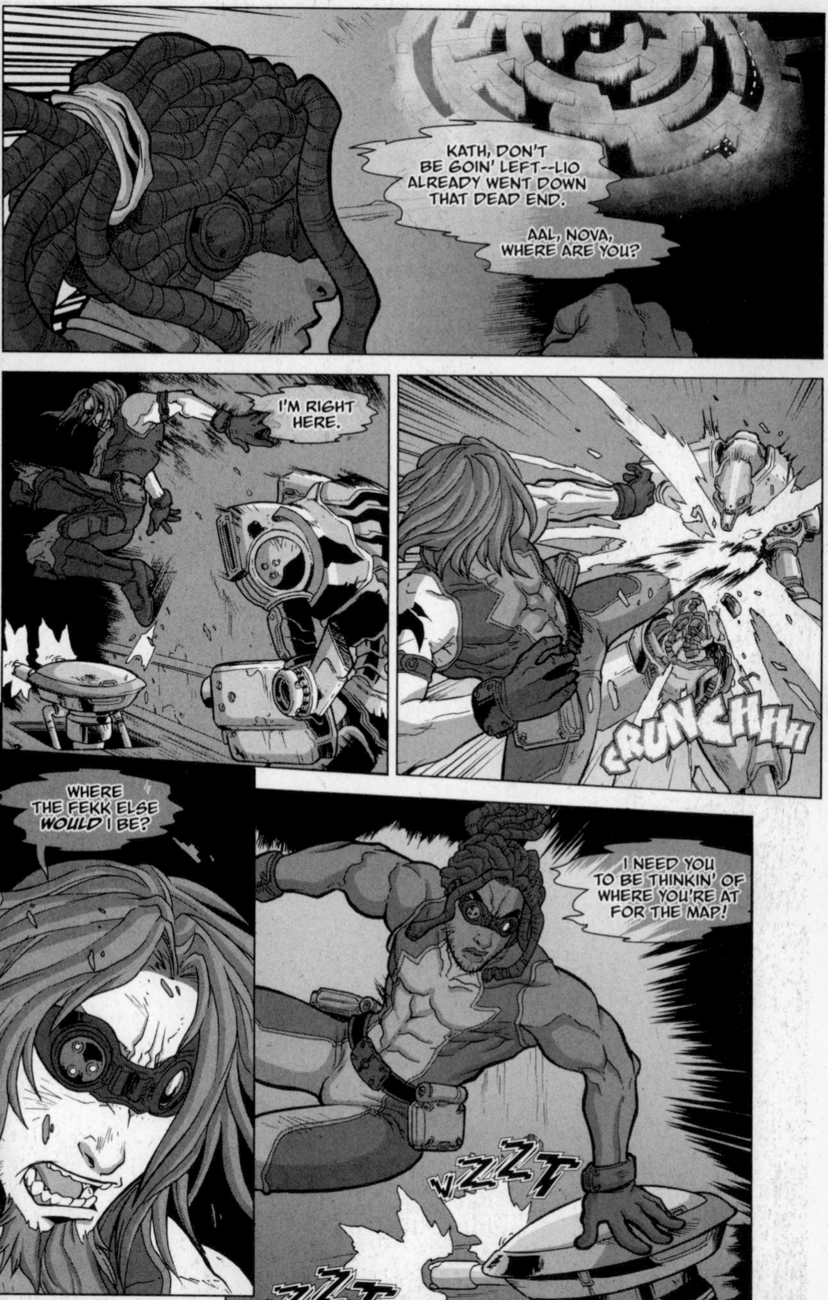
KATH, DON'T BE GOIN' LEFT--LIO ALREADY WENT DOWN THAT DEAD END.
AAL, NOVA, WHERE ARE YOU?
I'M RIGHT HERE.
CRUNCHHH
WHERE THE FEKK ELSE *WOULD* I BE?
I NEED YOU TO BE THINKIN' OF WHERE YOU'RE AT FOR THE MAP!
WZZZT
WZZZT

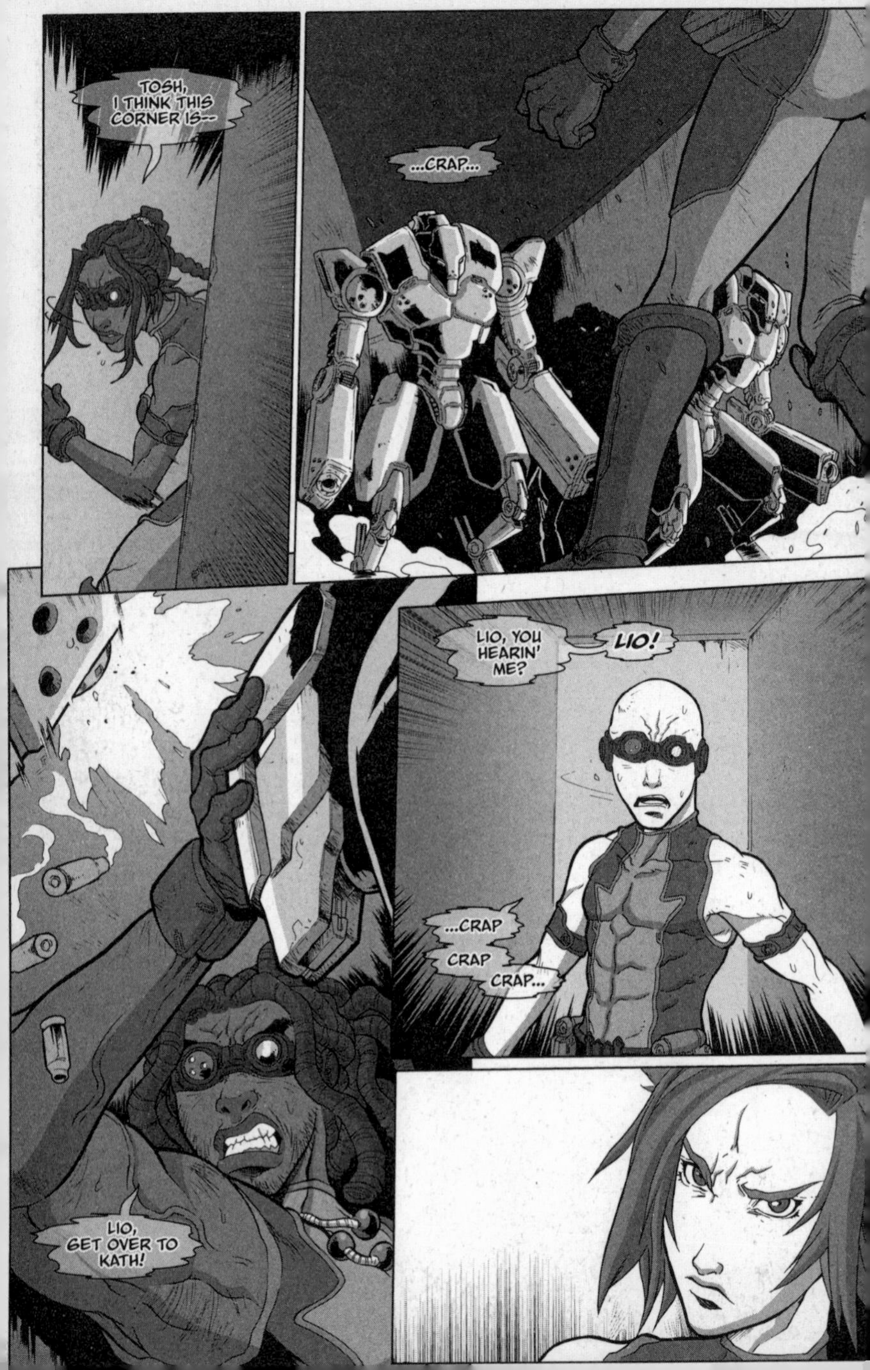
TOSH, I THINK THIS CORNER IS--
...CRAP...
LIO, YOU HEARIN' ME?
LIO!
...CRAP
CRAP
CRAP...
LIO, GET OVER TO KATH!

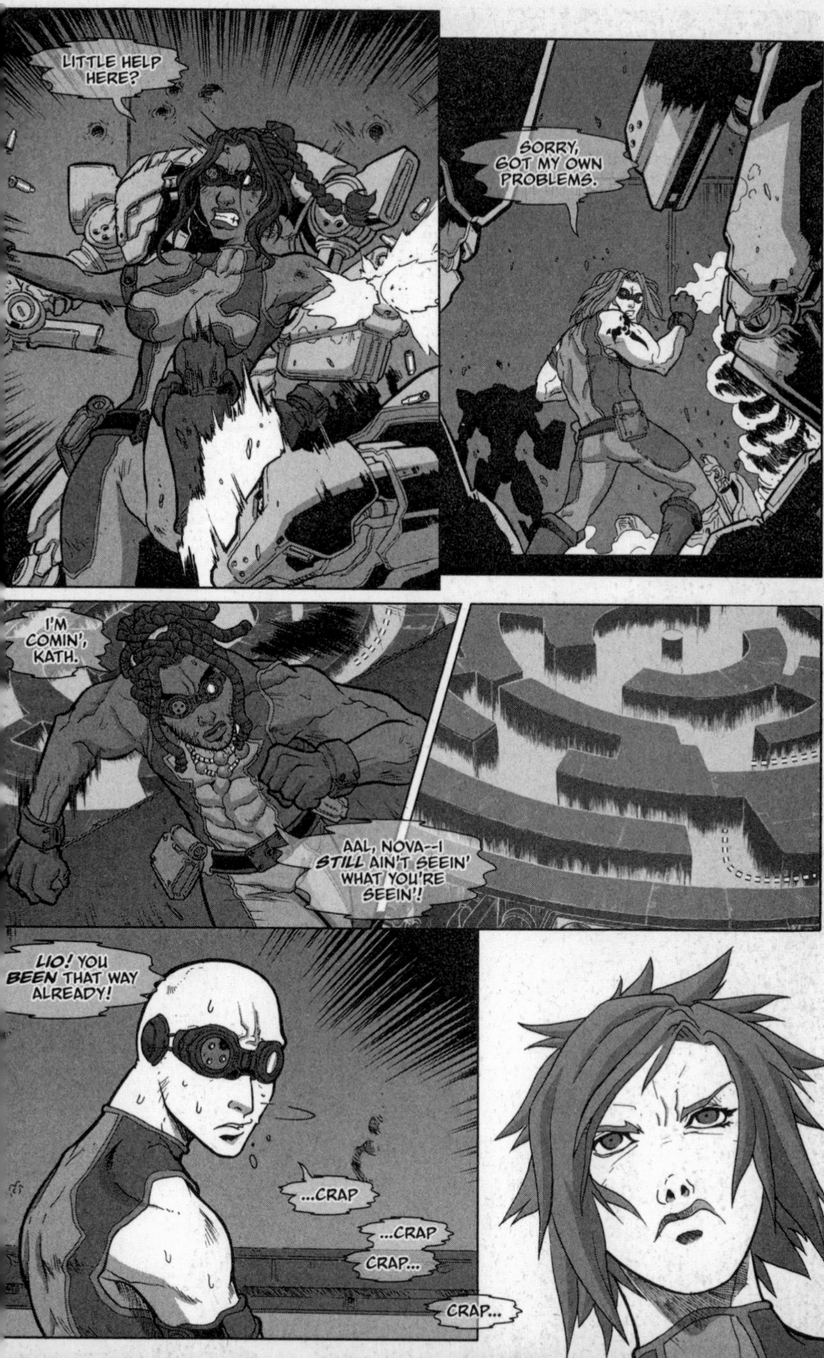
LITTLE HELP HERE?
SORRY, GOT MY OWN PROBLEMS.
I'M COMIN', KATH.
AAL, NOVA--I STILL AIN'T SEEIN' WHAT YOU'RE SEEIN'!
LIO! YOU BEEN THAT WAY ALREADY!
...CRAP
...CRAP
CRAP...
CRAP...

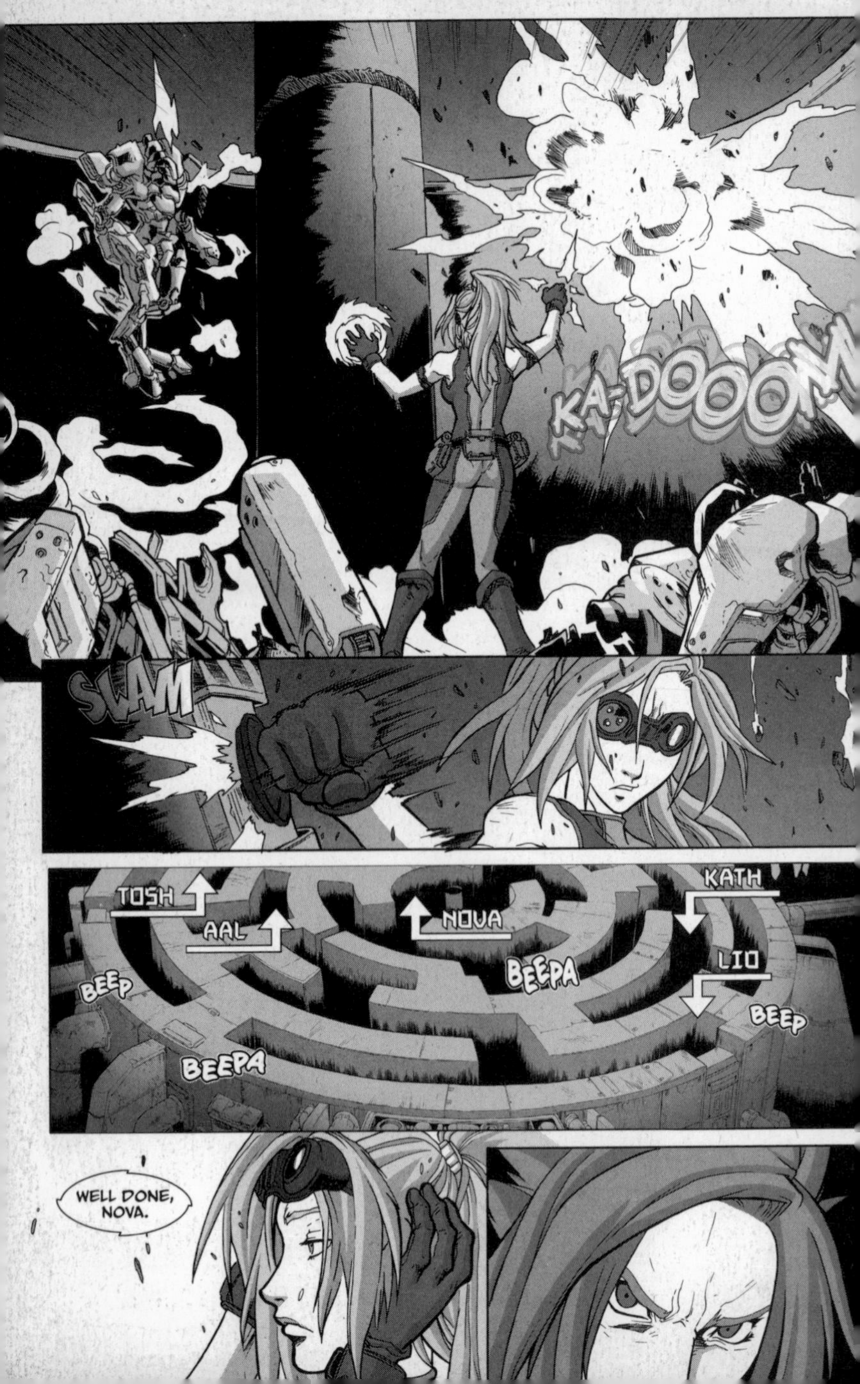
KA-DOOOOM
SLAM
TOSH
AAL
NOVA
KATH
LIO
BEEP
BEEPA
BEEPA
BEEP
WELL DONE, NOVA.

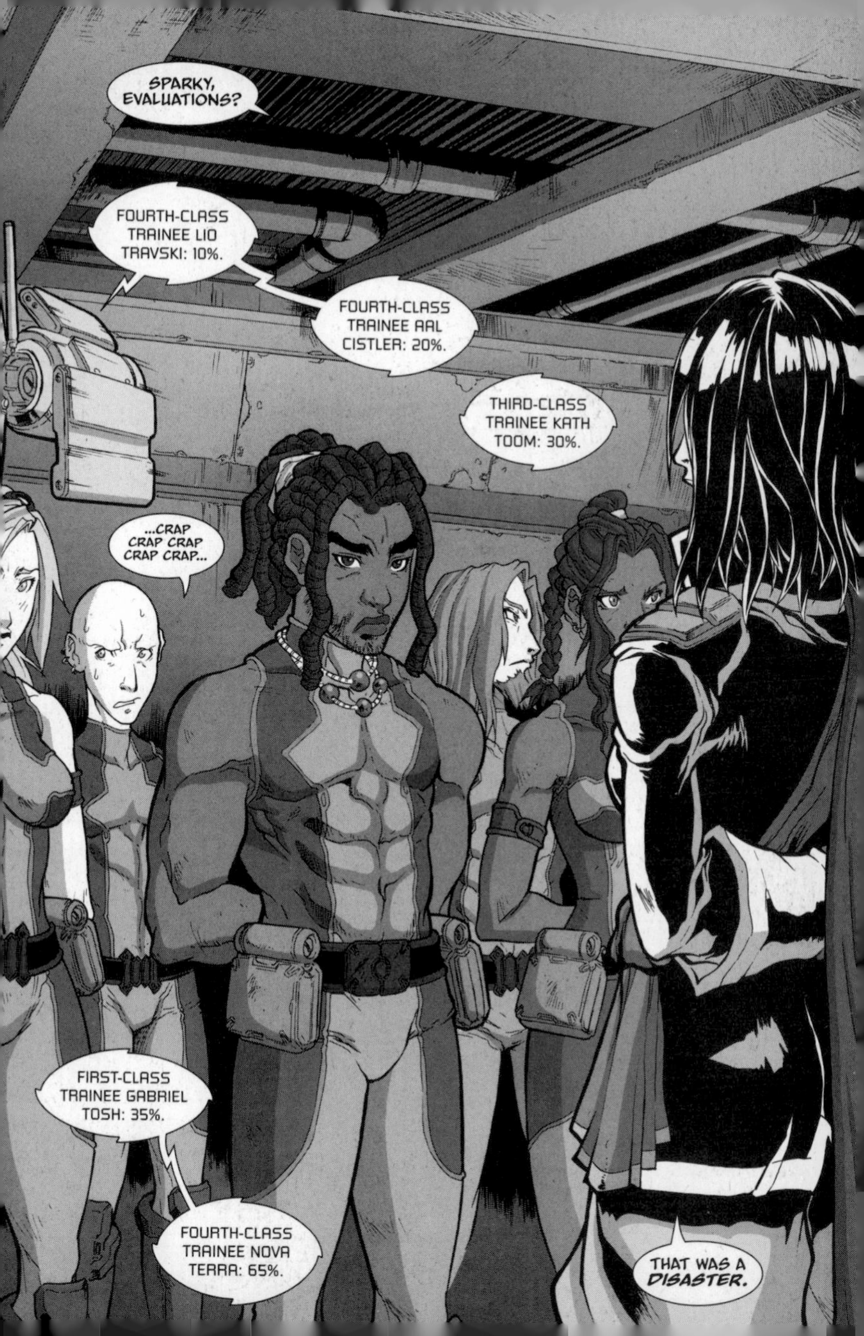
SPARKY, EVALUATIONS?
FOURTH-CLASS TRAINEE LIO TRAVSKI: 10%.
FOURTH-CLASS TRAINEE AAL CISTLER: 20%.
THIRD-CLASS TRAINEE KATH TOOM: 30%.
...CRAP CRAP CRAP CRAP CRAP...
FIRST-CLASS TRAINEE GABRIEL TOSH: 35%.
FOURTH-CLASS TRAINEE NOVA TERRA: 65%.
THAT WAS A *DISASTER.*

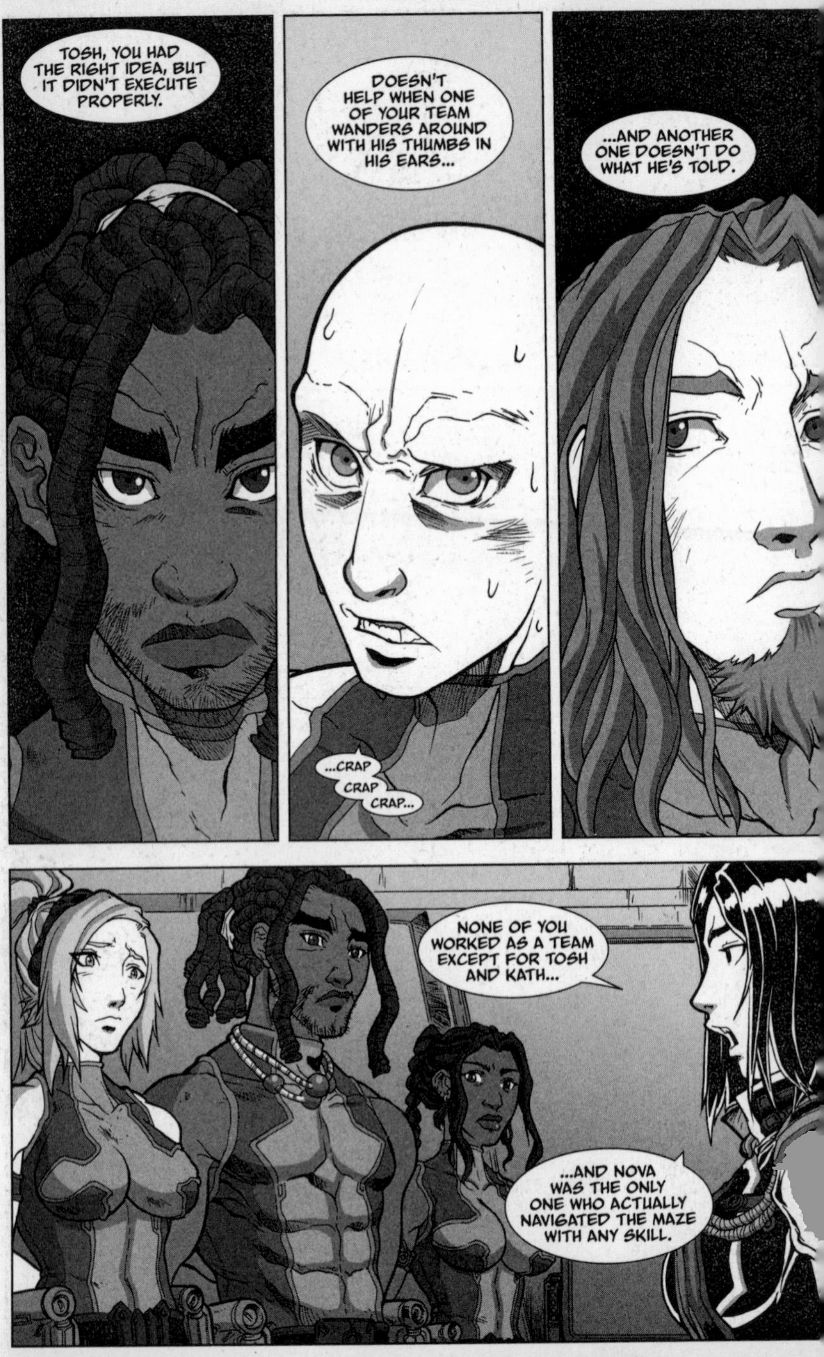

TOSH, YOU HAD THE RIGHT IDEA, BUT IT DIDN'T EXECUTE PROPERLY.
DOESN'T HELP WHEN ONE OF YOUR TEAM WANDERS AROUND WITH HIS THUMBS IN HIS EARS...
...CRAP CRAP CRAP...
...AND ANOTHER ONE DOESN'T DO WHAT HE'S TOLD.
NONE OF YOU WORKED AS A TEAM EXCEPT FOR TOSH AND KATH...
...AND NOVA WAS THE ONLY ONE WHO ACTUALLY NAVIGATED THE MAZE WITH ANY SKILL.

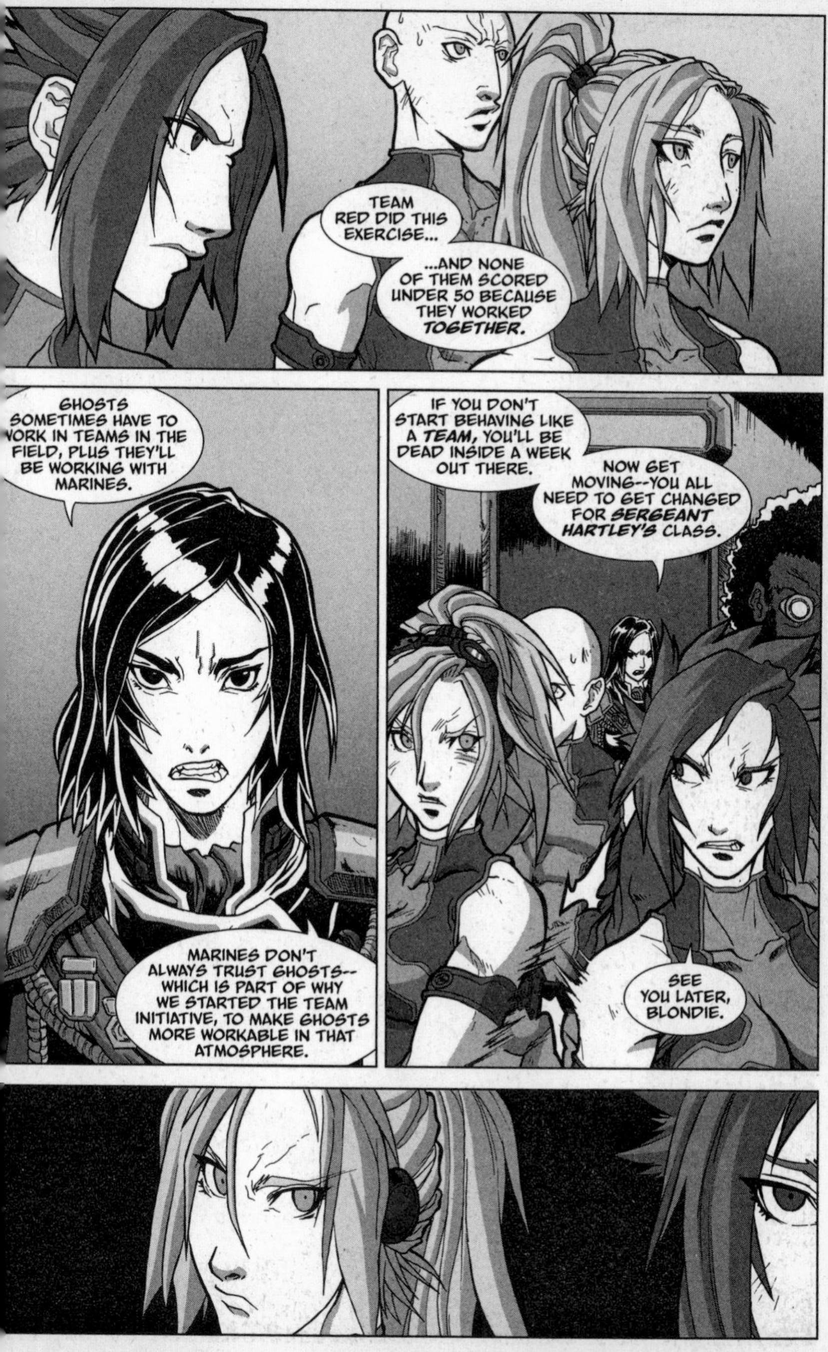
TEAM RED DID THIS EXERCISE...
...AND NONE OF THEM SCORED UNDER 50 BECAUSE THEY WORKED *TOGETHER.*
GHOSTS SOMETIMES HAVE TO WORK IN TEAMS IN THE FIELD, PLUS THEY'LL BE WORKING WITH MARINES.
MARINES DON'T ALWAYS TRUST GHOSTS-- WHICH IS PART OF WHY WE STARTED THE TEAM INITIATIVE, TO MAKE GHOSTS MORE WORKABLE IN THAT ATMOSPHERE.
IF YOU DON'T START BEHAVING LIKE A *TEAM,* YOU'LL BE DEAD INSIDE A WEEK OUT THERE.
NOW GET MOVING--YOU ALL NEED TO GET CHANGED FOR *SERGEANT HARTLEY'S* CLASS.
SEE YOU LATER, BLONDIE.

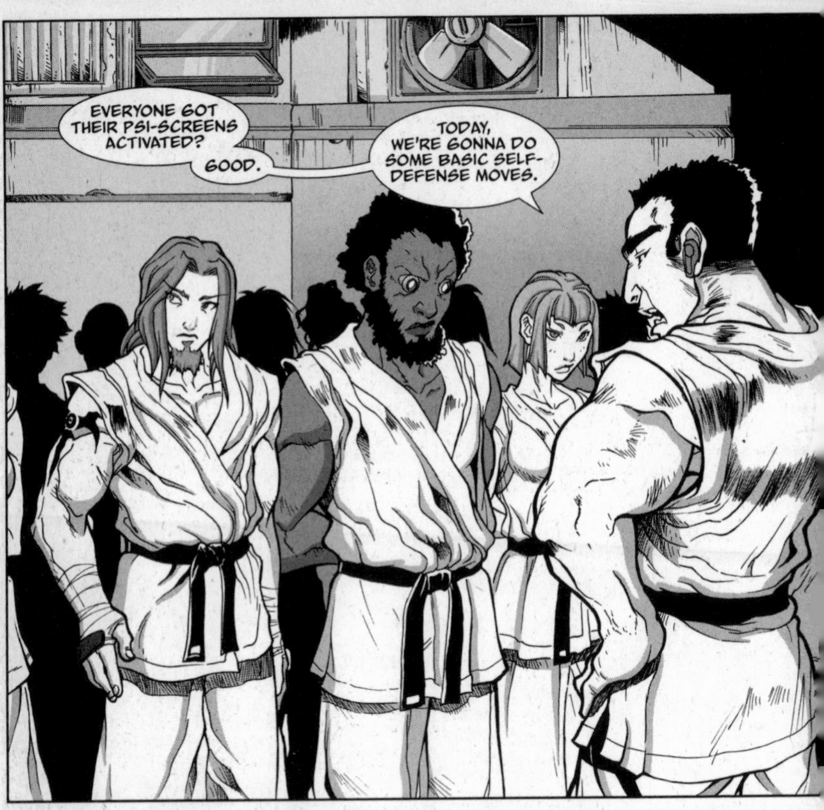
EVERYONE GOT THEIR PSI-SCREENS ACTIVATED?
GOOD.
TODAY, WE'RE GONNA DO SOME BASIC SELF-DEFENSE MOVES.
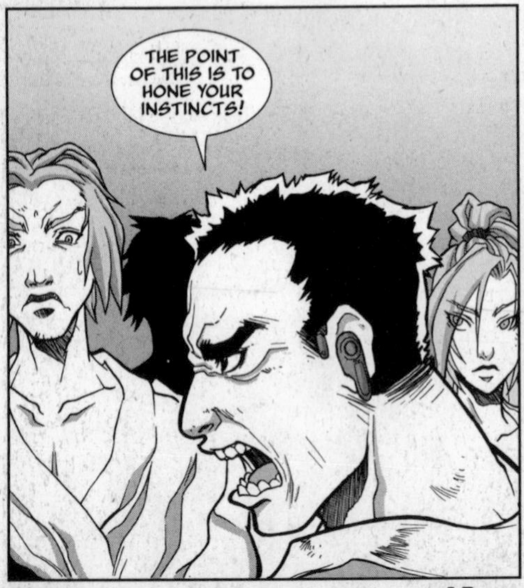
THE POINT OF THIS IS TO HONE YOUR INSTINCTS!
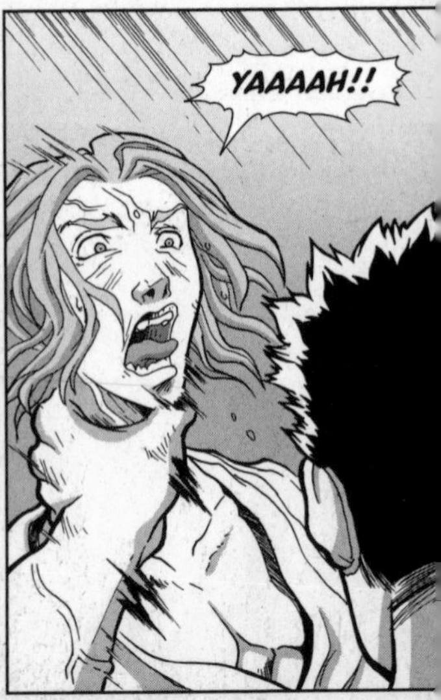
YAAAAH!!

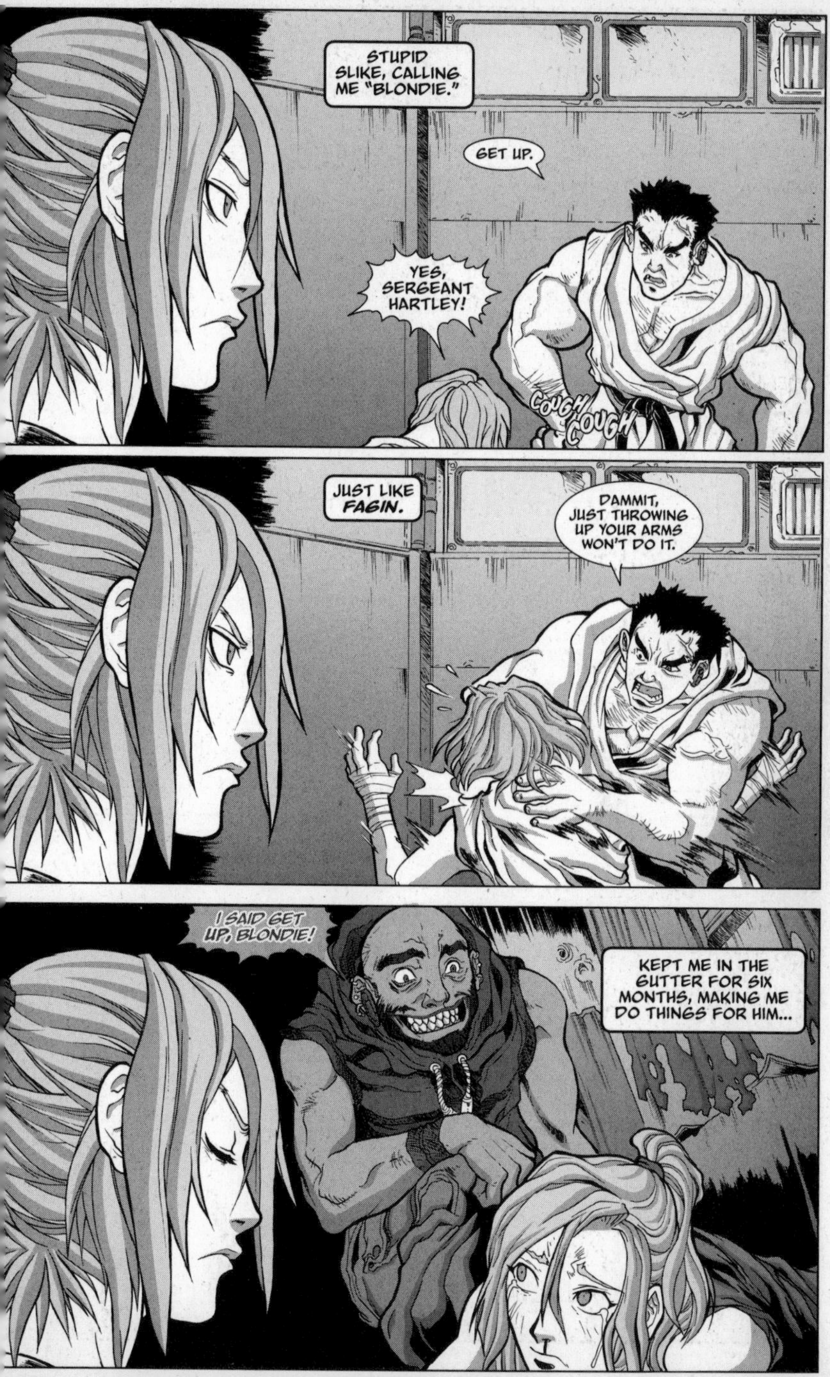
STUPID SLIKE, CALLING ME "BLONDIE."
GET UP.
YES, SERGEANT HARTLEY!
COUGH COUGH
JUST LIKE FAGIN.
DAMMIT, JUST THROWING UP YOUR ARMS WON'T DO IT.
I SAID GET UP, BLONDIE!
KEPT ME IN THE GUTTER FOR SIX MONTHS, MAKING ME DO THINGS FOR HIM...

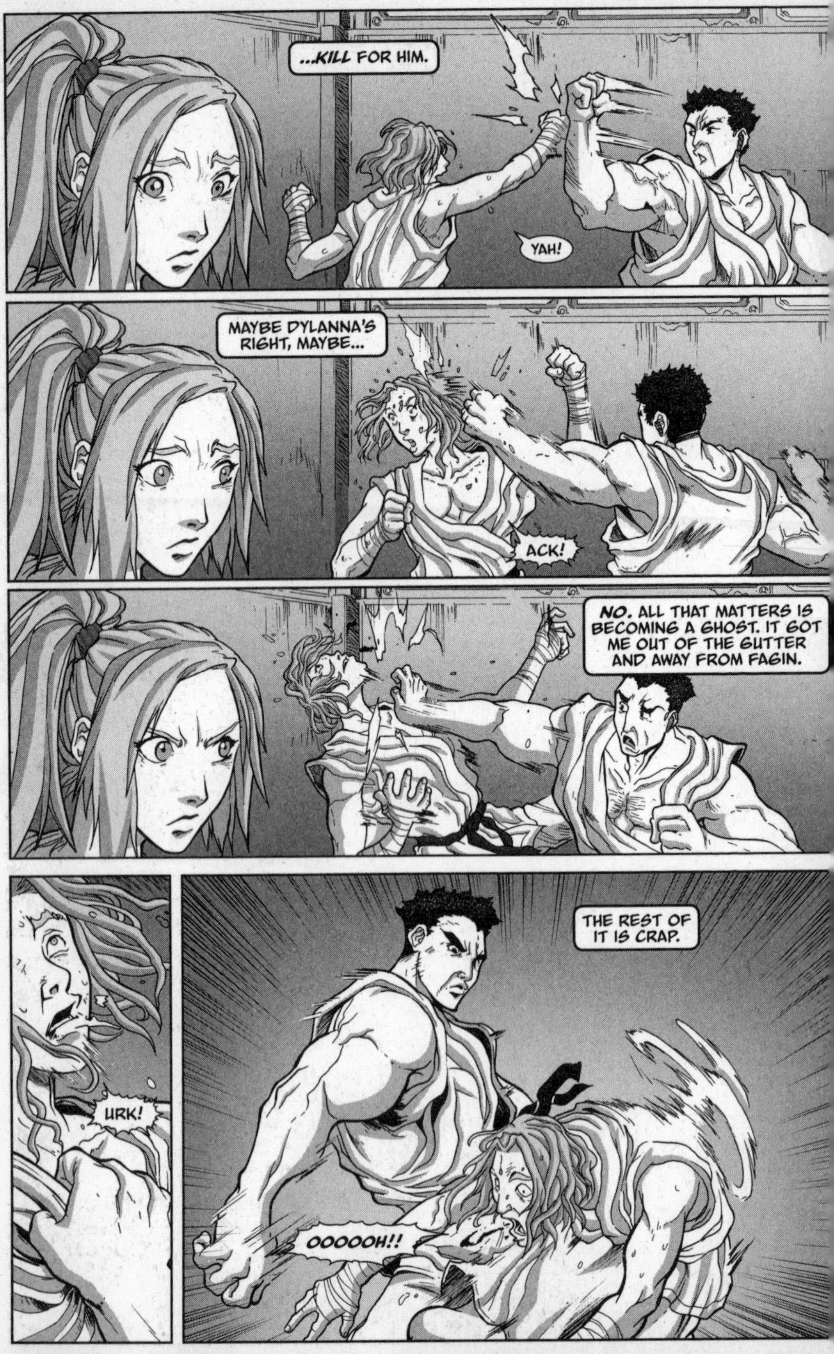
...KILL FOR HIM.
YAH!
MAYBE DYLANNA'S RIGHT, MAYBE...
ACK!
NO. ALL THAT MATTERS IS BECOMING A GHOST. IT GOT ME OUT OF THE GUTTER AND AWAY FROM FAGIN.
URK!
THE REST OF IT IS CRAP.
OOOOOH!!

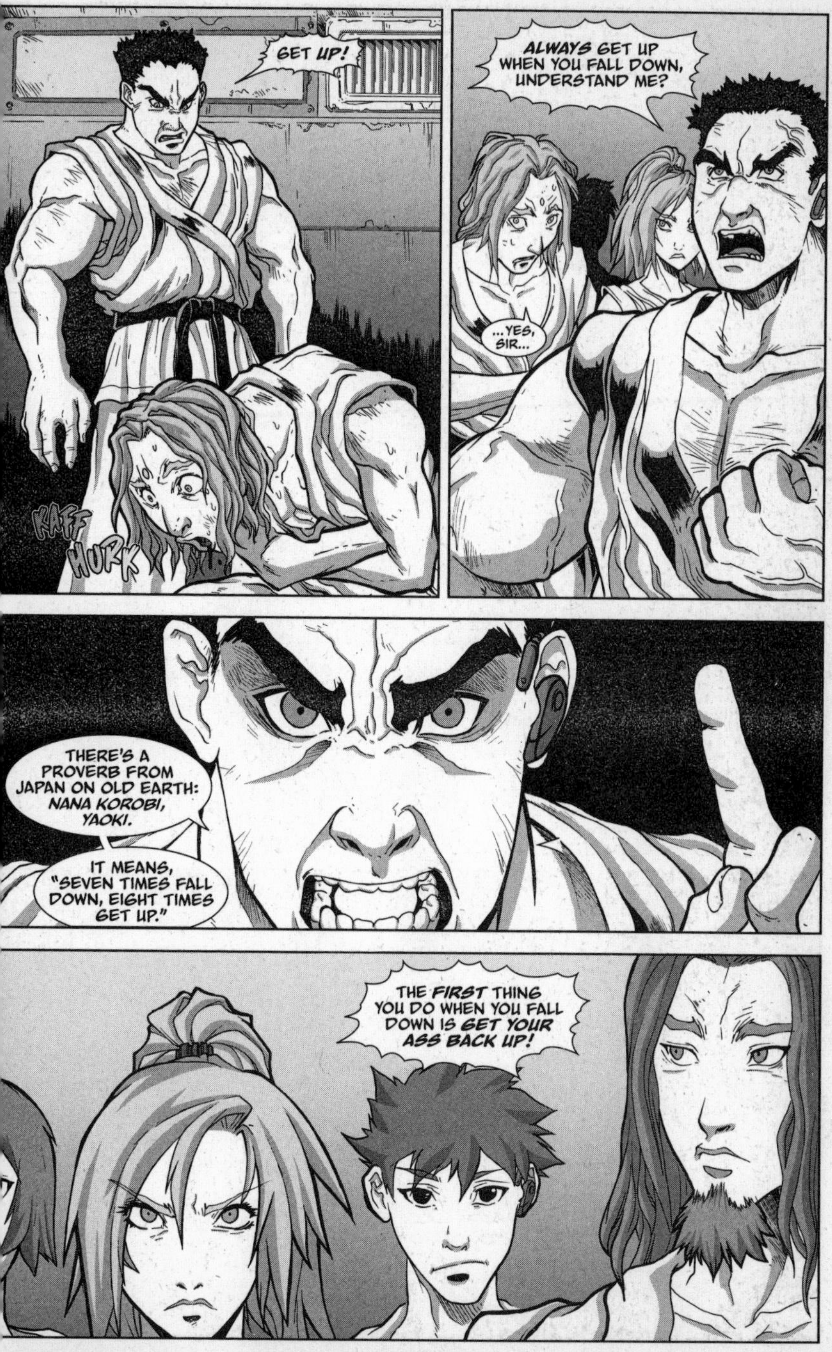
GET UP!
KAFF
HURK
ALWAYS GET UP WHEN YOU FALL DOWN, UNDERSTAND ME?
...YES, SIR...
THERE'S A PROVERB FROM JAPAN ON OLD EARTH: NANA KOROBI, YAOKI.
IT MEANS, "SEVEN TIMES FALL DOWN, EIGHT TIMES GET UP."
THE FIRST THING YOU DO WHEN YOU FALL DOWN IS GET YOUR ASS BACK UP!

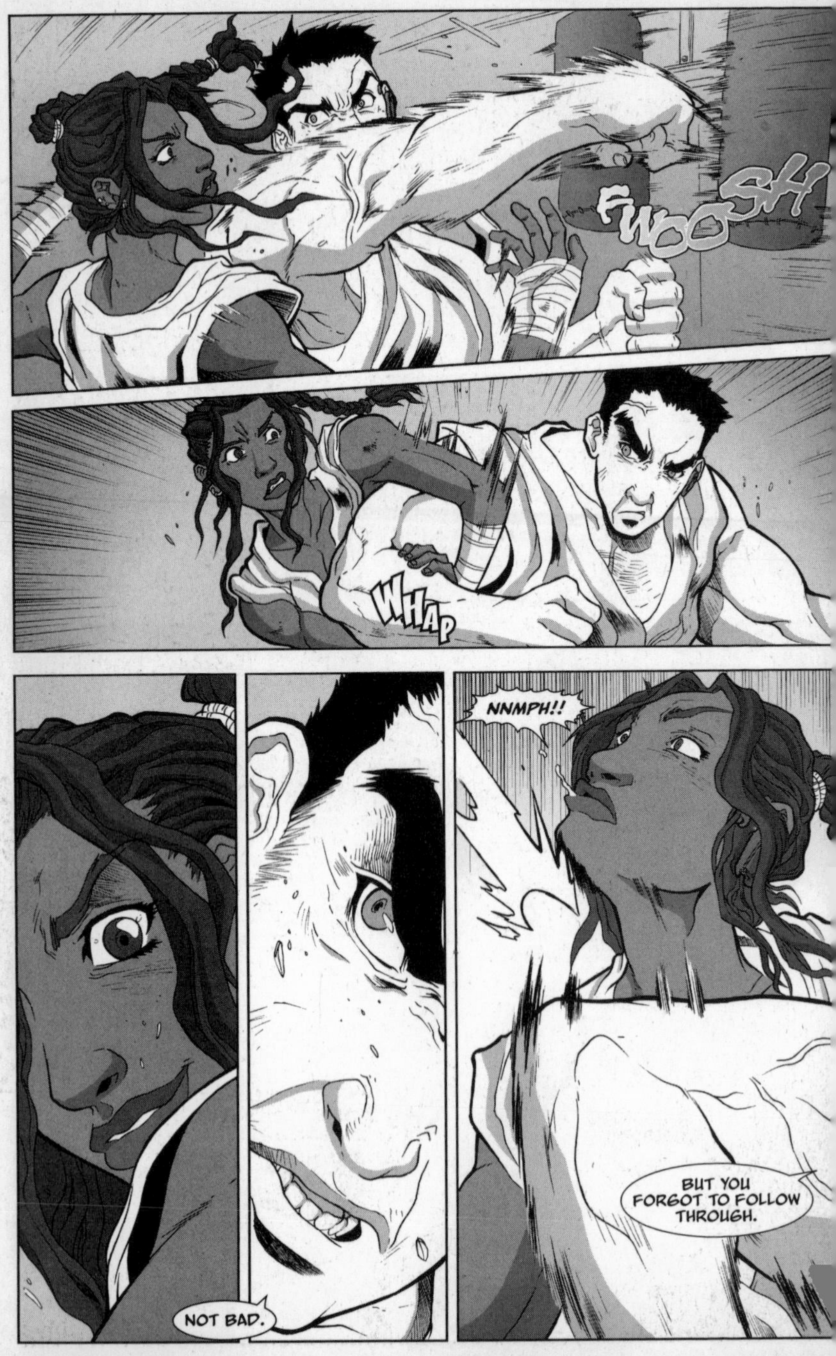
FWOOSH
WHAP
NOT BAD.
NNMPH!!
BUT YOU FORGOT TO FOLLOW THROUGH.

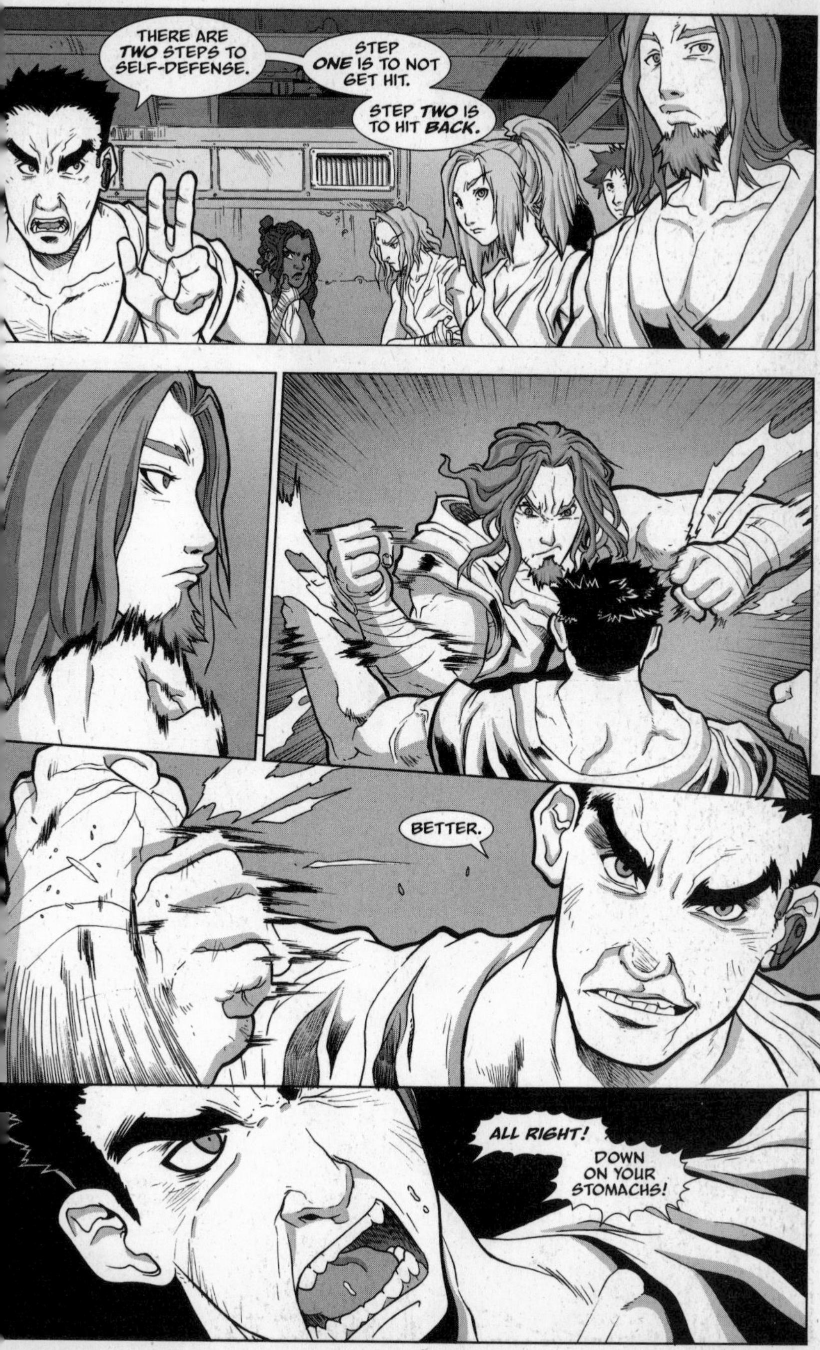
THERE ARE TWO STEPS TO SELF-DEFENSE.
STEP ONE IS TO NOT GET HIT.
STEP TWO IS TO HIT BACK.
BETTER.
ALL RIGHT!
DOWN ON YOUR STOMACHS!

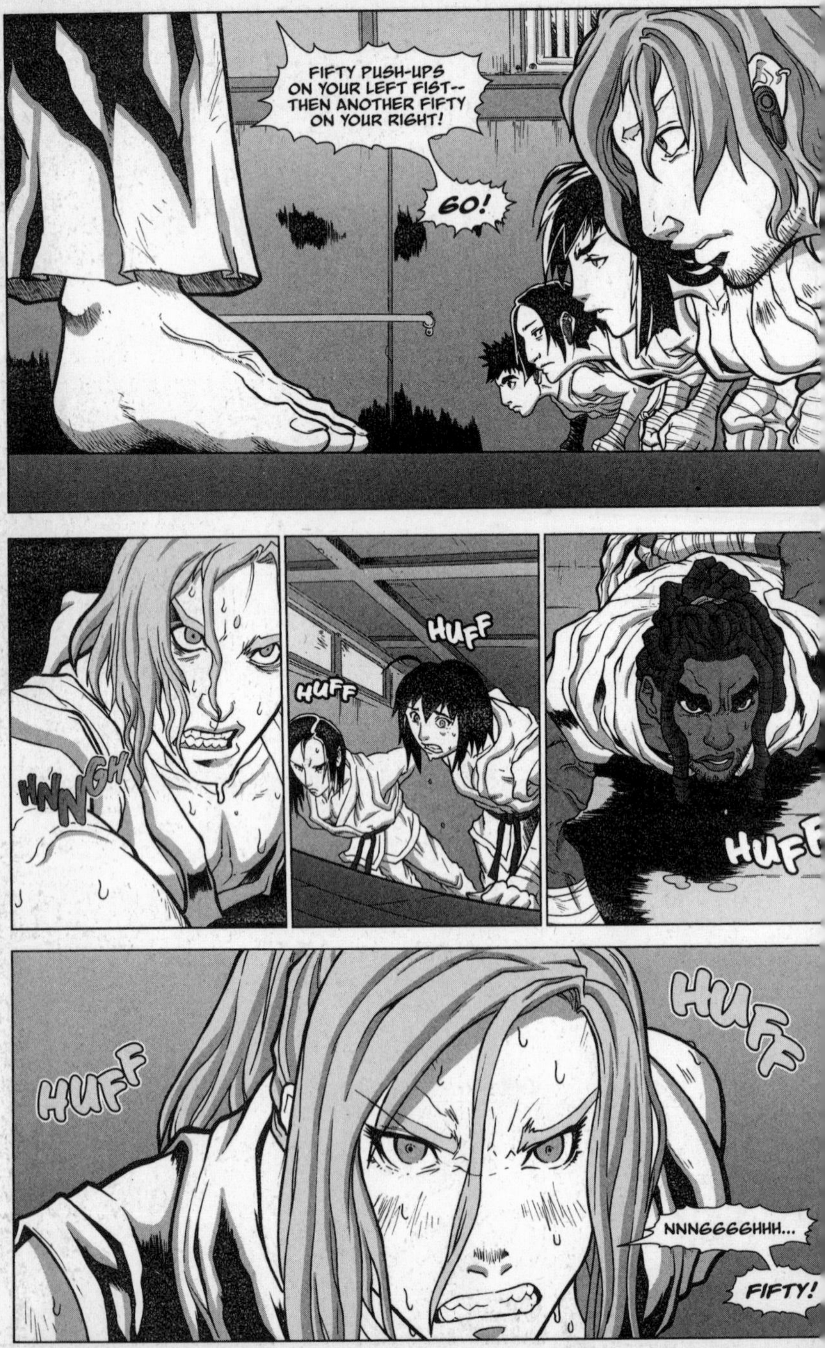
FIFTY PUSH-UPS ON YOUR LEFT FIST-- THEN ANOTHER FIFTY ON YOUR RIGHT!
GO!
HNNNGH
HUFF
HUFF
HUFF
HUFF
HUFF
NNNGGGGHHH...
FIFTY!

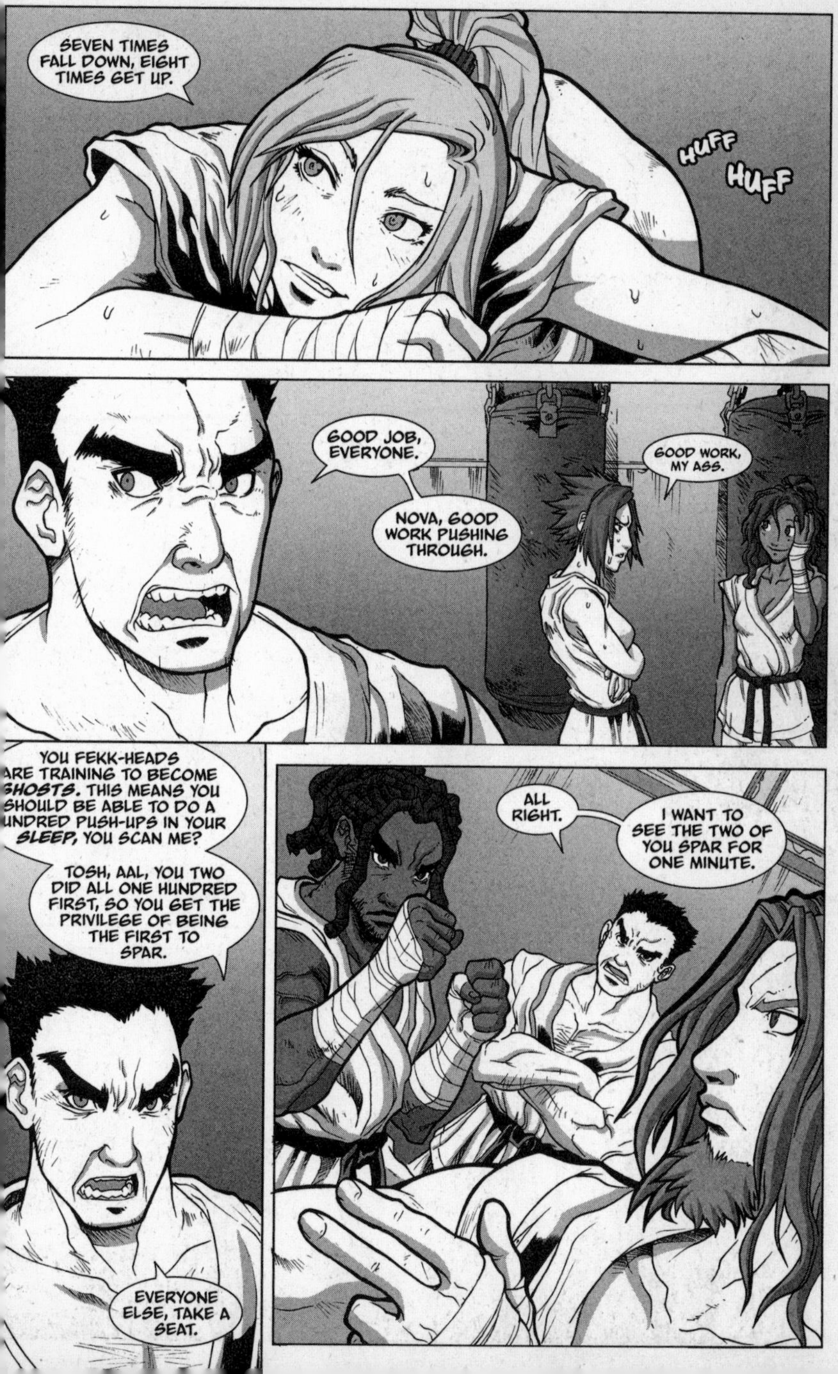
SEVEN TIMES FALL DOWN, EIGHT TIMES GET UP.
HUFF
HUFF
GOOD JOB, EVERYONE.
NOVA, GOOD WORK PUSHING THROUGH.
GOOD WORK, MY ASS.
YOU FEKK-HEADS ARE TRAINING TO BECOME GHOSTS. THIS MEANS YOU SHOULD BE ABLE TO DO A HUNDRED PUSH-UPS IN YOUR SLEEP, YOU SCAN ME?
TOSH, AAL, YOU TWO DID ALL ONE HUNDRED FIRST, SO YOU GET THE PRIVILEGE OF BEING THE FIRST TO SPAR.
EVERYONE ELSE, TAKE A SEAT.
ALL RIGHT.
I WANT TO SEE THE TWO OF YOU SPAR FOR ONE MINUTE.

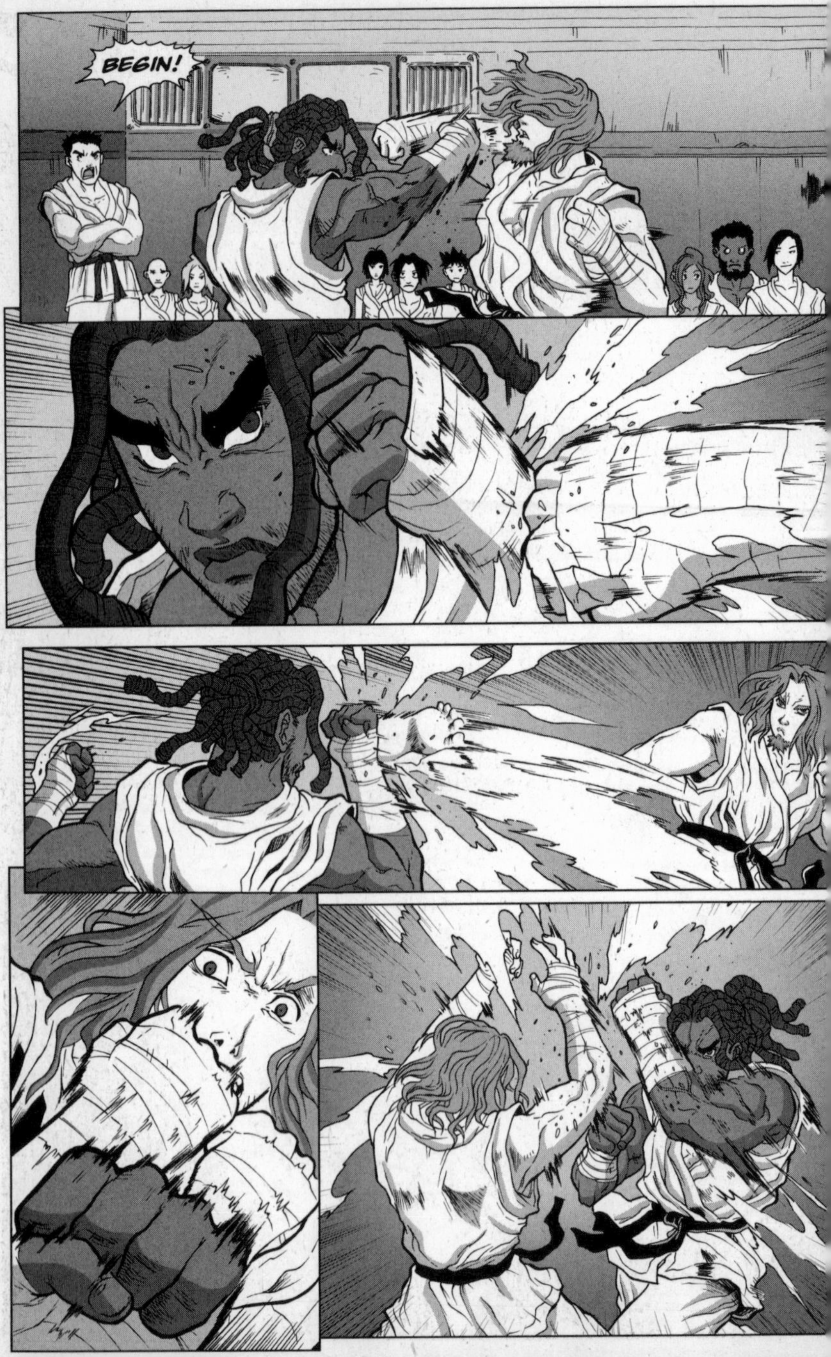
BEGIN!

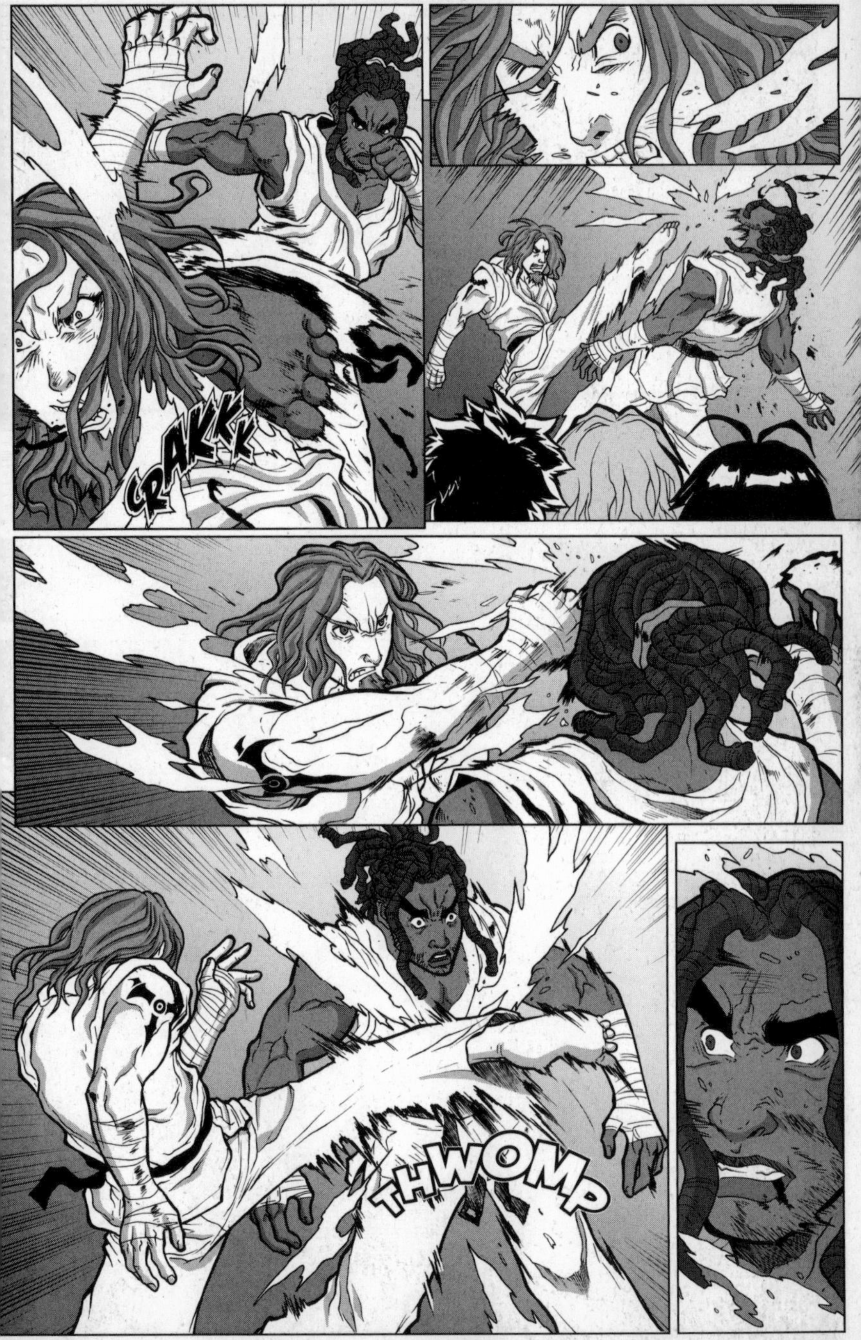
CRAKK
THWOMP

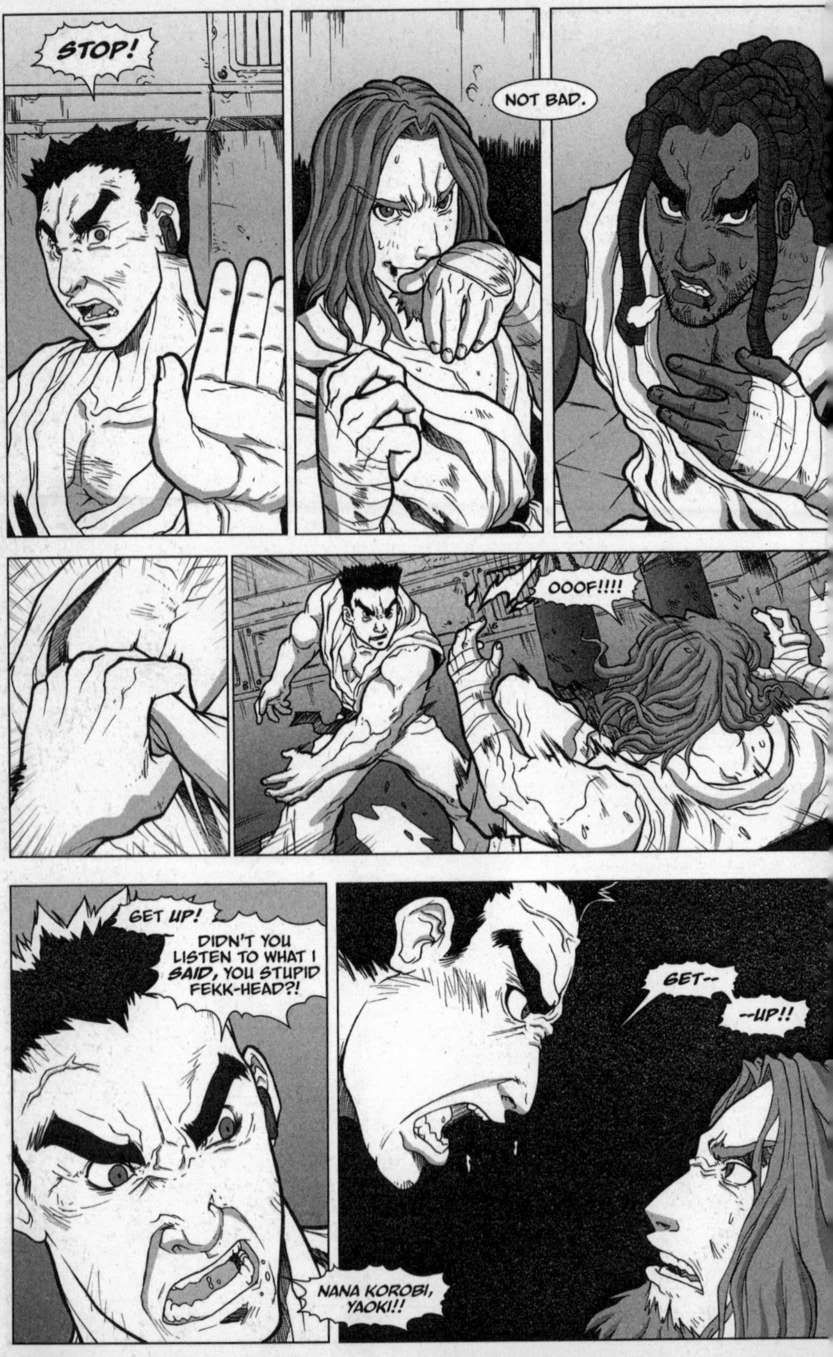
STOP!
NOT BAD.
OOOF!!!!
GET UP!
DIDN'T YOU LISTEN TO WHAT I SAID, YOU STUPID FEKK-HEAD?!
NANA KOROBI, YAOKI!!
GET--
--UP!!

WELL, AAL CAN FIGHT. I'LL GIVE HIM THAT.

YEAH, BUT YOU SAID HE'S ONLY A 4.5?

DAMN, WHAT A CLASS.

DIDN'T SEE THAT KICK COMIN' NO-HOW.

WHICH EXPLAINS WHY HE COULDN'T PROJECT RIGHT IN THE MAZE.

I KNOW, I ACHE IN PARTS OF MY BODY I DIDN'T KNOW I HAD.

THE FEKK IS HE EVEN *DOING* HERE?

HEY! BLONDIE!

I TOLD...

...MY NAME IS *NOVA*!

AND I TOLD *YOU* THAT I DON'T CARE.

WHATEVER! WHAT DO YOU WANT?

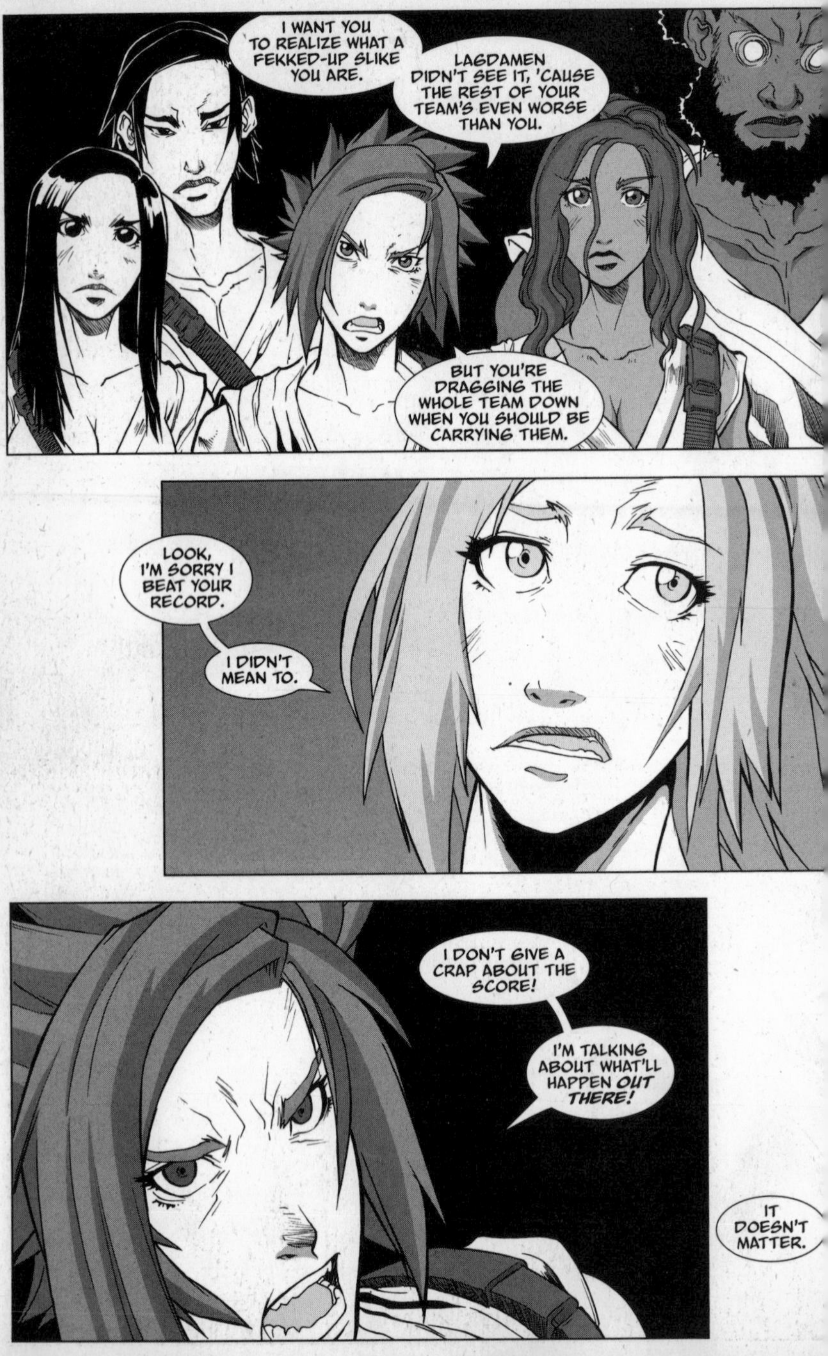
I WANT YOU TO REALIZE WHAT A FEKKED-UP SLIKE YOU ARE.
LAGDAMEN DIDN'T SEE IT, 'CAUSE THE REST OF YOUR TEAM'S EVEN WORSE THAN YOU.
BUT YOU'RE DRAGGING THE WHOLE TEAM DOWN WHEN YOU SHOULD BE CARRYING THEM.
LOOK, I'M SORRY I BEAT YOUR RECORD.
I DIDN'T MEAN TO.
I DON'T GIVE A CRAP ABOUT THE SCORE!
I'M TALKING ABOUT WHAT'LL HAPPEN *OUT THERE!*
IT DOESN'T MATTER.

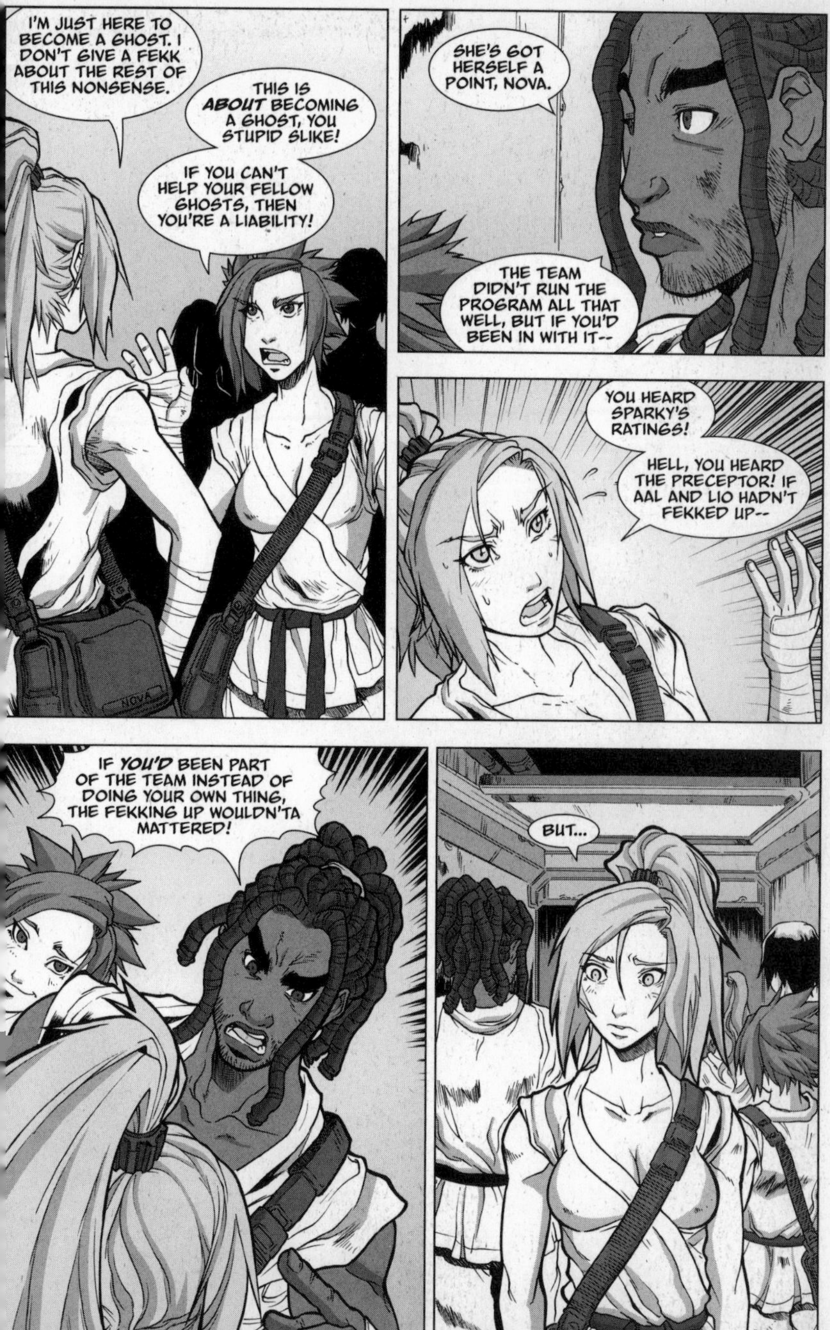

I'M JUST HERE TO BECOME A GHOST. I DON'T GIVE A FEKK ABOUT THE REST OF THIS NONSENSE.
THIS IS ABOUT BECOMING A GHOST, YOU STUPID SLIKE!
IF YOU CAN'T HELP YOUR FELLOW GHOSTS, THEN YOU'RE A LIABILITY!
NOVA
SHE'S GOT HERSELF A POINT, NOVA.
THE TEAM DIDN'T RUN THE PROGRAM ALL THAT WELL, BUT IF YOU'D BEEN IN WITH IT--
YOU HEARD SPARKY'S RATINGS!
HELL, YOU HEARD THE PRECEPTOR! IF AAL AND LIO HADN'T FEKKED UP--
IF YOU'D BEEN PART OF THE TEAM INSTEAD OF DOING YOUR OWN THING, THE FEKKING UP WOULDN'TA MATTERED!
BUT...

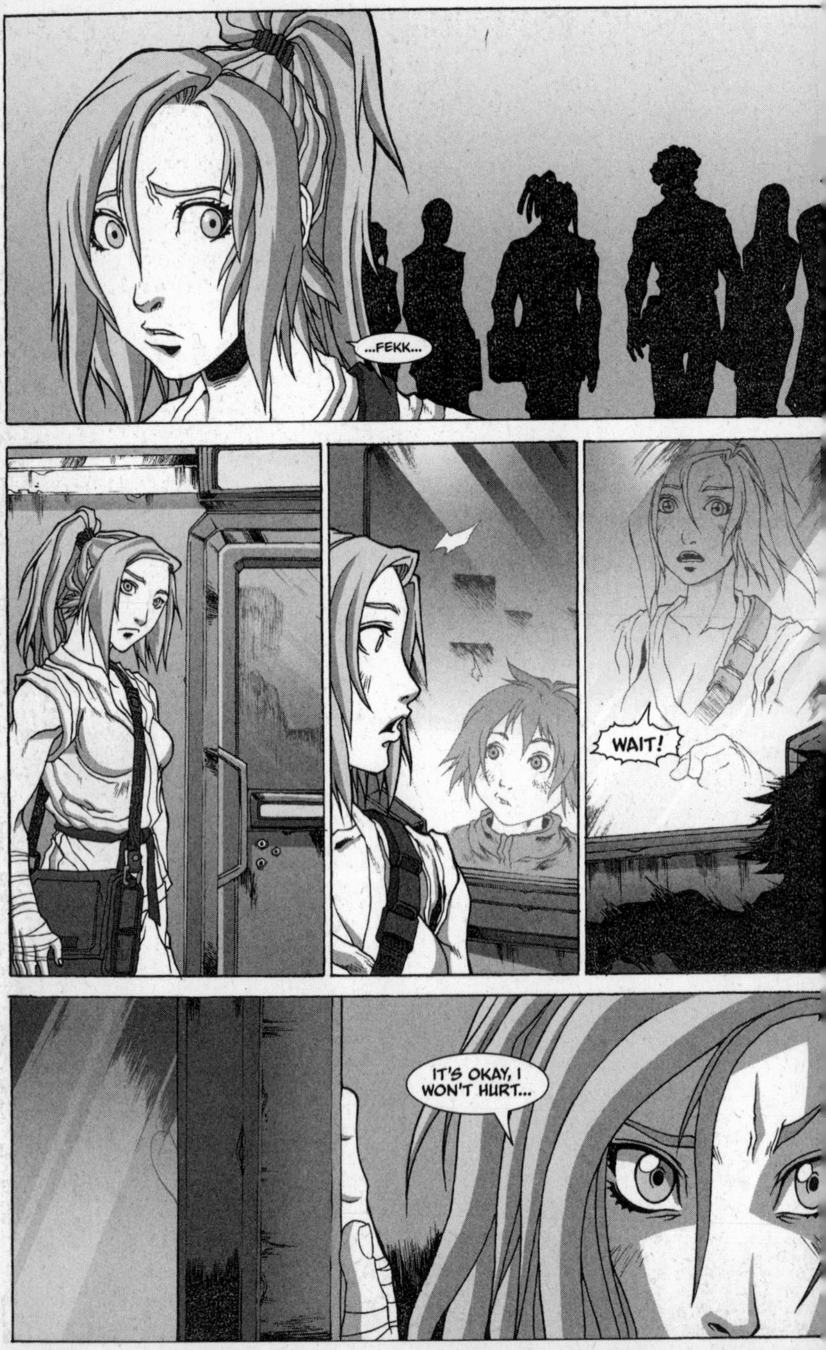
...FEKK...
WAIT!
IT'S OKAY, I WON'T HURT...

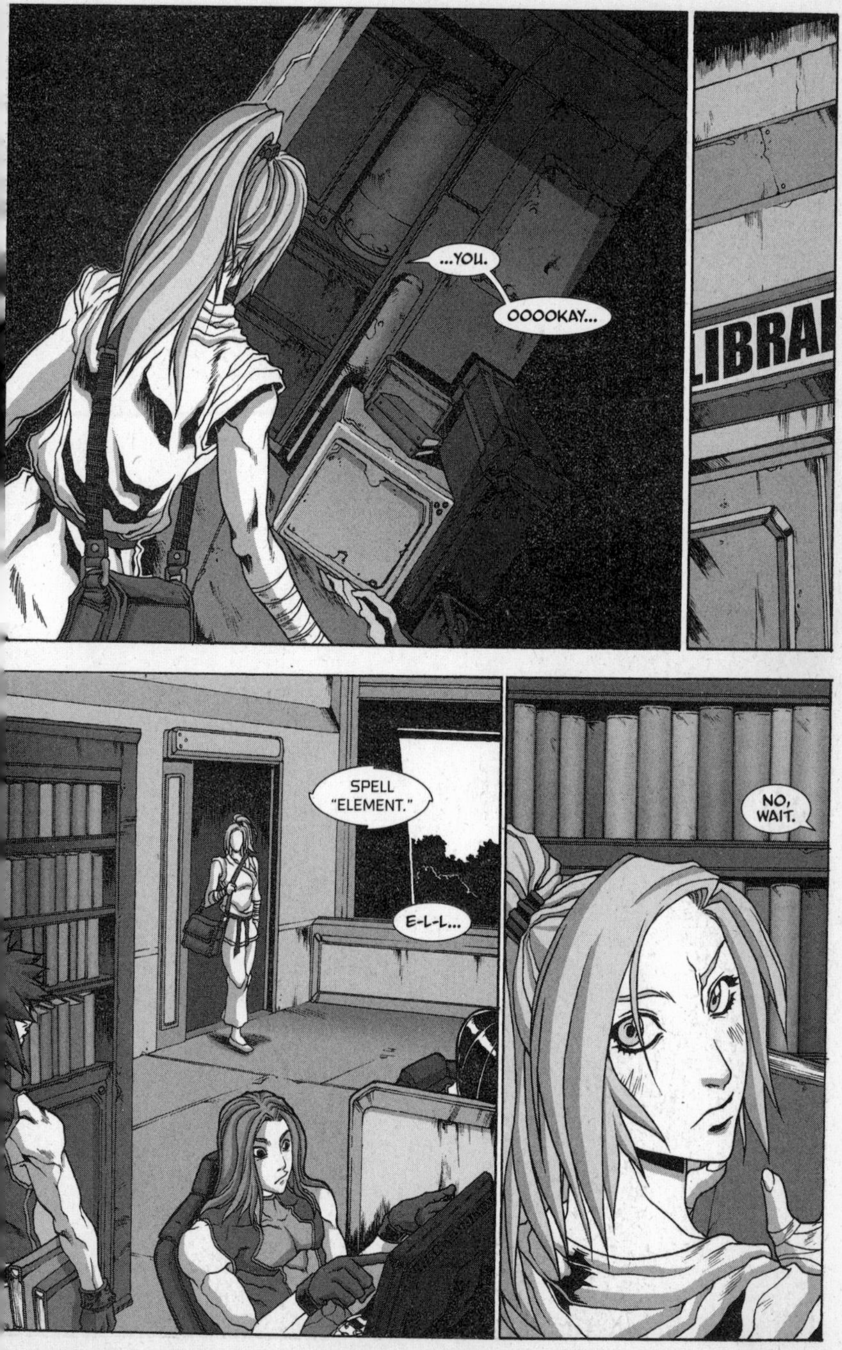
...YOU.
OOOOKAY...
LIBRA
SPELL "ELEMENT."
E-L-L...
NO, WAIT.

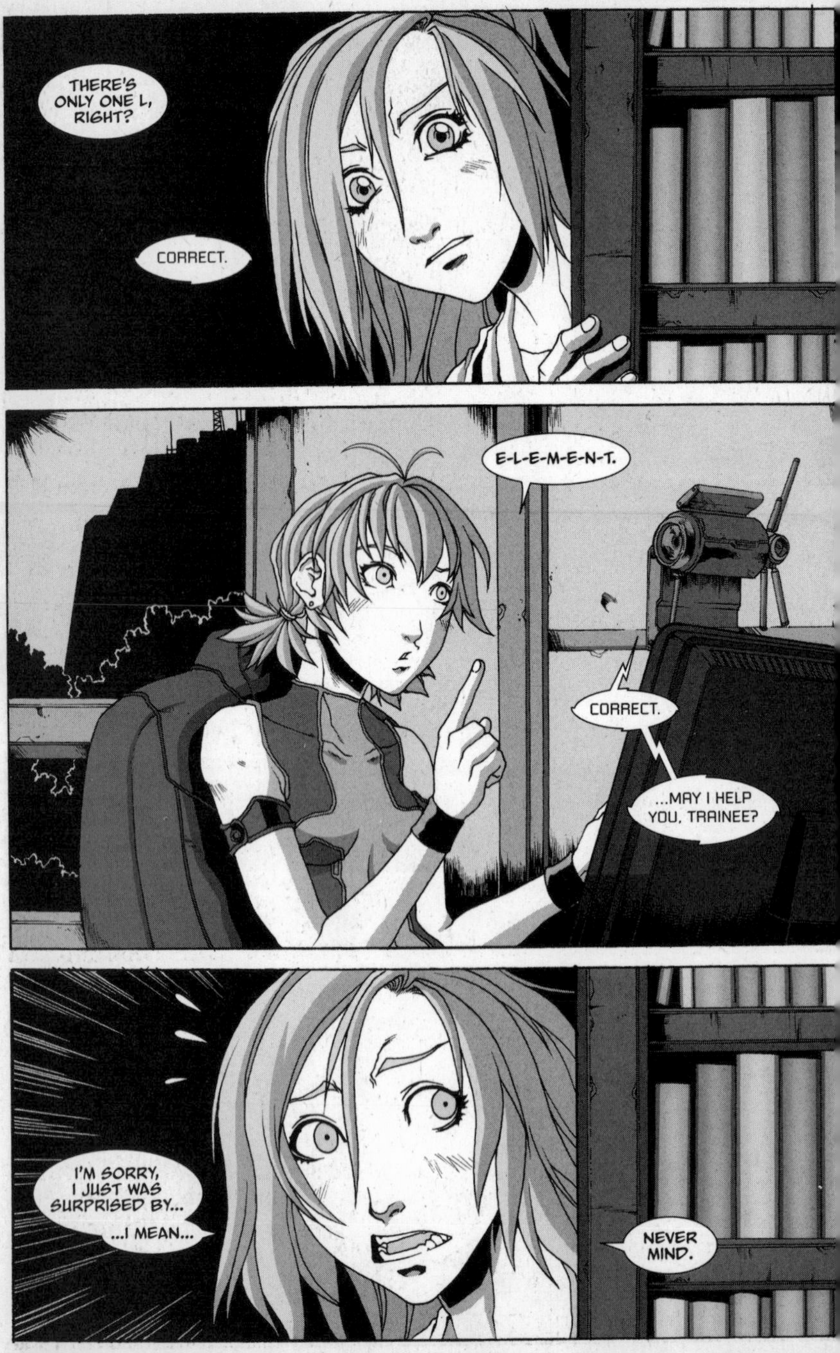
THERE'S ONLY ONE L, RIGHT?
CORRECT.
E-L-E-M-E-N-T.
CORRECT.
...MAY I HELP YOU, TRAINEE?
I'M SORRY, I JUST WAS SURPRISED BY...
...I MEAN...
NEVER MIND.

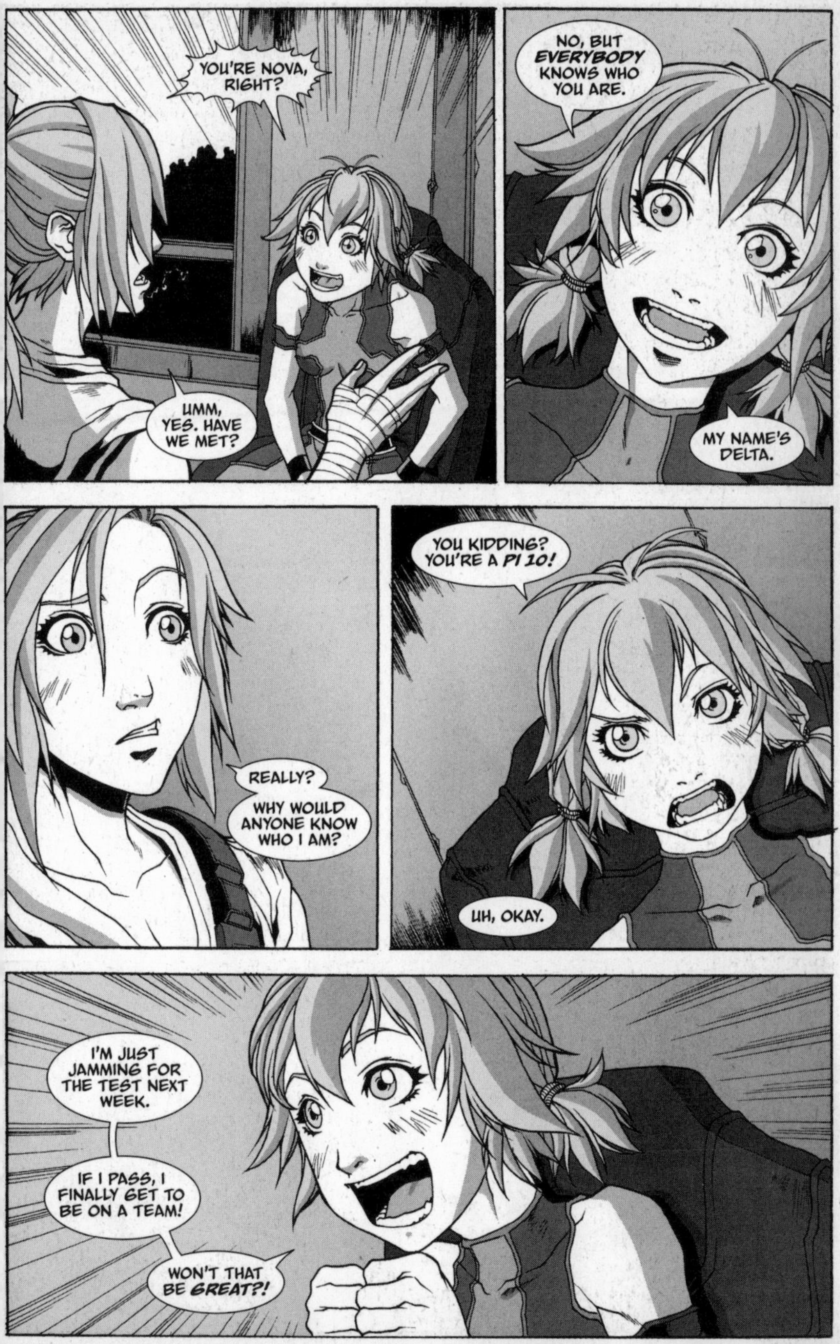
YOU'RE NOVA, RIGHT?
UMM, YES. HAVE WE MET?
NO, BUT EVERYBODY KNOWS WHO YOU ARE.
MY NAME'S DELTA.
REALLY?
WHY WOULD ANYONE KNOW WHO I AM?
YOU KIDDING? YOU'RE A PI 10!
UH, OKAY.
I'M JUST JAMMING FOR THE TEST NEXT WEEK.
IF I PASS, I FINALLY GET TO BE ON A TEAM!
WON'T THAT BE GREAT?!

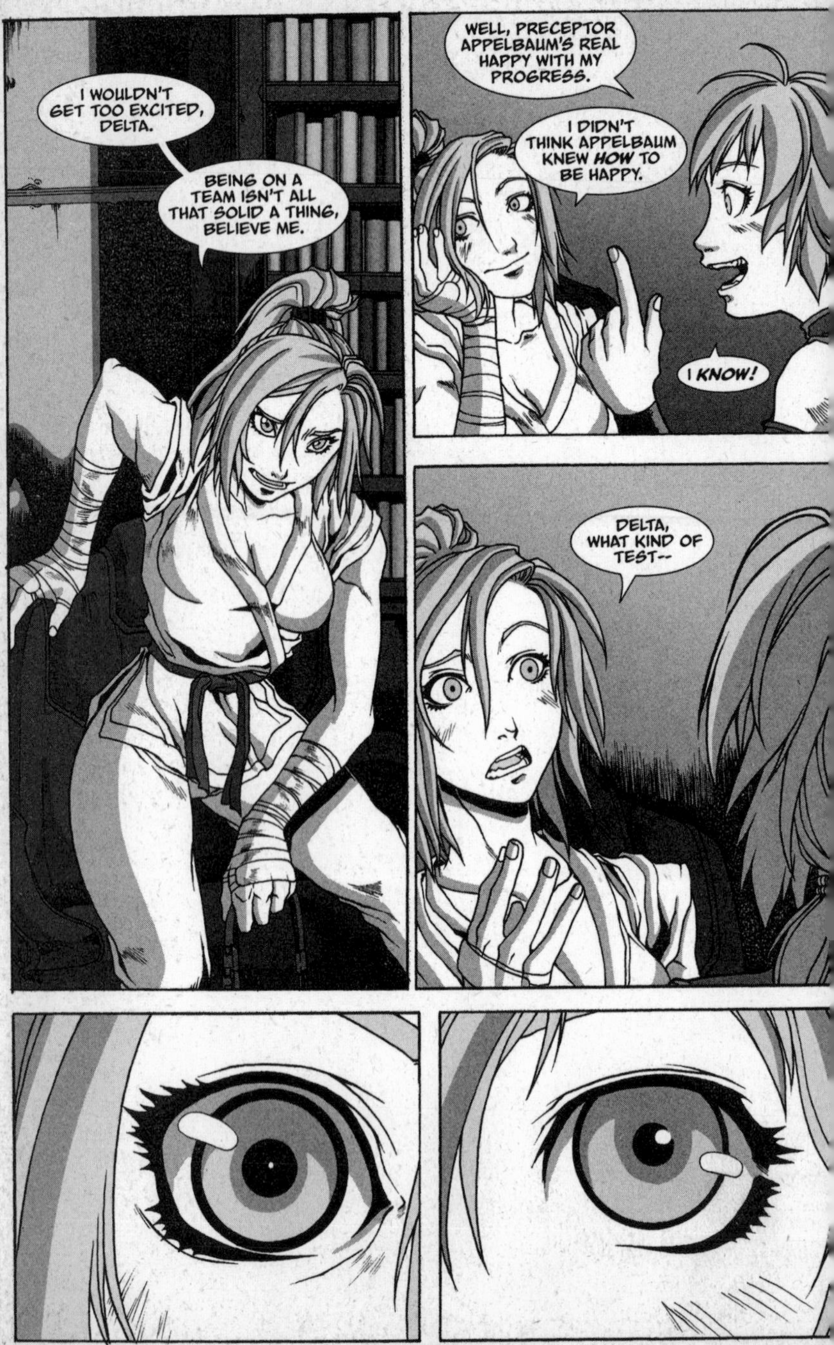
I WOULDN'T GET TOO EXCITED, DELTA.
BEING ON A TEAM ISN'T ALL THAT SOLID A THING, BELIEVE ME.
WELL, PRECEPTOR APPELBAUM'S REAL HAPPY WITH MY PROGRESS.
I DIDN'T THINK APPELBAUM KNEW *HOW* TO BE HAPPY.
I *KNOW!*
DELTA, WHAT KIND OF TEST--

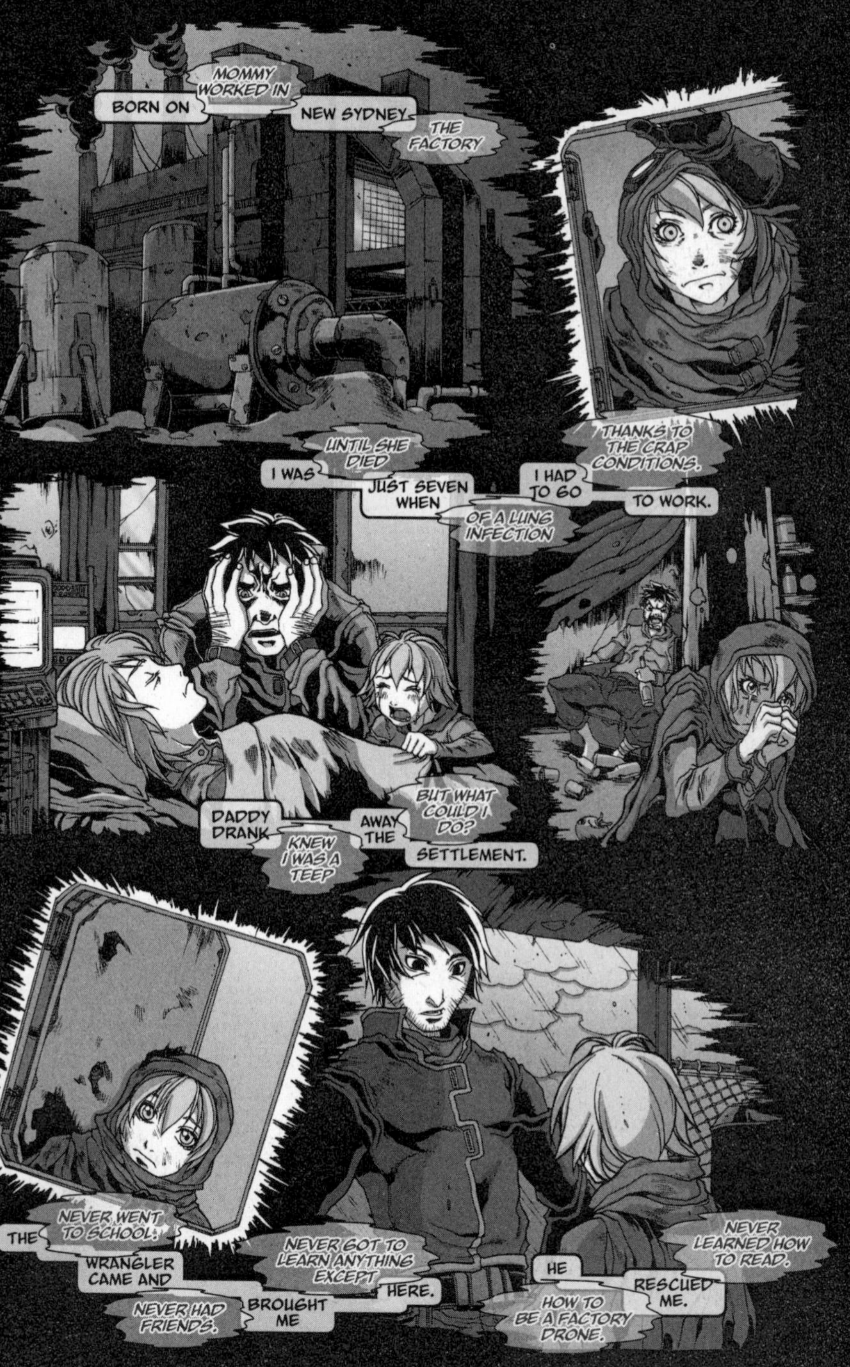

MOMMY WORKED IN
BORN ON
NEW SYDNEY
THE FACTORY
UNTIL SHE DIED
I WAS
JUST SEVEN WHEN
OF A LUNG INFECTION
THANKS TO THE CRAP CONDITIONS.
I HAD TO GO
TO WORK.
DADDY DRANK
KNEW I WAS A TEEP
AWAY
THE
BUT WHAT COULD I DO?
SETTLEMENT.
NEVER WENT TO SCHOOL.
THE
WRANGLER CAME AND
NEVER HAD FRIENDS.
BROUGHT ME
NEVER GOT TO LEARN ANYTHING EXCEPT
HERE.
NEVER LEARNED HOW TO READ.
HE
RESCUED ME.
HOW TO BE A FACTORY DRONE.

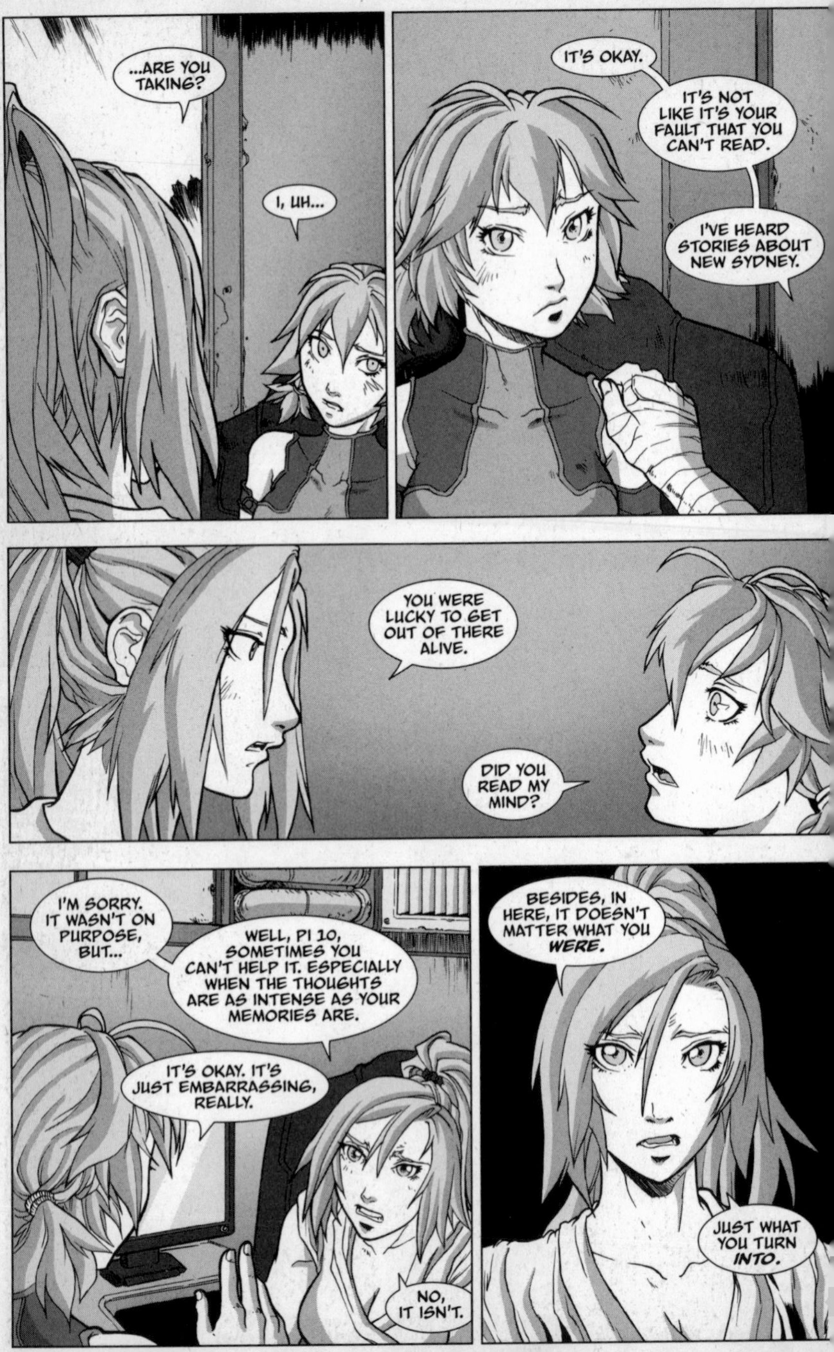
...ARE YOU TAKING?
I, UH...
IT'S OKAY.
IT'S NOT LIKE IT'S YOUR FAULT THAT YOU CAN'T READ.
I'VE HEARD STORIES ABOUT NEW SYDNEY.
YOU WERE LUCKY TO GET OUT OF THERE ALIVE.
DID YOU READ MY MIND?
I'M SORRY. IT WASN'T ON PURPOSE, BUT...
WELL, PI 10, SOMETIMES YOU CAN'T HELP IT. ESPECIALLY WHEN THE THOUGHTS ARE AS INTENSE AS YOUR MEMORIES ARE.
IT'S OKAY. IT'S JUST EMBARRASSING, REALLY.
NO, IT ISN'T.
BESIDES, IN HERE, IT DOESN'T MATTER WHAT YOU *WERE*.
JUST WHAT YOU TURN *INTO*.

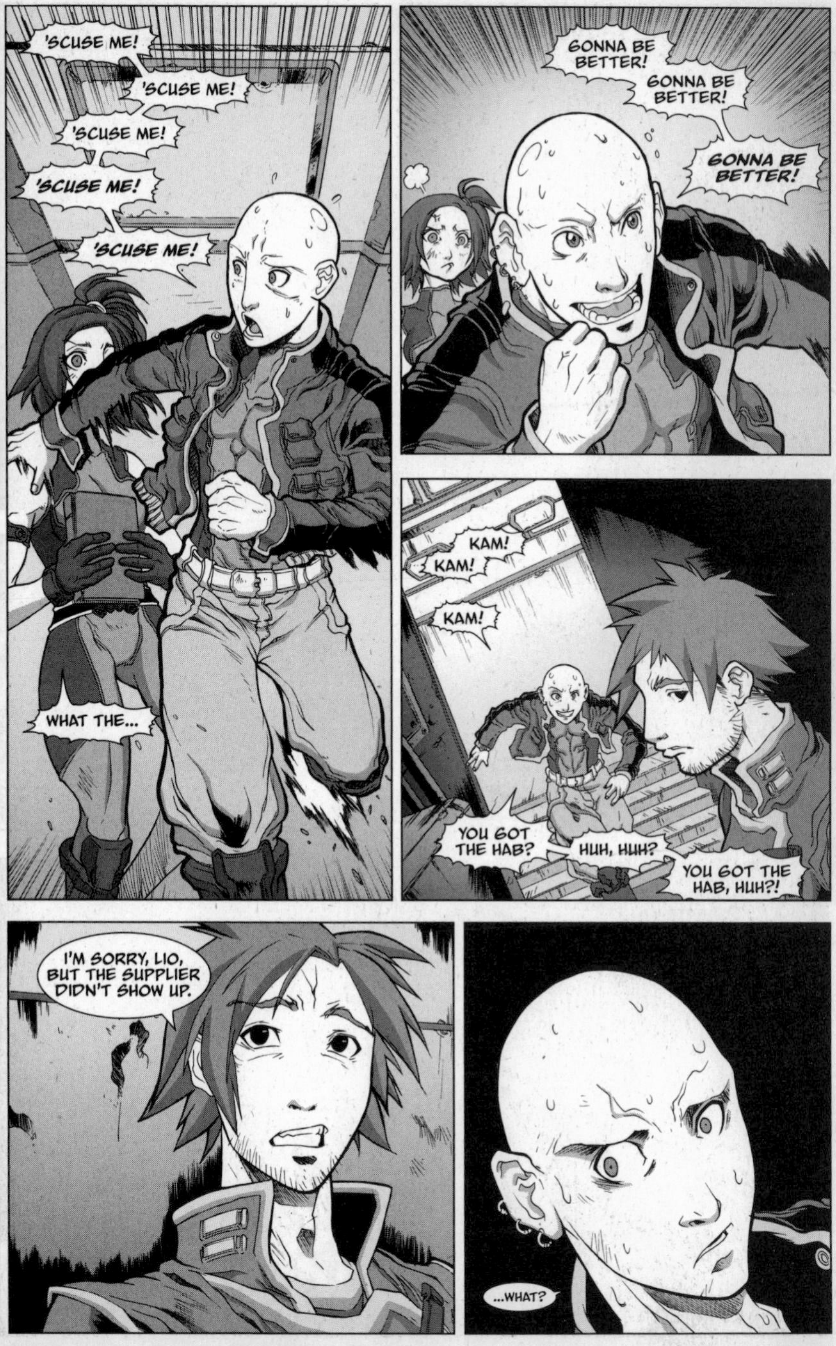
'SCUSE ME!
'SCUSE ME!
'SCUSE ME!
'SCUSE ME!
'SCUSE ME!
WHAT THE...
GONNA BE BETTER!
GONNA BE BETTER!
GONNA BE BETTER!
KAM!
KAM!
KAM!
YOU GOT THE HAB?
HUH, HUH?
YOU GOT THE HAB, HUH?!
I'M SORRY, LIO, BUT THE SUPPLIER DIDN'T SHOW UP.
...WHAT?

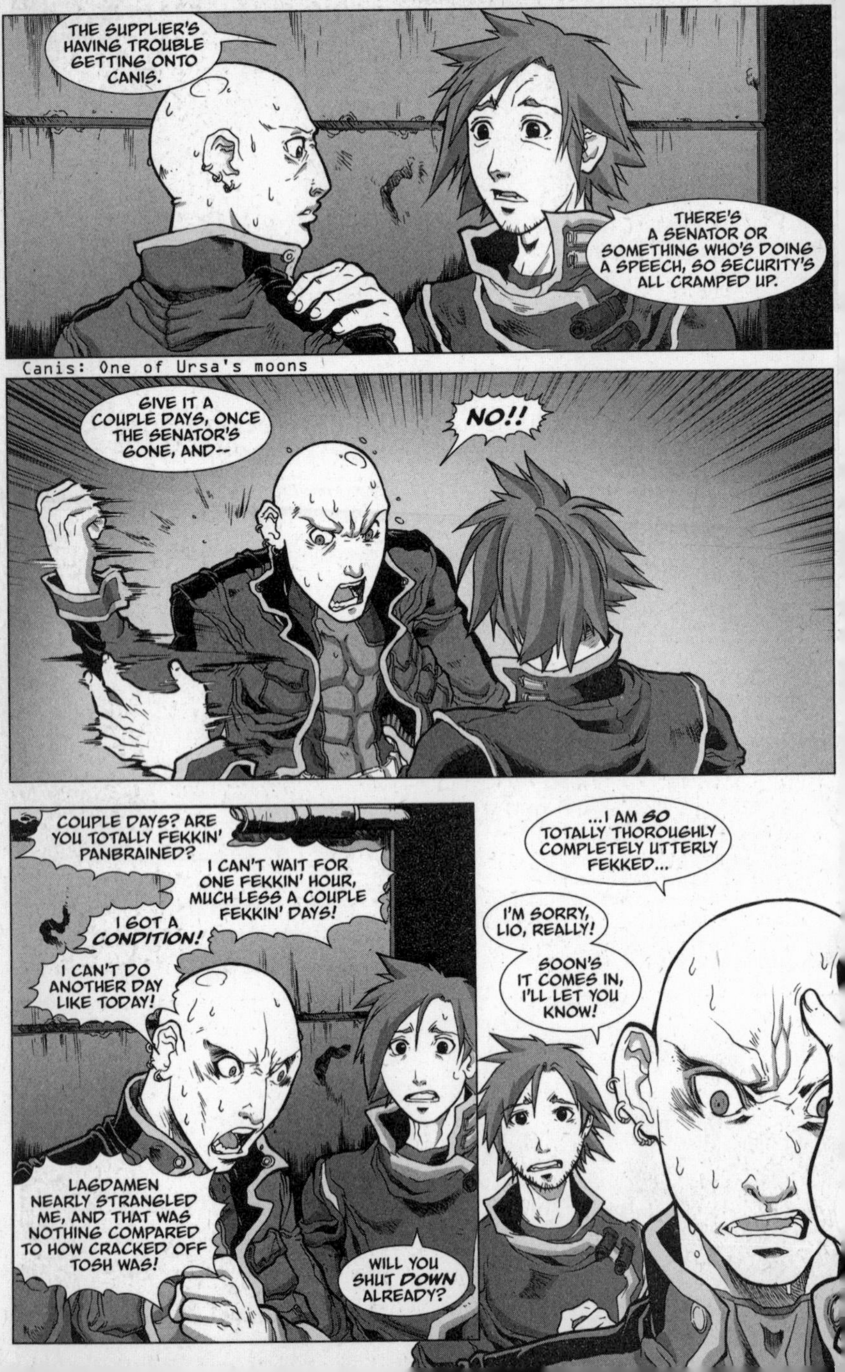
THE SUPPLIER'S HAVING TROUBLE GETTING ONTO CANIS.
THERE'S A SENATOR OR SOMETHING WHO'S DOING A SPEECH, SO SECURITY'S ALL CRAMPED UP.
Canis: One of Ursa's moons
GIVE IT A COUPLE DAYS, ONCE THE SENATOR'S GONE, AND--
NO!!
COUPLE DAYS? ARE YOU TOTALLY FEKKIN' PANBRAINED?
I CAN'T WAIT FOR ONE FEKKIN' HOUR, MUCH LESS A COUPLE FEKKIN' DAYS!
I GOT A *CONDITION!*
I CAN'T DO ANOTHER DAY LIKE TODAY!
LAGDAMEN NEARLY STRANGLED ME, AND THAT WAS NOTHING COMPARED TO HOW CRACKED OFF TOSH WAS!
WILL YOU SHUT *DOWN* ALREADY?
...I AM *SO* TOTALLY THOROUGHLY COMPLETELY UTTERLY FEKKED...
I'M SORRY, LIO, REALLY!
SOON'S IT COMES IN, I'LL LET YOU KNOW!

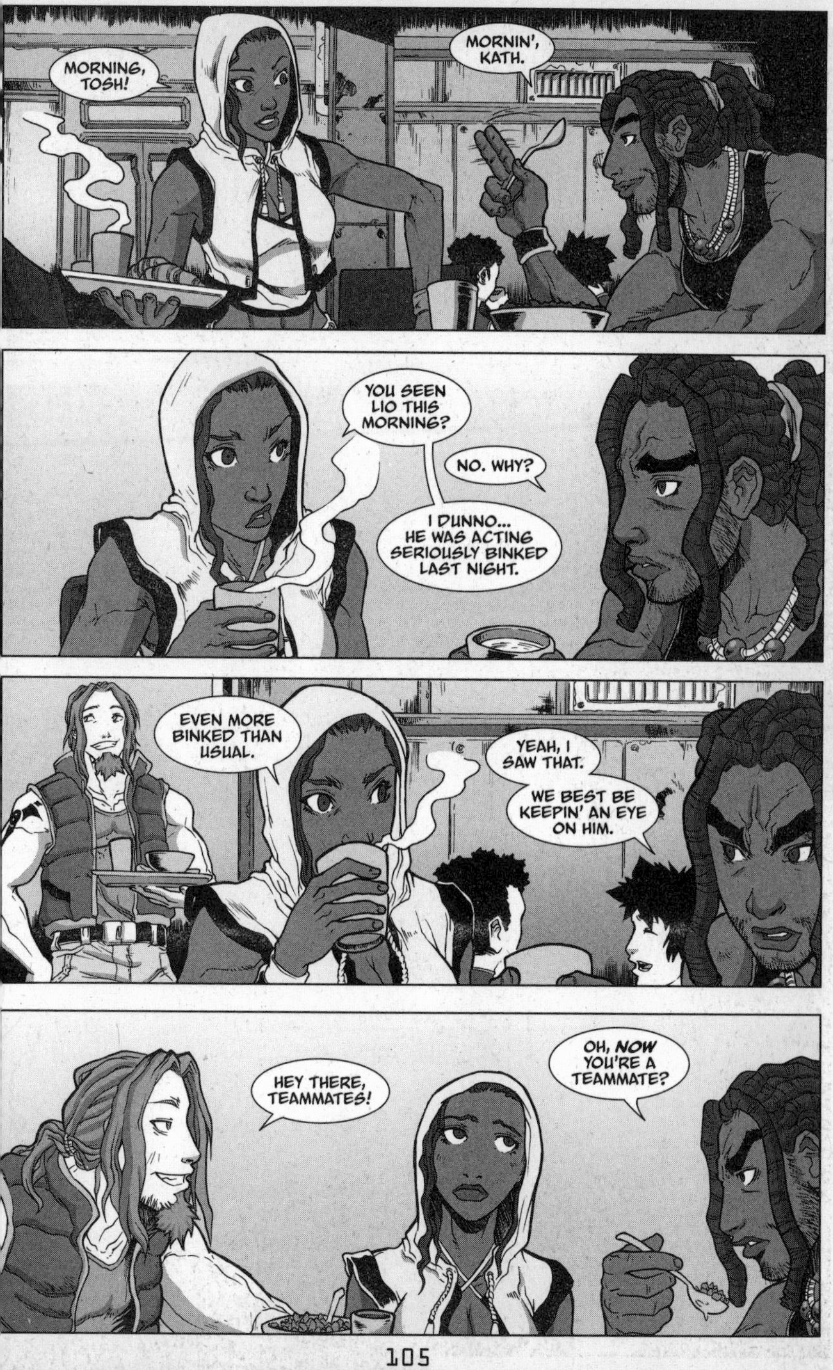
MORNING, TOSH!
MORNIN', KATH.
YOU SEEN LIO THIS MORNING?
NO. WHY?
I DUNNO... HE WAS ACTING SERIOUSLY BINKED LAST NIGHT.
EVEN MORE BINKED THAN USUAL.
YEAH, I SAW THAT.
WE BEST BE KEEPIN' AN EYE ON HIM.
HEY THERE, TEAMMATES!
OH, *NOW* YOU'RE A TEAMMATE?

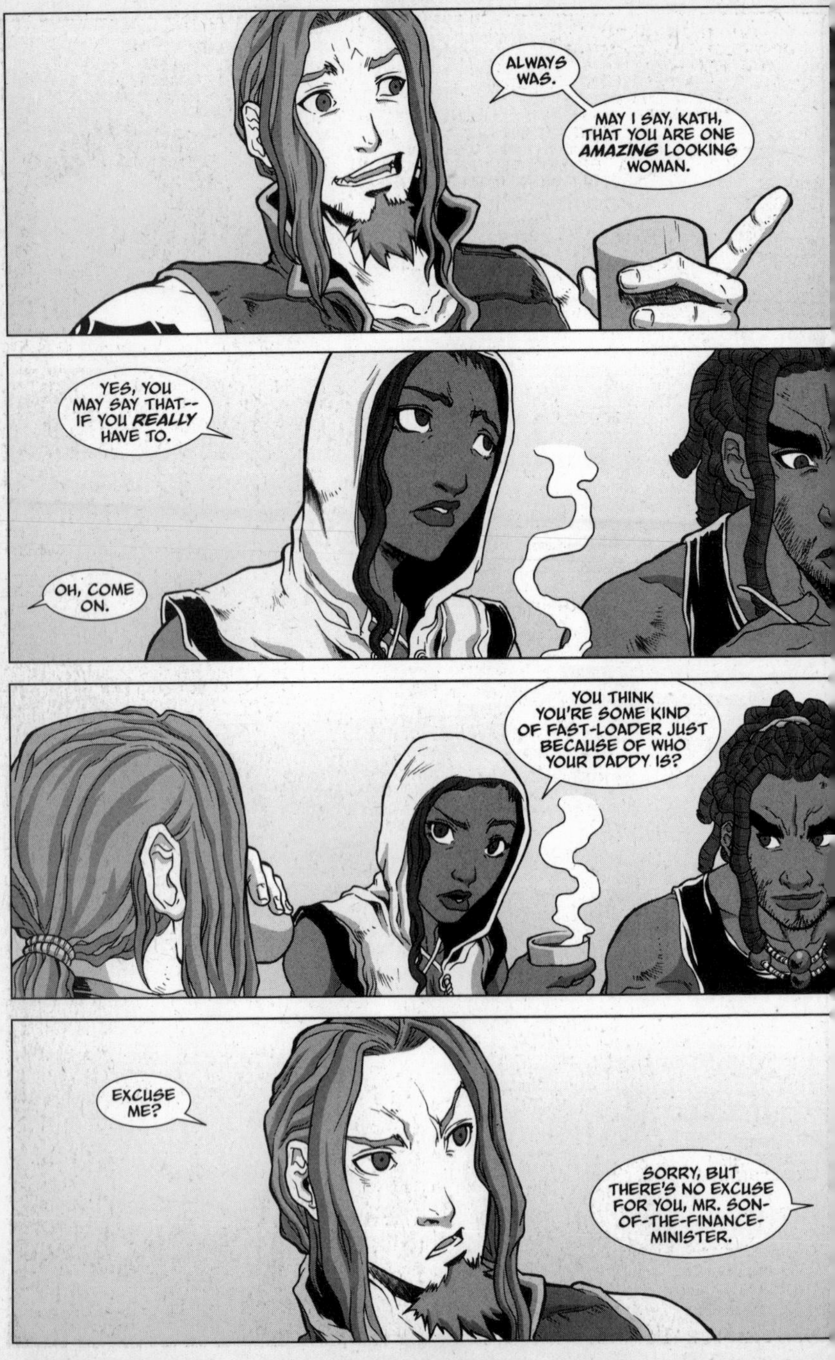
ALWAYS WAS.
MAY I SAY, KATH, THAT YOU ARE ONE ***AMAZING*** LOOKING WOMAN.
YES, YOU MAY SAY THAT-- IF YOU ***REALLY*** HAVE TO.
OH, COME ON.
YOU THINK YOU'RE SOME KIND OF FAST-LOADER JUST BECAUSE OF WHO YOUR DADDY IS?
EXCUSE ME?
SORRY, BUT THERE'S NO EXCUSE FOR YOU, MR. SON-OF-THE-FINANCE-MINISTER.

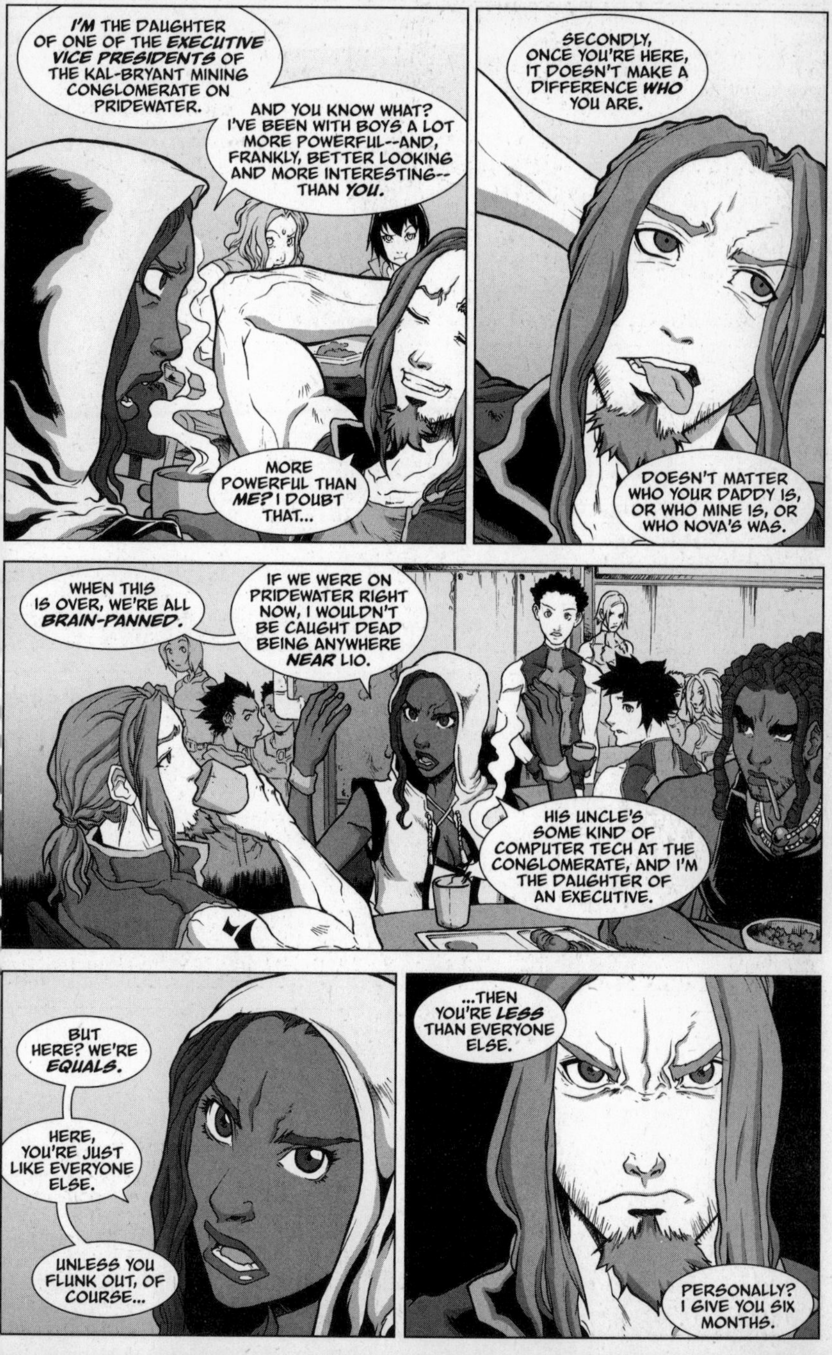
I'M THE DAUGHTER OF ONE OF THE EXECUTIVE VICE PRESIDENTS OF THE KAL-BRYANT MINING CONGLOMERATE ON PRIDEWATER.
AND YOU KNOW WHAT? I'VE BEEN WITH BOYS A LOT MORE POWERFUL--AND, FRANKLY, BETTER LOOKING AND MORE INTERESTING--THAN YOU.
MORE POWERFUL THAN ME? I DOUBT THAT...
SECONDLY, ONCE YOU'RE HERE, IT DOESN'T MAKE A DIFFERENCE WHO YOU ARE.
DOESN'T MATTER WHO YOUR DADDY IS, OR WHO MINE IS, OR WHO NOVA'S WAS.
WHEN THIS IS OVER, WE'RE ALL BRAIN-PANNED.
IF WE WERE ON PRIDEWATER RIGHT NOW, I WOULDN'T BE CAUGHT DEAD BEING ANYWHERE NEAR LIO.
HIS UNCLE'S SOME KIND OF COMPUTER TECH AT THE CONGLOMERATE, AND I'M THE DAUGHTER OF AN EXECUTIVE.
BUT HERE? WE'RE EQUALS.
HERE, YOU'RE JUST LIKE EVERYONE ELSE.
UNLESS YOU FLUNK OUT, OF COURSE...
...THEN YOU'RE LESS THAN EVERYONE ELSE.
PERSONALLY? I GIVE YOU SIX MONTHS.

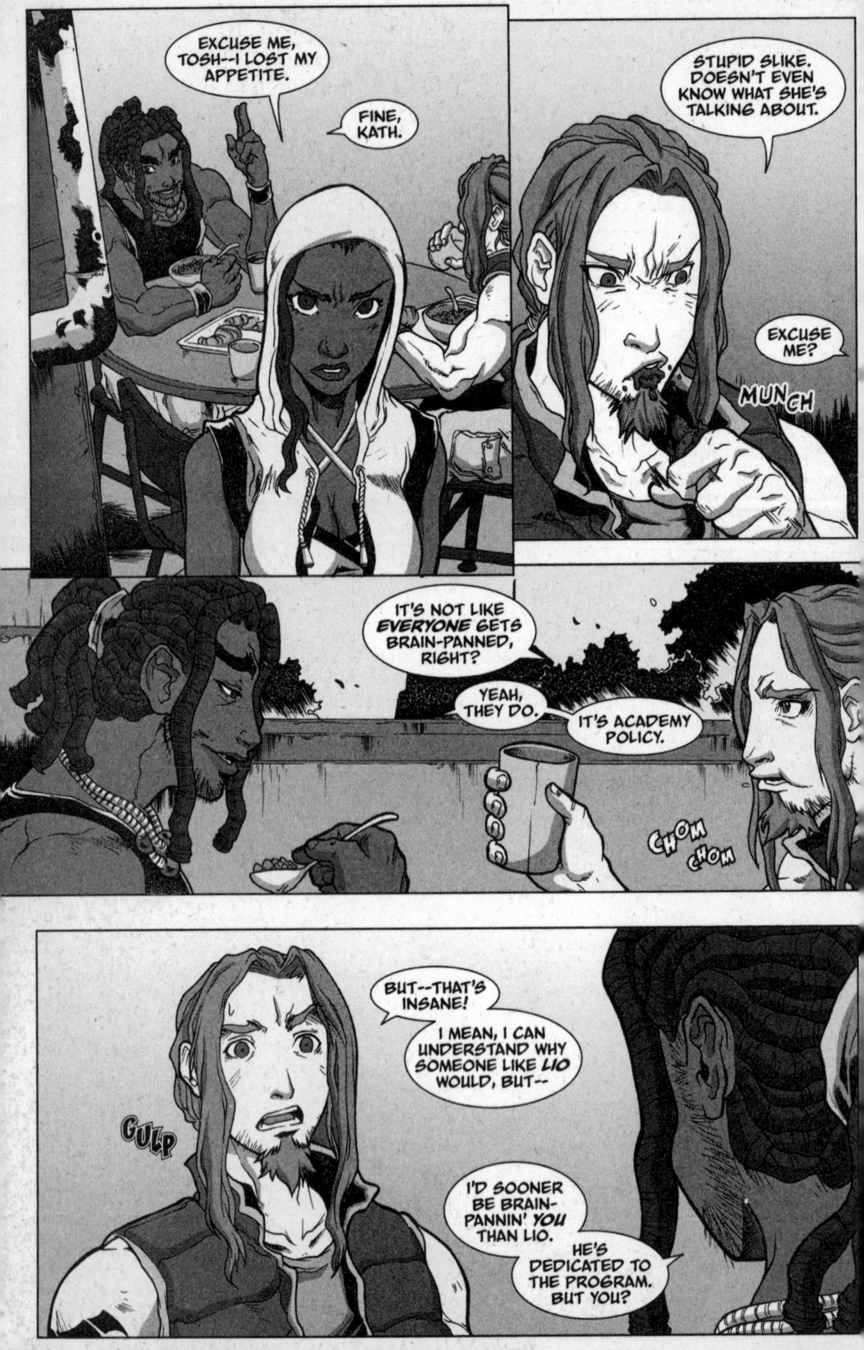
EXCUSE ME, TOSH--I LOST MY APPETITE.
FINE, KATH.
STUPID SLIKE. DOESN'T EVEN KNOW WHAT SHE'S TALKING ABOUT.
EXCUSE ME?
MUNCH
IT'S NOT LIKE *EVERYONE* GETS BRAIN-PANNED, RIGHT?
YEAH, THEY DO.
IT'S ACADEMY POLICY.
CHOM CHOM
BUT--THAT'S INSANE!
I MEAN, I CAN UNDERSTAND WHY SOMEONE LIKE *LIO* WOULD, BUT--
GULP
I'D SOONER BE BRAIN-PANNIN' *YOU* THAN LIO.
HE'S DEDICATED TO THE PROGRAM. BUT YOU?

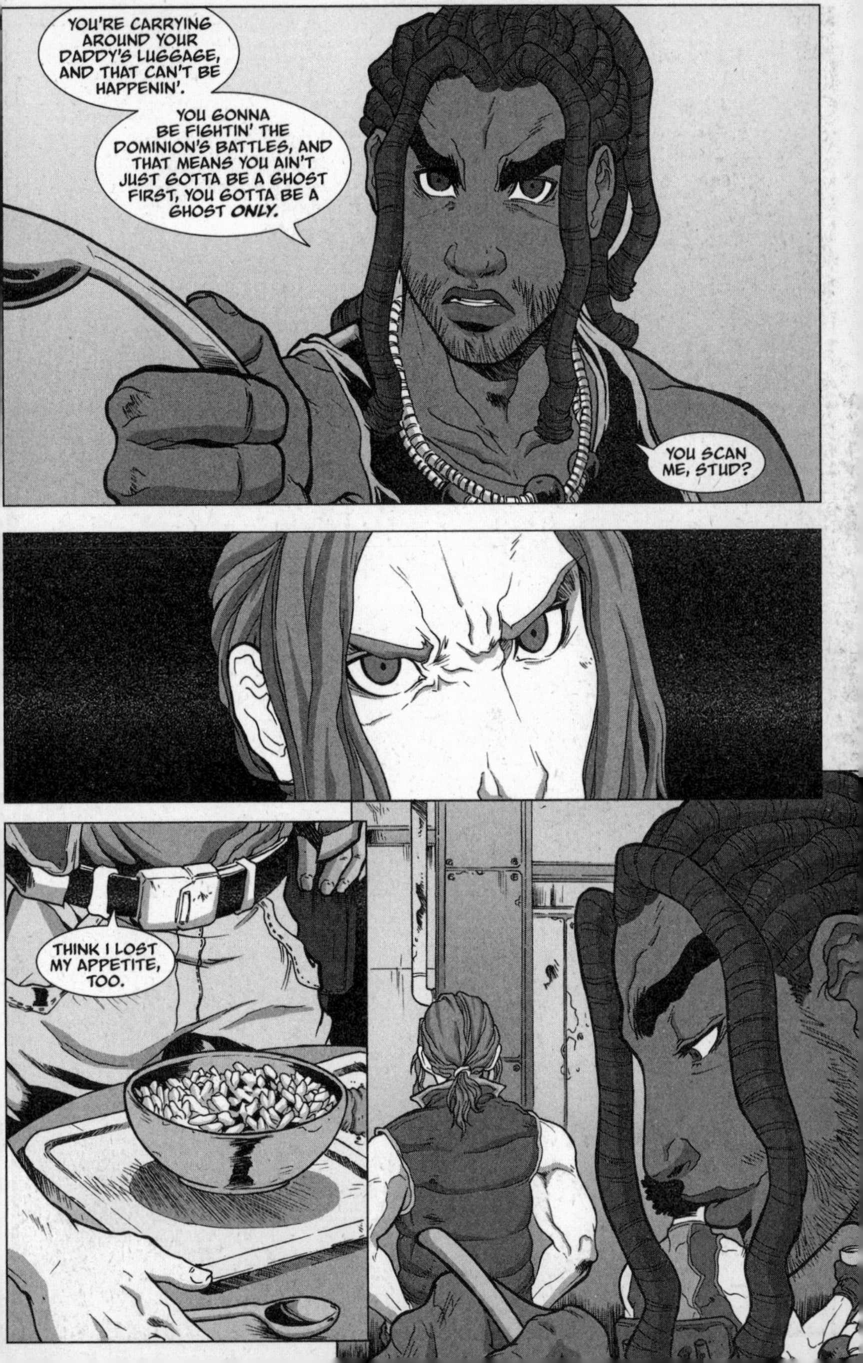
YOU'RE CARRYING AROUND YOUR DADDY'S LUGGAGE, AND THAT CAN'T BE HAPPENIN'.
YOU GONNA BE FIGHTIN' THE DOMINION'S BATTLES, AND THAT MEANS YOU AIN'T JUST GOTTA BE A GHOST FIRST, YOU GOTTA BE A GHOST *ONLY.*
YOU SCAN ME, STUD?
THINK I LOST MY APPETITE, TOO.

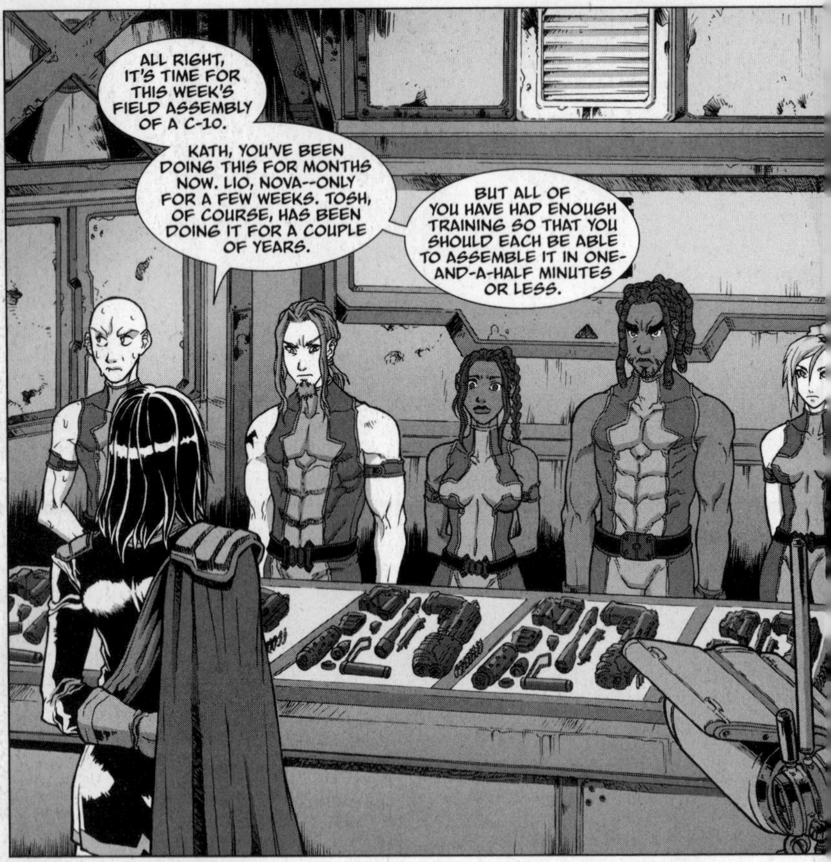
ALL RIGHT, IT'S TIME FOR THIS WEEK'S FIELD ASSEMBLY OF A C-10.
KATH, YOU'VE BEEN DOING THIS FOR MONTHS NOW. LIO, NOVA--ONLY FOR A FEW WEEKS. TOSH, OF COURSE, HAS BEEN DOING IT FOR A COUPLE OF YEARS.
BUT ALL OF YOU HAVE HAD ENOUGH TRAINING SO THAT YOU SHOULD EACH BE ABLE TO ASSEMBLE IT IN ONE-AND-A-HALF MINUTES OR LESS.
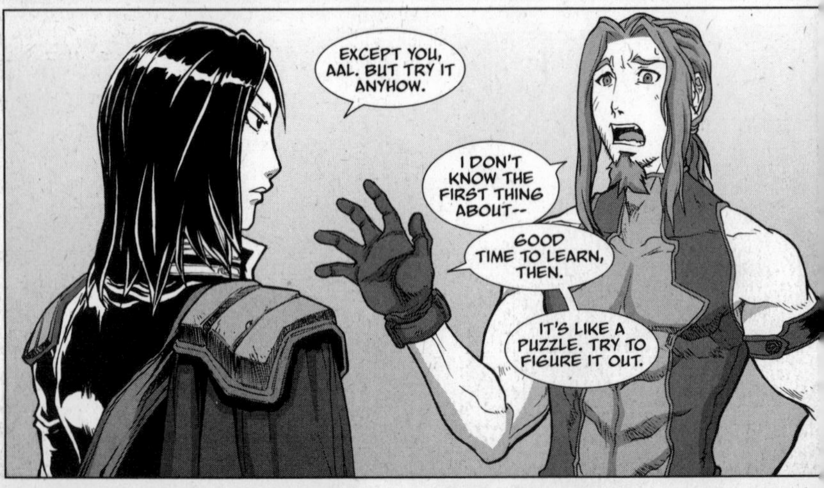
EXCEPT YOU, AAL. BUT TRY IT ANYHOW.
I DON'T KNOW THE FIRST THING ABOUT--
GOOD TIME TO LEARN, THEN.
IT'S LIKE A PUZZLE. TRY TO FIGURE IT OUT.

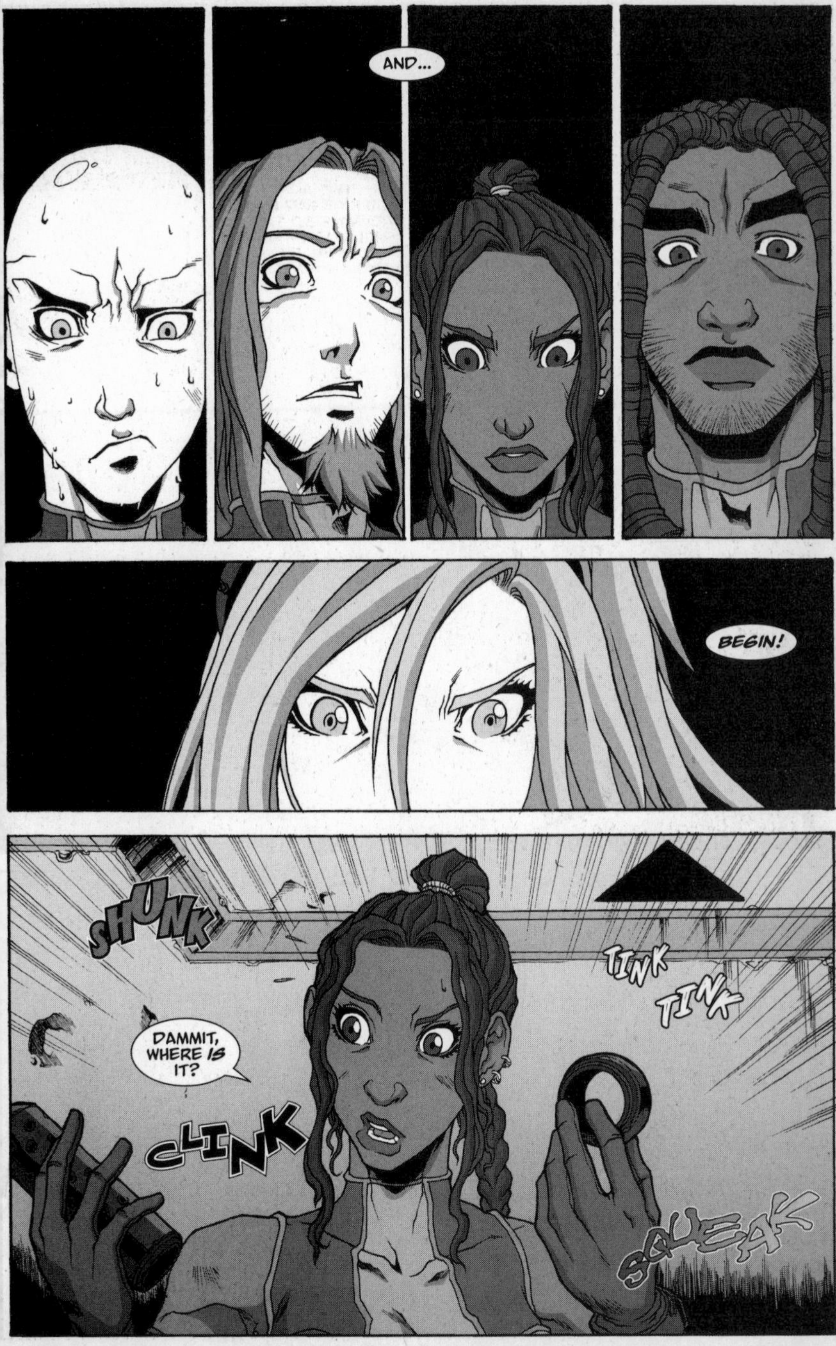
AND...
BEGIN!
SHUNK
TINK
TINK
DAMMIT, WHERE IS IT?
CLINK
SQUEAK

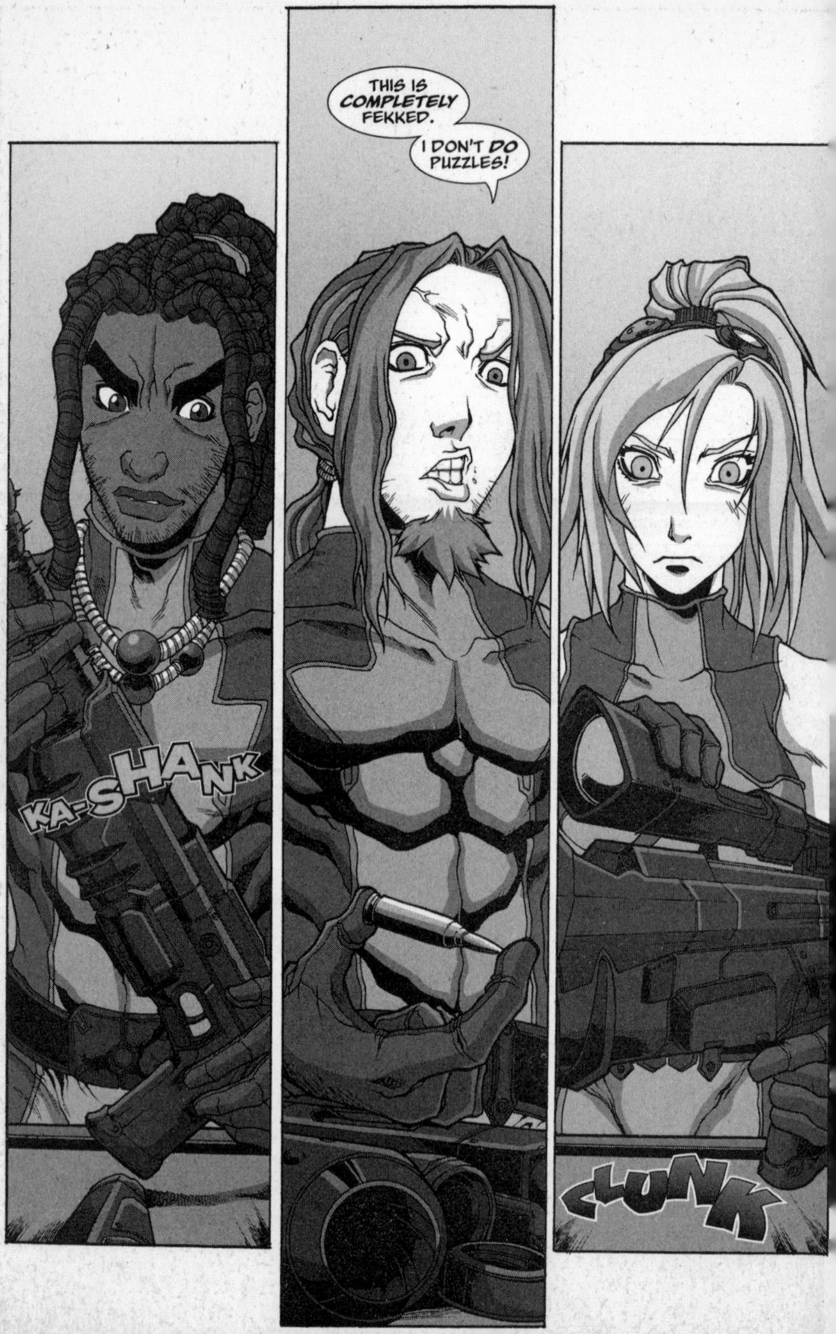
KA-SHANK
THIS IS COMPLETELY FEKKED.
I DON'T DO PUZZLES!
CLUNK

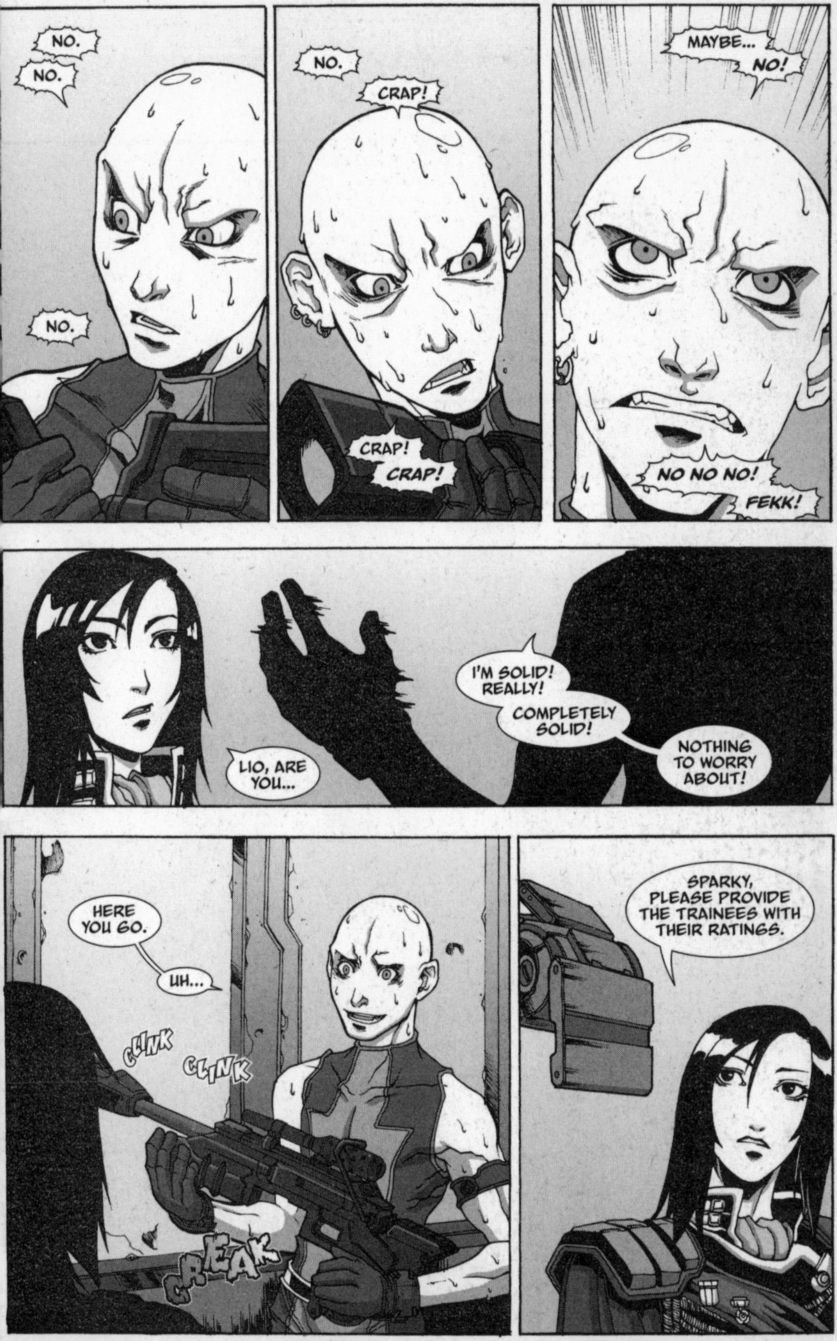
NO.
NO.
NO.
NO.
CRAP!
CRAP!
CRAP!
MAYBE...
NO!
NO NO NO!
FEKK!
LIO, ARE YOU...
I'M SOLID! REALLY!
COMPLETELY SOLID!
NOTHING TO WORRY ABOUT!
HERE YOU GO.
UH...
CLINK
CLINK
CREAK
SPARKY, PLEASE PROVIDE THE TRAINEES WITH THEIR RATINGS.

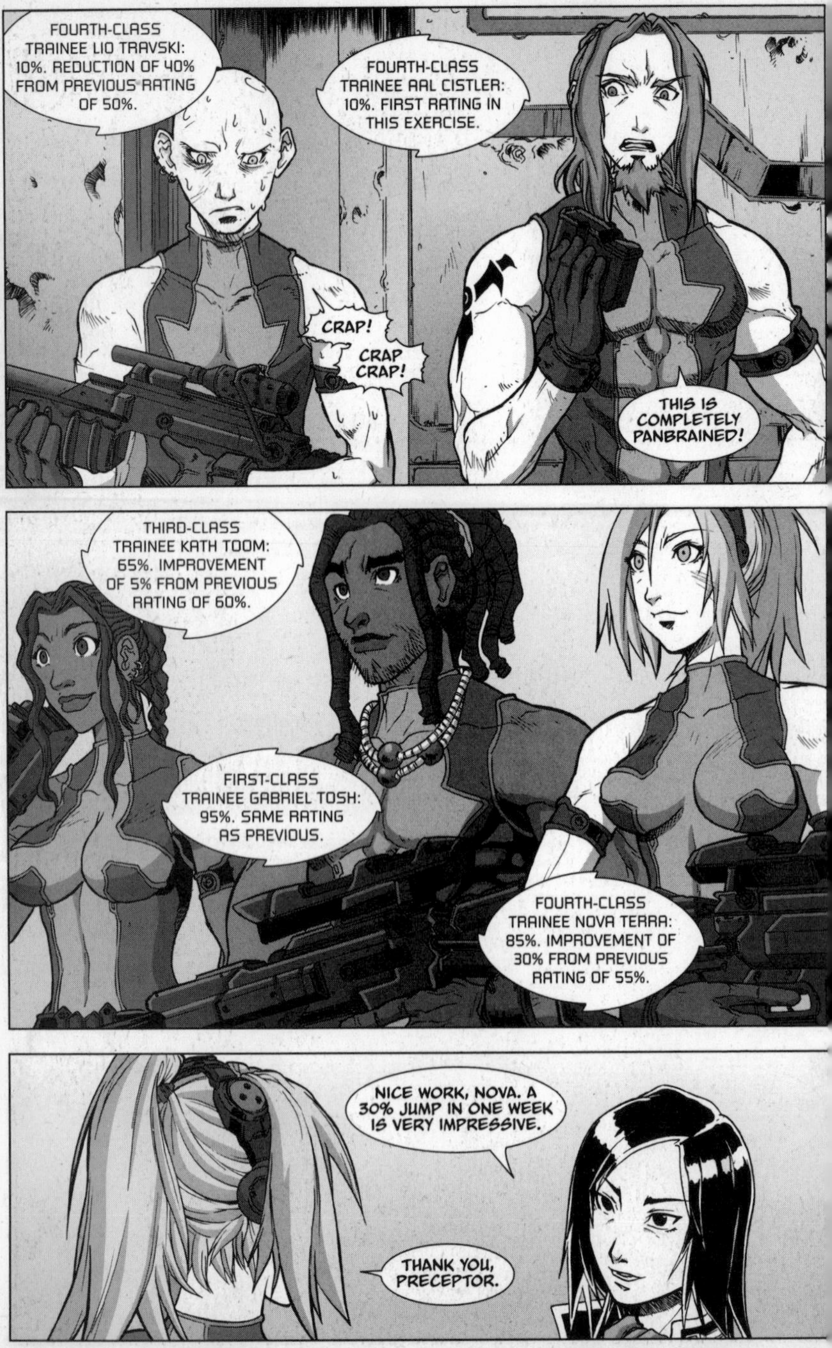
FOURTH-CLASS TRAINEE LIO TRAVSKI: 10%. REDUCTION OF 40% FROM PREVIOUS RATING OF 50%.
FOURTH-CLASS TRAINEE AAL CISTLER: 10%. FIRST RATING IN THIS EXERCISE.
CRAP!
CRAP CRAP!
THIS IS COMPLETELY PANBRAINED!
THIRD-CLASS TRAINEE KATH TOOM: 65%. IMPROVEMENT OF 5% FROM PREVIOUS RATING OF 60%.
FIRST-CLASS TRAINEE GABRIEL TOSH: 95%. SAME RATING AS PREVIOUS.
FOURTH-CLASS TRAINEE NOVA TERRA: 85%. IMPROVEMENT OF 30% FROM PREVIOUS RATING OF 55%.
NICE WORK, NOVA. A 30% JUMP IN ONE WEEK IS VERY IMPRESSIVE.
THANK YOU, PRECEPTOR.

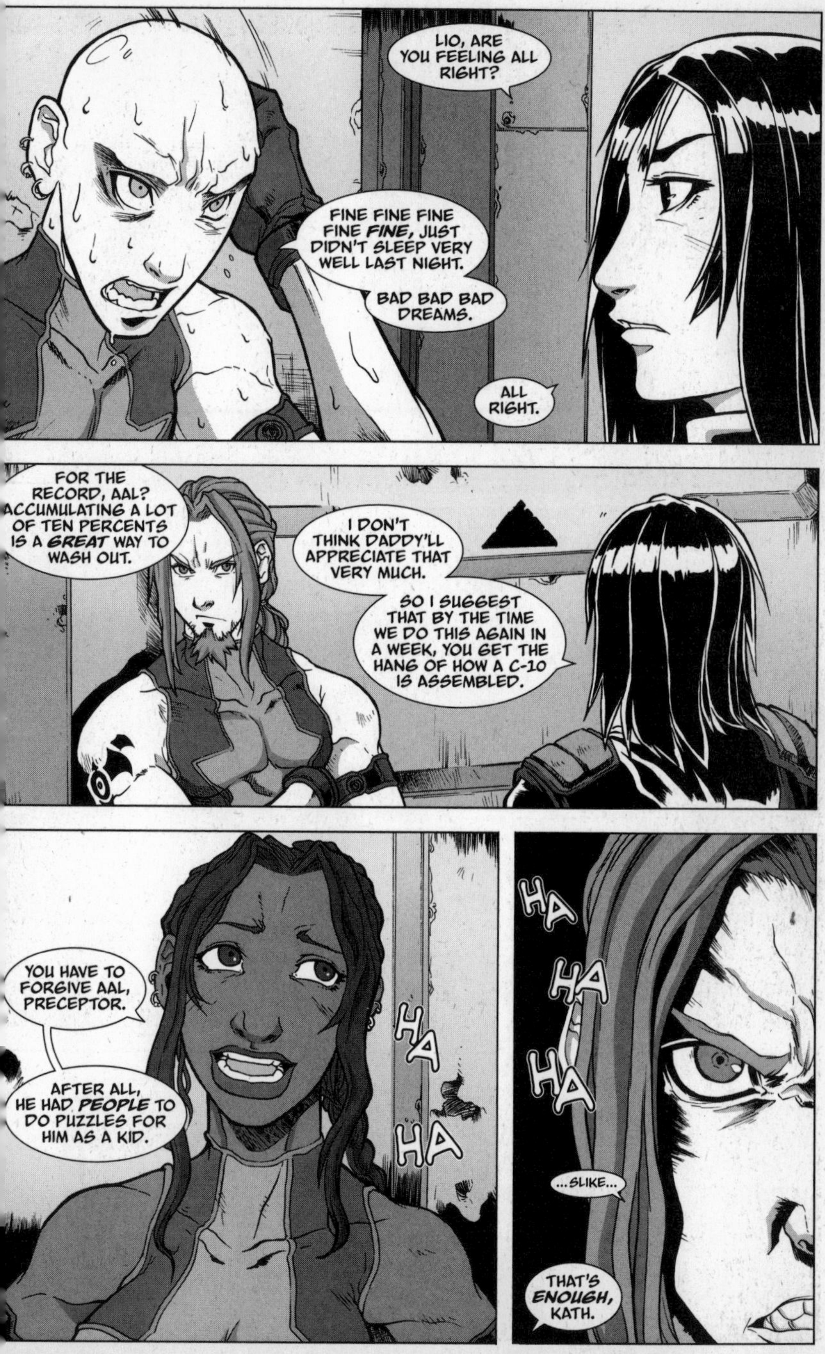
LIO, ARE YOU FEELING ALL RIGHT?
FINE FINE FINE FINE *FINE*, JUST DIDN'T SLEEP VERY WELL LAST NIGHT.
BAD BAD BAD DREAMS.
ALL RIGHT.
FOR THE RECORD, AAL? ACCUMULATING A LOT OF TEN PERCENTS IS A *GREAT* WAY TO WASH OUT.
I DON'T THINK DADDY'LL APPRECIATE THAT VERY MUCH.
SO I SUGGEST THAT BY THE TIME WE DO THIS AGAIN IN A WEEK, YOU GET THE HANG OF HOW A C-10 IS ASSEMBLED.
YOU HAVE TO FORGIVE AAL, PRECEPTOR.
AFTER ALL, HE HAD *PEOPLE* TO DO PUZZLES FOR HIM AS A KID.
HA
HA
HA
HA
HA
...SLIKE...
THAT'S *ENOUGH*, KATH.

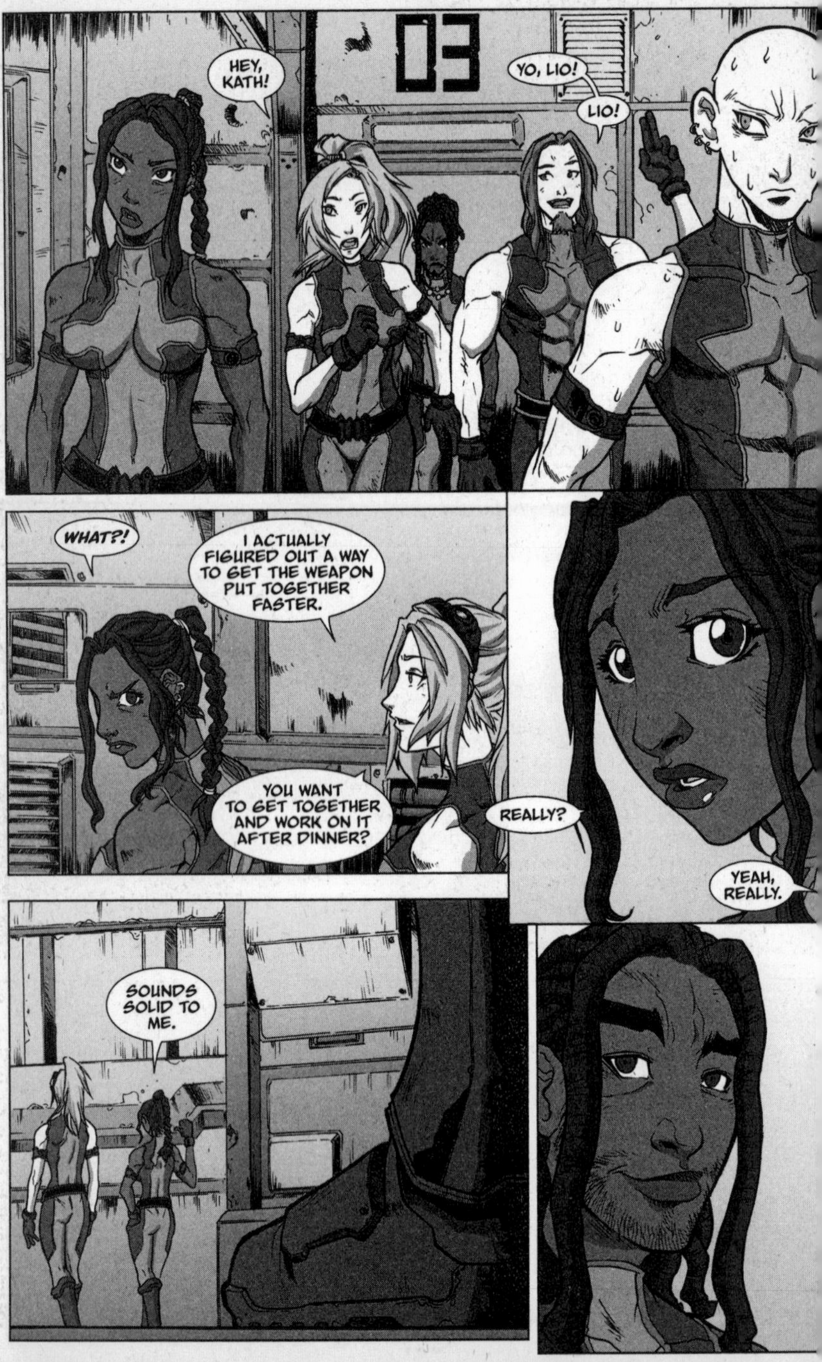
HEY, KATH!
YO, LIO!
LIO!
WHAT?!
I ACTUALLY FIGURED OUT A WAY TO GET THE WEAPON PUT TOGETHER FASTER.
YOU WANT TO GET TOGETHER AND WORK ON IT AFTER DINNER?
REALLY?
YEAH, REALLY.
SOUNDS SOLID TO ME.

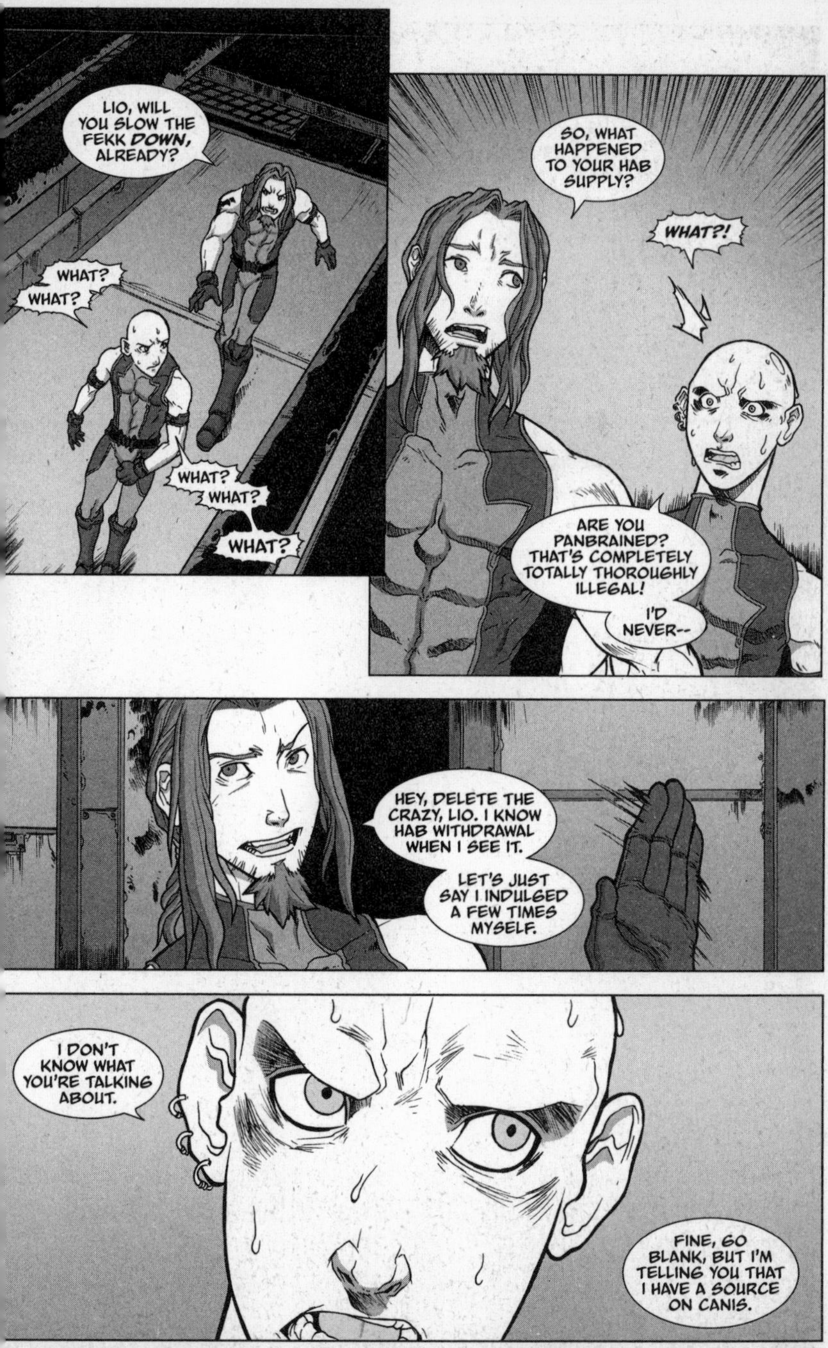
LIO, WILL YOU SLOW THE FEKK *DOWN*, ALREADY?
WHAT?
WHAT?
WHAT?
WHAT?
WHAT?
SO, WHAT HAPPENED TO YOUR HAB SUPPLY?
WHAT?!
ARE YOU PANBRAINED? THAT'S COMPLETELY TOTALLY THOROUGHLY ILLEGAL!
I'D NEVER--
HEY, DELETE THE CRAZY, LIO. I KNOW HAB WITHDRAWAL WHEN I SEE IT.
LET'S JUST SAY I INDULGED A FEW TIMES MYSELF.
I DON'T KNOW WHAT YOU'RE TALKING ABOUT.
FINE, GO BLANK, BUT I'M TELLING YOU THAT I HAVE A SOURCE ON CANIS.

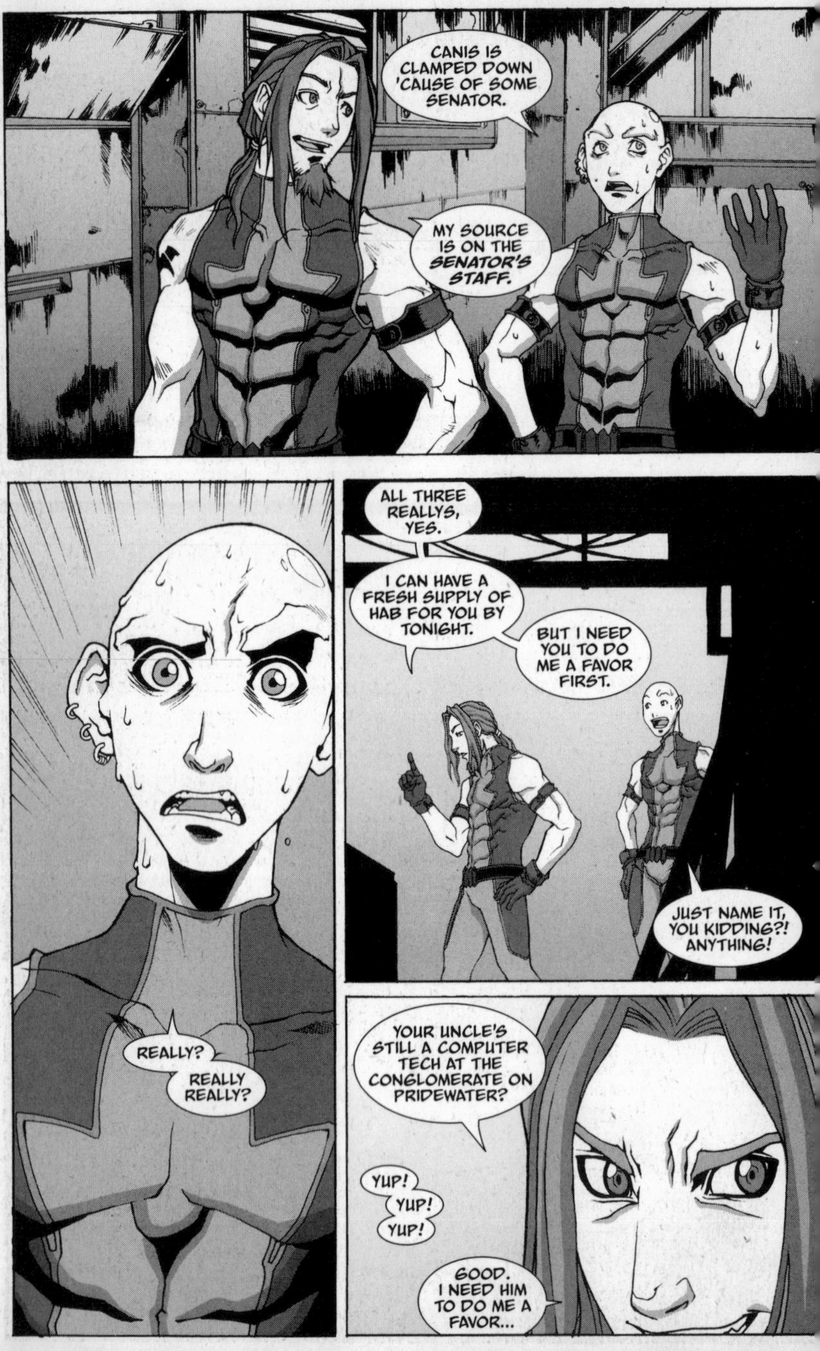
CANIS IS CLAMPED DOWN 'CAUSE OF SOME SENATOR.
MY SOURCE IS ON THE *SENATOR'S STAFF.*
REALLY?
REALLY REALLY?
ALL THREE REALLYS, YES.
I CAN HAVE A FRESH SUPPLY OF HAB FOR YOU BY TONIGHT.
BUT I NEED YOU TO DO ME A FAVOR FIRST.
JUST NAME IT, YOU KIDDING?! ANYTHING!
YOUR UNCLE'S STILL A COMPUTER TECH AT THE CONGLOMERATE ON PRIDEWATER?
YUP!
YUP!
YUP!
GOOD. I NEED HIM TO DO ME A FAVOR...

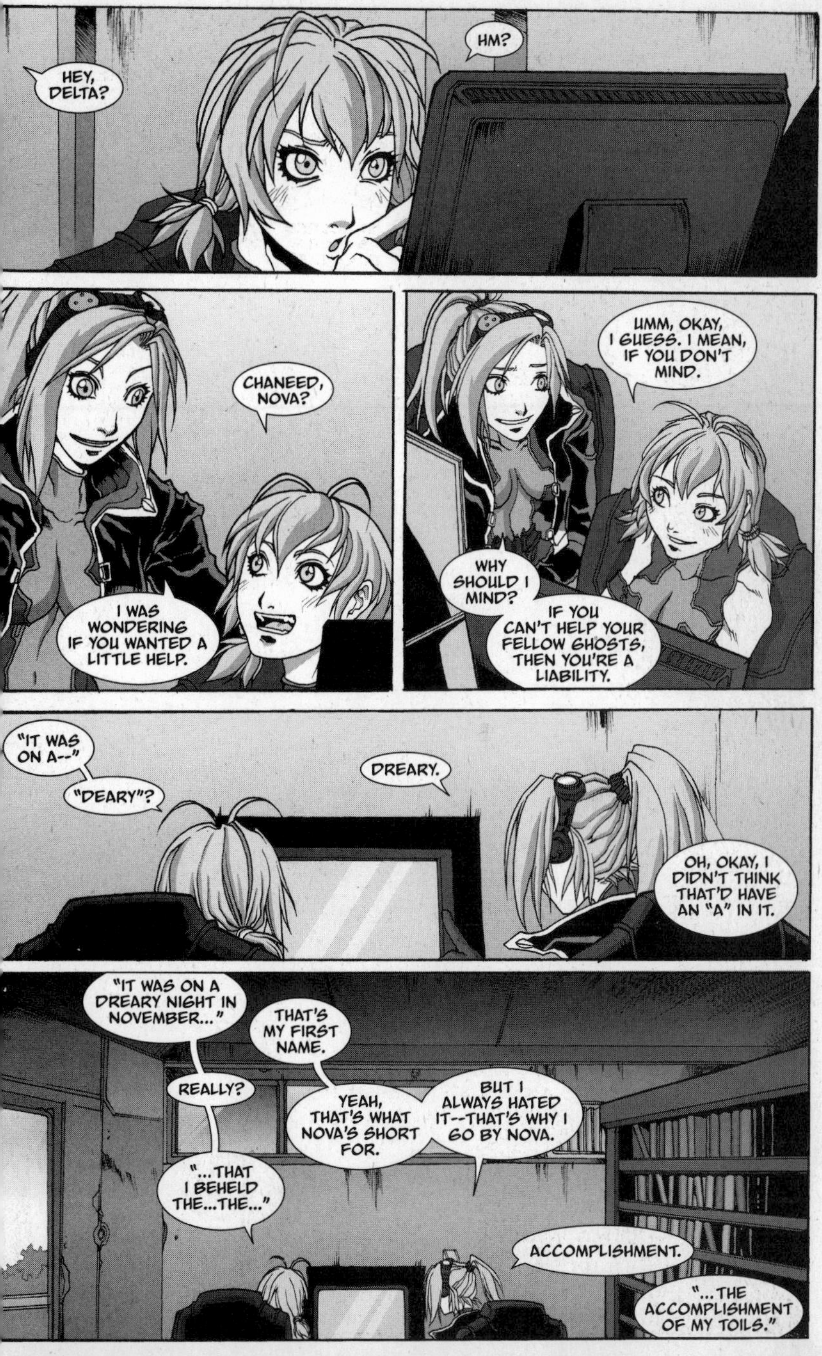
HEY, DELTA?
HM?
CHANEED, NOVA?
I WAS WONDERING IF YOU WANTED A LITTLE HELP.
UMM, OKAY, I GUESS. I MEAN, IF YOU DON'T MIND.
WHY SHOULD I MIND?
IF YOU CAN'T HELP YOUR FELLOW GHOSTS, THEN YOU'RE A LIABILITY.
"IT WAS ON A--"
"DEARY"?
DREARY.
OH, OKAY, I DIDN'T THINK THAT'D HAVE AN "A" IN IT.
"IT WAS ON A DREARY NIGHT IN NOVEMBER..."
THAT'S MY FIRST NAME.
REALLY?
YEAH, THAT'S WHAT NOVA'S SHORT FOR.
BUT I ALWAYS HATED IT--THAT'S WHY I GO BY NOVA.
"...THAT I BEHELD THE...THE..."
ACCOMPLISHMENT.
"...THE ACCOMPLISHMENT OF MY TOILS."

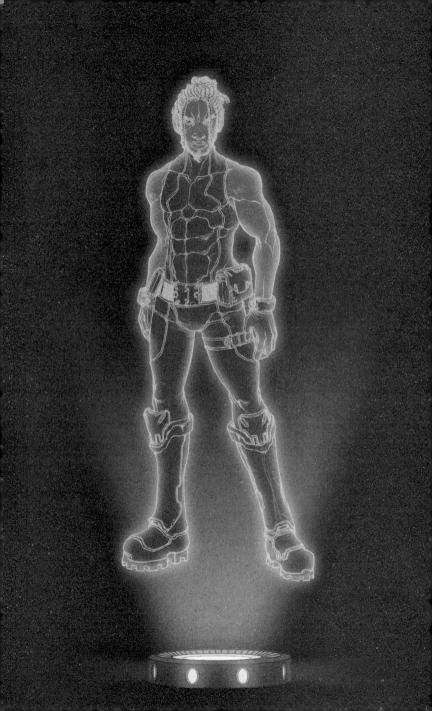

CHAPTER 4

ALL I HAVE TO DO IS DREAM

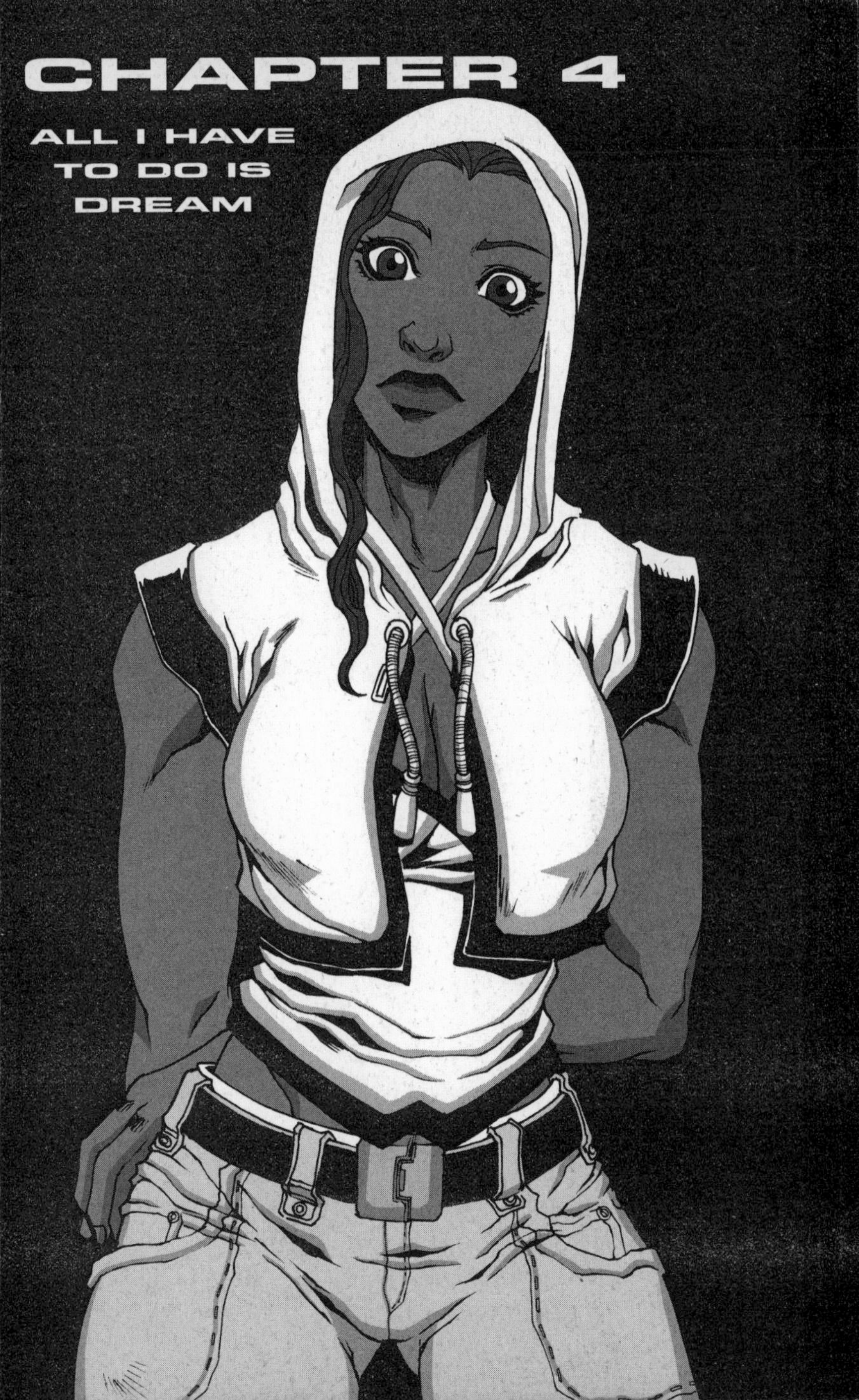

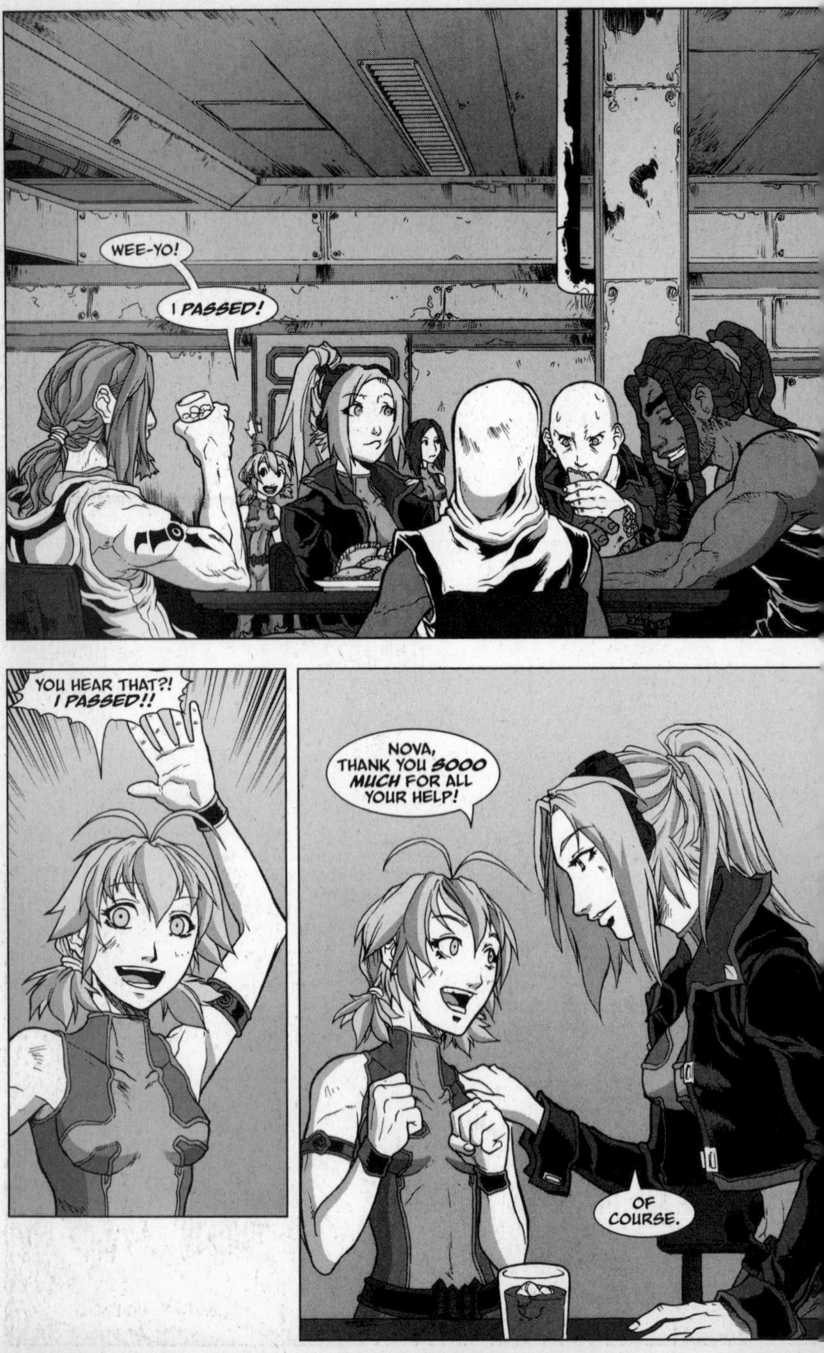
WEE-YO!
I PASSED!
YOU HEAR THAT?! I PASSED!!
NOVA, THANK YOU SOOO MUCH FOR ALL YOUR HELP!
OF COURSE.

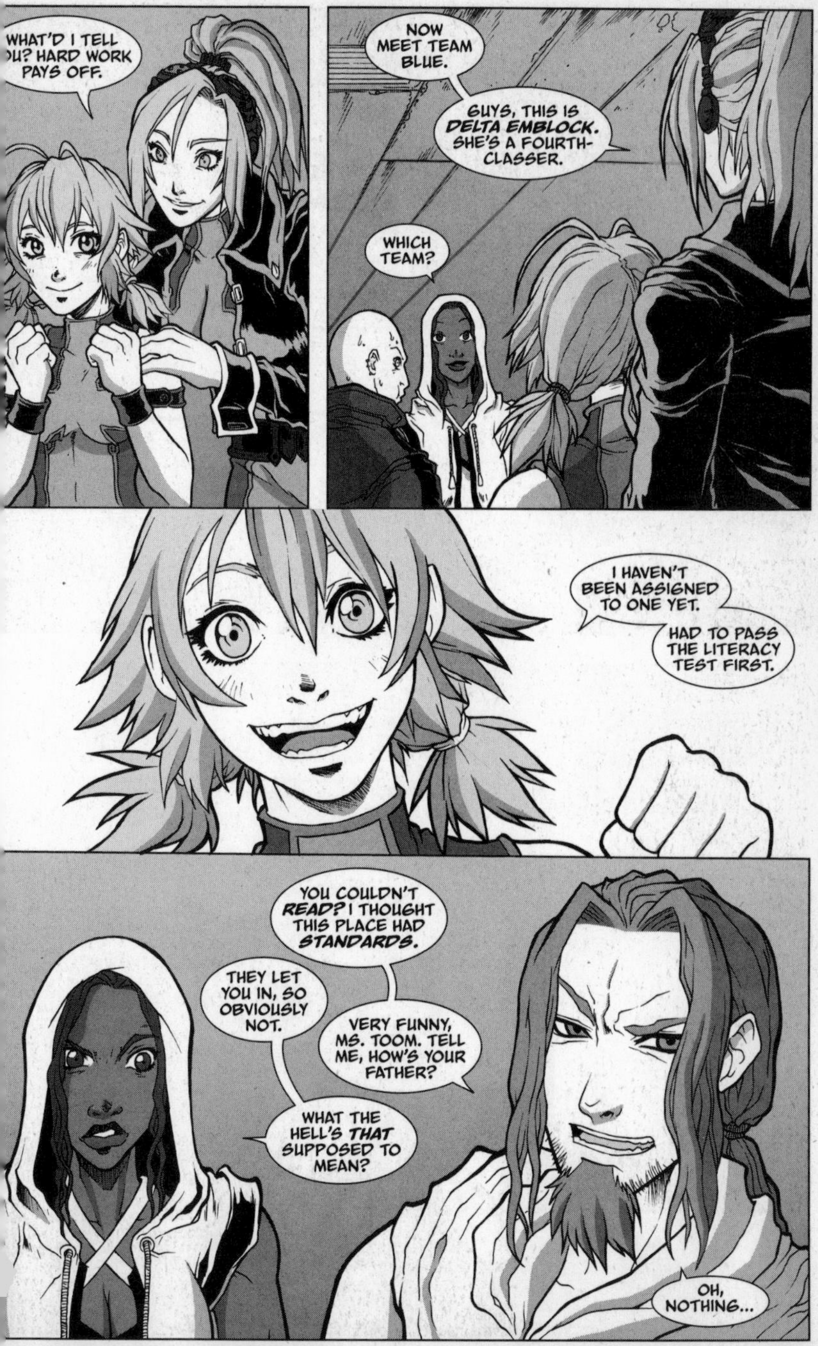
WHAT'D I TELL OU? HARD WORK PAYS OFF.
NOW MEET TEAM BLUE.
GUYS, THIS IS DELTA EMBLOCK. SHE'S A FOURTH-CLASSER.
WHICH TEAM?
I HAVEN'T BEEN ASSIGNED TO ONE YET.
HAD TO PASS THE LITERACY TEST FIRST.
YOU COULDN'T READ? I THOUGHT THIS PLACE HAD STANDARDS.
THEY LET YOU IN, SO OBVIOUSLY NOT.
VERY FUNNY, MS. TOOM. TELL ME, HOW'S YOUR FATHER?
WHAT THE HELL'S THAT SUPPOSED TO MEAN?
OH, NOTHING...

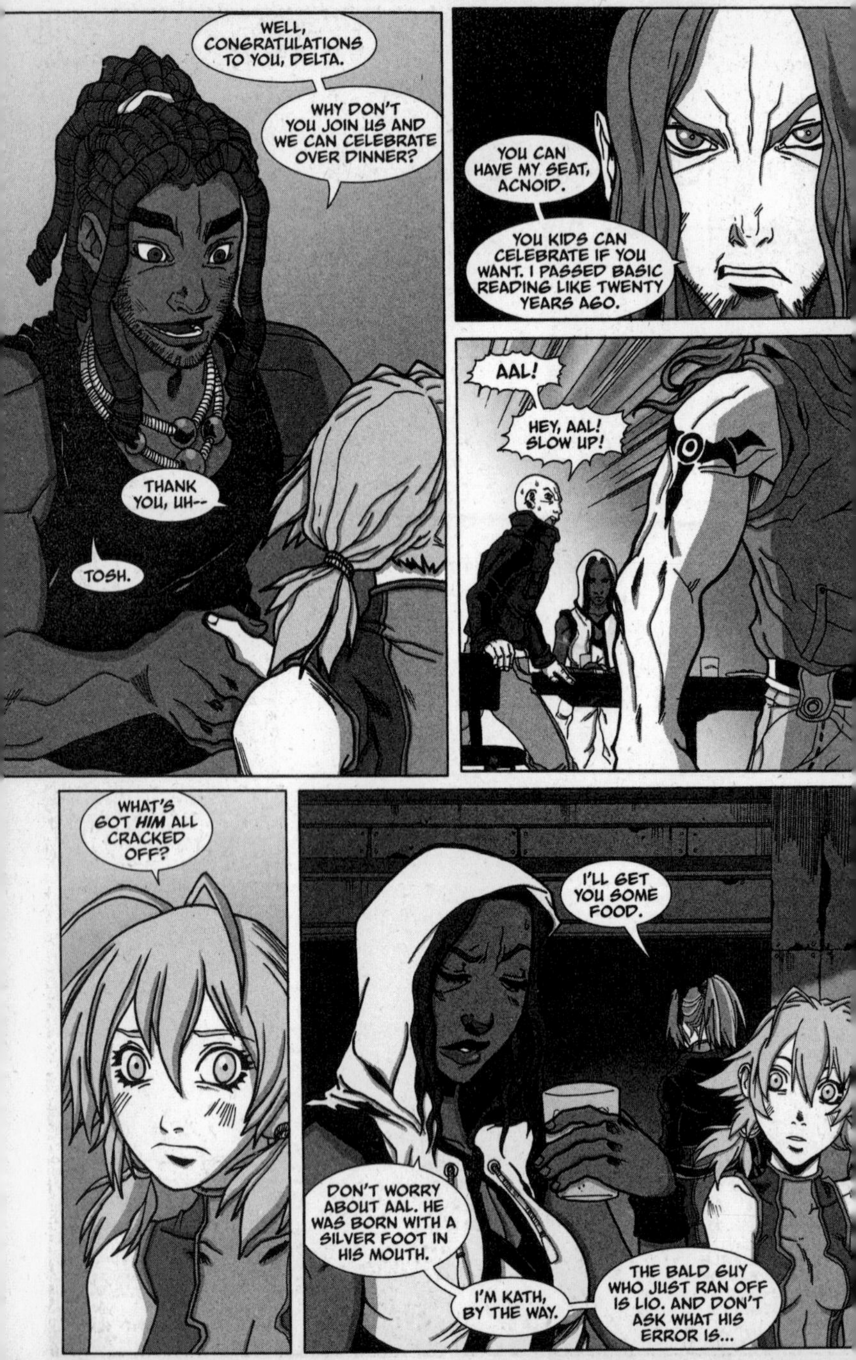
WELL, CONGRATULATIONS TO YOU, DELTA.
WHY DON'T YOU JOIN US AND WE CAN CELEBRATE OVER DINNER?
THANK YOU, UH--
TOSH.
YOU CAN HAVE MY SEAT, ACNOID.
YOU KIDS CAN CELEBRATE IF YOU WANT. I PASSED BASIC READING LIKE TWENTY YEARS AGO.
AAL!
HEY, AAL! SLOW UP!
WHAT'S GOT HIM ALL CRACKED OFF?
I'LL GET YOU SOME FOOD.
DON'T WORRY ABOUT AAL. HE WAS BORN WITH A SILVER FOOT IN HIS MOUTH.
I'M KATH, BY THE WAY.
THE BALD GUY WHO JUST RAN OFF IS LIO. AND DON'T ASK WHAT HIS ERROR IS...

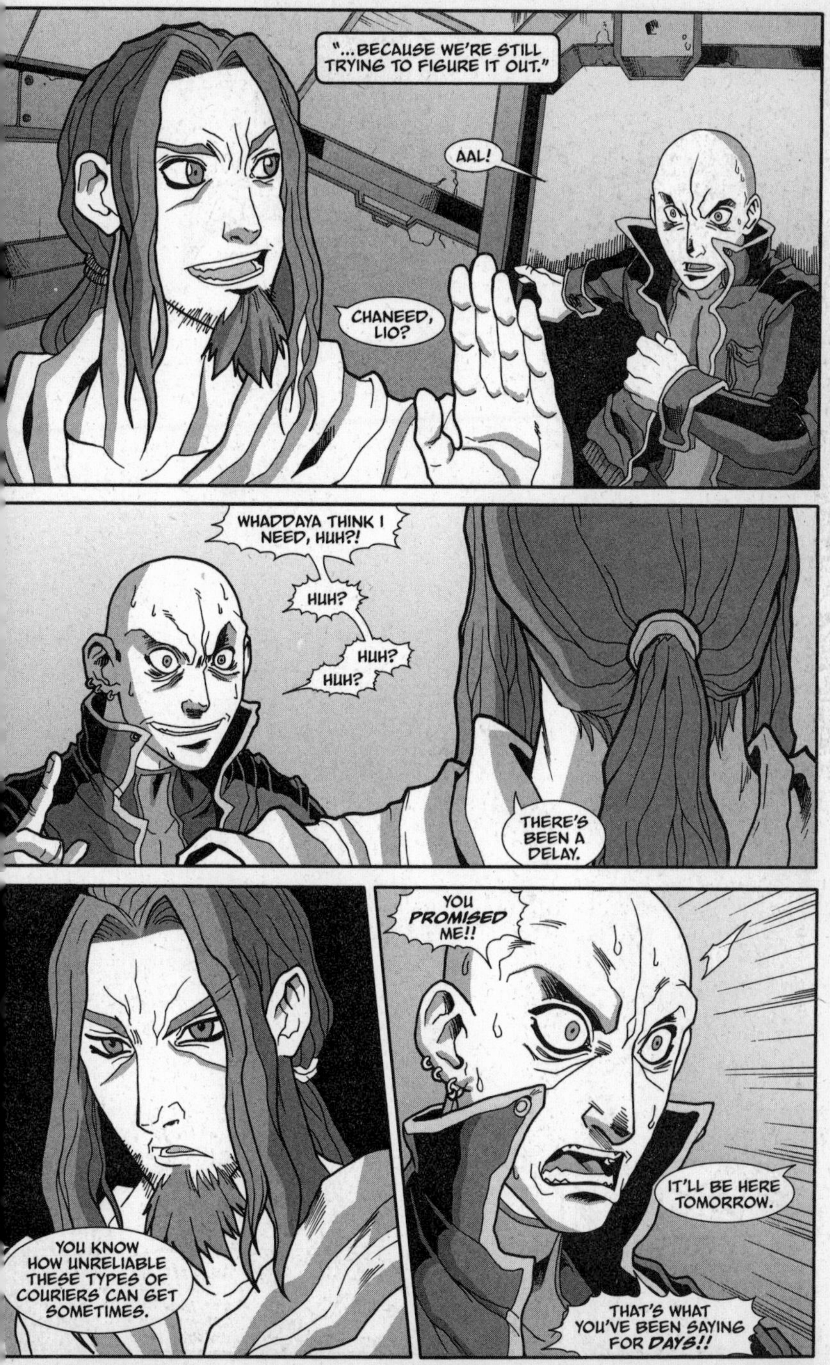
"...BECAUSE WE'RE STILL TRYING TO FIGURE IT OUT."
AAL!
CHANEED, LIO?
WHADDAYA THINK I NEED, HUH?!
HUH?
HUH?
HUH?
THERE'S BEEN A DELAY.
YOU KNOW HOW UNRELIABLE THESE TYPES OF COURIERS CAN GET SOMETIMES.
YOU *PROMISED* ME!!
IT'LL BE HERE TOMORROW.
THAT'S WHAT YOU'VE BEEN SAYING FOR *DAYS*!!

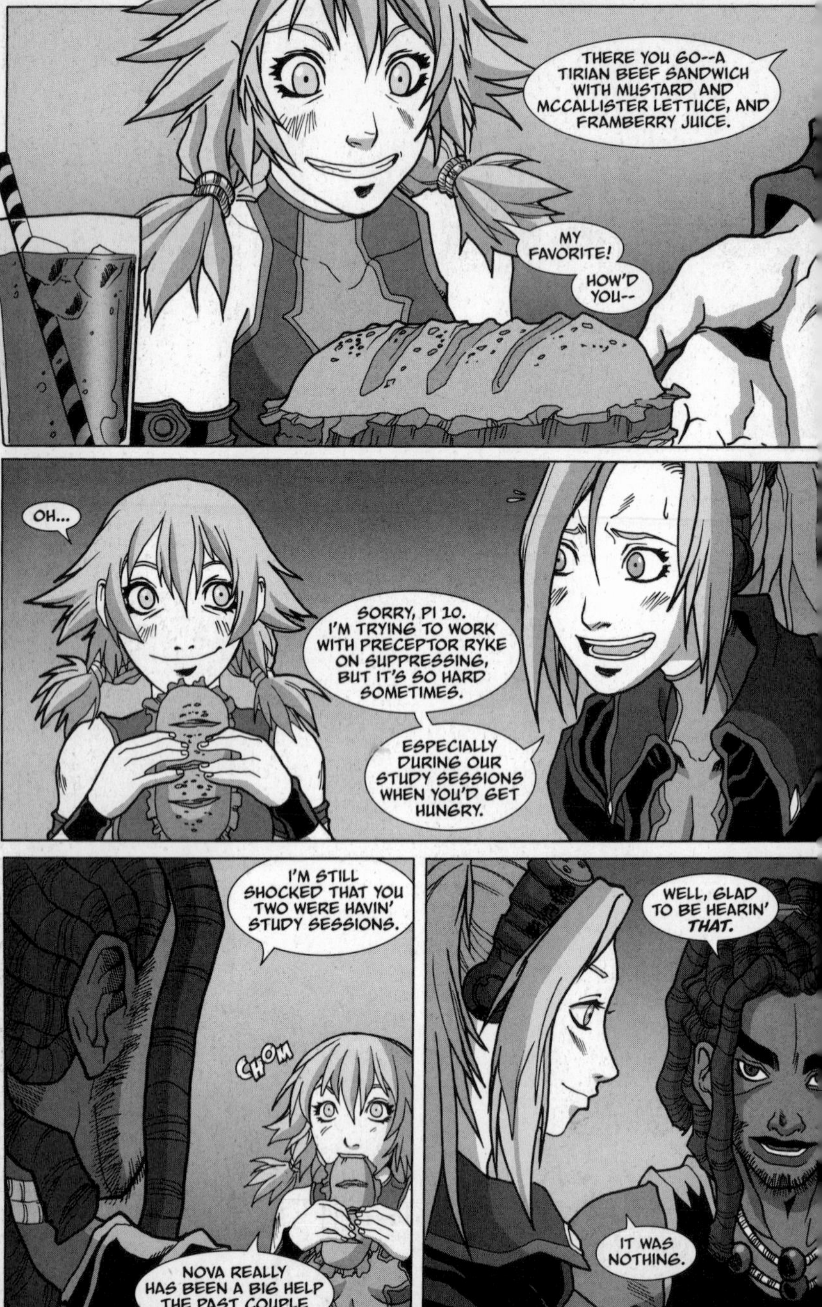
THERE YOU GO--A TIRIAN BEEF SANDWICH WITH MUSTARD AND MCCALLISTER LETTUCE, AND FRAMBERRY JUICE.
MY FAVORITE!
HOW'D YOU--
OH...
SORRY, PI 10. I'M TRYING TO WORK WITH PRECEPTOR RYKE ON SUPPRESSING, BUT IT'S SO HARD SOMETIMES.
ESPECIALLY DURING OUR STUDY SESSIONS WHEN YOU'D GET HUNGRY.
I'M STILL SHOCKED THAT YOU TWO WERE HAVIN' STUDY SESSIONS.
CHOM
NOVA REALLY HAS BEEN A BIG HELP THE PAST COUPLE OF DAYS.
WELL, GLAD TO BE HEARIN' *THAT.*
IT WAS NOTHING.

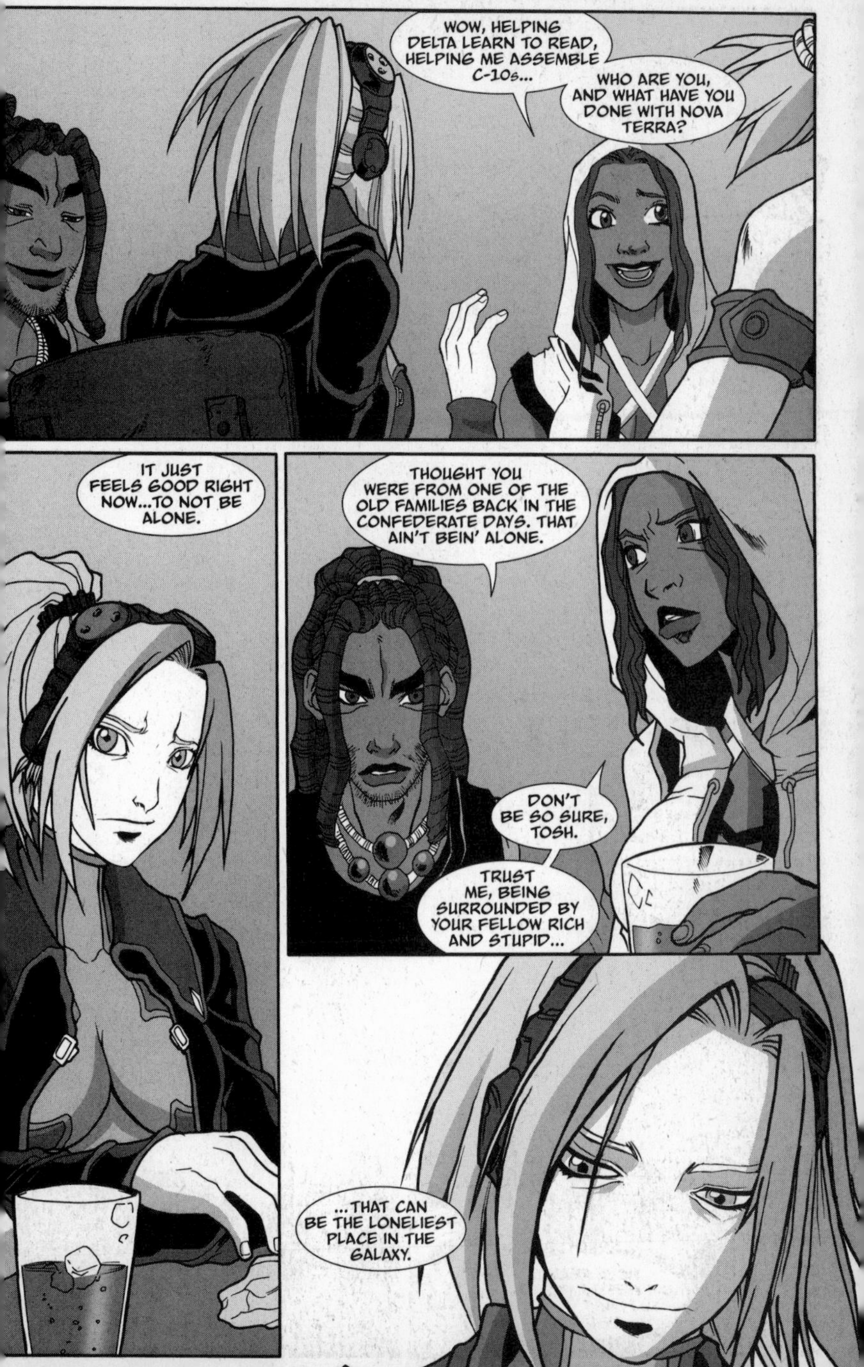
WOW, HELPING DELTA LEARN TO READ, HELPING ME ASSEMBLE C-10s...
WHO ARE YOU, AND WHAT HAVE YOU DONE WITH NOVA TERRA?
IT JUST FEELS GOOD RIGHT NOW...TO NOT BE ALONE.
THOUGHT YOU WERE FROM ONE OF THE OLD FAMILIES BACK IN THE CONFEDERATE DAYS. THAT AIN'T BEIN' ALONE.
DON'T BE SO SURE, TOSH.
TRUST ME, BEING SURROUNDED BY YOUR FELLOW RICH AND STUPID...
...THAT CAN BE THE LONELIEST PLACE IN THE GALAXY.

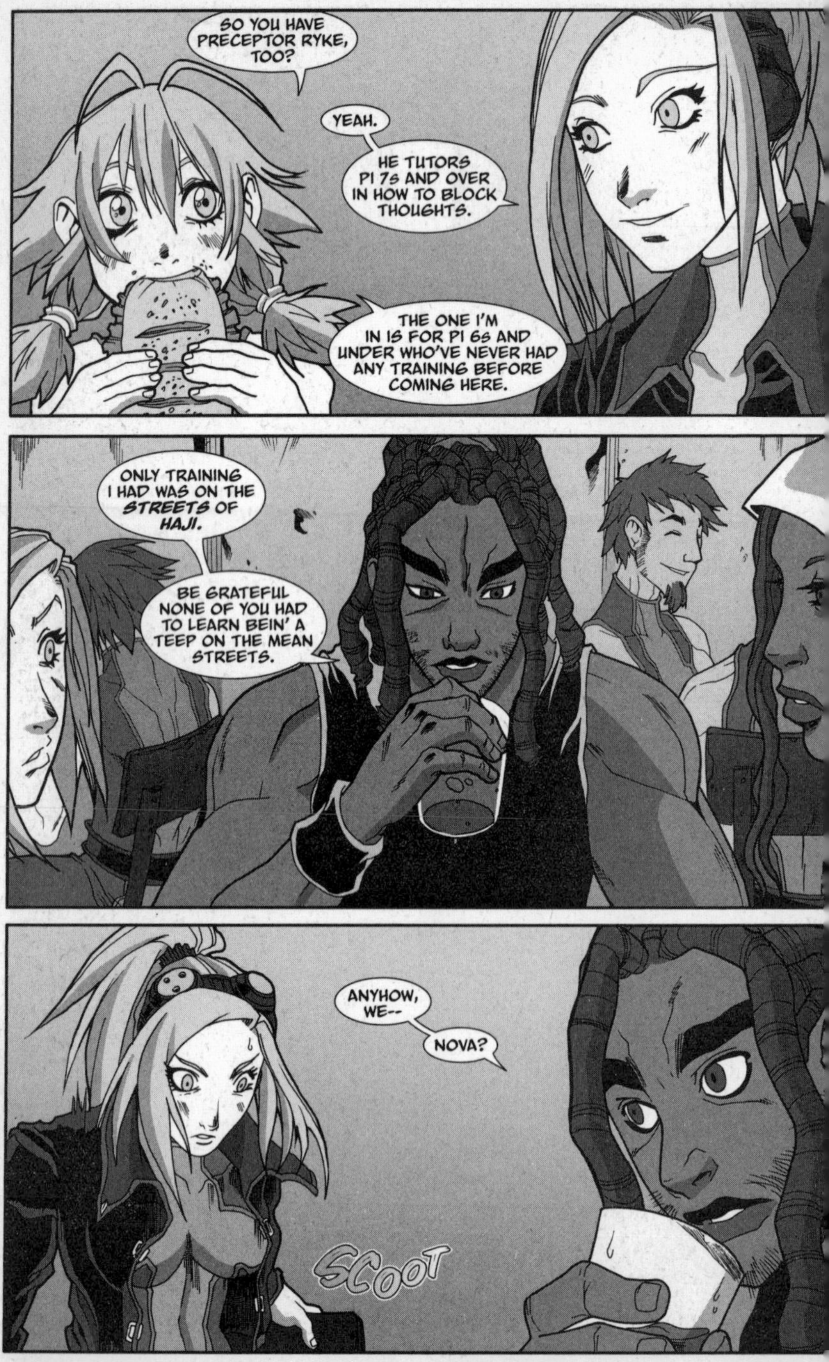
SO YOU HAVE PRECEPTOR RYKE, TOO?
YEAH.
HE TUTORS PI 7s AND OVER IN HOW TO BLOCK THOUGHTS.
THE ONE I'M IN IS FOR PI 6s AND UNDER WHO'VE NEVER HAD ANY TRAINING BEFORE COMING HERE.
ONLY TRAINING I HAD WAS ON THE *STREETS* OF *HAJI.*
BE GRATEFUL NONE OF YOU HAD TO LEARN BEIN' A TEEP ON THE MEAN STREETS.
ANYHOW, WE--
NOVA?
SCOOT

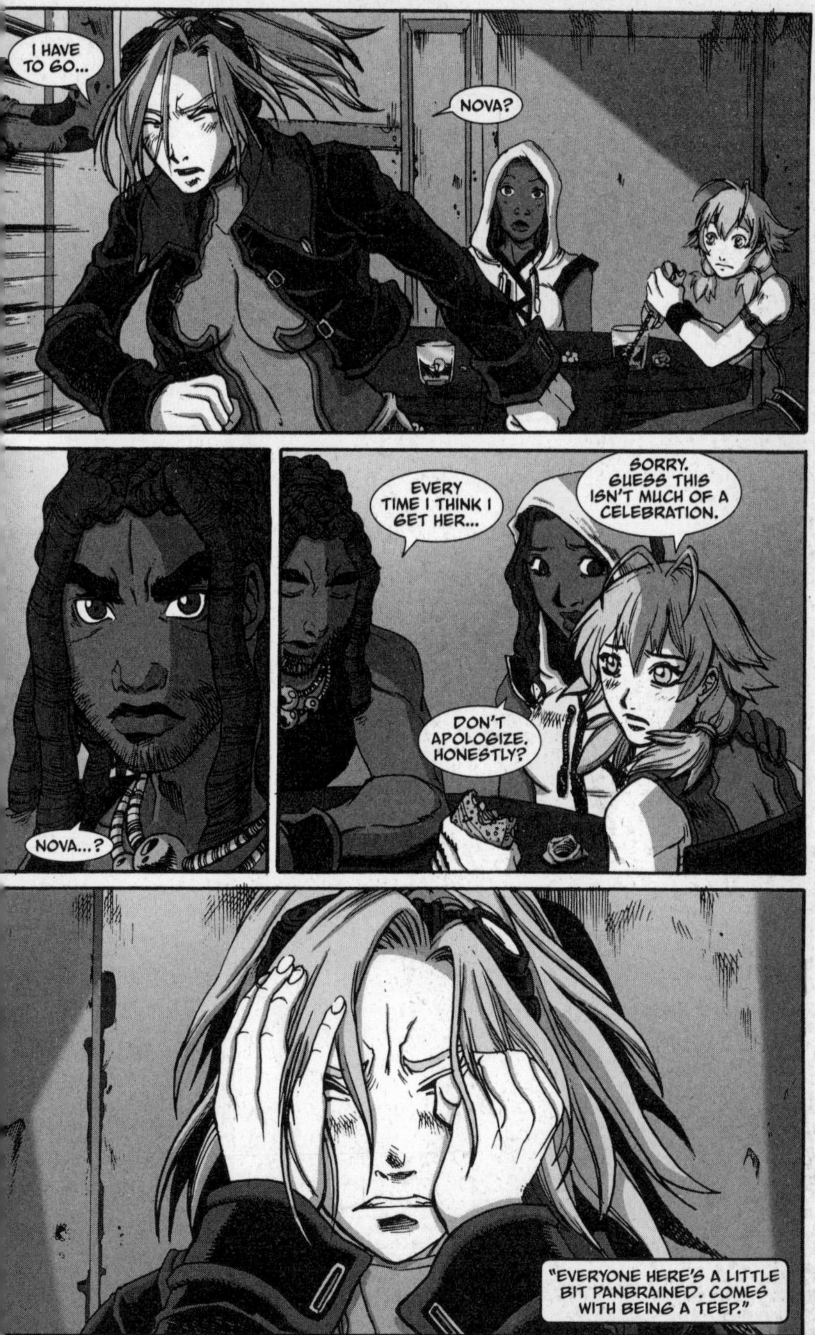
I HAVE TO GO...
NOVA?
NOVA...?
EVERY TIME I THINK I GET HER...
SORRY. GUESS THIS ISN'T MUCH OF A CELEBRATION.
DON'T APOLOGIZE. HONESTLY?
"EVERYONE HERE'S A LITTLE BIT PANBRAINED. COMES WITH BEING A TEEP."

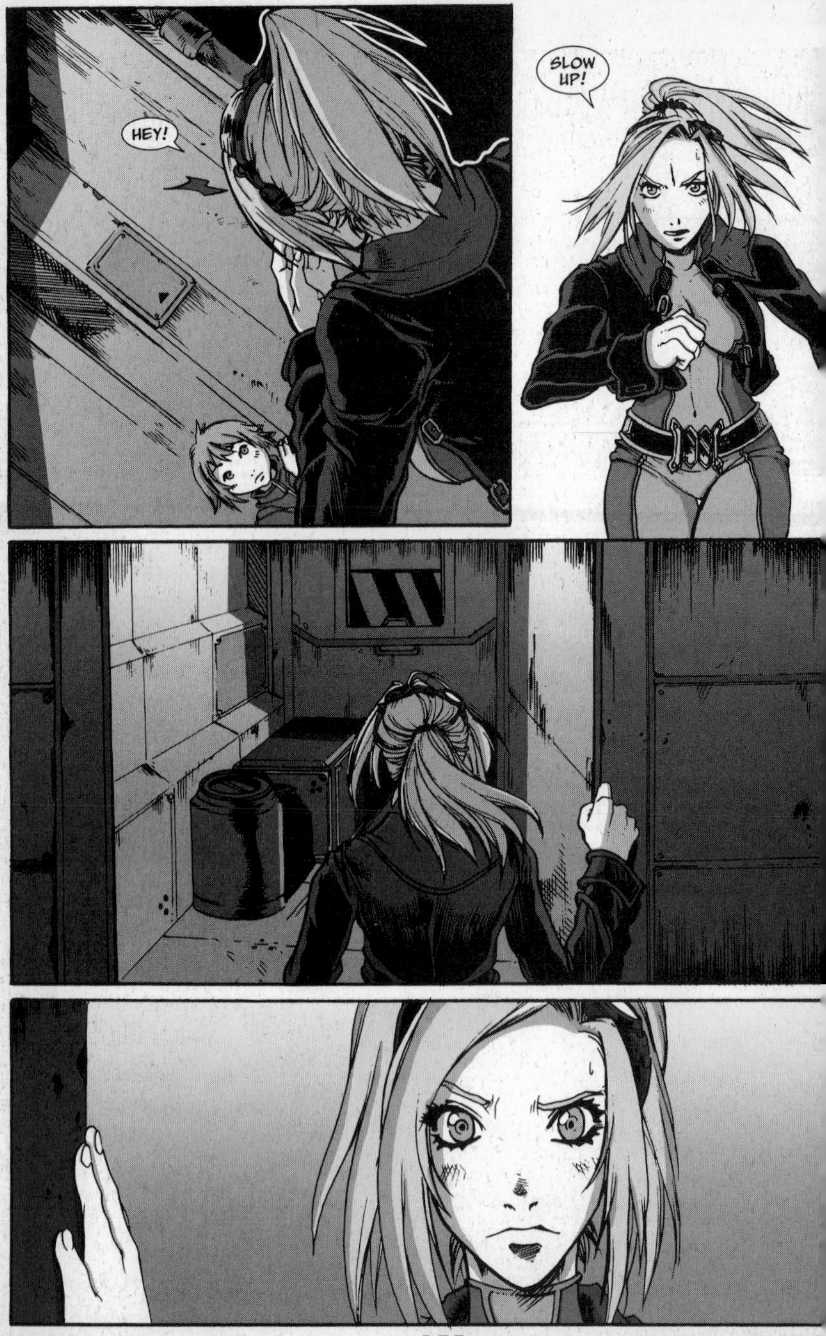
HEY!
SLOW UP!

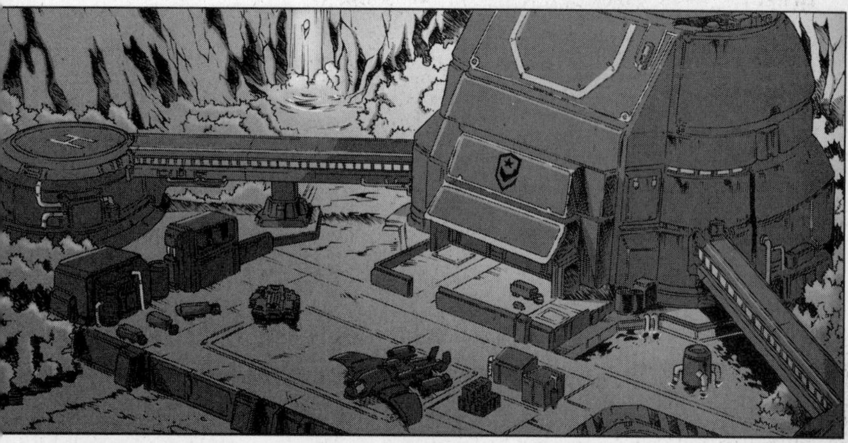

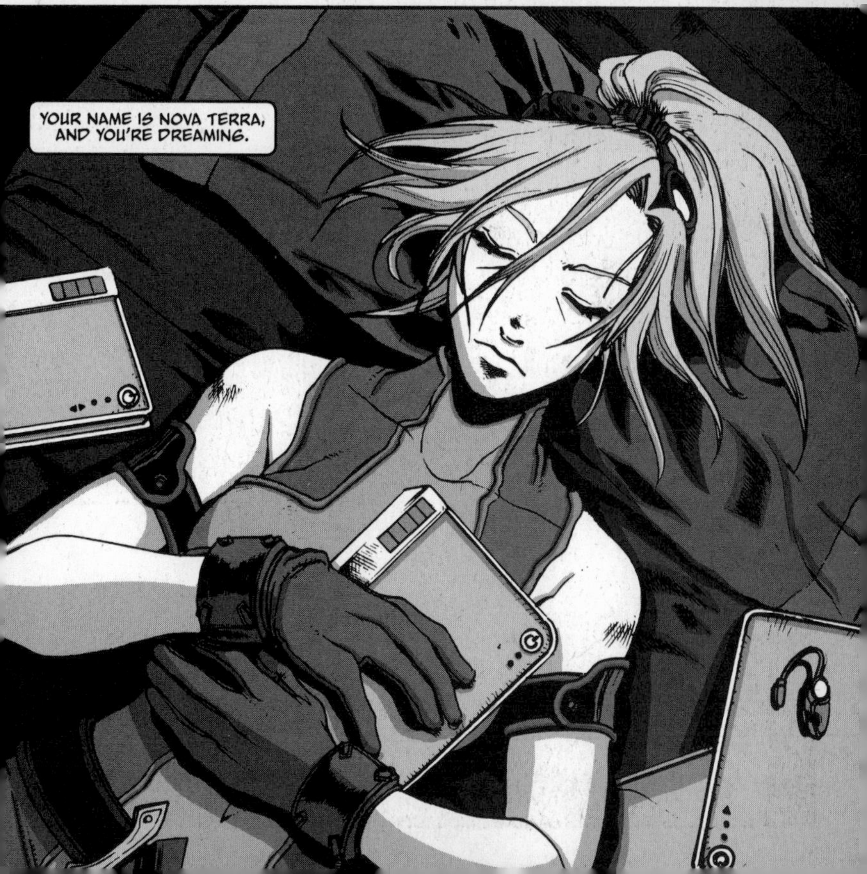
YOUR NAME IS NOVA TERRA, AND YOU'RE DREAMING.

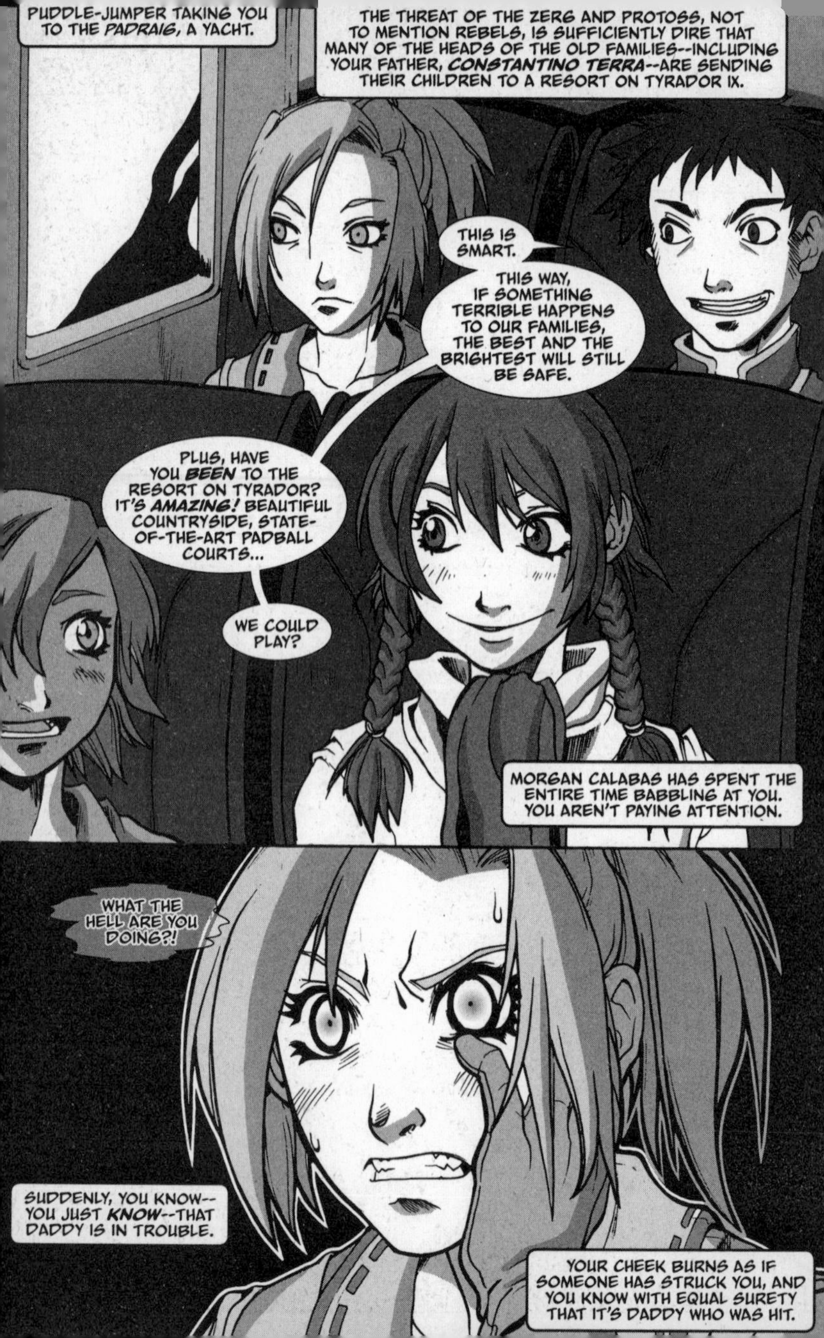
PUDDLE-JUMPER TAKING YOU TO THE *PADRAIG*, A YACHT.
THE THREAT OF THE ZERG AND PROTOSS, NOT TO MENTION REBELS, IS SUFFICIENTLY DIRE THAT MANY OF THE HEADS OF THE OLD FAMILIES--INCLUDING YOUR FATHER, ***CONSTANTINO TERRA***--ARE SENDING THEIR CHILDREN TO A RESORT ON TYRADOR IX.
THIS IS SMART.
THIS WAY, IF SOMETHING TERRIBLE HAPPENS TO OUR FAMILIES, THE BEST AND THE BRIGHTEST WILL STILL BE SAFE.
PLUS, HAVE YOU ***BEEN*** TO THE RESORT ON TYRADOR? IT'S ***AMAZING!*** BEAUTIFUL COUNTRYSIDE, STATE-OF-THE-ART PADBALL COURTS...
WE COULD PLAY?
MORGAN CALABAS HAS SPENT THE ENTIRE TIME BABBLING AT YOU. YOU AREN'T PAYING ATTENTION.
WHAT THE HELL ARE YOU DOING?!
SUDDENLY, YOU KNOW--YOU JUST ***KNOW***--THAT DADDY IS IN TROUBLE.
YOUR CHEEK BURNS AS IF SOMEONE HAS STRUCK YOU, AND YOU KNOW WITH EQUAL SURETY THAT IT'S DADDY WHO WAS HIT.

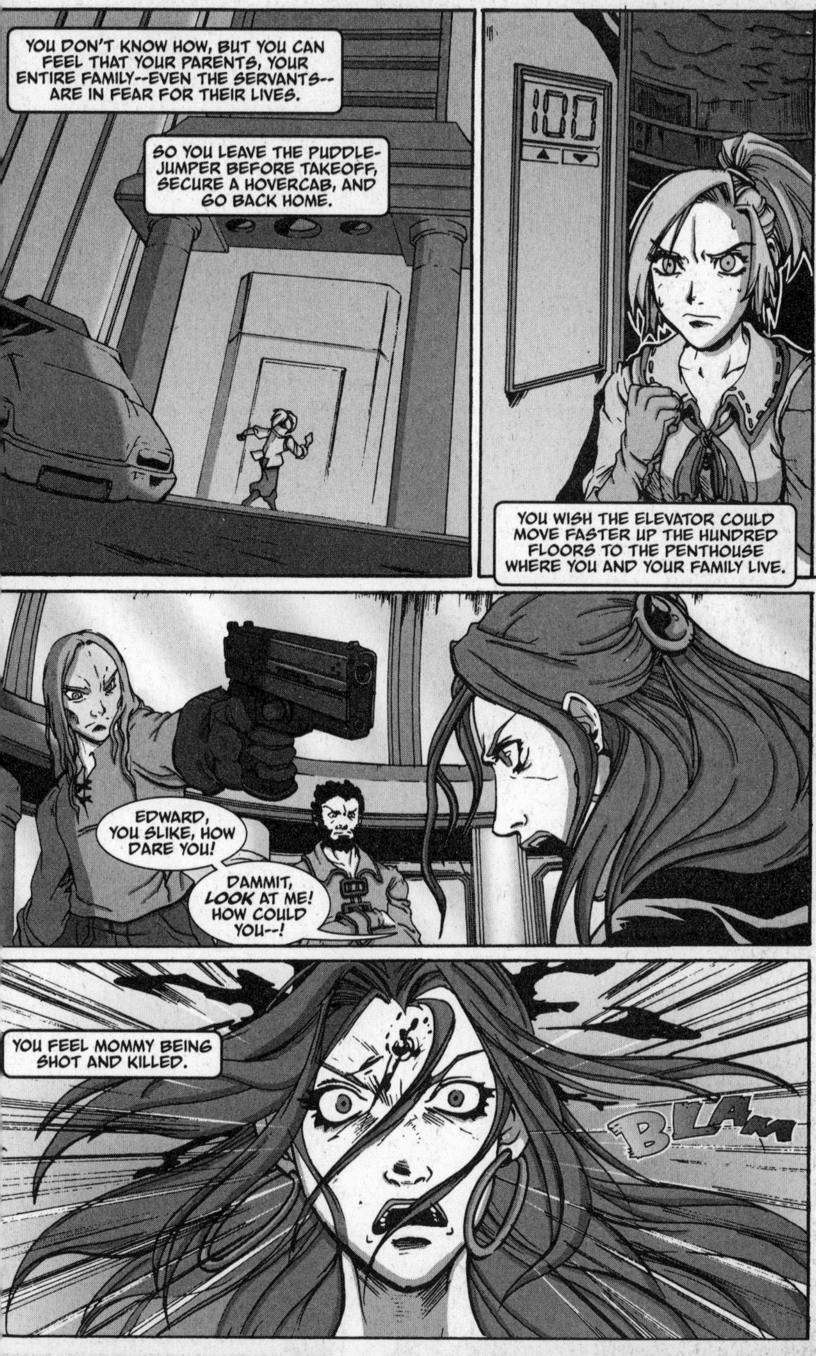
YOU DON'T KNOW HOW, BUT YOU CAN FEEL THAT YOUR PARENTS, YOUR ENTIRE FAMILY--EVEN THE SERVANTS--ARE IN FEAR FOR THEIR LIVES.
SO YOU LEAVE THE PUDDLE-JUMPER BEFORE TAKEOFF, SECURE A HOVERCAB, AND GO BACK HOME.
100
YOU WISH THE ELEVATOR COULD MOVE FASTER UP THE HUNDRED FLOORS TO THE PENTHOUSE WHERE YOU AND YOUR FAMILY LIVE.
EDWARD, YOU SLIKE, HOW DARE YOU!
DAMMIT, LOOK AT ME! HOW COULD YOU--!
YOU FEEL MOMMY BEING SHOT AND KILLED.
BLAM

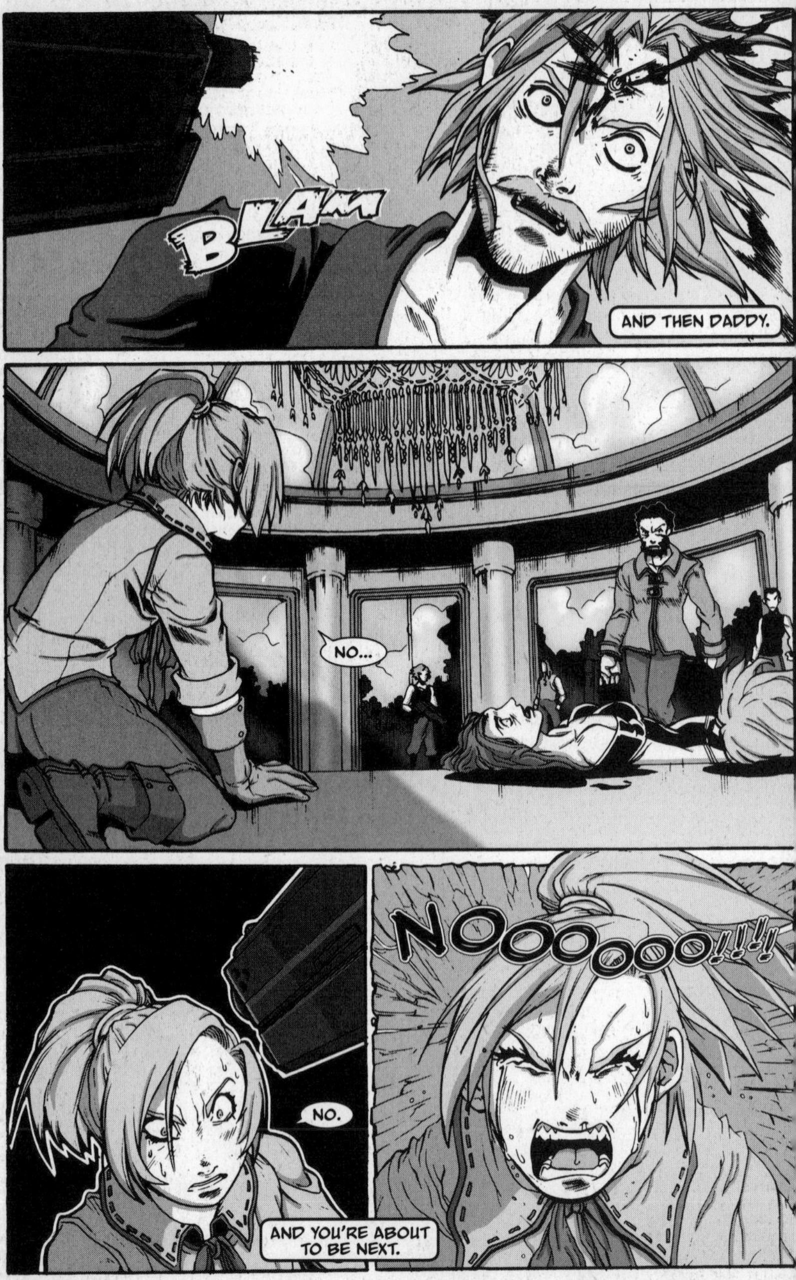

BLAM
AND THEN DADDY.
NO...
NO.
AND YOU'RE ABOUT TO BE NEXT.
NOOOOOOO!!!!

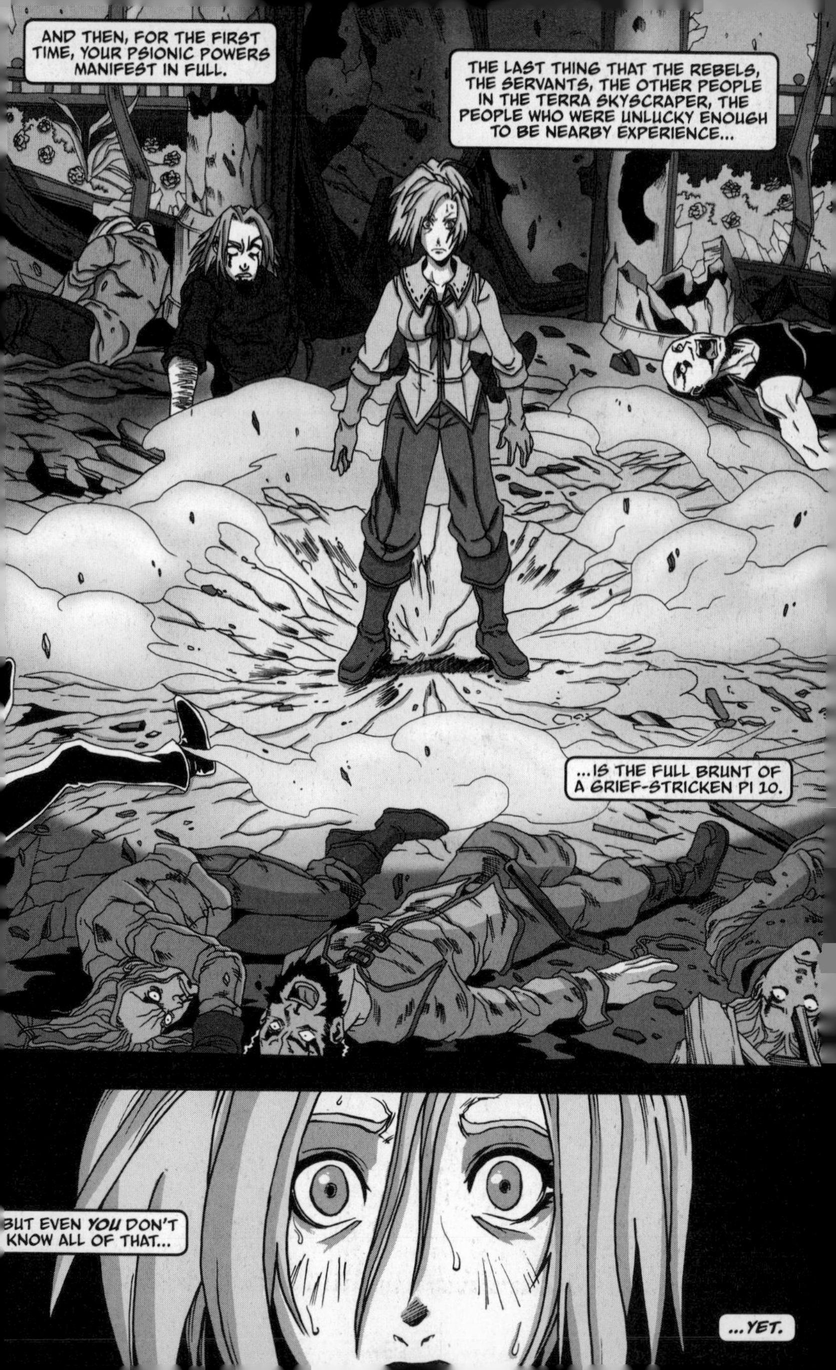
AND THEN, FOR THE FIRST TIME, YOUR PSIONIC POWERS MANIFEST IN FULL.
THE LAST THING THAT THE REBELS, THE SERVANTS, THE OTHER PEOPLE IN THE TERRA SKYSCRAPER, THE PEOPLE WHO WERE UNLUCKY ENOUGH TO BE NEARBY EXPERIENCE...
...IS THE FULL BRUNT OF A GRIEF-STRICKEN PI 10.
BUT EVEN YOU DON'T KNOW ALL OF THAT...
...YET.

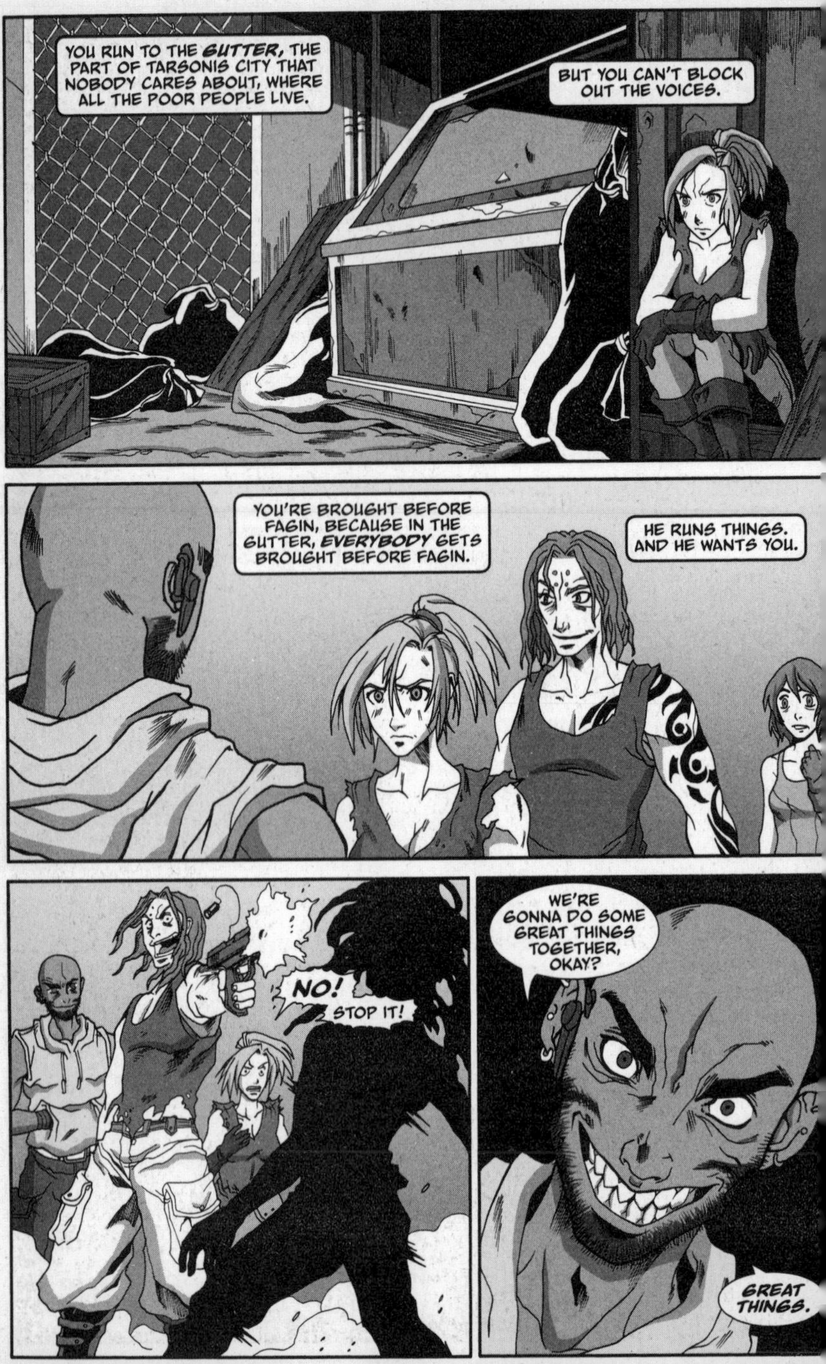
YOU RUN TO THE GUTTER, THE PART OF TARSONIS CITY THAT NOBODY CARES ABOUT, WHERE ALL THE POOR PEOPLE LIVE.
BUT YOU CAN'T BLOCK OUT THE VOICES.
YOU'RE BROUGHT BEFORE FAGIN, BECAUSE IN THE GUTTER, EVERYBODY GETS BROUGHT BEFORE FAGIN.
HE RUNS THINGS. AND HE WANTS YOU.
NO!
STOP IT!
WE'RE GONNA DO SOME GREAT THINGS TOGETHER, OKAY?
GREAT THINGS.

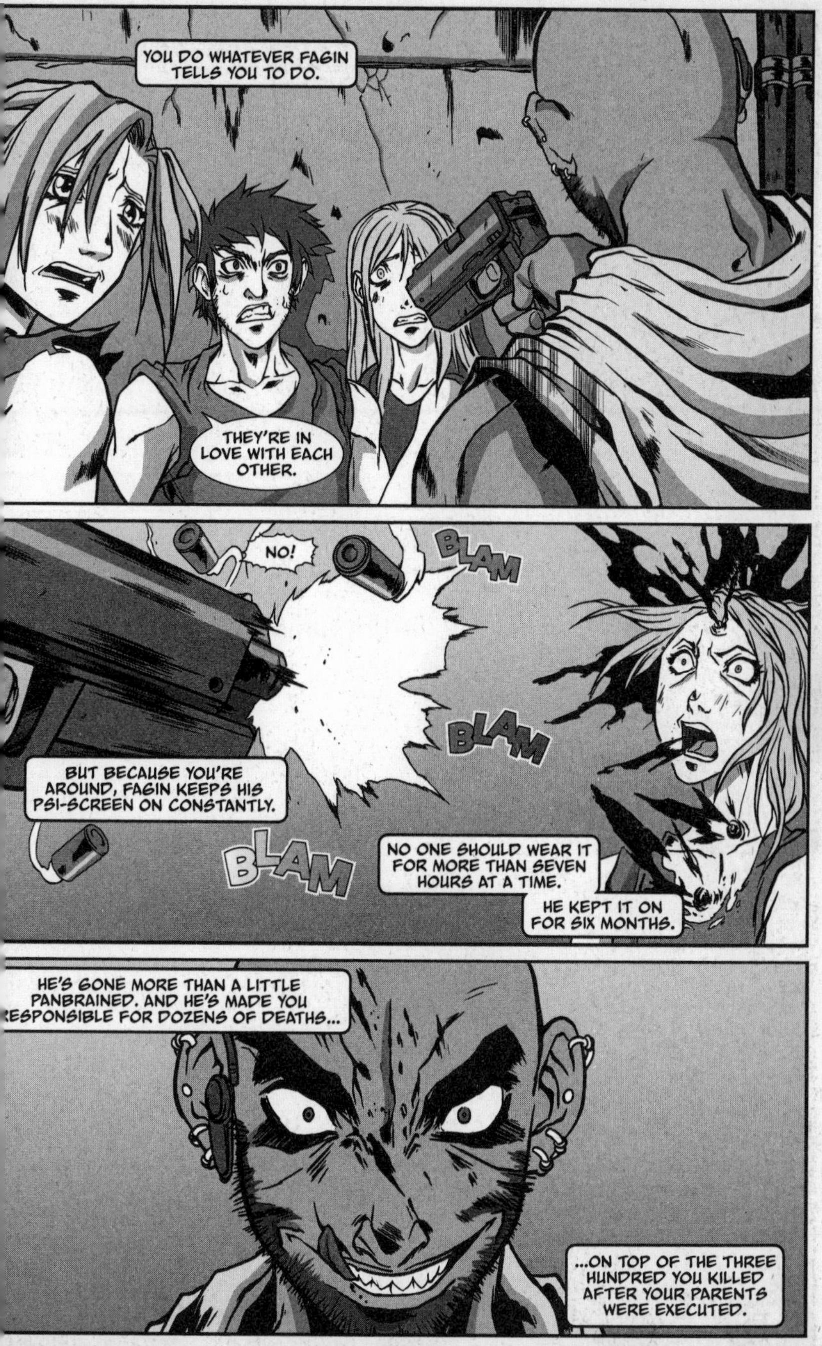
YOU DO WHATEVER FAGIN TELLS YOU TO DO.
THEY'RE IN LOVE WITH EACH OTHER.
NO!
BLAM
BLAM
BUT BECAUSE YOU'RE AROUND, FAGIN KEEPS HIS PSI-SCREEN ON CONSTANTLY.
BLAM
NO ONE SHOULD WEAR IT FOR MORE THAN SEVEN HOURS AT A TIME.
HE KEPT IT ON FOR SIX MONTHS.
HE'S GONE MORE THAN A LITTLE PANBRAINED. AND HE'S MADE YOU RESPONSIBLE FOR DOZENS OF DEATHS...
...ON TOP OF THE THREE HUNDRED YOU KILLED AFTER YOUR PARENTS WERE EXECUTED.

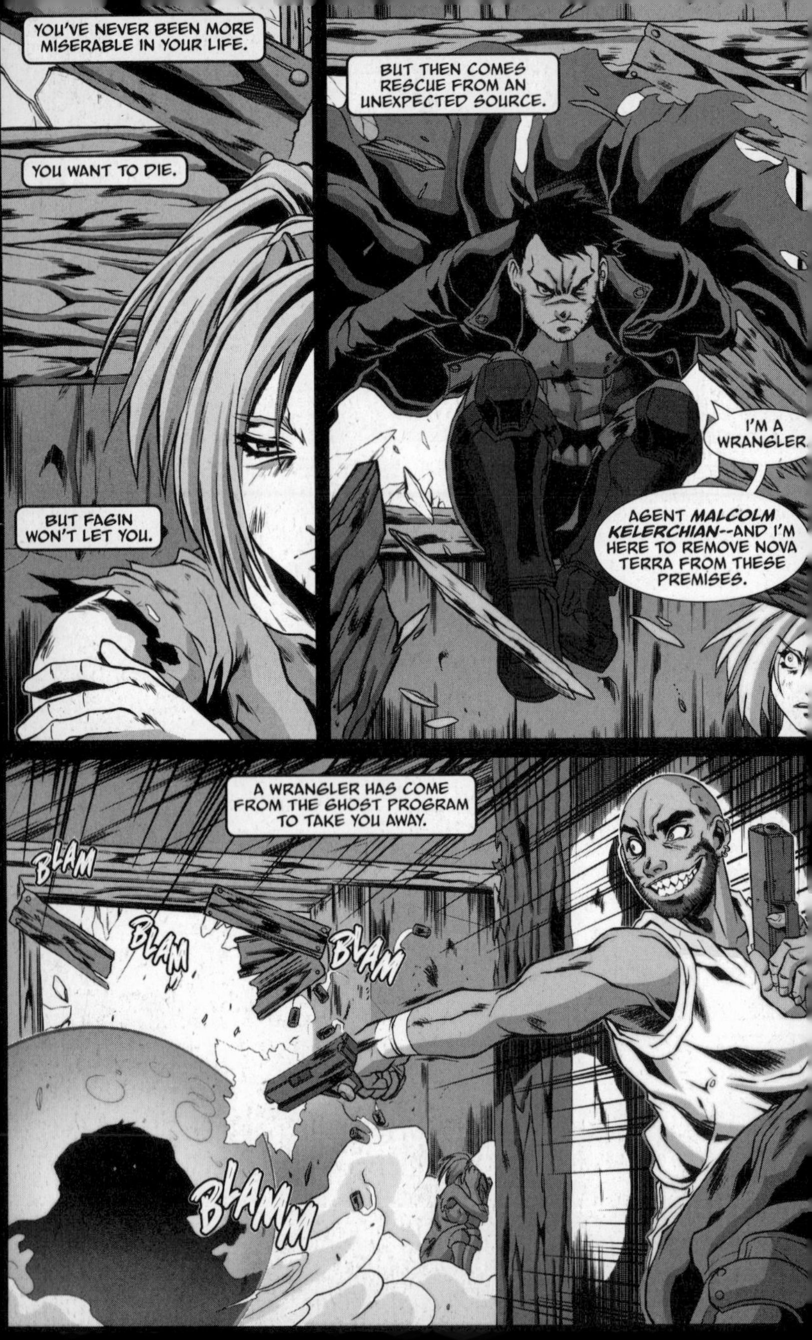
YOU'VE NEVER BEEN MORE MISERABLE IN YOUR LIFE.
YOU WANT TO DIE.
BUT FAGIN WON'T LET YOU.
BUT THEN COMES RESCUE FROM AN UNEXPECTED SOURCE.
I'M A WRANGLER.
AGENT MALCOLM KELERCHIAN--AND I'M HERE TO REMOVE NOVA TERRA FROM THESE PREMISES.
A WRANGLER HAS COME FROM THE GHOST PROGRAM TO TAKE YOU AWAY.
BLAM
BLAM
BLAM
BLAMM

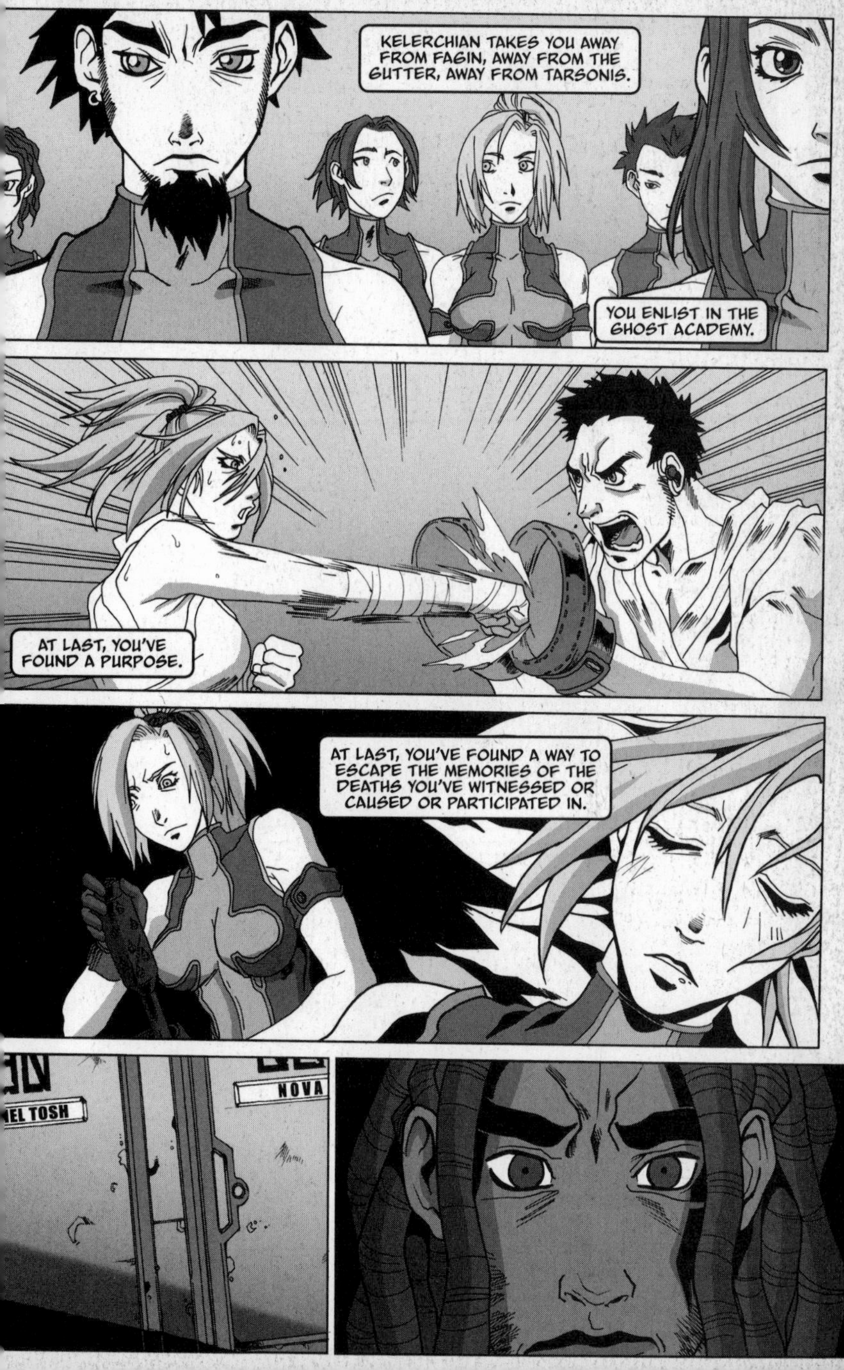
KELERCHIAN TAKES YOU AWAY FROM FAGIN, AWAY FROM THE GUTTER, AWAY FROM TARSONIS.
YOU ENLIST IN THE GHOST ACADEMY.
AT LAST, YOU'VE FOUND A PURPOSE.
AT LAST, YOU'VE FOUND A WAY TO ESCAPE THE MEMORIES OF THE DEATHS YOU'VE WITNESSED OR CAUSED OR PARTICIPATED IN.
EL TOSH
NOVA

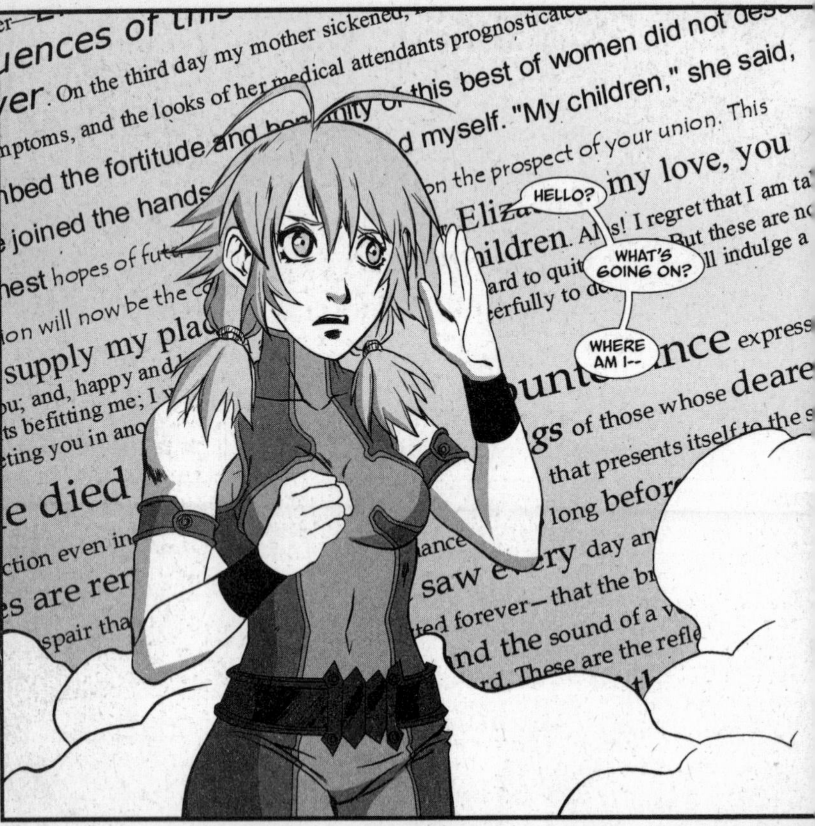
HELLO?
WHAT'S GOING ON?
WHERE AM I--

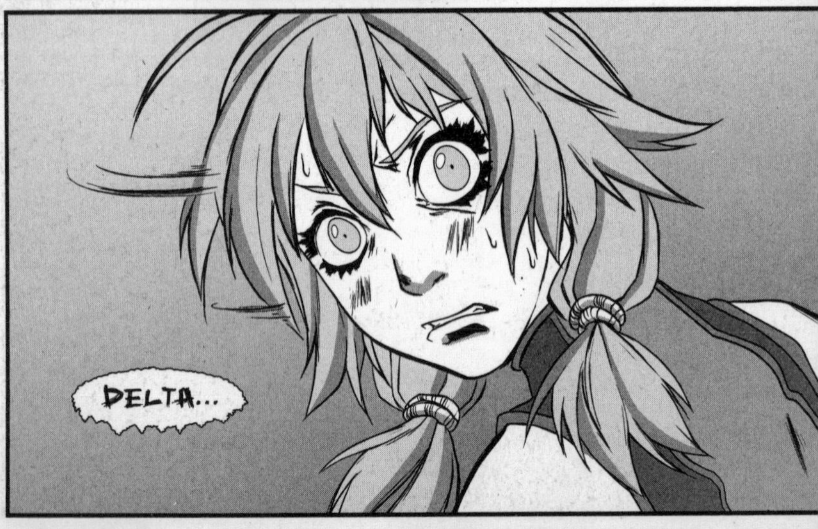
DELTA...

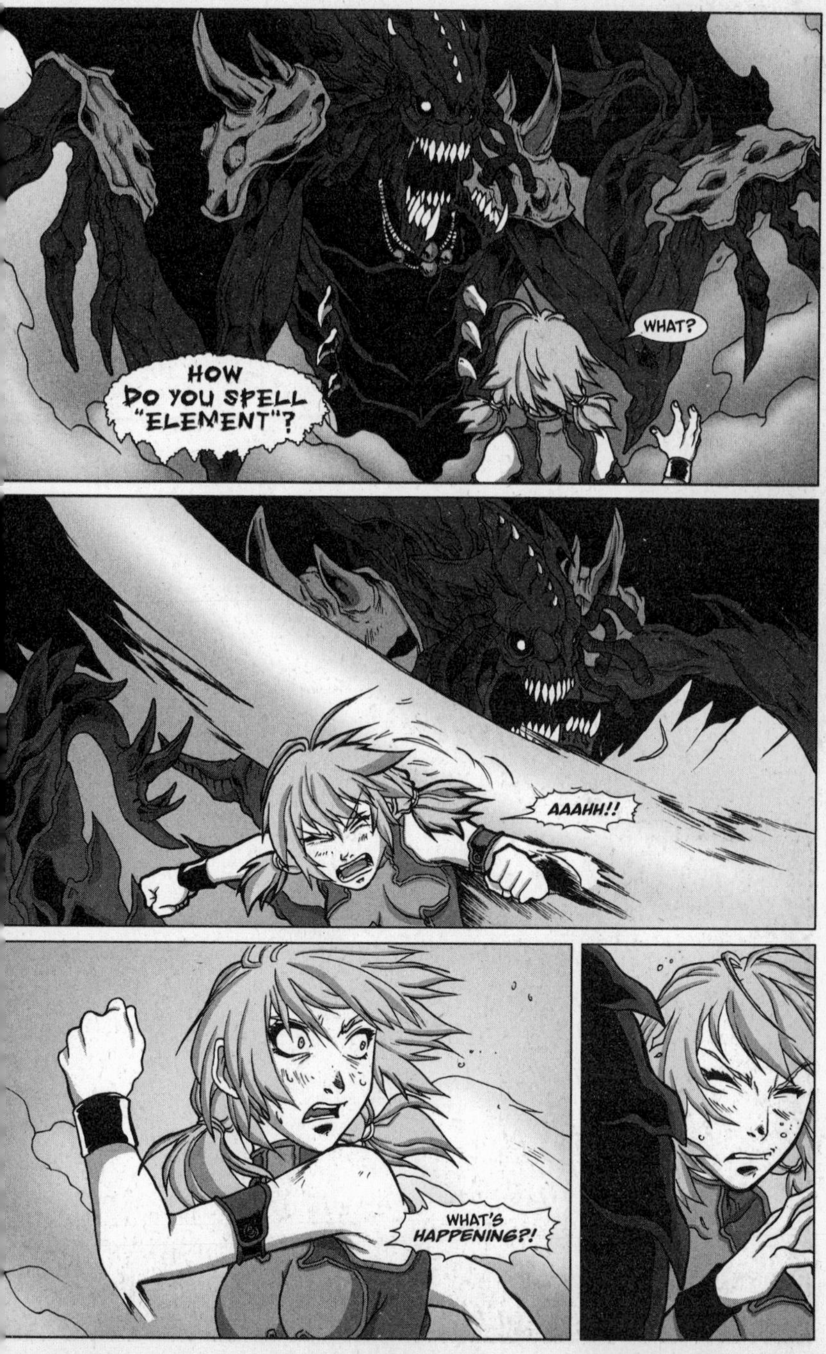
WHAT?
HOW DO YOU SPELL "ELEMENT"?
AAAHH!!
WHAT'S HAPPENING?!

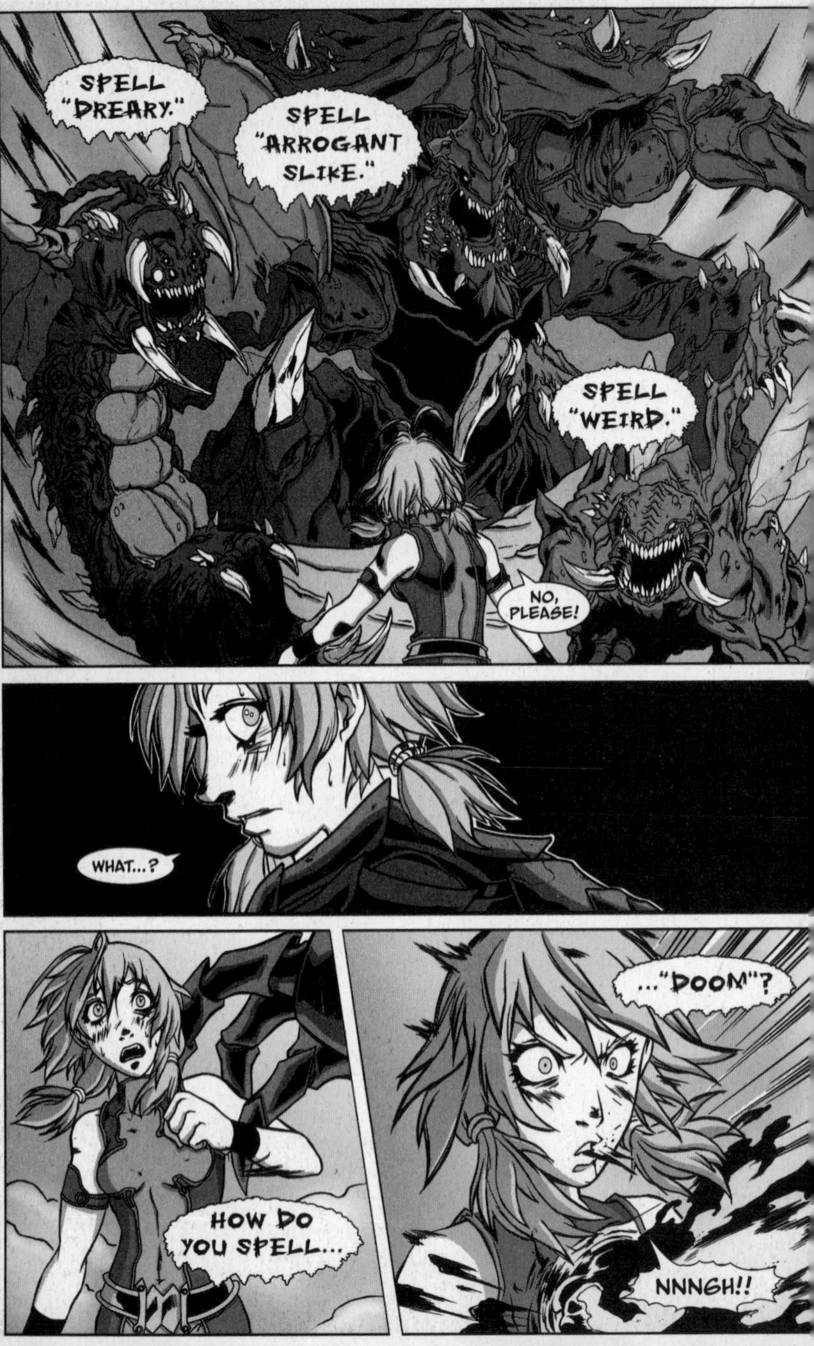
SPELL "DREARY."
SPELL "ARROGANT SLIKE."
SPELL "WEIRD."
NO, PLEASE!
WHAT...?
HOW DO YOU SPELL...
..."DOOM"?
NNNGH!!

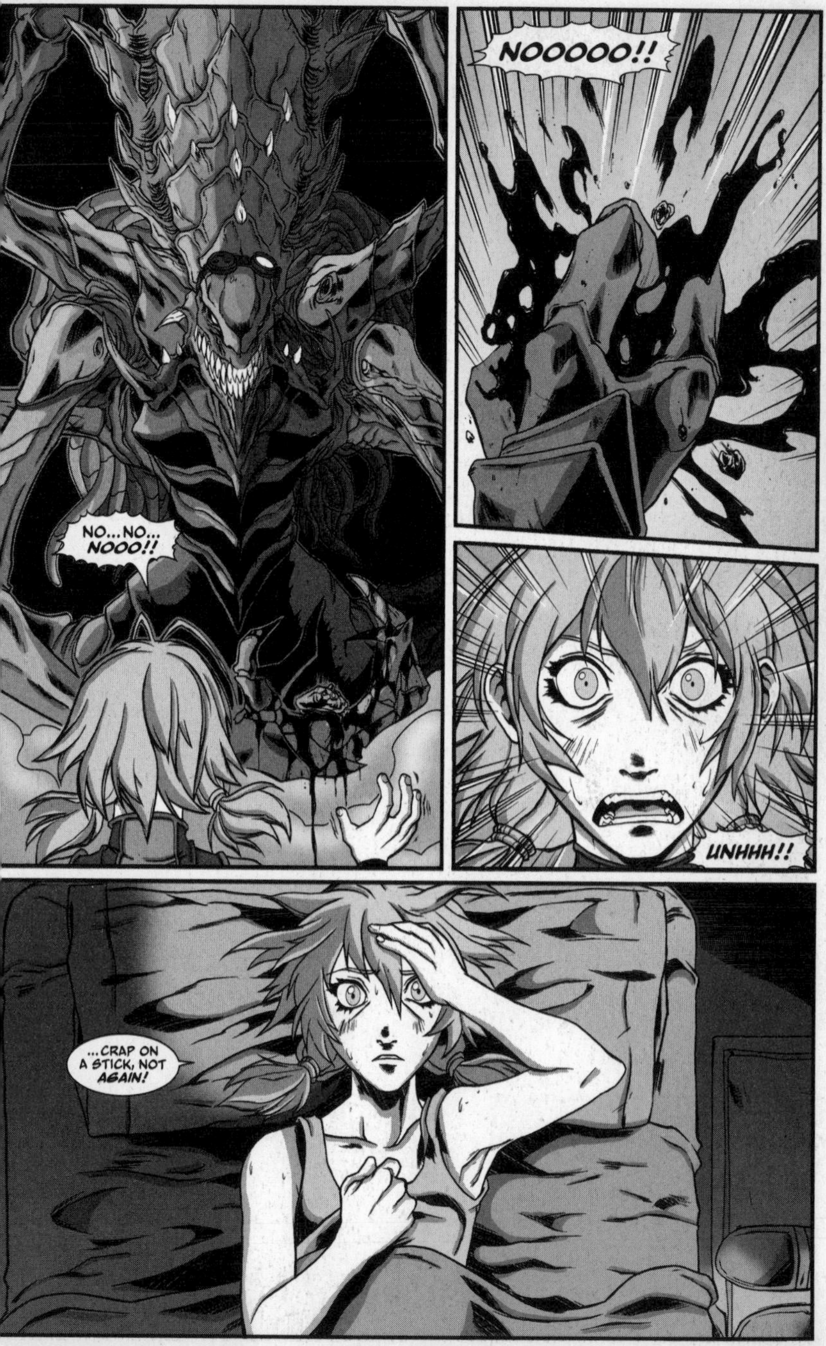
NO... NO... NOOO!!
NOOOOO!!
UNHHH!!
...CRAP ON A STICK, NOT AGAIN!

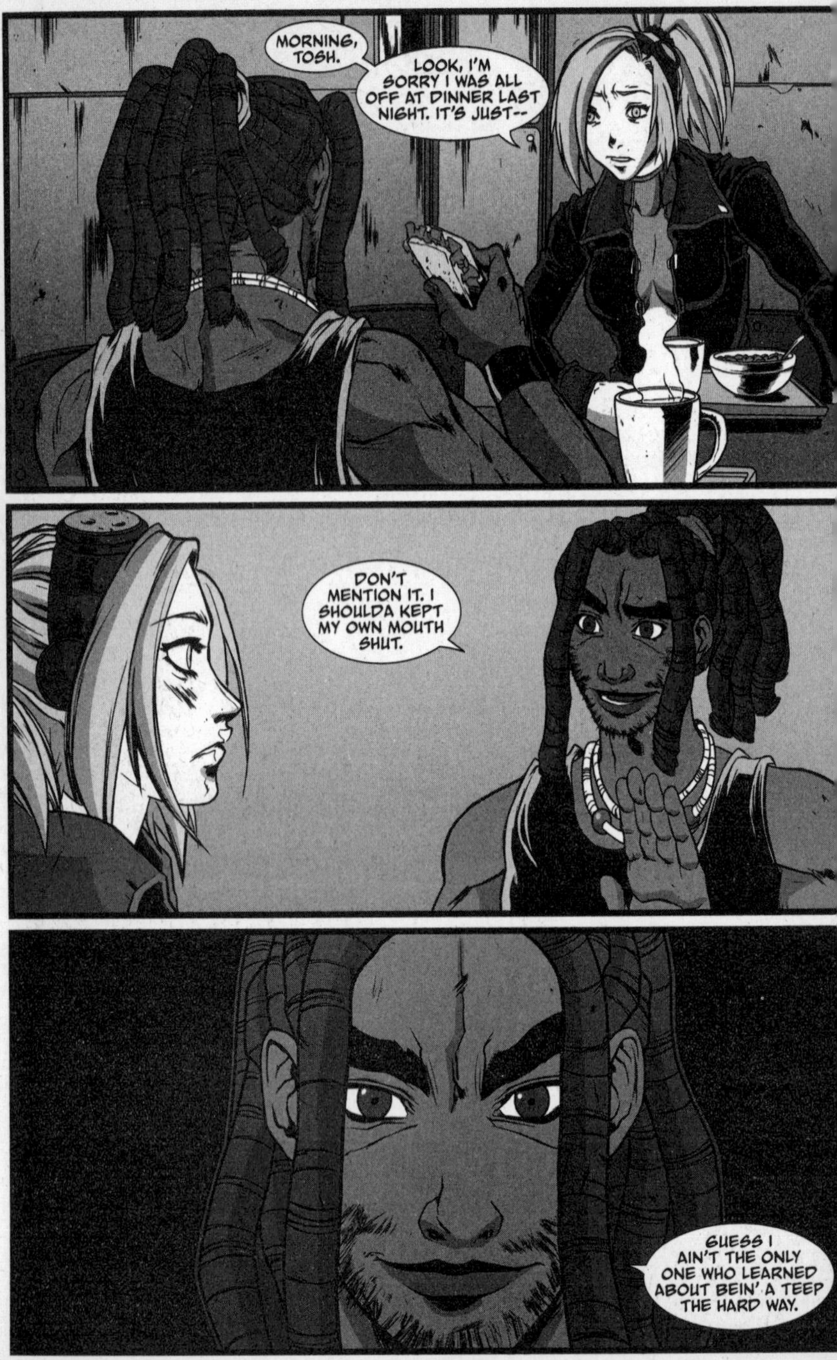
MORNING, TOSH.
LOOK, I'M SORRY I WAS ALL OFF AT DINNER LAST NIGHT. IT'S JUST--
DON'T MENTION IT. I SHOULDA KEPT MY OWN MOUTH SHUT.
GUESS I AIN'T THE ONLY ONE WHO LEARNED ABOUT BEIN' A TEEP THE HARD WAY.

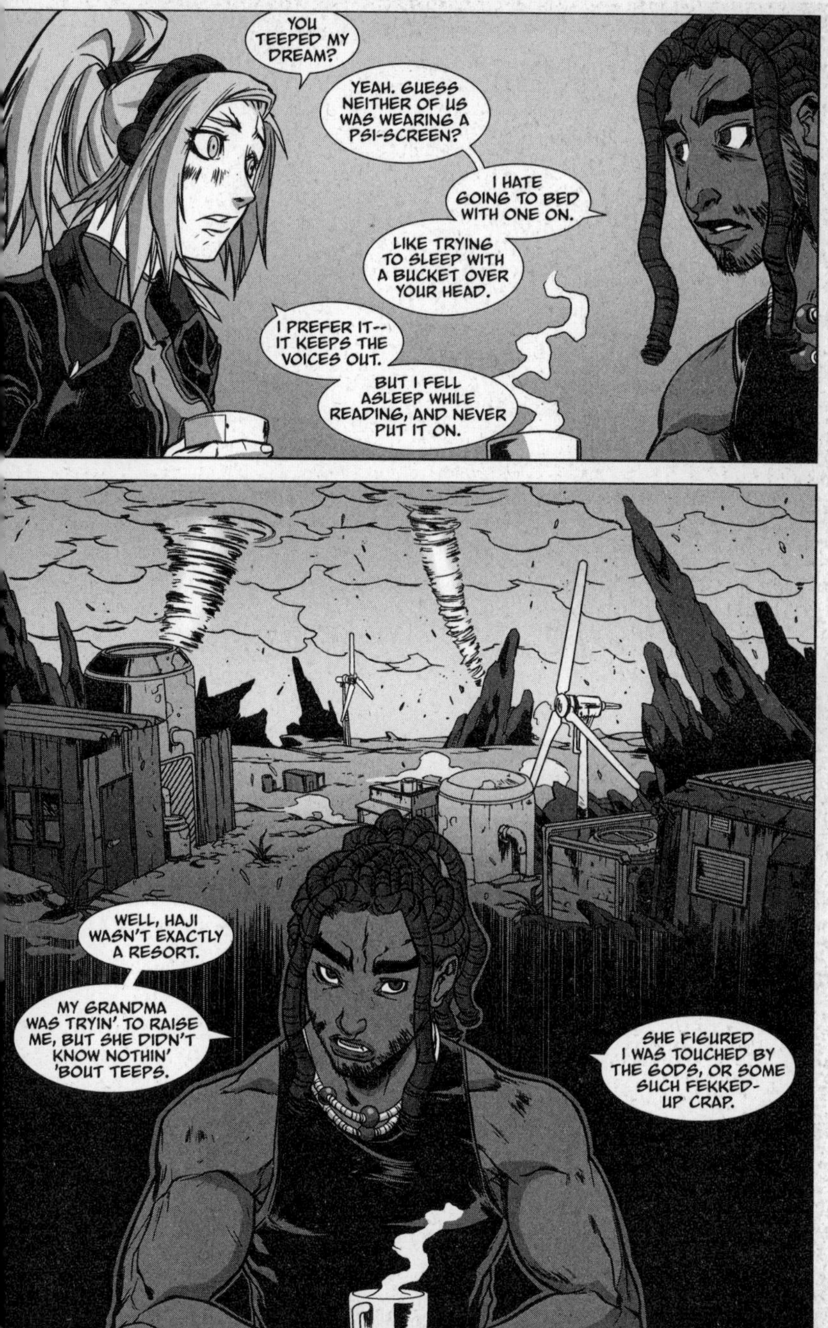
YOU TEEPED MY DREAM?
YEAH. GUESS NEITHER OF US WAS WEARING A PSI-SCREEN?
I HATE GOING TO BED WITH ONE ON.
LIKE TRYING TO SLEEP WITH A BUCKET OVER YOUR HEAD.
I PREFER IT-- IT KEEPS THE VOICES OUT.
BUT I FELL ASLEEP WHILE READING, AND NEVER PUT IT ON.
WELL, HAJI WASN'T EXACTLY A RESORT.
MY GRANDMA WAS TRYIN' TO RAISE ME, BUT SHE DIDN'T KNOW NOTHIN' 'BOUT TEEPS.
SHE FIGURED I WAS TOUCHED BY THE GODS, OR SOME SUCH FEKKED-UP CRAP.

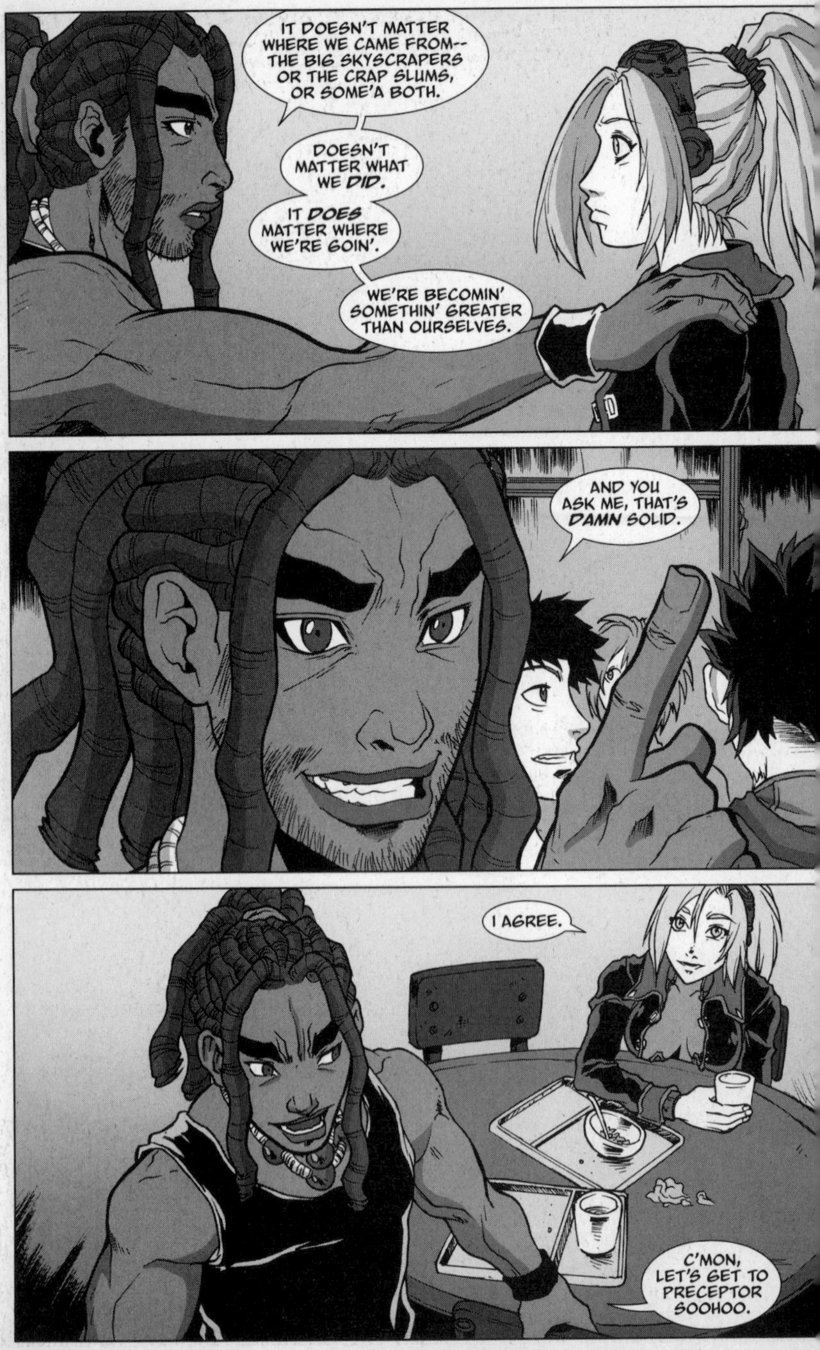
IT DOESN'T MATTER WHERE WE CAME FROM-- THE BIG SKYSCRAPERS OR THE CRAP SLUMS, OR SOME'A BOTH.
DOESN'T MATTER WHAT WE DID.
IT DOES MATTER WHERE WE'RE GOIN'.
WE'RE BECOMIN' SOMETHIN' GREATER THAN OURSELVES.
AND YOU ASK ME, THAT'S DAMN SOLID.
I AGREE.
C'MON, LET'S GET TO PRECEPTOR SOOHOO.

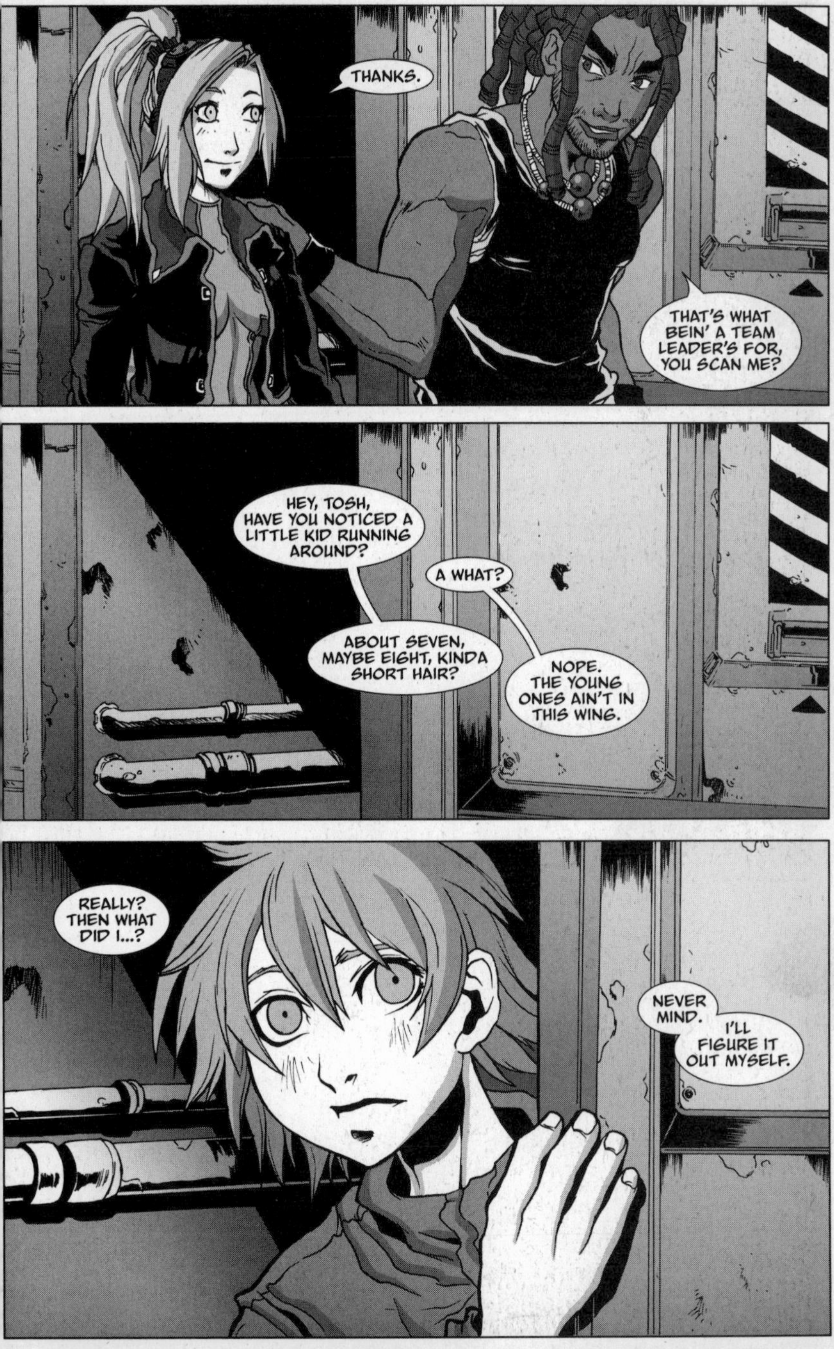
THANKS.
THAT'S WHAT BEIN' A TEAM LEADER'S FOR, YOU SCAN ME?
HEY, TOSH, HAVE YOU NOTICED A LITTLE KID RUNNING AROUND?
A WHAT?
ABOUT SEVEN, MAYBE EIGHT, KINDA SHORT HAIR?
NOPE. THE YOUNG ONES AIN'T IN THIS WING.
REALLY? THEN WHAT DID I...?
NEVER MIND.
I'LL FIGURE IT OUT MYSELF.

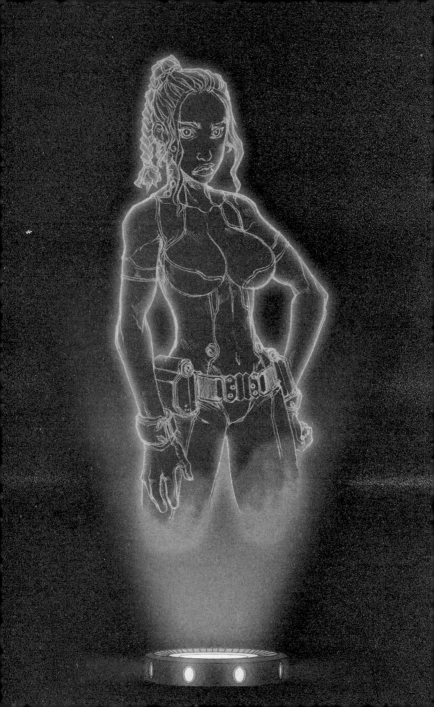

CHAPTER 5
REDEMPTION

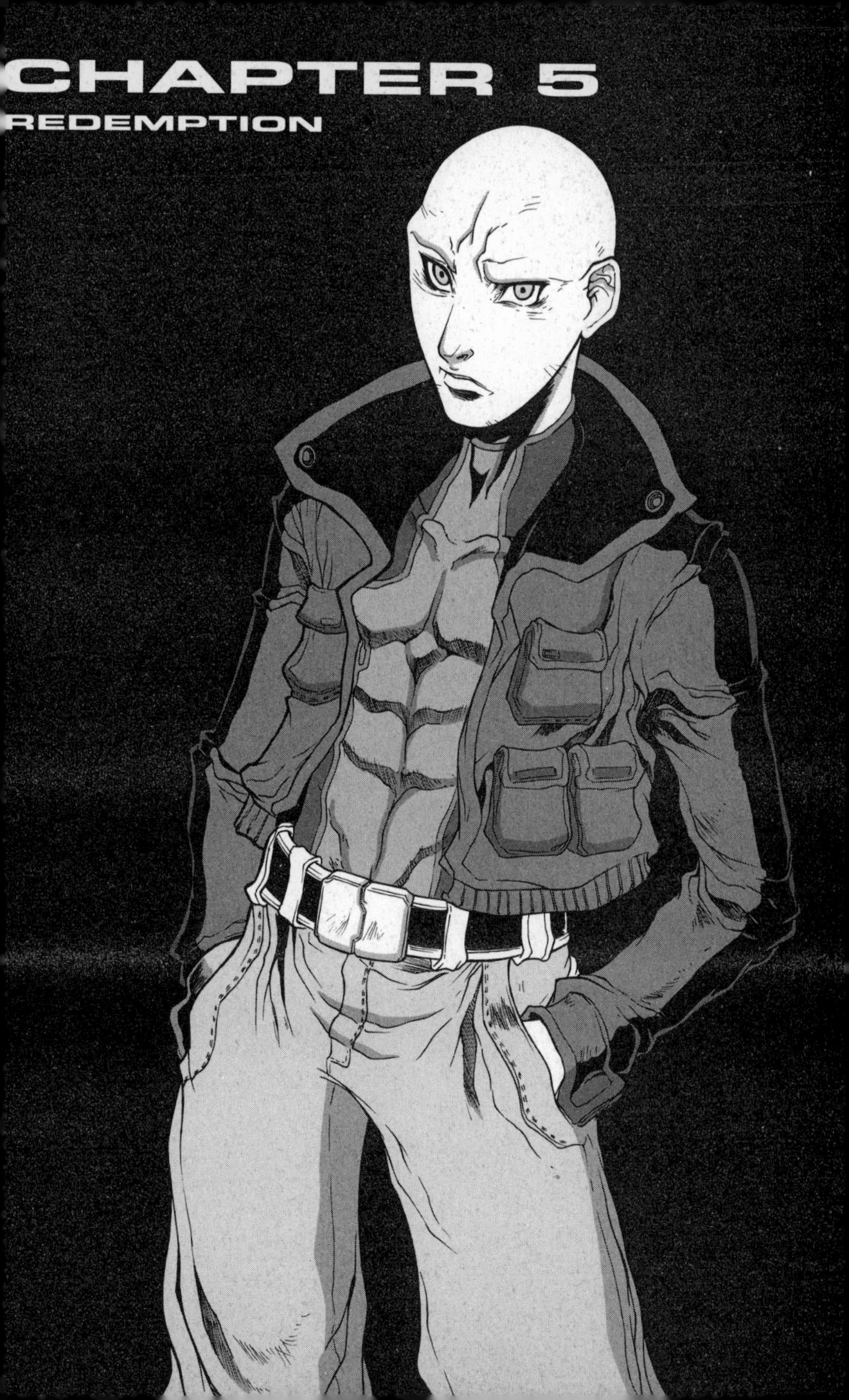

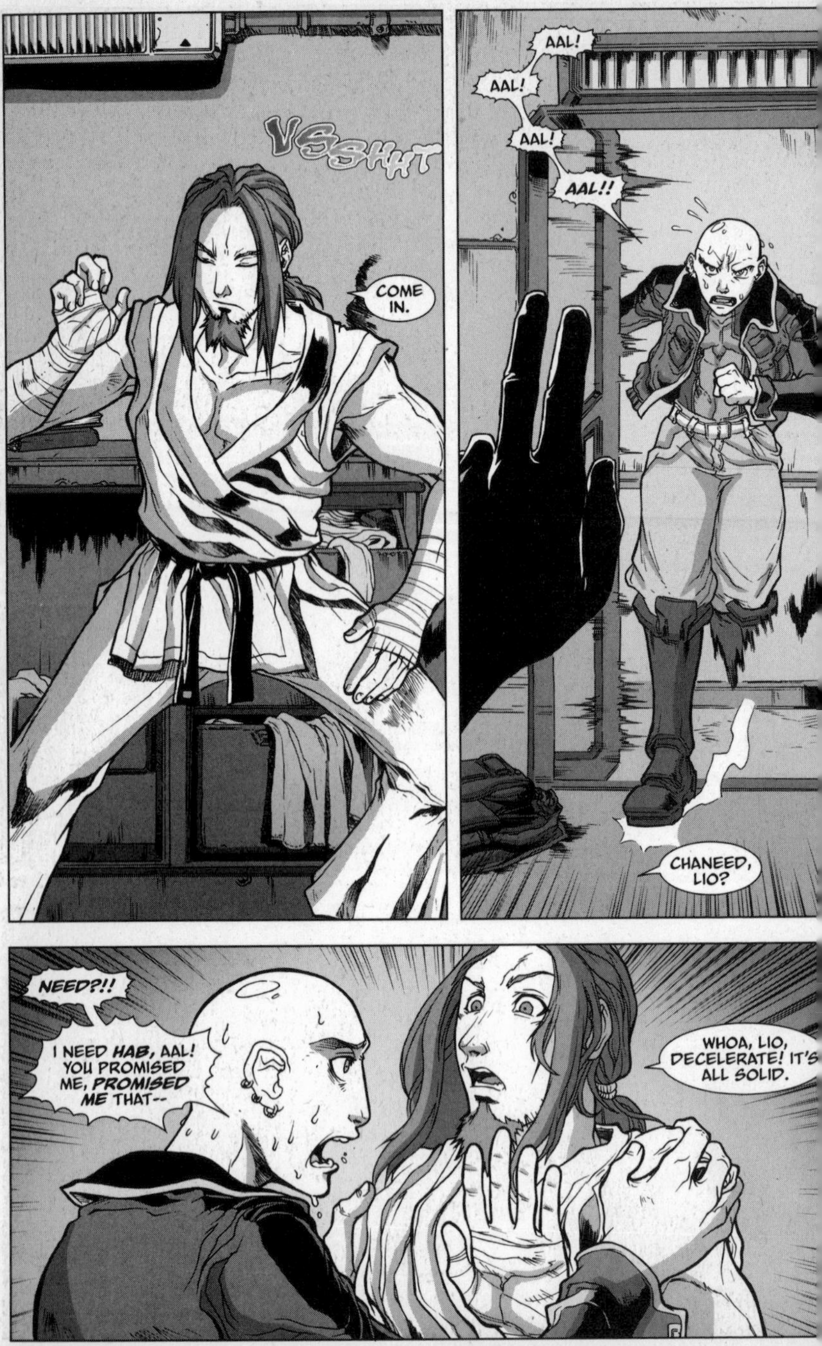
VSSHHT
COME IN.
AAL!
AAL!
AAL!
AAL!!
CHANEED, LIO?
NEED?!!
I NEED HAB, AAL! YOU PROMISED ME, PROMISED ME THAT--
WHOA, LIO, DECELERATE! IT'S ALL SOLID.

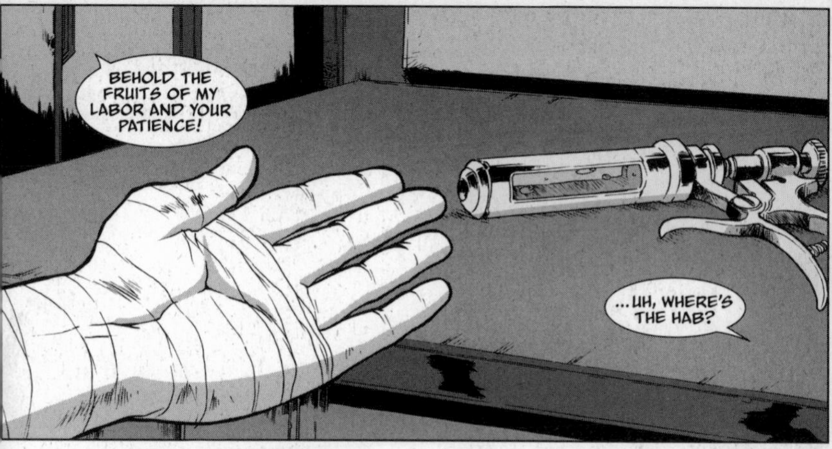
BEHOLD THE FRUITS OF MY LABOR AND YOUR PATIENCE!
...UH, WHERE'S THE HAB?

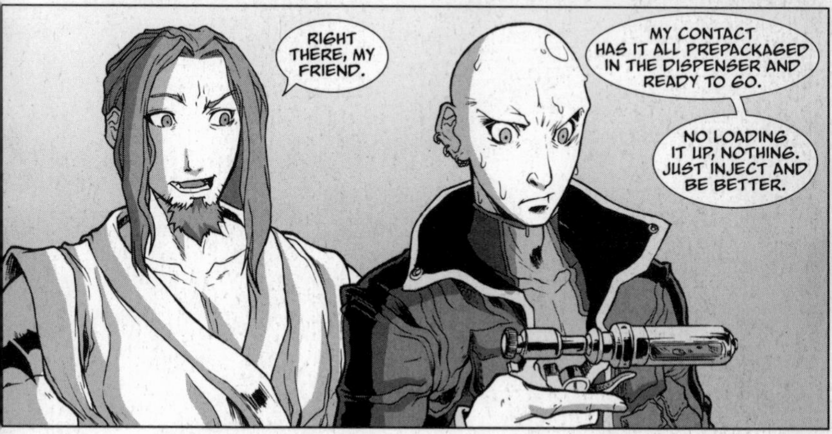
RIGHT THERE, MY FRIEND.
MY CONTACT HAS IT ALL PREPACKAGED IN THE DISPENSER AND READY TO GO.
NO LOADING IT UP, NOTHING. JUST INJECT AND BE BETTER.

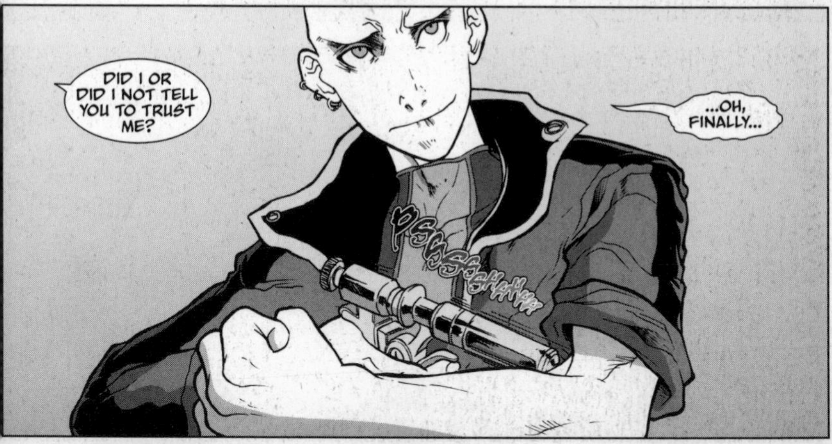
DID I OR DID I NOT TELL YOU TO TRUST ME?
...OH, FINALLY...

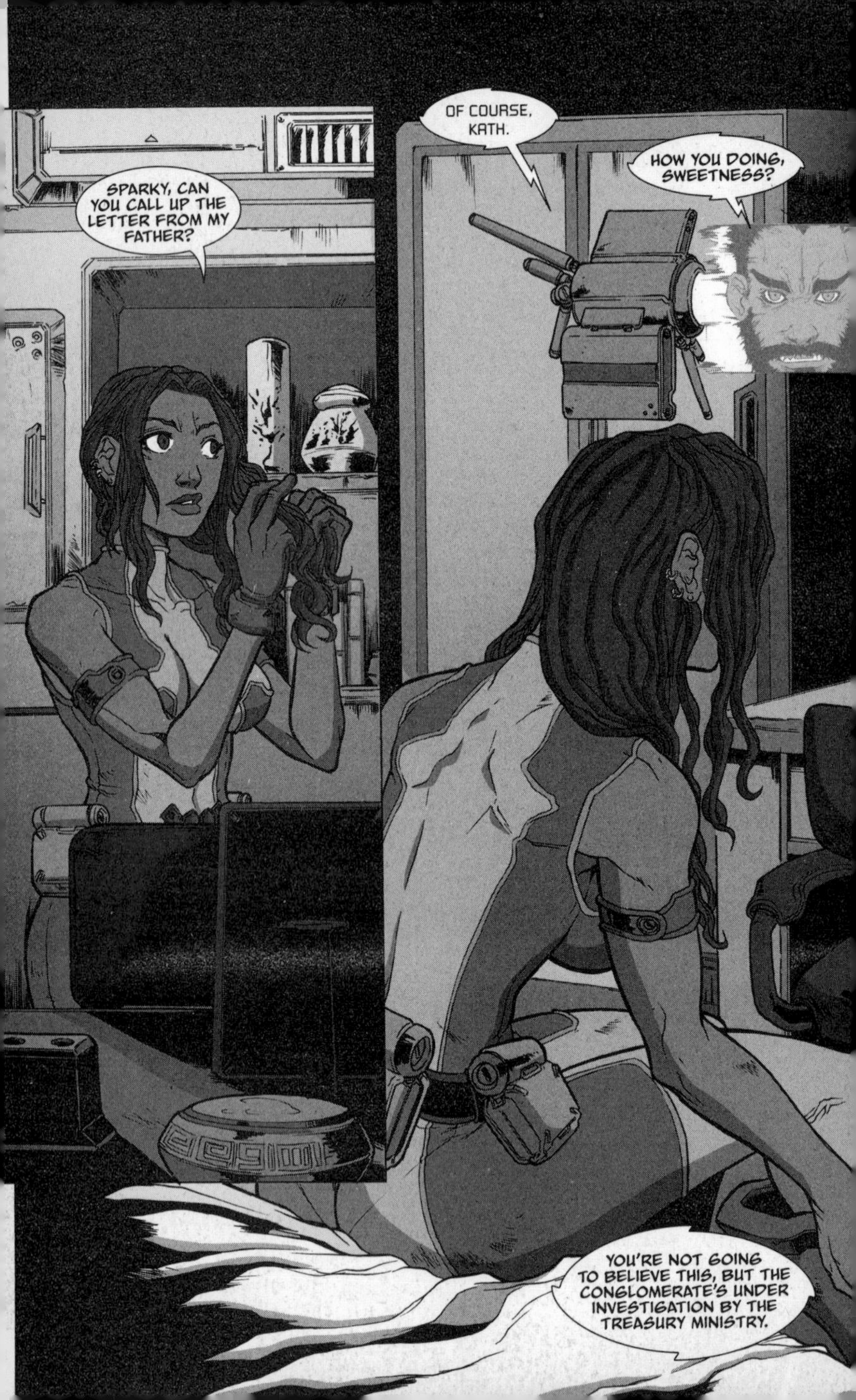
SPARKY, CAN YOU CALL UP THE LETTER FROM MY FATHER?
OF COURSE, KATH.
HOW YOU DOING, SWEETNESS?
YOU'RE NOT GOING TO BELIEVE THIS, BUT THE CONGLOMERATE'S UNDER INVESTIGATION BY THE TREASURY MINISTRY.

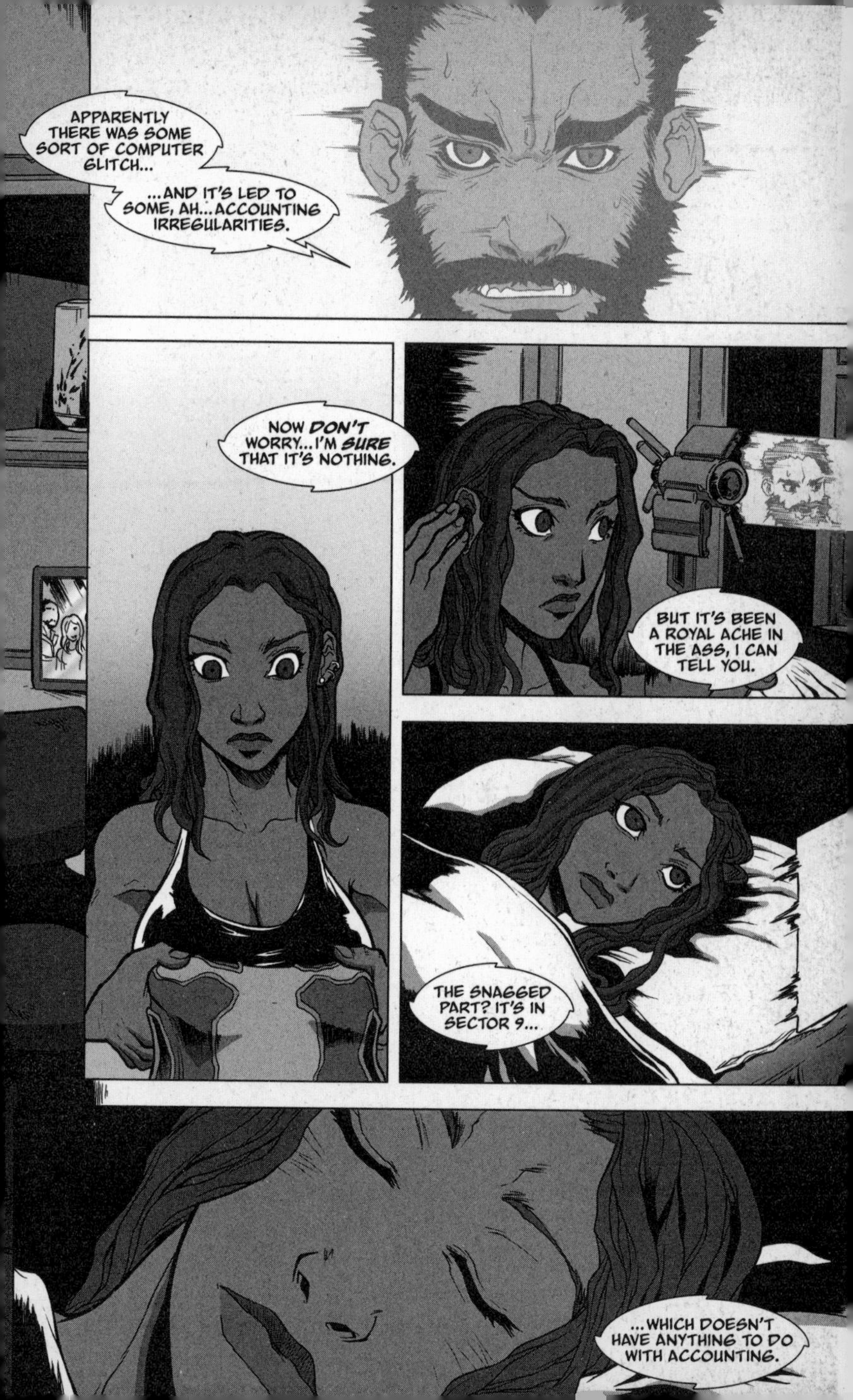
APPARENTLY THERE WAS SOME SORT OF COMPUTER GLITCH...
...AND IT'S LED TO SOME, AH...ACCOUNTING IRREGULARITIES.
NOW DON'T WORRY...I'M SURE THAT IT'S NOTHING.
BUT IT'S BEEN A ROYAL ACHE IN THE ASS, I CAN TELL YOU.
THE SNAGGED PART? IT'S IN SECTOR 9...
...WHICH DOESN'T HAVE ANYTHING TO DO WITH ACCOUNTING.

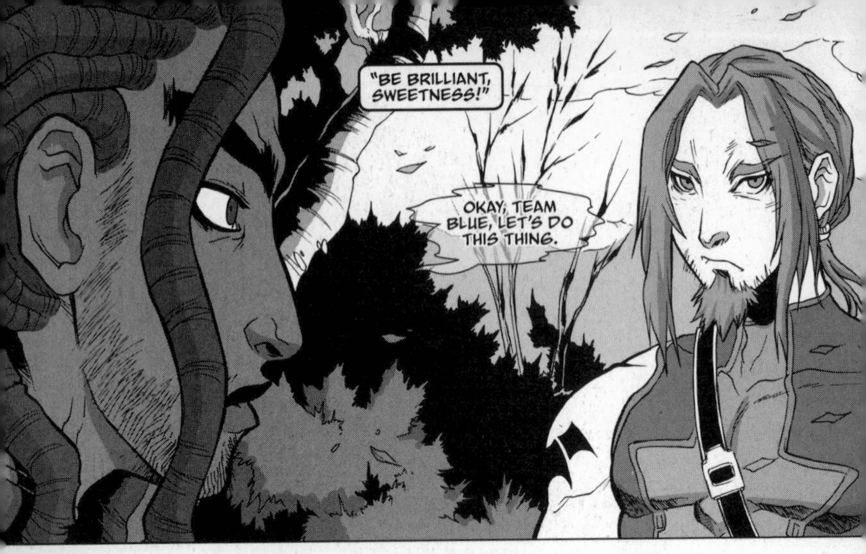
"BE BRILLIANT, SWEETNESS!"
OKAY, TEAM BLUE, LET'S DO THIS THING.
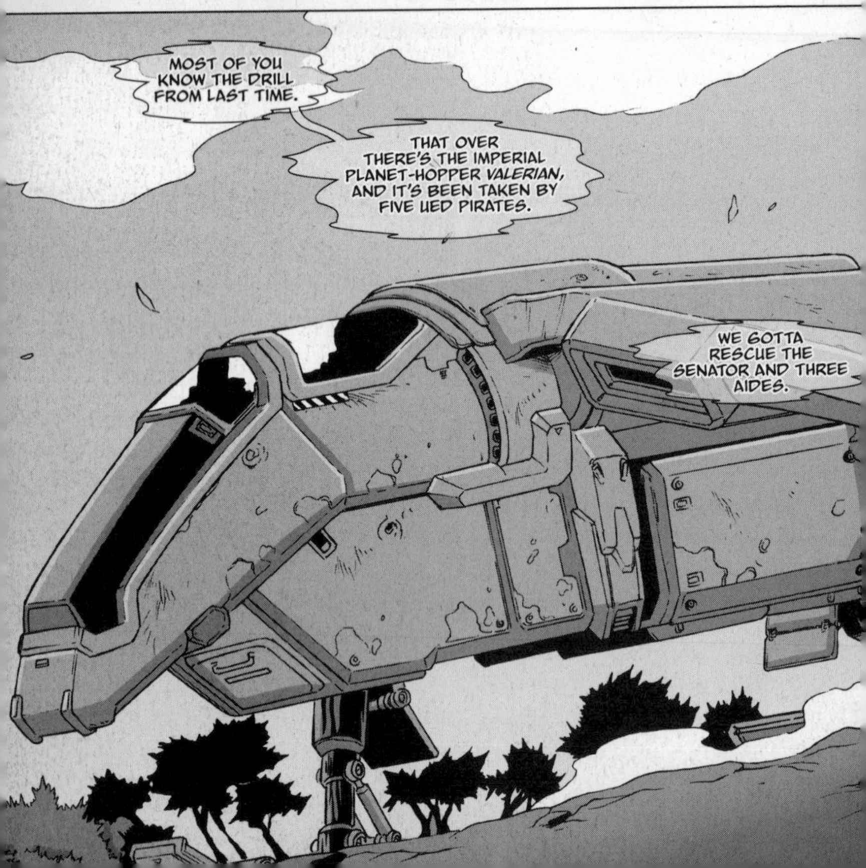
MOST OF YOU KNOW THE DRILL FROM LAST TIME.
THAT OVER THERE'S THE IMPERIAL PLANET-HOPPER *VALERIAN*, AND IT'S BEEN TAKEN BY FIVE UED PIRATES.
WE GOTTA RESCUE THE SENATOR AND THREE AIDES.

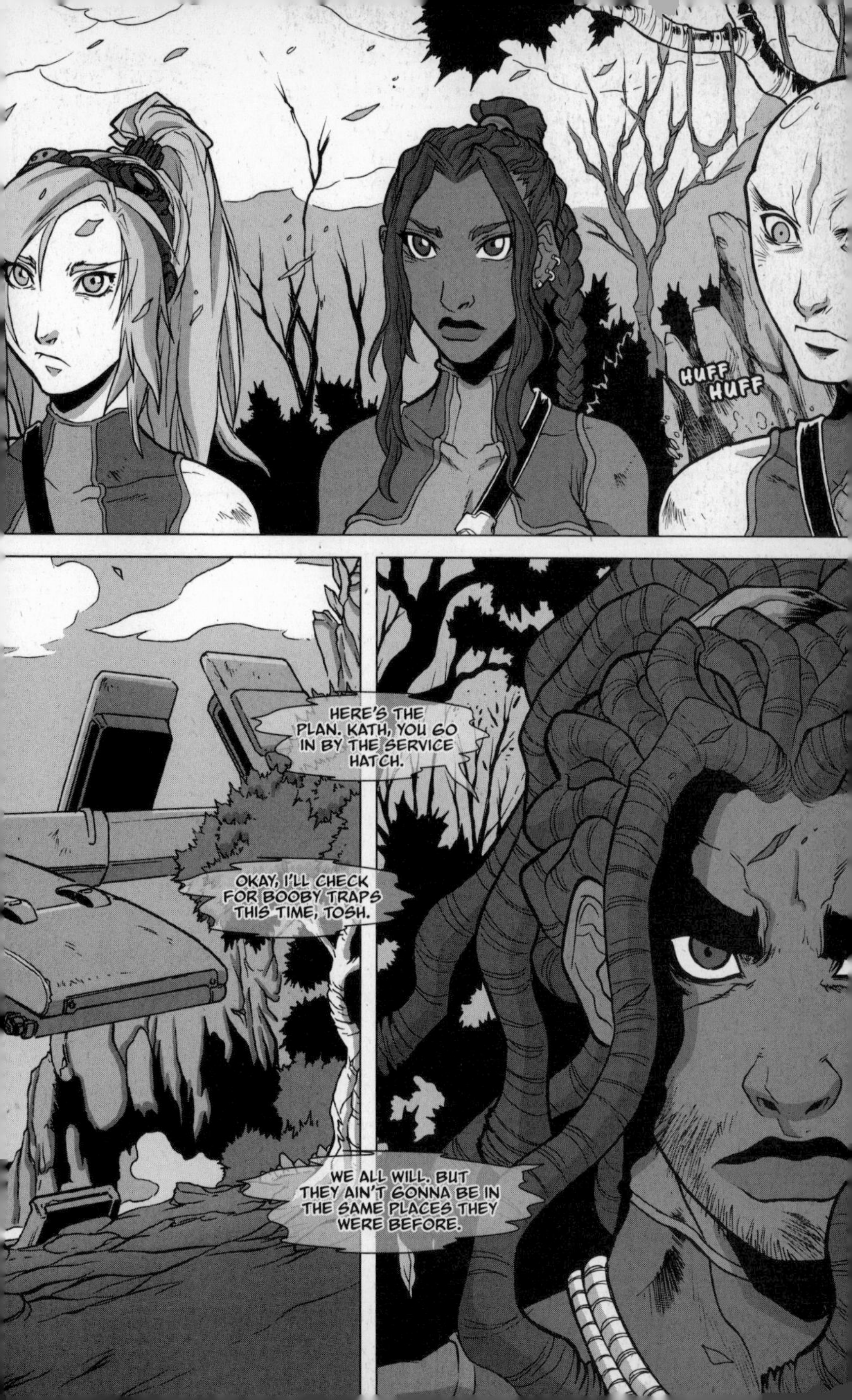
HUFF HUFF
HERE'S THE PLAN. KATH, YOU GO IN BY THE SERVICE HATCH.
OKAY, I'LL CHECK FOR BOOBY TRAPS THIS TIME, TOSH.
WE ALL WILL. BUT THEY AIN'T GONNA BE IN THE SAME PLACES THEY WERE BEFORE.

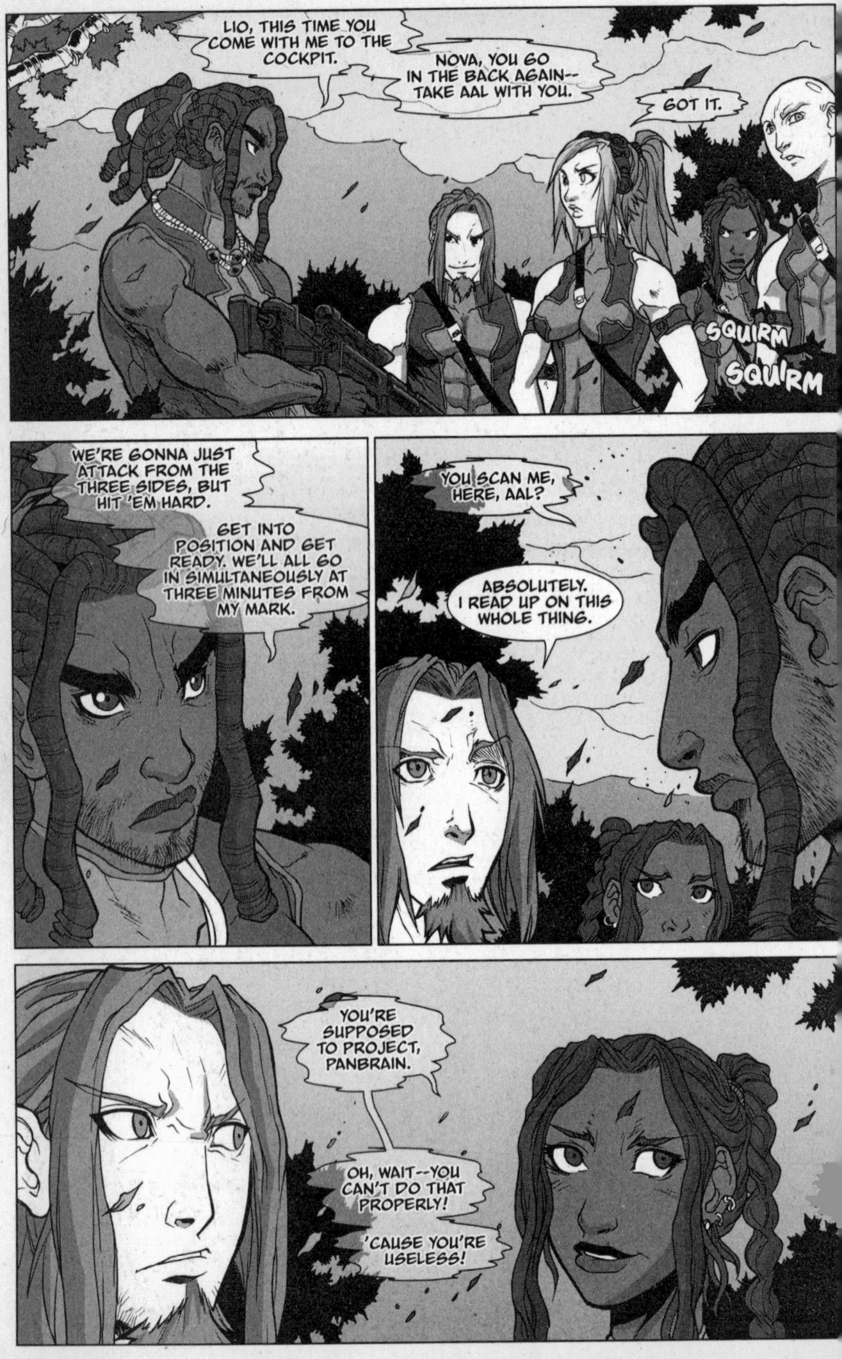
LIO, THIS TIME YOU COME WITH ME TO THE COCKPIT.
NOVA, YOU GO IN THE BACK AGAIN-- TAKE AAL WITH YOU.
GOT IT.
SQUIRM
SQUIRM
WE'RE GONNA JUST ATTACK FROM THE THREE SIDES, BUT HIT 'EM HARD.
GET INTO POSITION AND GET READY. WE'LL ALL GO IN SIMULTANEOUSLY AT THREE MINUTES FROM MY MARK.
YOU SCAN ME, HERE, AAL?
ABSOLUTELY. I READ UP ON THIS WHOLE THING.
YOU'RE SUPPOSED TO PROJECT, PANBRAIN.
OH, WAIT--YOU CAN'T DO THAT PROPERLY!
'CAUSE YOU'RE USELESS!

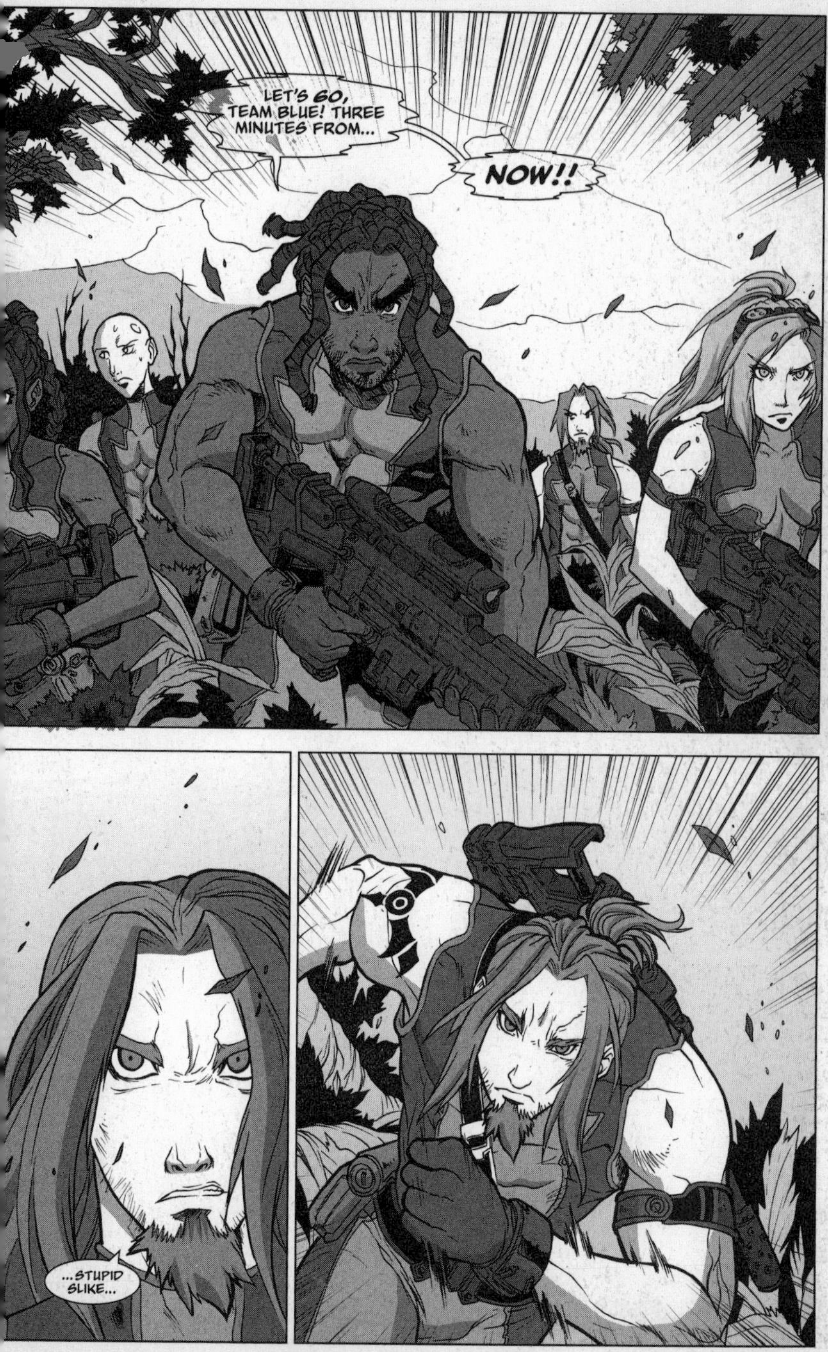
LET'S GO, TEAM BLUE! THREE MINUTES FROM...
NOW!!
...STUPID SLIKE...

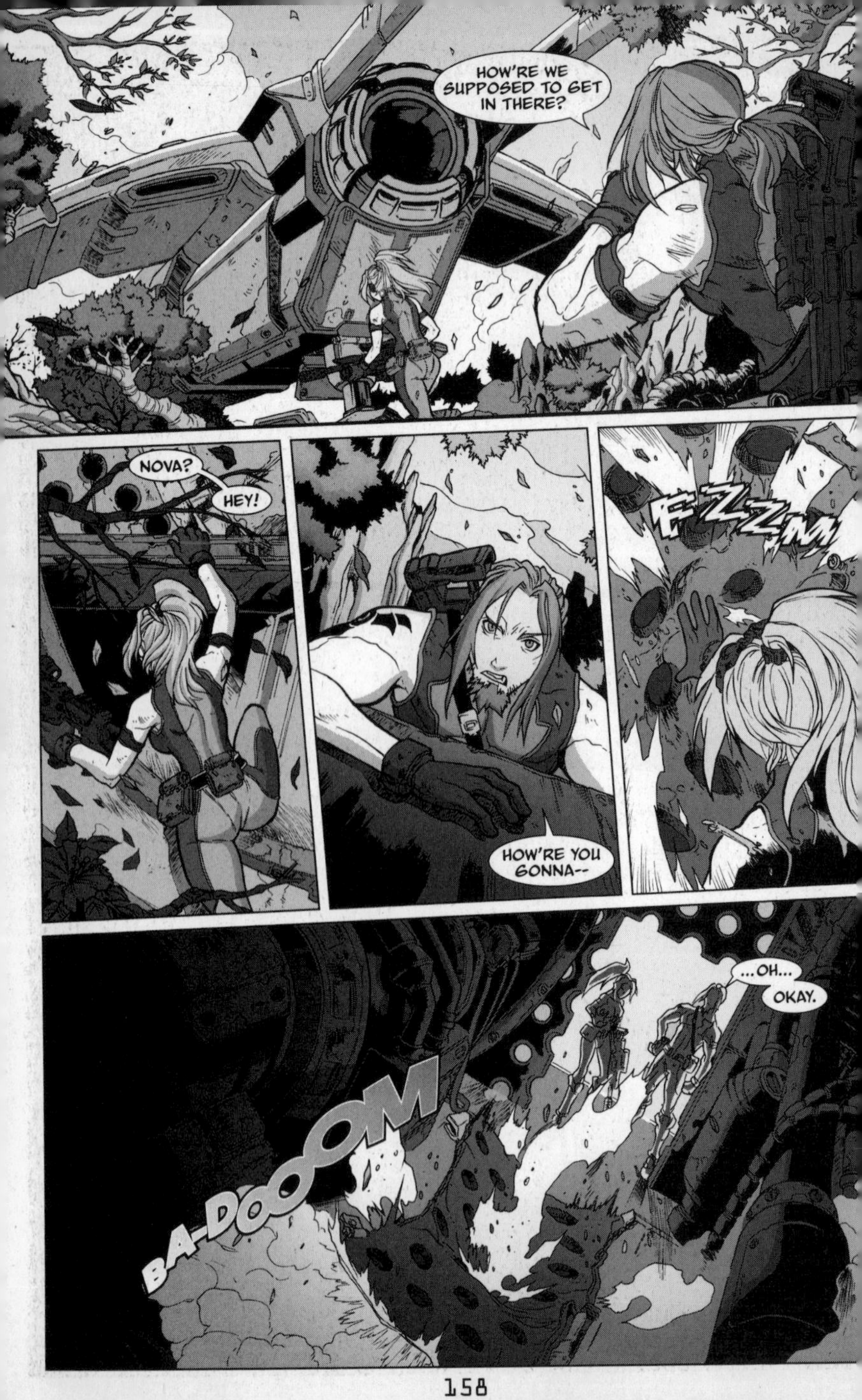
HOW'RE WE SUPPOSED TO GET IN THERE?
NOVA?
HEY!
HOW'RE YOU GONNA--
FZZZM
...OH... OKAY.
BA-DOOOOM

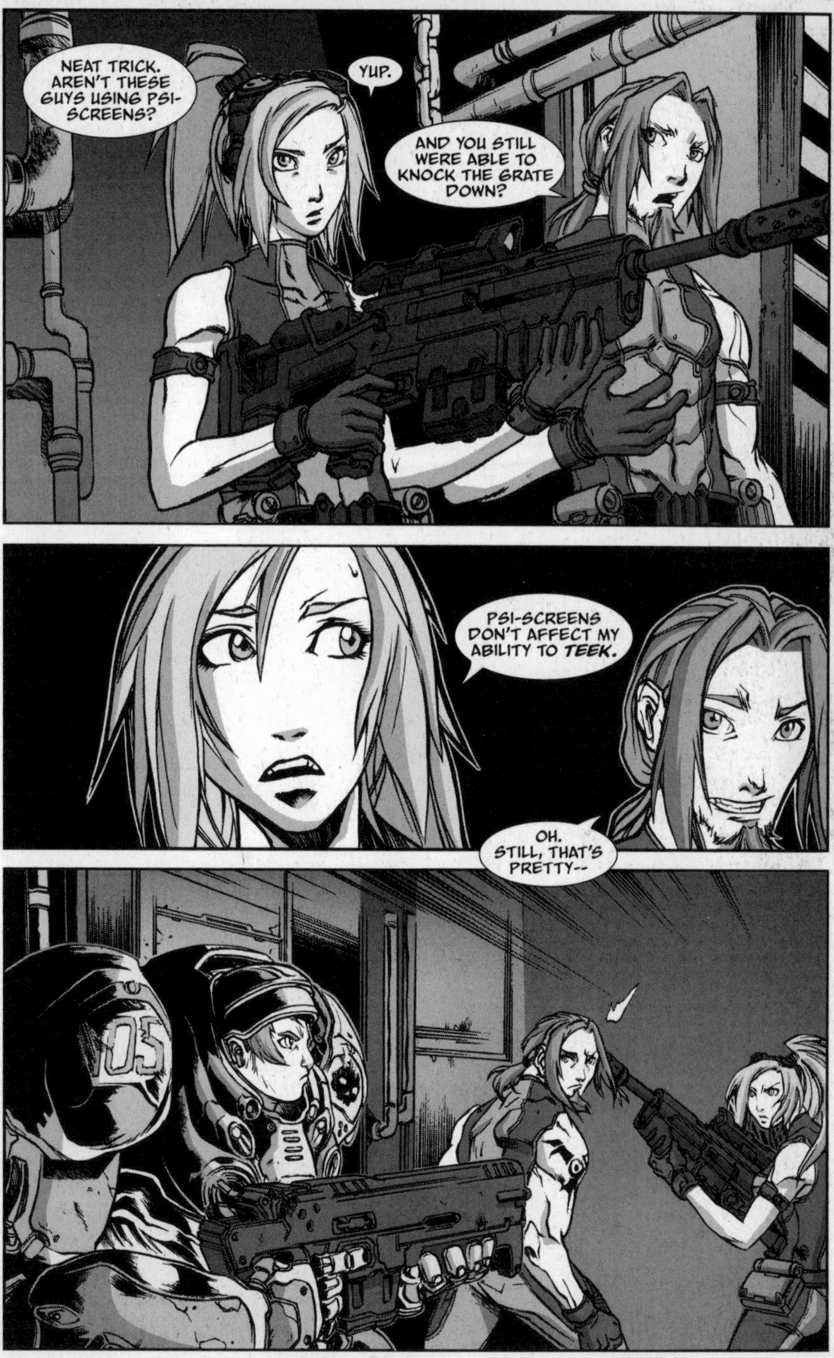
NEAT TRICK. AREN'T THESE GUYS USING PSI-SCREENS?
YUP.
AND YOU STILL WERE ABLE TO KNOCK THE GRATE DOWN?
PSI-SCREENS DON'T AFFECT MY ABILITY TO *TEEK*.
OH. STILL, THAT'S PRETTY--
05

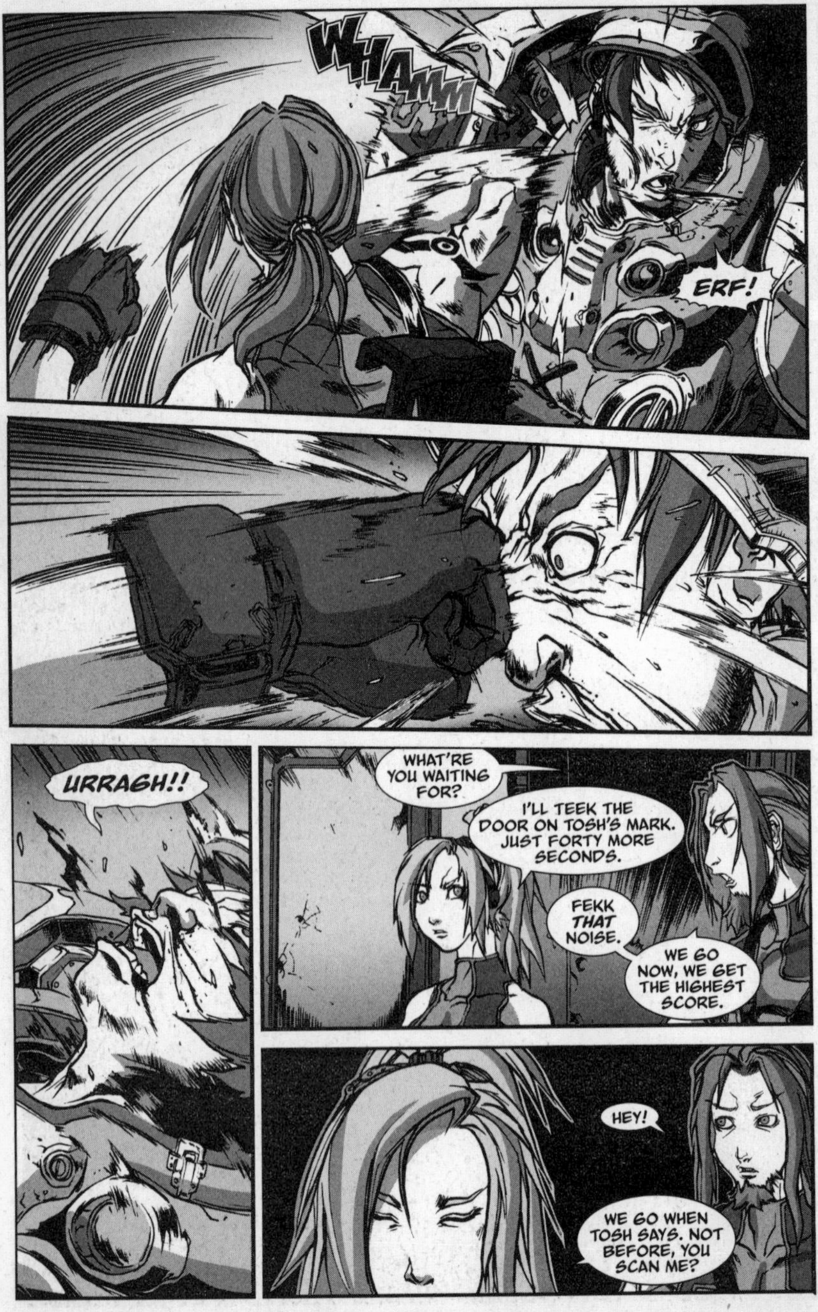
WHAMM
ERF!
URRAGH!!
WHAT'RE YOU WAITING FOR?
I'LL TEEK THE DOOR ON TOSH'S MARK. JUST FORTY MORE SECONDS.
FEKK THAT NOISE.
WE GO NOW, WE GET THE HIGHEST SCORE.
HEY!
WE GO WHEN TOSH SAYS. NOT BEFORE, YOU SCAN ME?

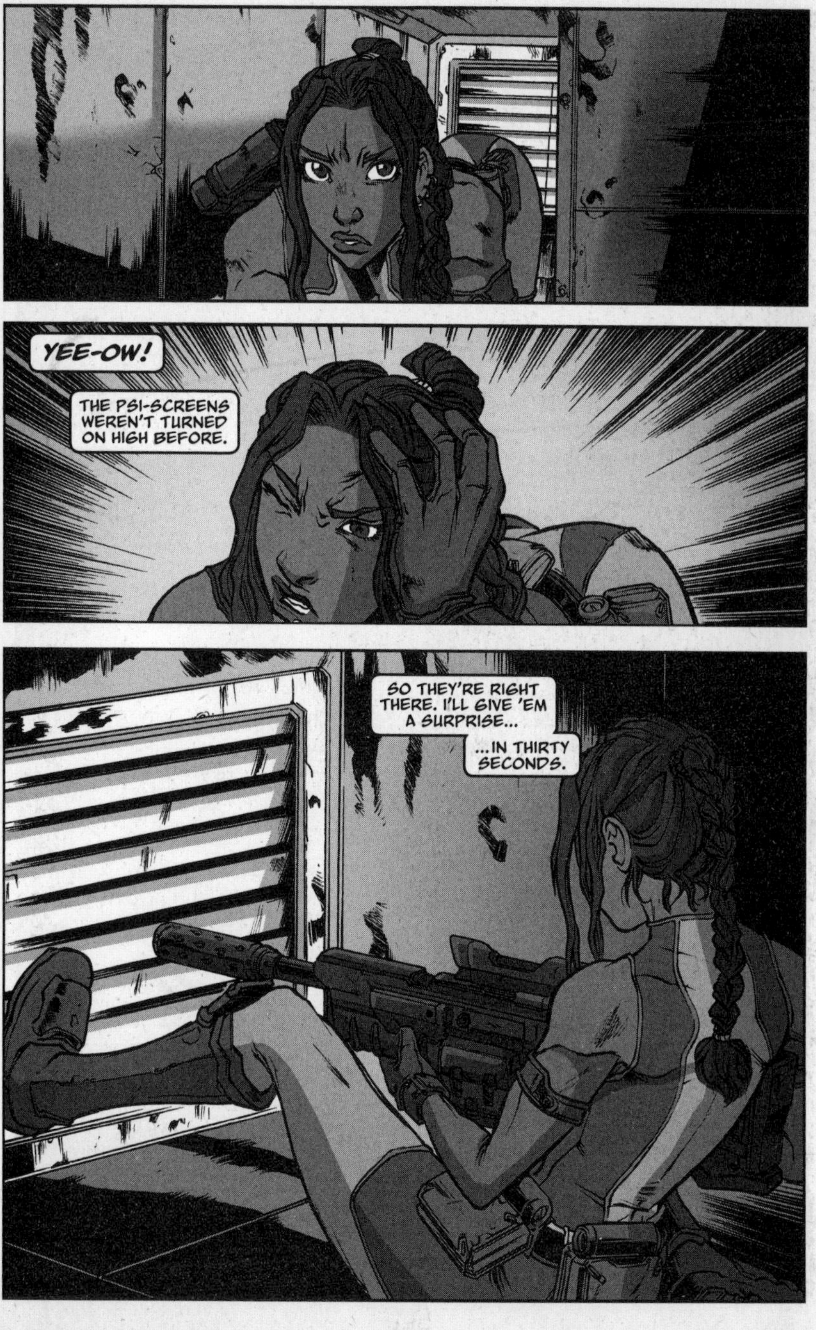
YEE-OW!
THE PSI-SCREENS WEREN'T TURNED ON HIGH BEFORE.
SO THEY'RE RIGHT THERE. I'LL GIVE 'EM A SURPRISE...
...IN THIRTY SECONDS.

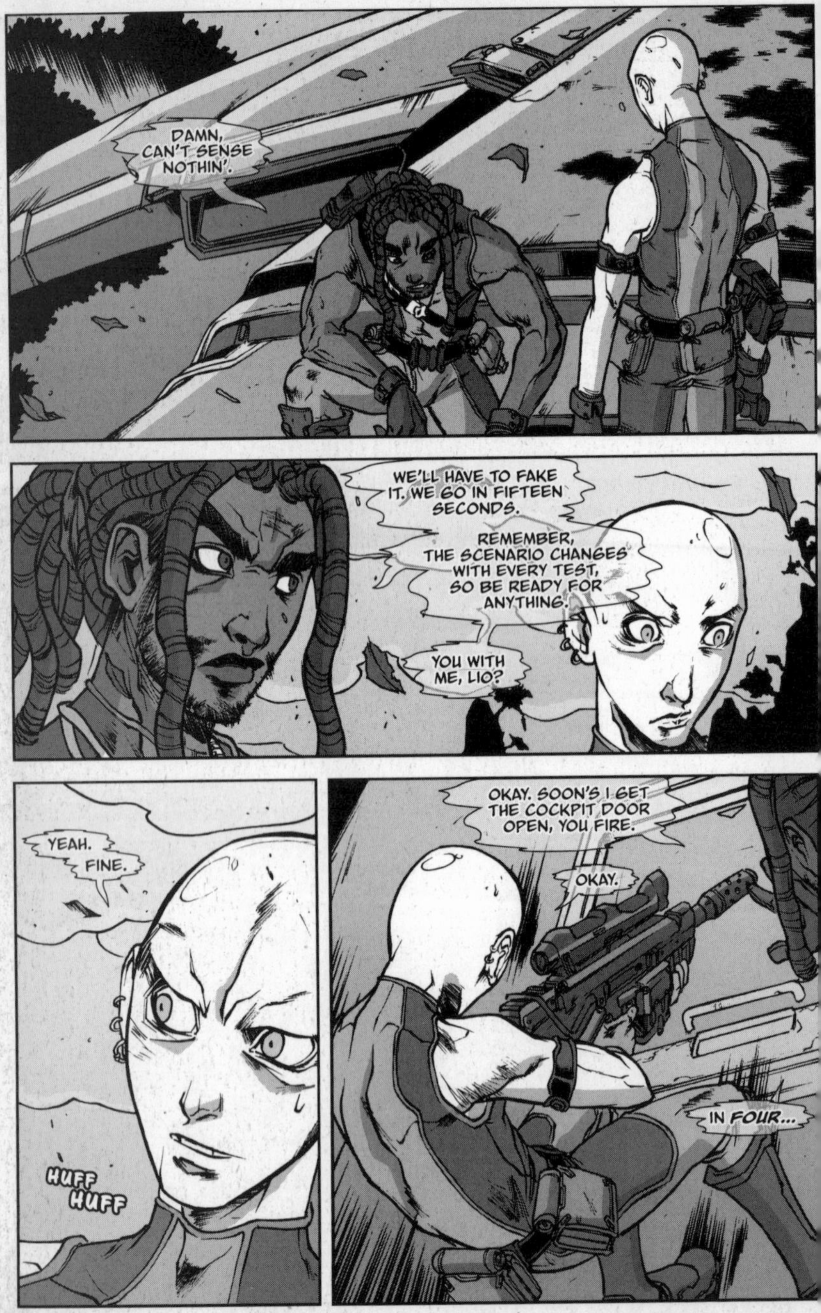
DAMN, CAN'T SENSE NOTHIN'.
WE'LL HAVE TO FAKE IT. WE GO IN FIFTEEN SECONDS.
REMEMBER, THE SCENARIO CHANGES WITH EVERY TEST, SO BE READY FOR ANYTHING.
YOU WITH ME, LIO?
YEAH.
FINE.
HUFF HUFF
OKAY. SOON'S I GET THE COCKPIT DOOR OPEN, YOU FIRE.
OKAY.
IN FOUR...

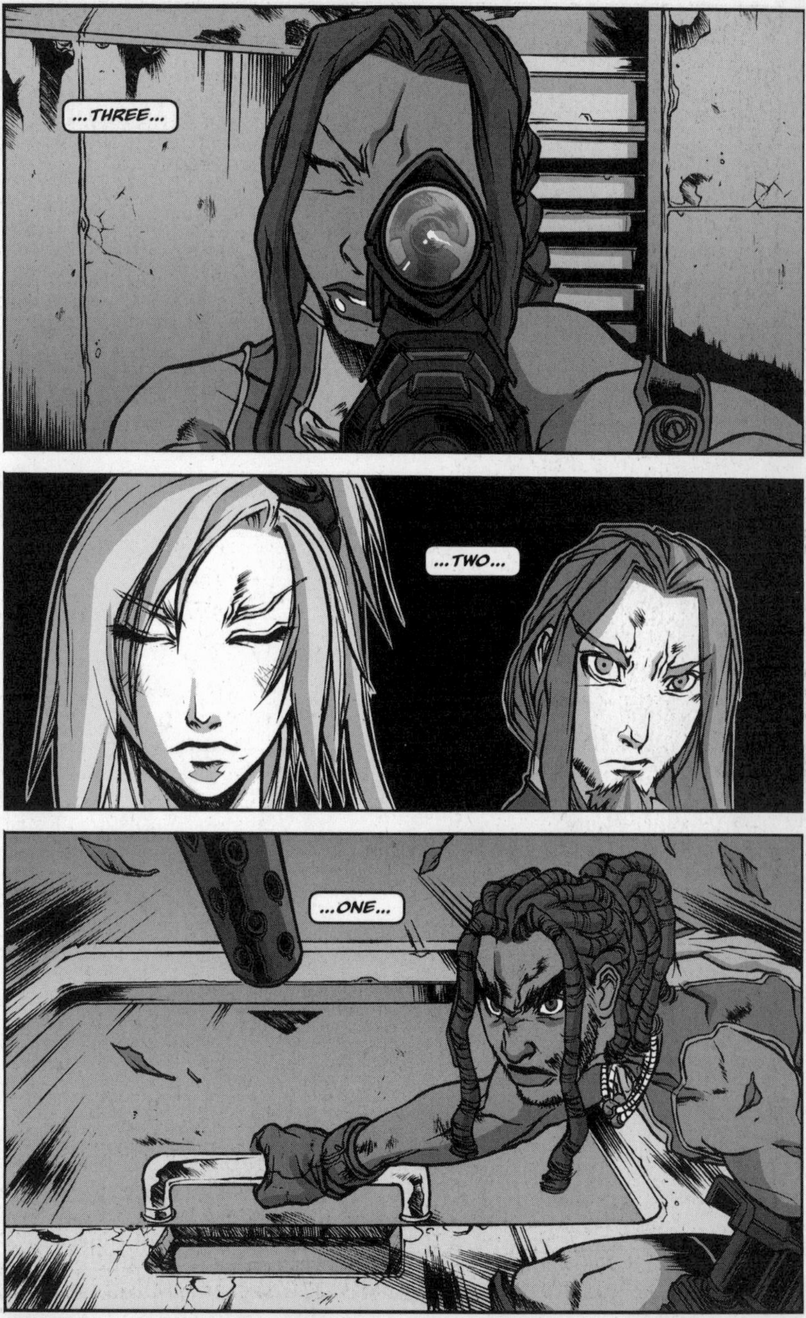
...THREE...
...TWO...
...ONE...

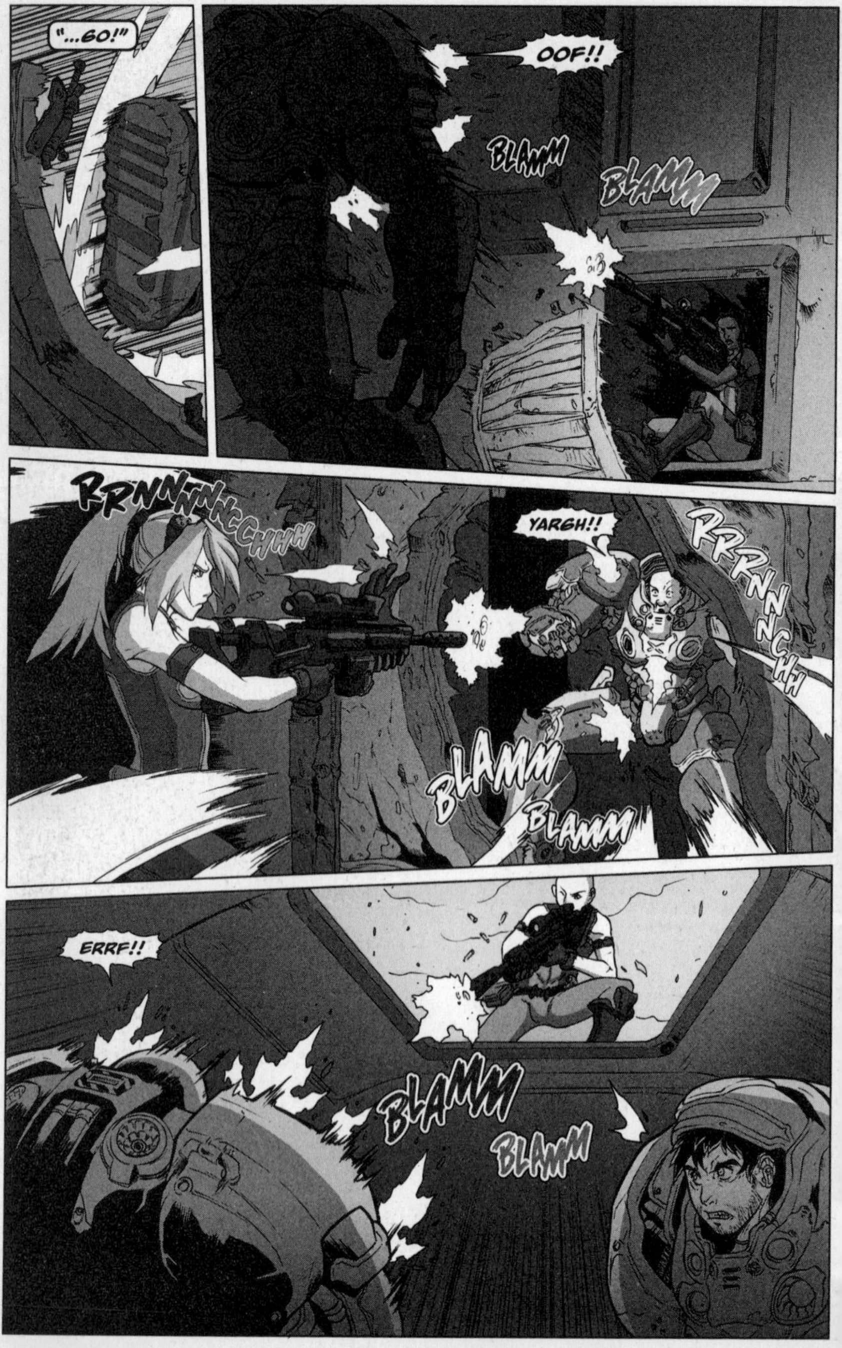
"...GO!"
OOF!!
BLAMM
BLAMM
RRNNNNNCHHH
YARGH!!
RRRNNNNCHH
BLAMM
BLAMM
ERRF!!
BLAMM
BLAMM

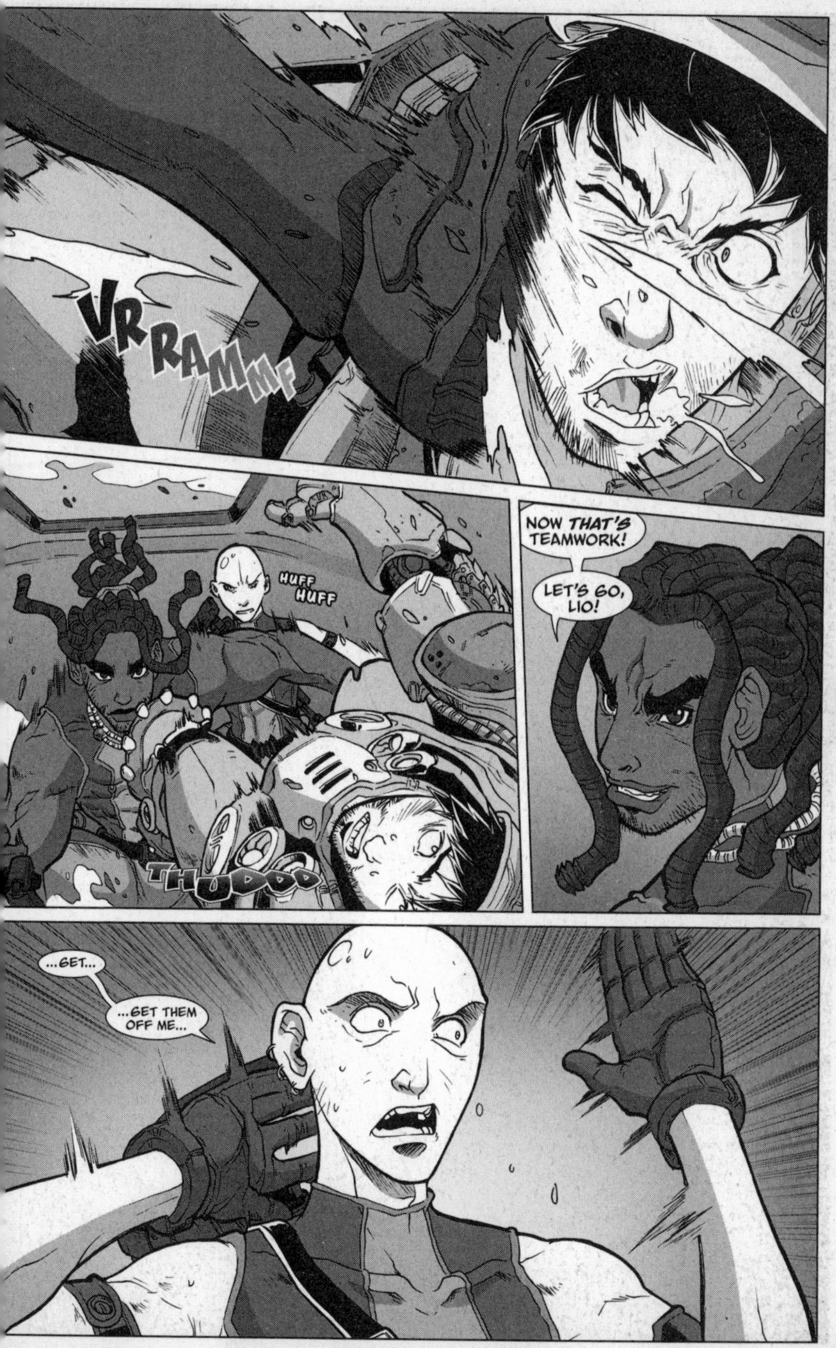
VRRAMMF
HUFF HUFF
THUDDD
NOW THAT'S TEAMWORK!
LET'S GO, LIO!
...GET...
...GET THEM OFF ME...

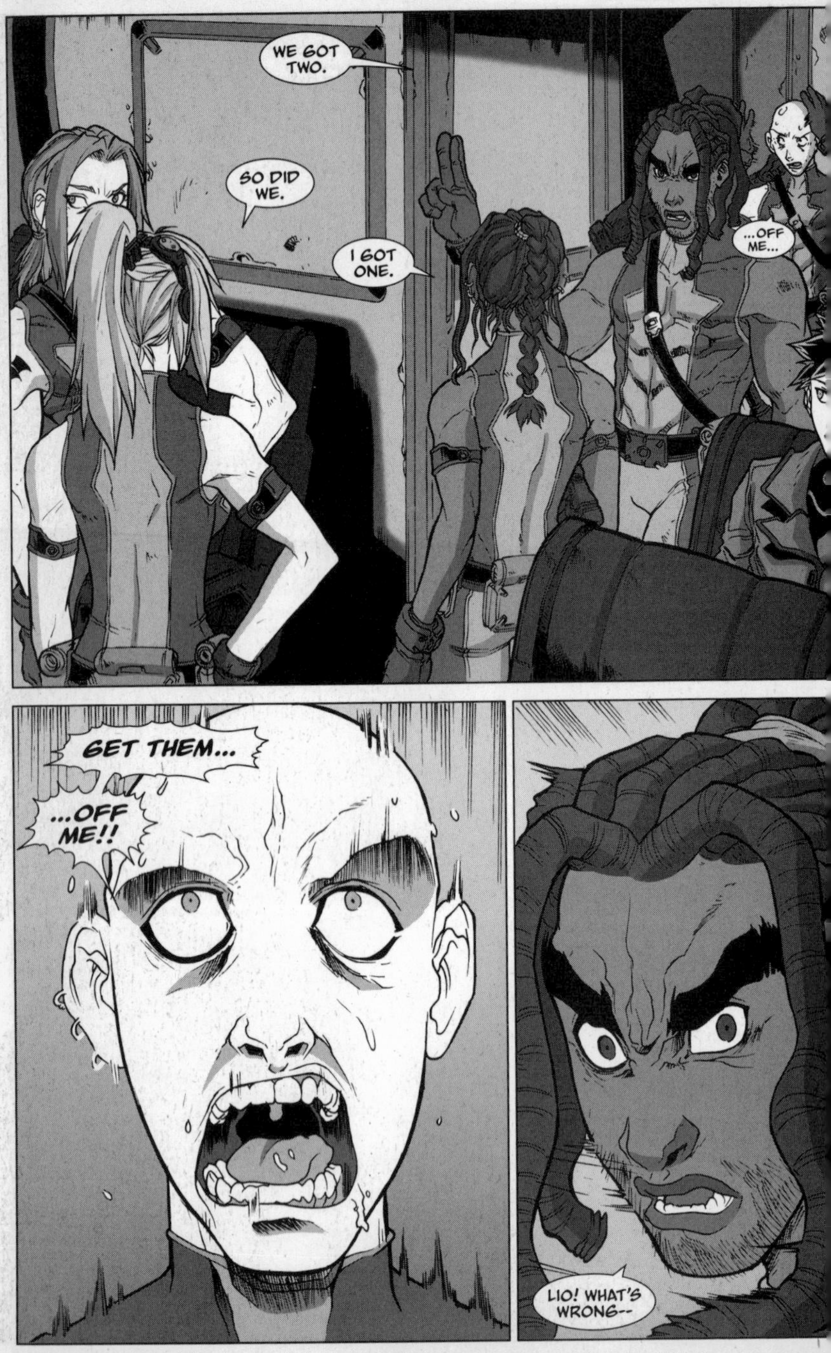
WE GOT TWO.
SO DID WE.
I GOT ONE.
...OFF ME...
GET THEM...
...OFF ME!!
LIO! WHAT'S WRONG--

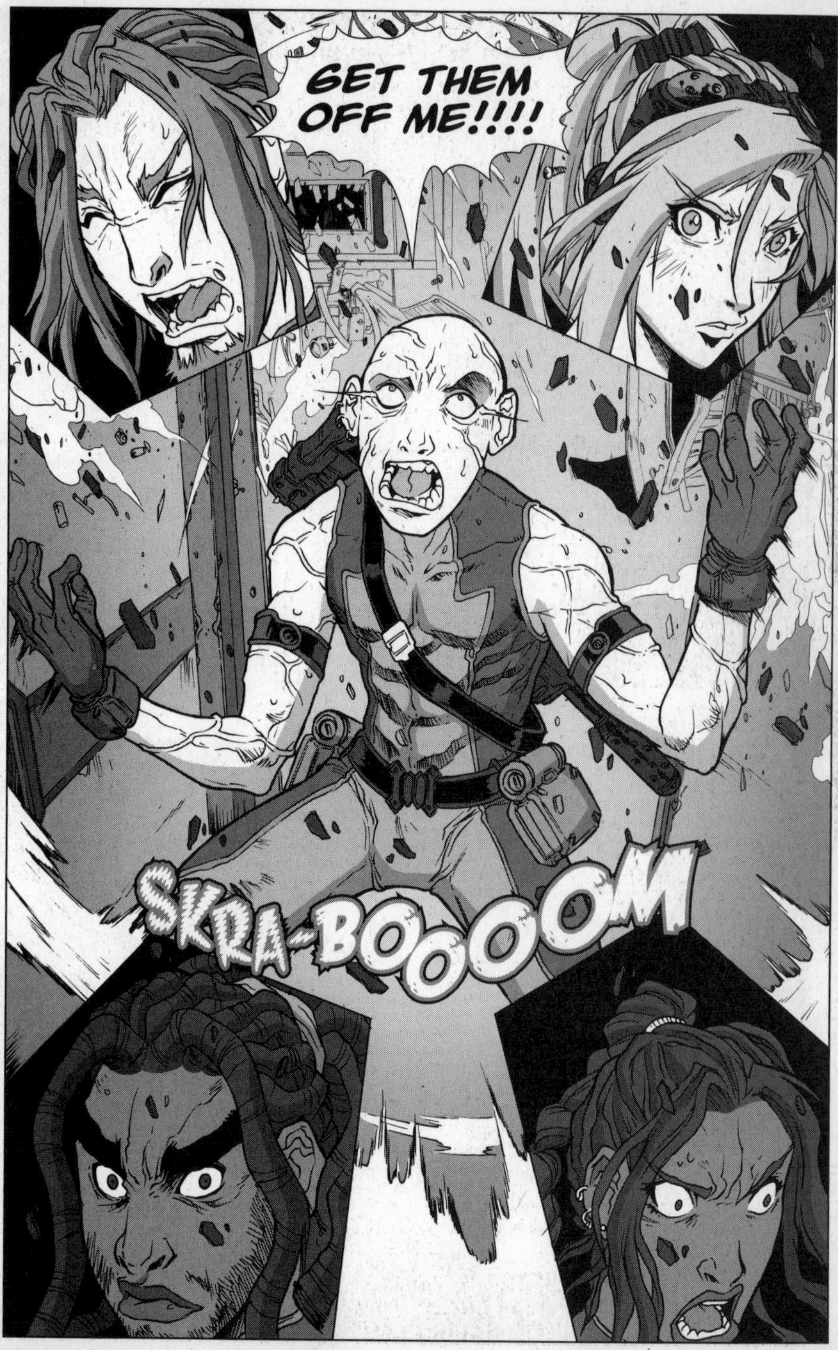
GET THEM OFF ME!!!!
SKRA-BOOOOOM

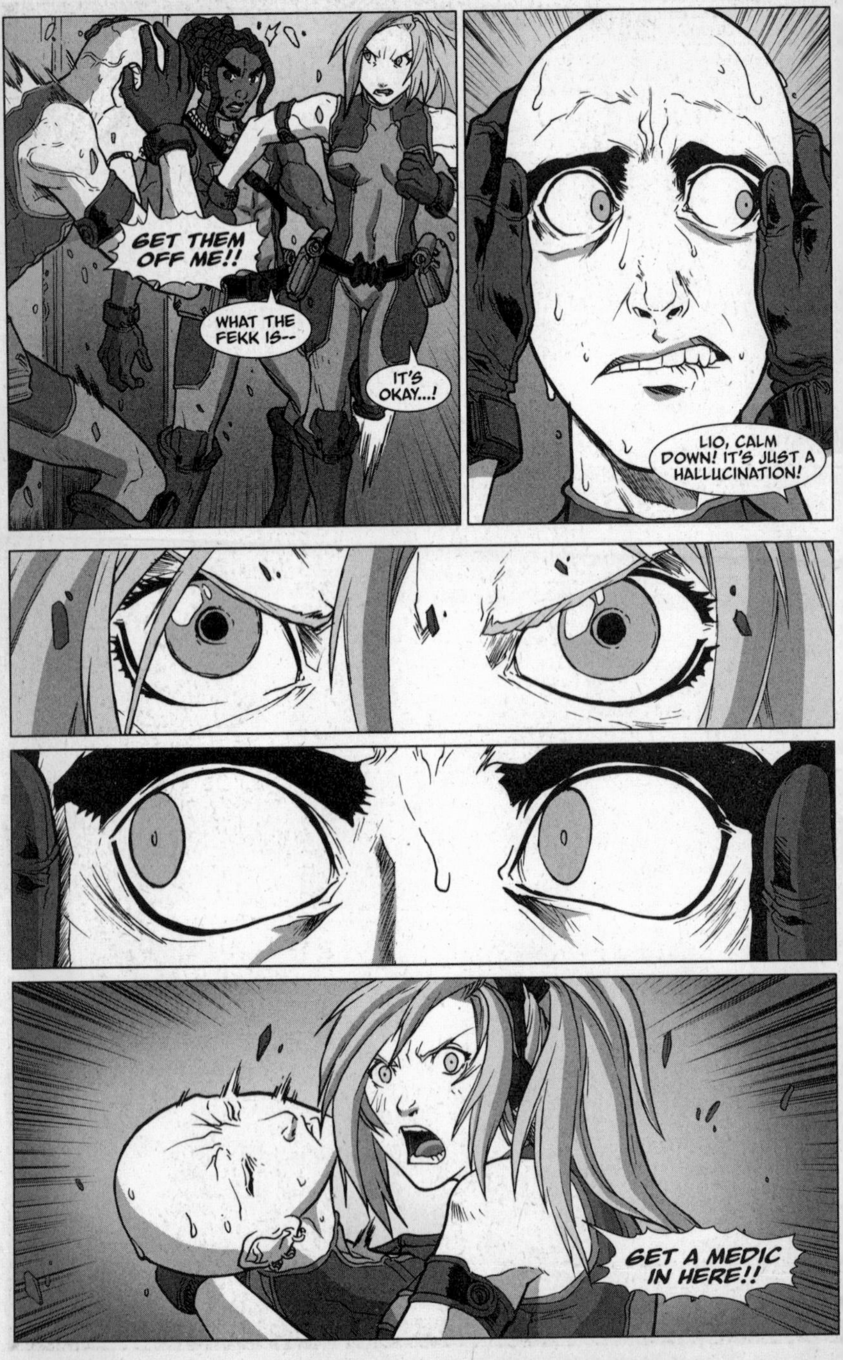
GET THEM OFF ME!!
WHAT THE FEKK IS--
IT'S OKAY...!
LIO, CALM DOWN! IT'S JUST A HALLUCINATION!
GET A MEDIC IN HERE!!

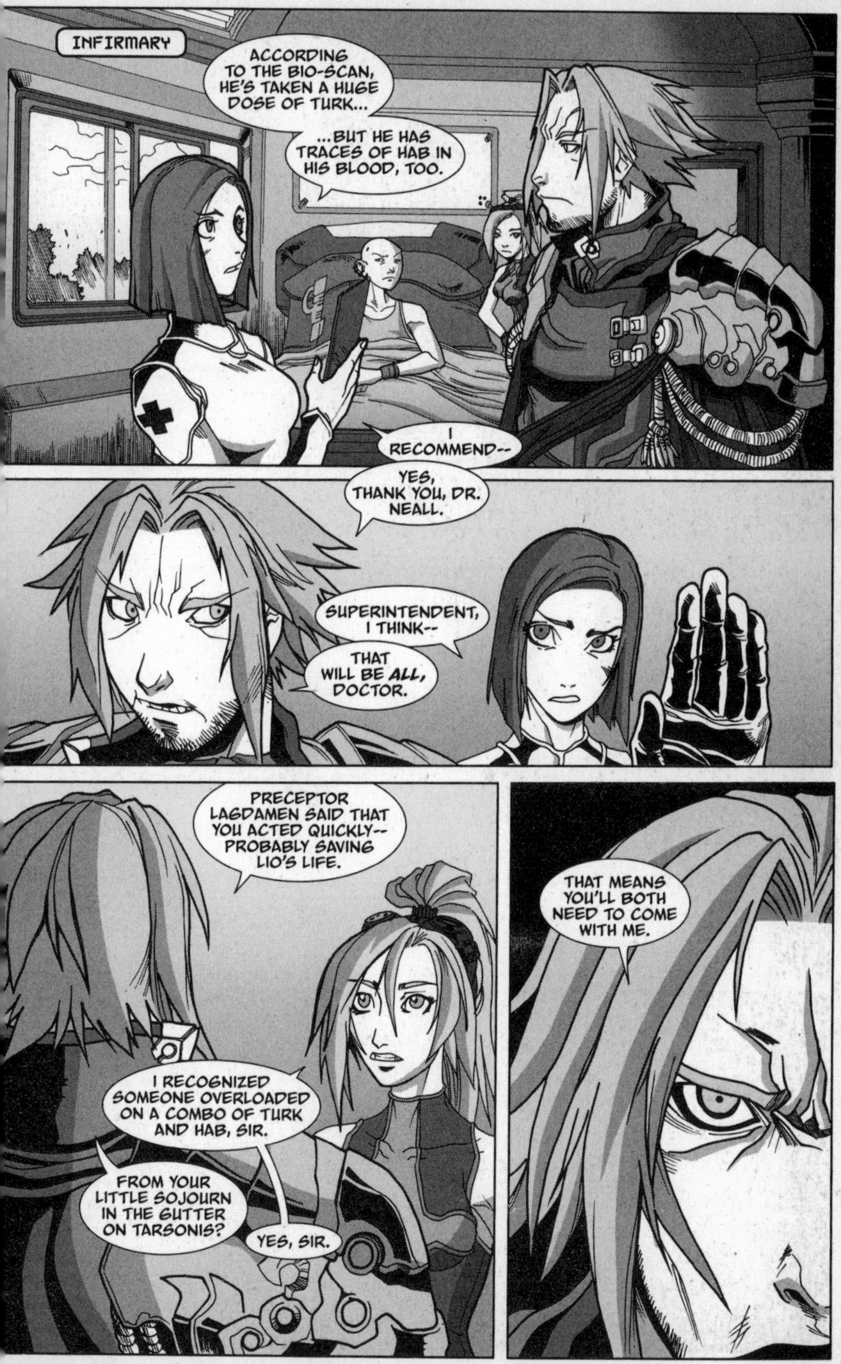
INFIRMARY
ACCORDING TO THE BIO-SCAN, HE'S TAKEN A HUGE DOSE OF TURK...
...BUT HE HAS TRACES OF HAB IN HIS BLOOD, TOO.
I RECOMMEND--
YES, THANK YOU, DR. NEALL.
SUPERINTENDENT, I THINK--
THAT WILL BE *ALL*, DOCTOR.
PRECEPTOR LAGDAMEN SAID THAT YOU ACTED QUICKLY--PROBABLY SAVING LIO'S LIFE.
I RECOGNIZED SOMEONE OVERLOADED ON A COMBO OF TURK AND HAB, SIR.
FROM YOUR LITTLE SOJOURN IN THE GUTTER ON TARSONIS?
YES, SIR.
THAT MEANS YOU'LL BOTH NEED TO COME WITH ME.

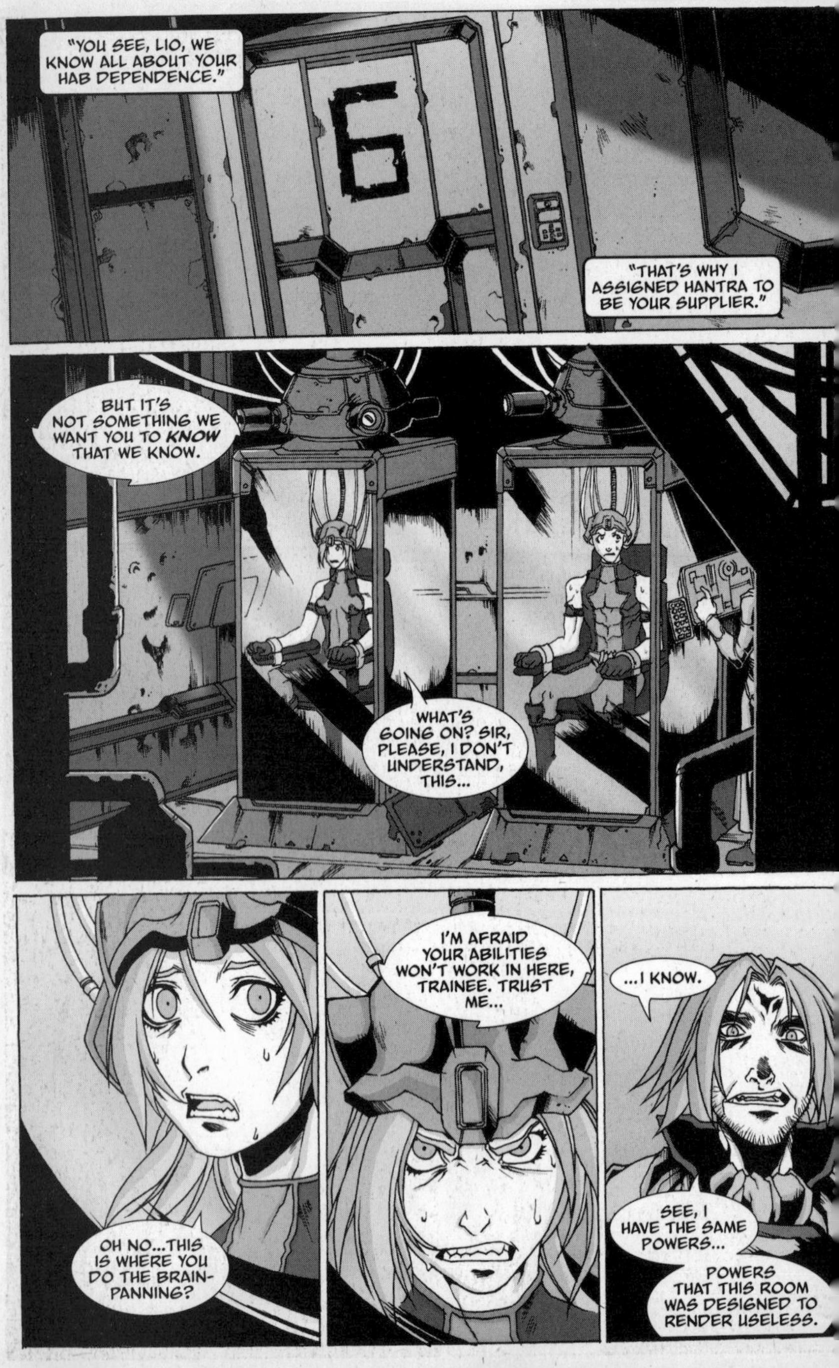
"YOU SEE, LIO, WE KNOW ALL ABOUT YOUR HAB DEPENDENCE."
"THAT'S WHY I ASSIGNED HANTRA TO BE YOUR SUPPLIER."
BUT IT'S NOT SOMETHING WE WANT YOU TO *KNOW* THAT WE KNOW.
WHAT'S GOING ON? SIR, PLEASE, I DON'T UNDERSTAND, THIS...
OH NO...THIS IS WHERE YOU DO THE BRAIN-PANNING?
I'M AFRAID YOUR ABILITIES WON'T WORK IN HERE, TRAINEE. TRUST ME...
...I KNOW.
SEE, I HAVE THE SAME POWERS...
POWERS THAT THIS ROOM WAS DESIGNED TO RENDER USELESS.

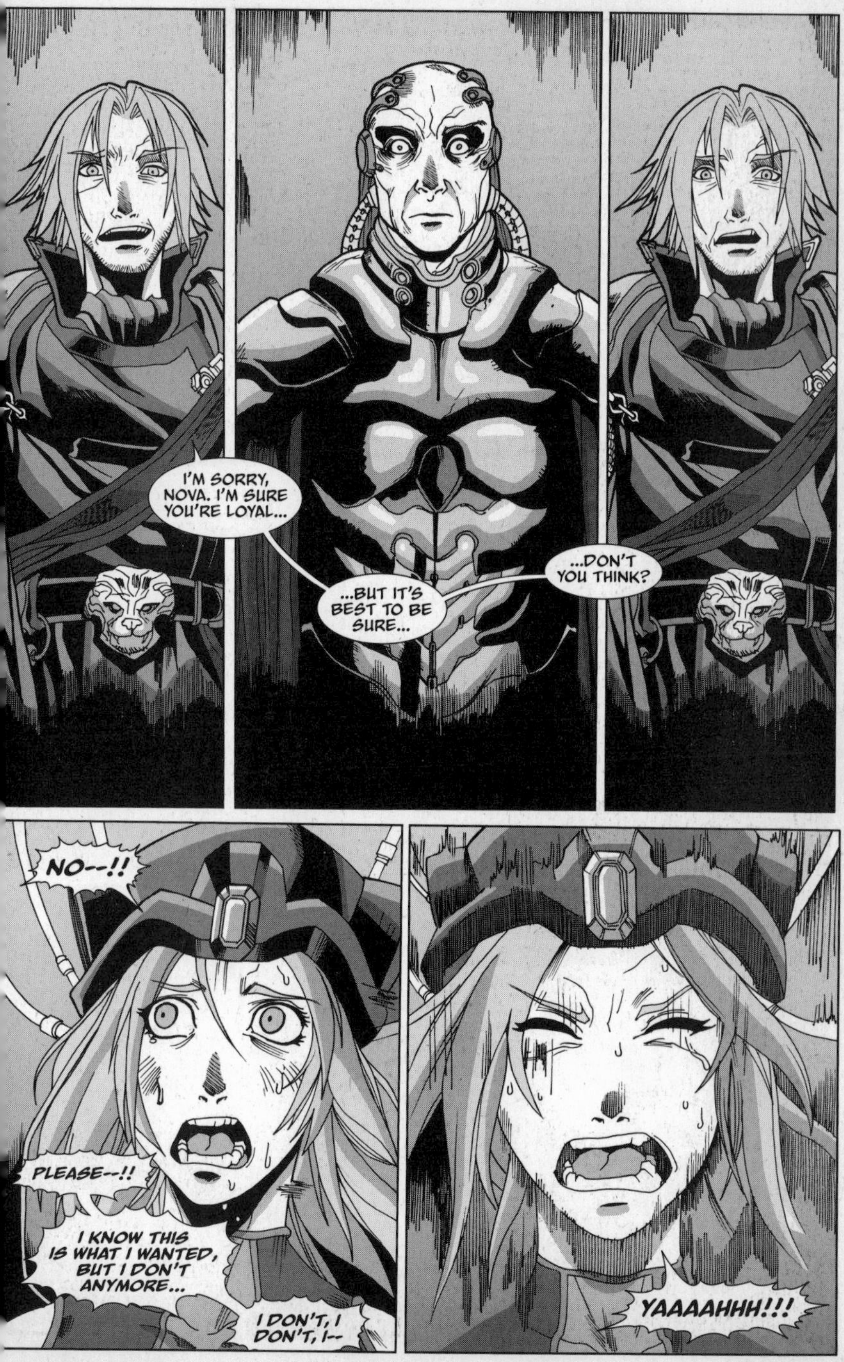
I'M SORRY, NOVA. I'M SURE YOU'RE LOYAL...
...BUT IT'S BEST TO BE SURE...
...DON'T YOU THINK?
NO--!!
PLEASE--!!
I KNOW THIS IS WHAT I WANTED, BUT I DON'T ANYMORE...
I DON'T, I DON'T, I--
YAAAAHHH!!!

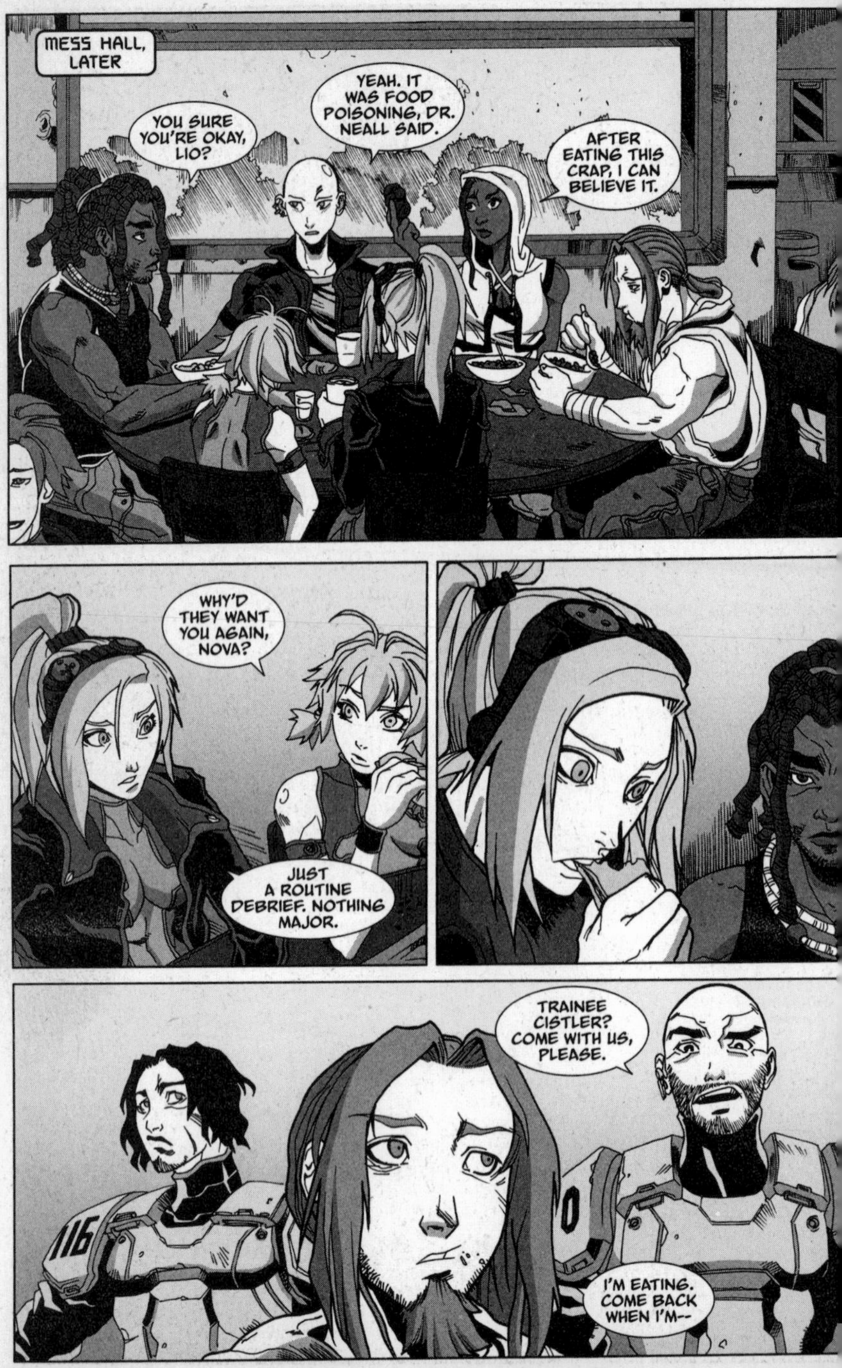
MESS HALL, LATER
YOU SURE YOU'RE OKAY, LIO?
YEAH. IT WAS FOOD POISONING, DR. NEALL SAID.
AFTER EATING THIS CRAP, I CAN BELIEVE IT.
WHY'D THEY WANT YOU AGAIN, NOVA?
JUST A ROUTINE DEBRIEF. NOTHING MAJOR.
TRAINEE CISTLER? COME WITH US, PLEASE.
116
I'M EATING. COME BACK WHEN I'M--

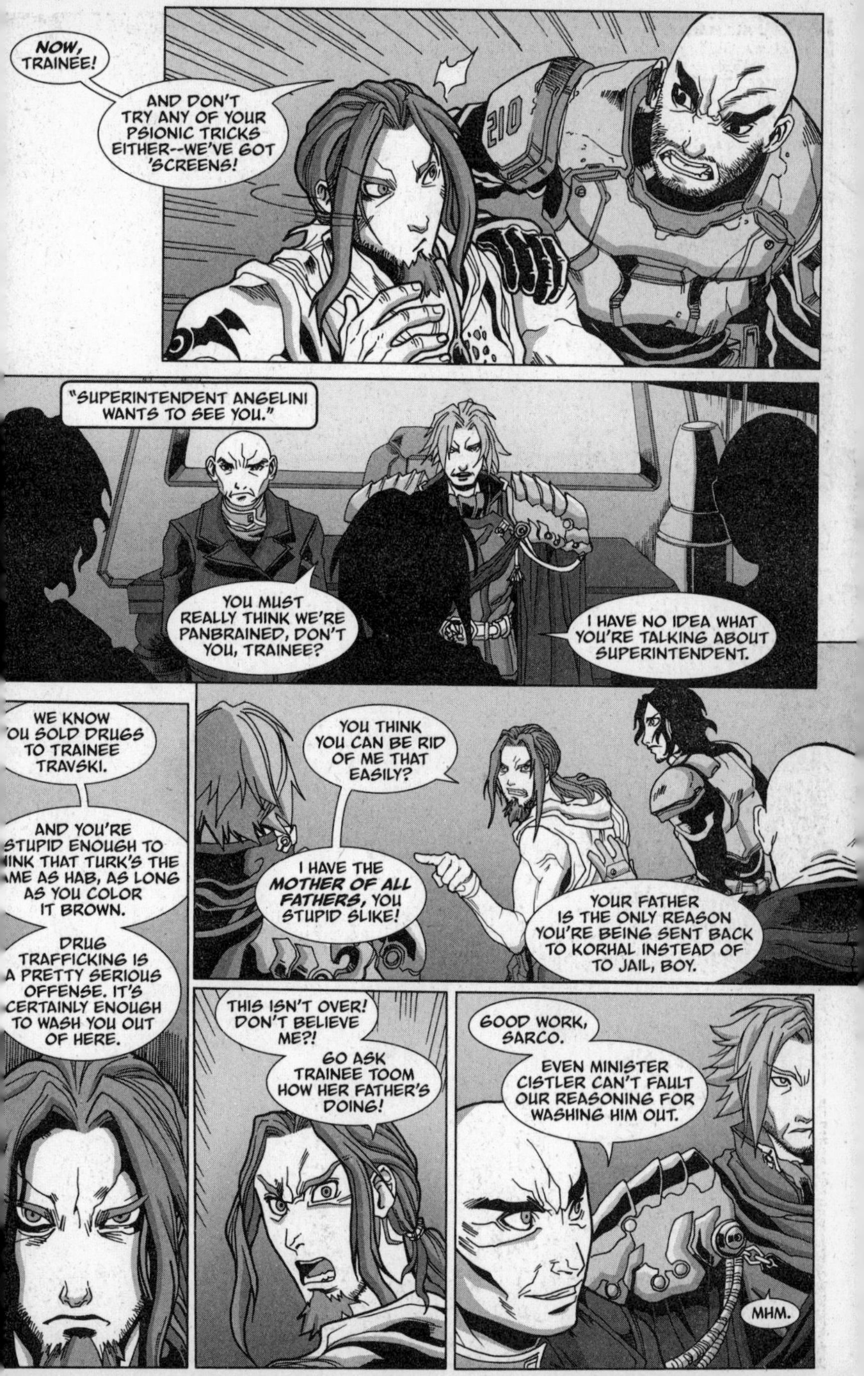
NOW, TRAINEE!
AND DON'T TRY ANY OF YOUR PSIONIC TRICKS EITHER--WE'VE GOT 'SCREENS!
210
"SUPERINTENDENT ANGELINI WANTS TO SEE YOU."
YOU MUST REALLY THINK WE'RE PANBRAINED, DON'T YOU, TRAINEE?
I HAVE NO IDEA WHAT YOU'RE TALKING ABOUT SUPERINTENDENT.
WE KNOW YOU SOLD DRUGS TO TRAINEE TRAVSKI.
AND YOU'RE STUPID ENOUGH TO THINK THAT TURK'S THE SAME AS HAB, AS LONG AS YOU COLOR IT BROWN.
DRUG TRAFFICKING IS A PRETTY SERIOUS OFFENSE. IT'S CERTAINLY ENOUGH TO WASH YOU OUT OF HERE.
YOU THINK YOU CAN BE RID OF ME THAT EASILY?
I HAVE THE *MOTHER OF ALL FATHERS,* YOU STUPID SLIKE!
YOUR FATHER IS THE ONLY REASON YOU'RE BEING SENT BACK TO KORHAL INSTEAD OF TO JAIL, BOY.
THIS ISN'T OVER! DON'T BELIEVE ME?!
GO ASK TRAINEE TOOM HOW HER FATHER'S DOING!
GOOD WORK, SARCO.
EVEN MINISTER CISTLER CAN'T FAULT OUR REASONING FOR WASHING HIM OUT.
MHM.

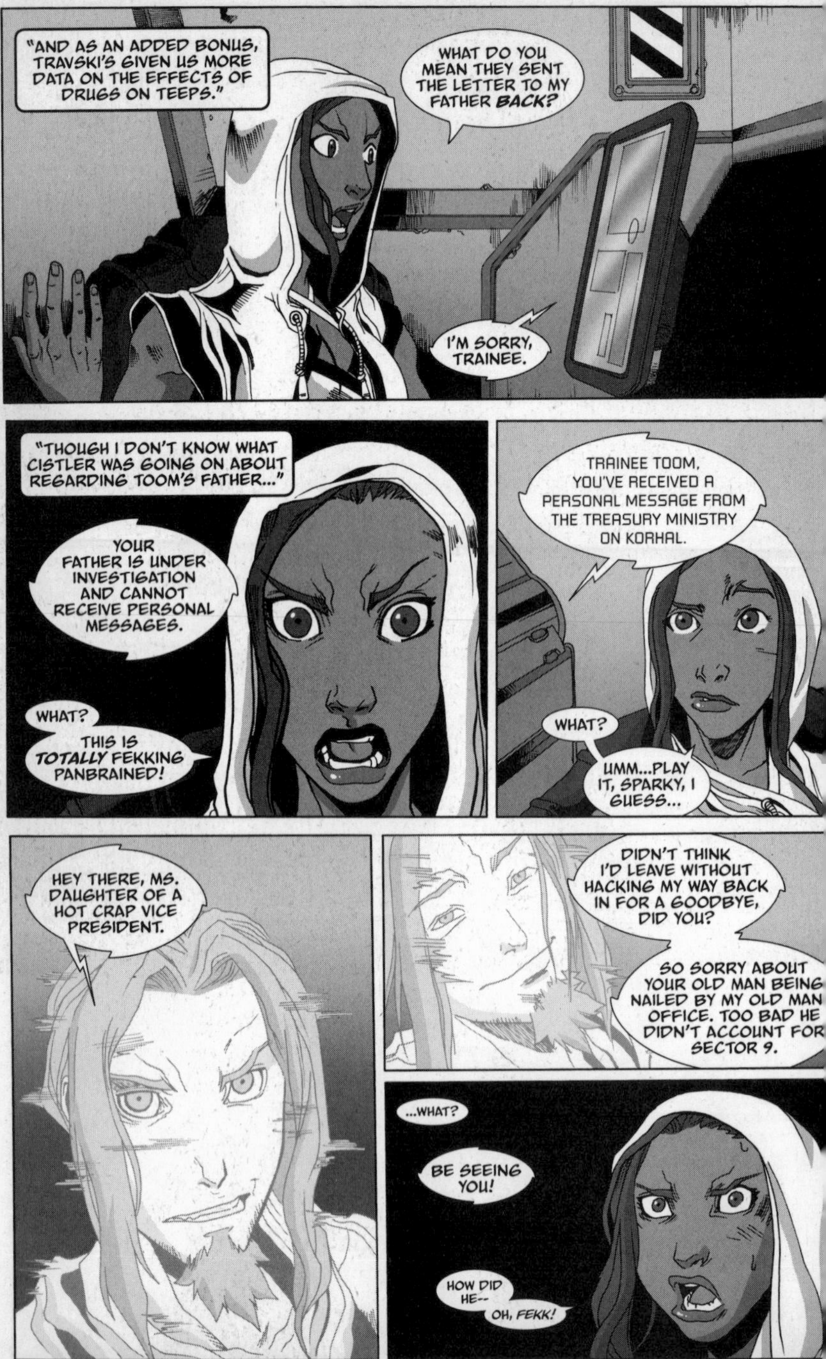
"AND AS AN ADDED BONUS, TRAVSKI'S GIVEN US MORE DATA ON THE EFFECTS OF DRUGS ON TEEPS."
WHAT DO YOU MEAN THEY SENT THE LETTER TO MY FATHER *BACK*?
I'M SORRY, TRAINEE.
"THOUGH I DON'T KNOW WHAT CISTLER WAS GOING ON ABOUT REGARDING TOOM'S FATHER..."
YOUR FATHER IS UNDER INVESTIGATION AND CANNOT RECEIVE PERSONAL MESSAGES.
WHAT?
THIS IS *TOTALLY* FEKKING PANBRAINED!
TRAINEE TOOM, YOU'VE RECEIVED A PERSONAL MESSAGE FROM THE TREASURY MINISTRY ON KORHAL.
WHAT?
UMM...PLAY IT, SPARKY, I GUESS...
HEY THERE, MS. DAUGHTER OF A HOT CRAP VICE PRESIDENT.
DIDN'T THINK I'D LEAVE WITHOUT HACKING MY WAY BACK IN FOR A GOODBYE, DID YOU?
SO SORRY ABOUT YOUR OLD MAN BEING NAILED BY MY OLD MAN OFFICE. TOO BAD HE DIDN'T ACCOUNT FOR SECTOR 9.
...WHAT?
BE SEEING YOU!
HOW DID HE--
OH, *FEKK*!

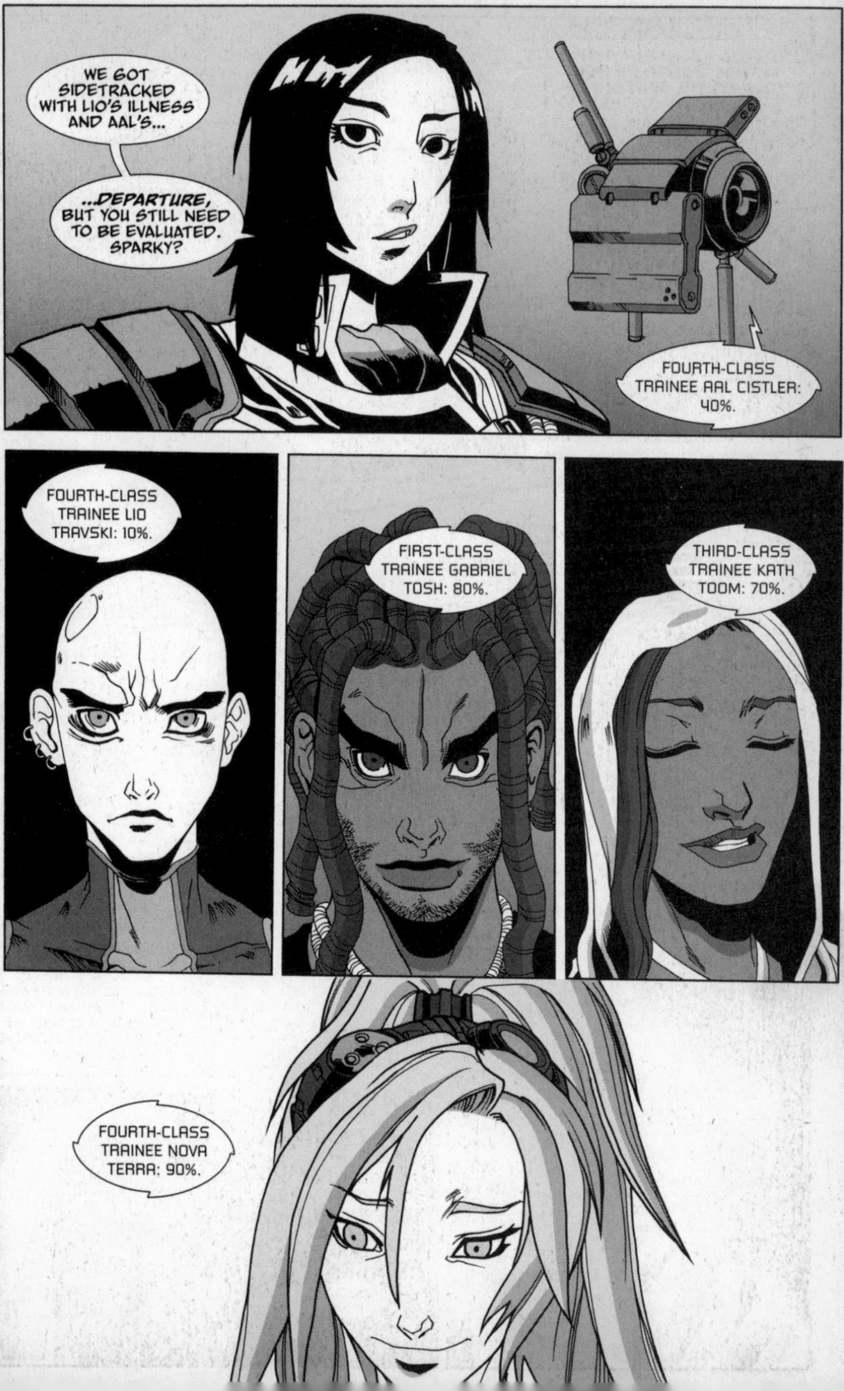
WE GOT SIDETRACKED WITH LIO'S ILLNESS AND AAL'S...
...DEPARTURE, BUT YOU STILL NEED TO BE EVALUATED. SPARKY?
FOURTH-CLASS TRAINEE AAL CISTLER: 40%.
FOURTH-CLASS TRAINEE LIO TRAVSKI: 10%.
FIRST-CLASS TRAINEE GABRIEL TOSH: 80%.
THIRD-CLASS TRAINEE KATH TOOM: 70%.
FOURTH-CLASS TRAINEE NOVA TERRA: 90%.

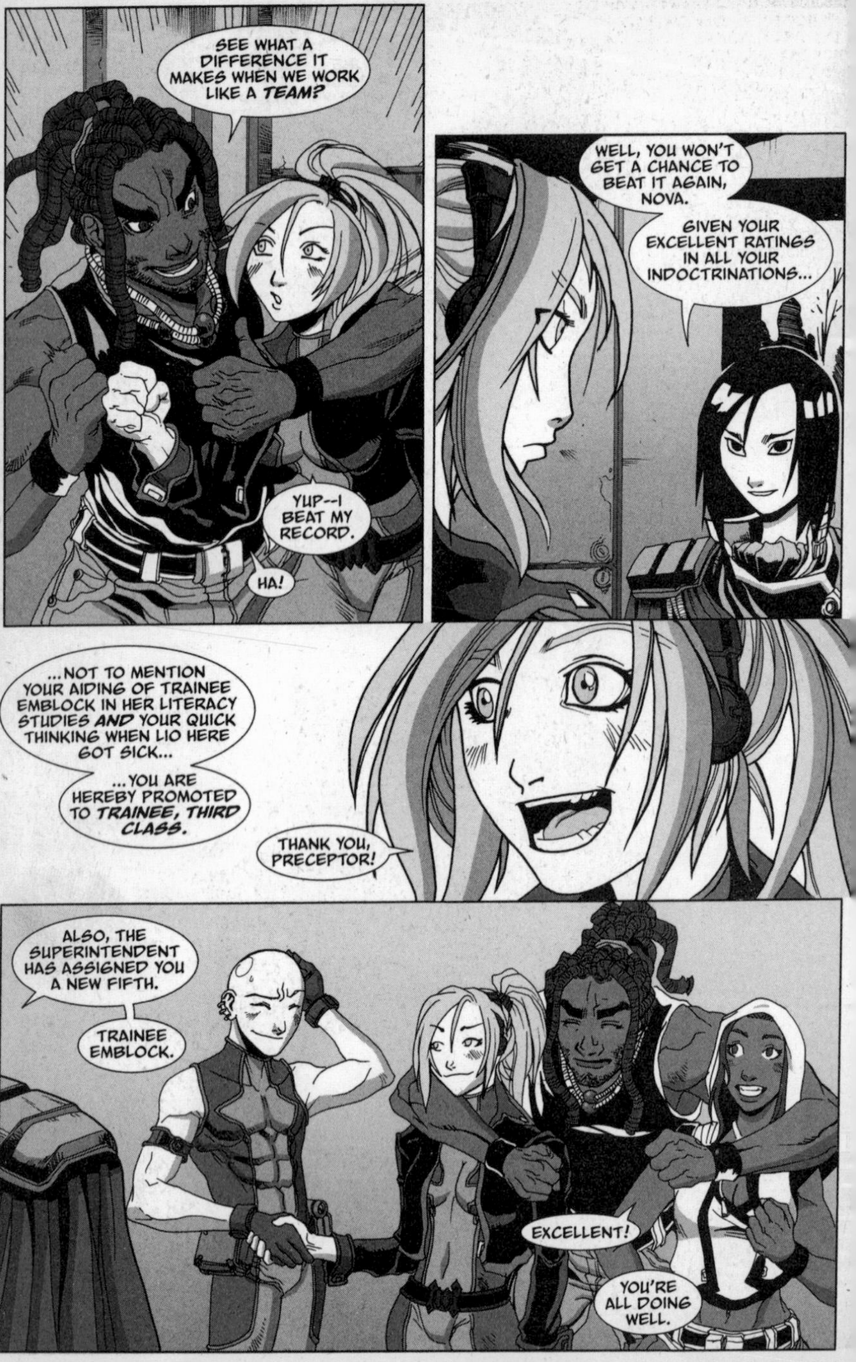
SEE WHAT A DIFFERENCE IT MAKES WHEN WE WORK LIKE A *TEAM?*
YUP--I BEAT MY RECORD.
HA!
WELL, YOU WON'T GET A CHANCE TO BEAT IT AGAIN, NOVA.
GIVEN YOUR EXCELLENT RATINGS IN ALL YOUR INDOCTRINATIONS...
...NOT TO MENTION YOUR AIDING OF TRAINEE EMBLOCK IN HER LITERACY STUDIES ***AND*** YOUR QUICK THINKING WHEN LIO HERE GOT SICK...
...YOU ARE HEREBY PROMOTED TO ***TRAINEE, THIRD CLASS.***
THANK YOU, PRECEPTOR!
ALSO, THE SUPERINTENDENT HAS ASSIGNED YOU A NEW FIFTH.
TRAINEE EMBLOCK.
EXCELLENT!
YOU'RE ALL DOING WELL.

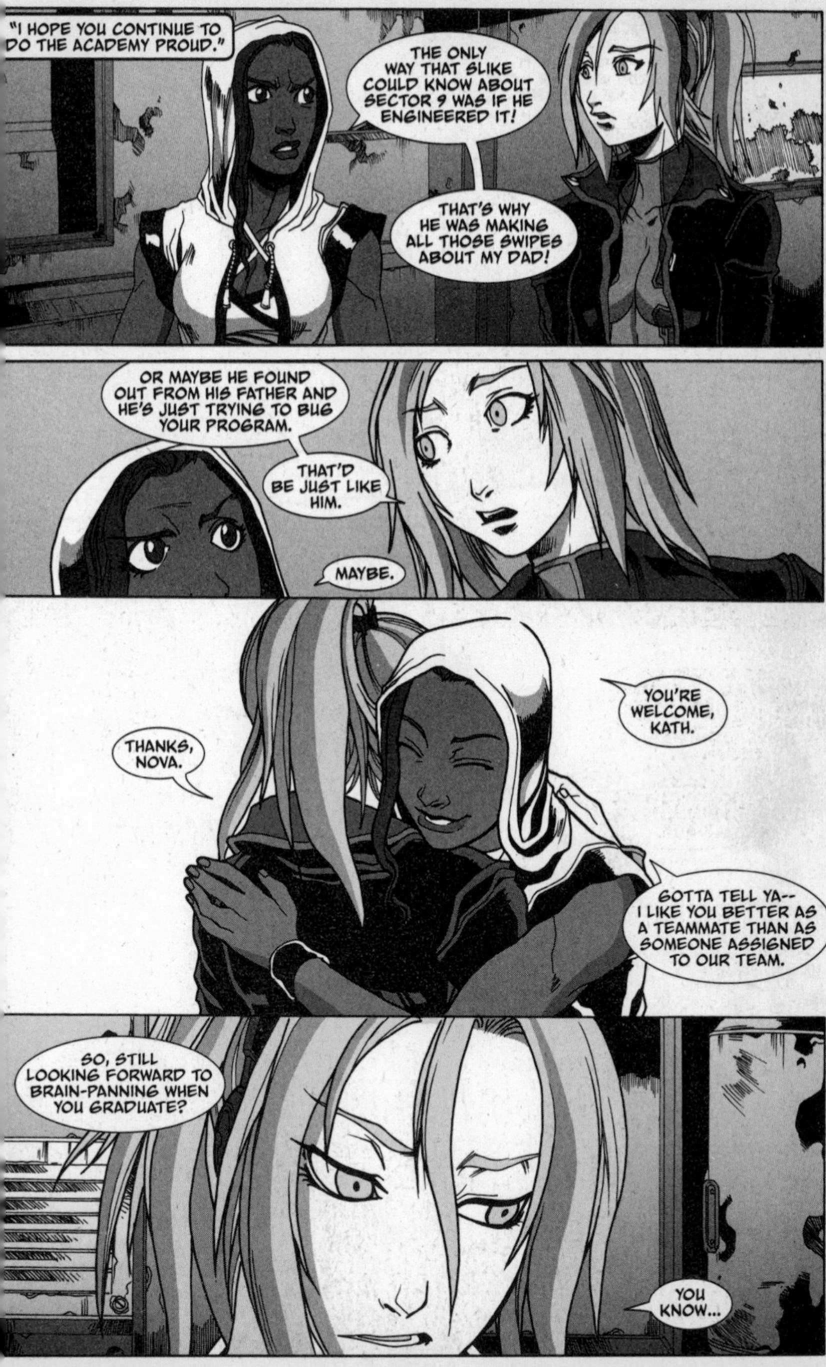
"I HOPE YOU CONTINUE TO DO THE ACADEMY PROUD."
THE ONLY WAY THAT SLIKE COULD KNOW ABOUT SECTOR 9 WAS IF HE ENGINEERED IT!
THAT'S WHY HE WAS MAKING ALL THOSE SWIPES ABOUT MY DAD!
OR MAYBE HE FOUND OUT FROM HIS FATHER AND HE'S JUST TRYING TO BUG YOUR PROGRAM.
THAT'D BE JUST LIKE HIM.
MAYBE.
THANKS, NOVA.
YOU'RE WELCOME, KATH.
GOTTA TELL YA-- I LIKE YOU BETTER AS A TEAMMATE THAN AS SOMEONE ASSIGNED TO OUR TEAM.
SO, STILL LOOKING FORWARD TO BRAIN-PANNING WHEN YOU GRADUATE?
YOU KNOW...

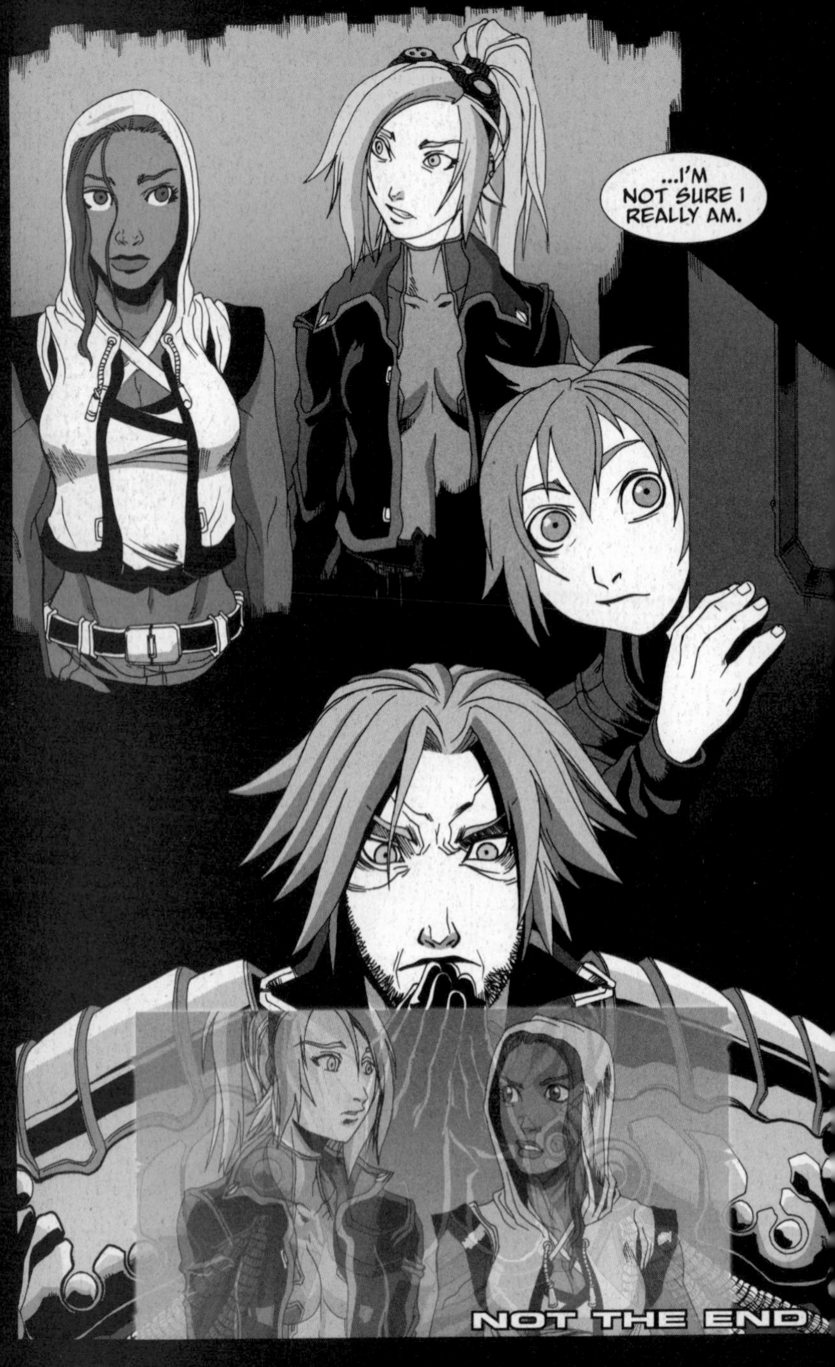
...I'M NOT SURE I REALLY AM.
NOT THE END

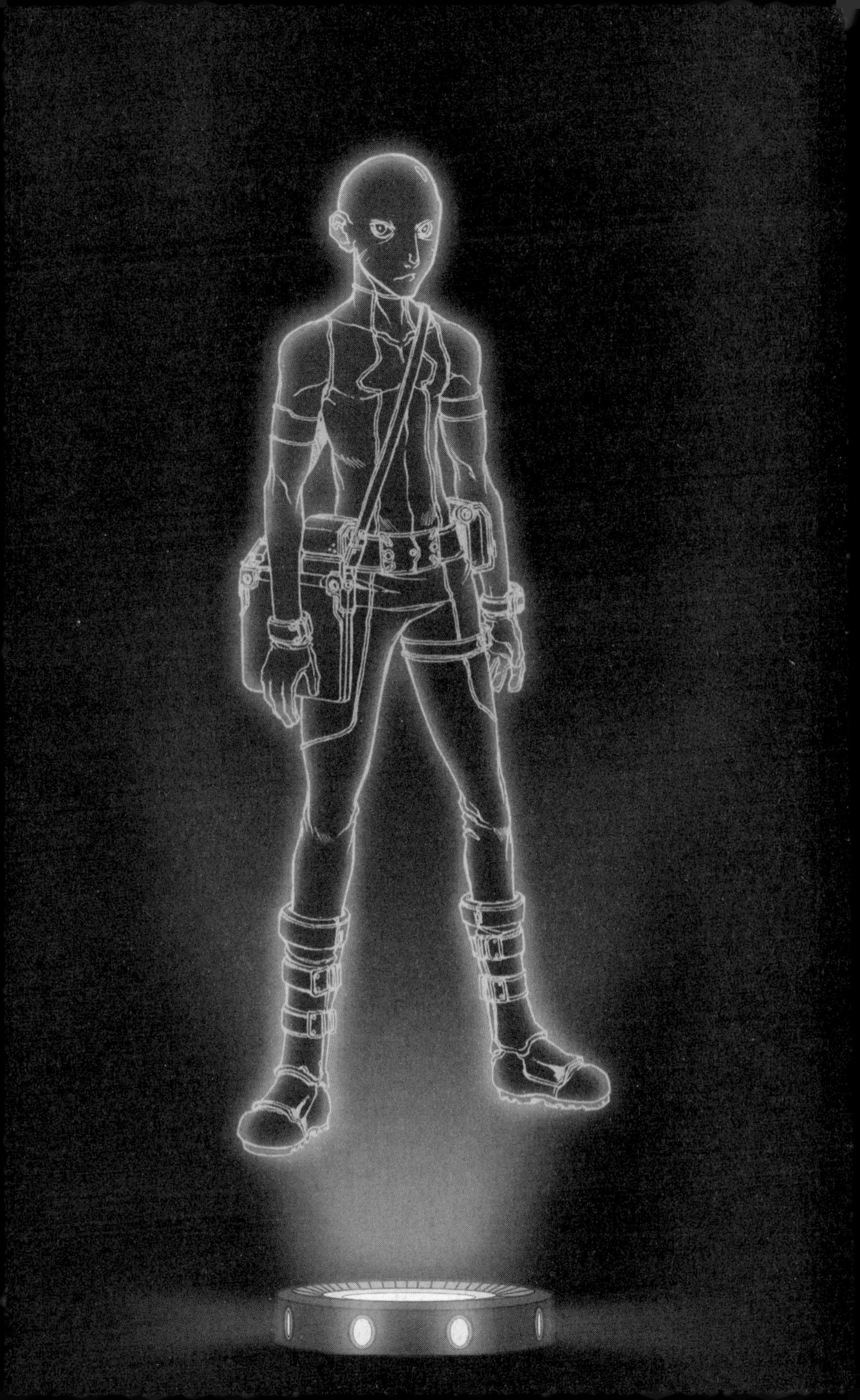

The Administrative Office of the Ghost Academy

Dear Ghost Academy Educators and Staff,

In light of the recent events involving Aal Cistler possessing and distributing the illegal substance hab to another Ghost Academy trainee, the following actions will be taken in the next term:

-Trainee Cistler has been expelled from the Ghost Academy. Any records of trainee Cistler are to be deleted. His team, Team Blue, will be assigned a new fifth member.

-We appreciate your compassion and cooperation as Lio Travski undergoes detox and rehabilitation from the drug hab.

Finally, a friendly reminder: this academy has regulations against romantic relationships. It is the responsibility of the staff to redirect our trainees' adolescent exuberance in productive directions. We cannot afford to have the Dominion's best and brightest engaged in distracting and messy romantic entanglements.

Fondly,

Director Kevin Bick

THANKS FOR PICKING UP
STARCRAFT: GHOST ACADEMY!

StarCraft:Ghost Academy represents the fruition of a bond between TOKYOPOP and Blizzard Entertainment in which ideas flow like wine and the party goes all night long! Well...maybe the partnership resembles a flow of emails and work going into the wee hours of the morning. But hey, you get the idea!

The notion for a series focusing on the Ghost Academy was born at a meeting back in spring 2008, as groundwork for the **StarCraft: Frontline** and **Warcraft: Legends** series was being hammered out. In brainstorming the "what ifs" of the **StarCraft** universe, the concept of going more in-depth with the Ghost Academy appealed to everyone's curiosity.

For those of you who haven't read the **StarCraft: Ghost: Nova** novel, there's a conspicuous gap between ghost prodigy Nova's entrance into and exit from the Ghost Academy. What happened during that time? TOKYOPOP is extremely pleased to finally bring you this lost period of Nova's life. Volume 1 is just the beginning—there are two more volumes hitting stores in the coming year!

This project would not be possible without the thorough and considerable contributions of the Blizzard creative team. I'd like to thank our immediate contacts at Blizzard—Jason Bischoff, Micky Neilson, James Waugh, Rob Tokar, Evelyn Fredericksen and Sean Copeland, as well as Senior Vice President, Creative Development Chris Metzen—for their insightful feedback and excellent suggestions. We're grateful for their input, which represents the creative endeavors of hundreds of other inventive minds at Blizzard.

Last, but not least, thanks to the people who made this book happen—the writer and artists. I'd like to thank Keith R.A. DeCandido for sharing and building upon the world of **Nova**. Fernando Heinz Furukawa—you're solid, stud. You must have gone through ghost training of your own, since you finish pages before anyone even knows you've started. The superhuman efforts of everyone who contributed to the book—and that includes you, Matias Timarchi—are amazing on a level I cannot possibly convey. Whatever ghosts feel upon calling down a nuclear strike, that's what it feels like to direct this team towards a project.

Finally, thanks to my fellow team members at TOKYOPOP: Troy Lewter, who actually oversaw much of the production of the book, and **StarCraft** expert and invaluable layout ninja Michael Paolilli. And, oh yeah, we **did** call for an exterminator. How'd you know?

Hope Donovan
Editor

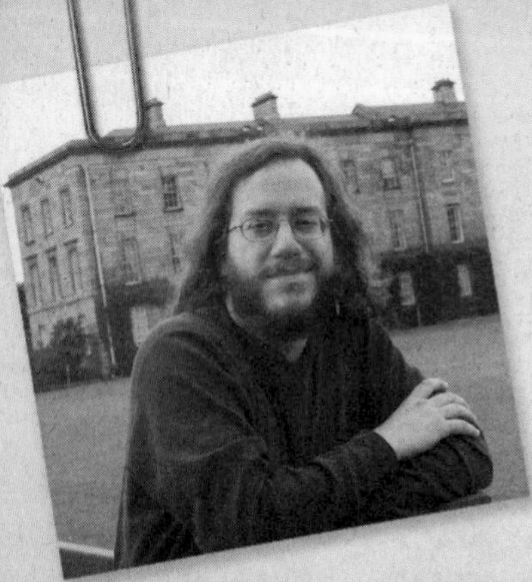

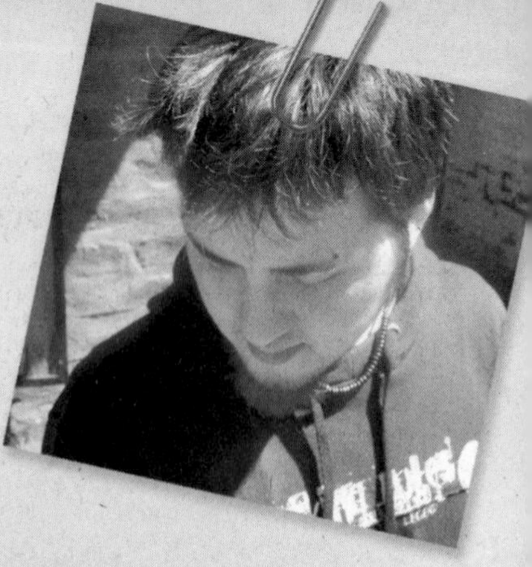

WRITER:
KEITH R.A. DECANDIDO

Keith R.A. DeCandido has also written two ***StarCraft*** novels: ***Nova*** (2006) and ***Spectres*** (forthcoming in 2010), as well as the 2006 ***World of Warcraft*** novel ***Cycle of Hatred.*** Outside of Blizzard Games, Keith has written more than 40 novels, as well as a mess of short stories, eBooks, novellas, comic books, and nonfiction in a wide variety of media universes—among them ***Star Trek*** (most recently the novella "The Unhappy Ones" in ***Seven Deadly Sins), Buffy the Vampire Slayer*** (the novels ***Blackout*** and ***The Deathless***), ***CSI: NY*** (the novel ***Four Walls***), ***Doctor Who*** (the anthologies ***Destination Prague*** and ***The Quality of Leadership), Farscape*** (scripting the monthly comic book in collaboration with series creator Rockne S. O'Bannon), ***Resident Evil*** (the novelizations of all three films), ***Supernatural*** (the novels ***Nevermore, Bone Key,*** and ***Heart of the Dragon***) and more. He is also a longtime editor, having put together a dozen anthologies. In 2009, Keith was generously granted a Lifetime Achievement Award by the International Association of Media Tie-in Writers, which obviously means that he doesn't need to achieve anything ever again. He is also a professional percussionist, currently with the parody band Boogie Knights (www.boogie-knights.org), and a black belt in Kenshikai karate. Find out more at his web site at DeCandido.net or read his inane ramblings at kradical.livejournal.com.

ARTIST:
FERNANDO HEINZ FURUKAWA

Born in Argentina, **Fernando Heinz Furukawa** is the son of a German father and a Japanese mother. Fernando has been drawing since he was a small child and furthered his artistic education under the tutelage of local art professors, Pier Brito and Feliciano Garcia Zecchin. He began his professional artist career at age nineteen and was published in several local magazines. This led to him publishing his own series (along with writer Mauro Mantella and artist Rocio Zucchi) ***TIME: 5***. His recent works include his job as lead artist for an online web series, drawing the TOKYOPOP manga ***Tantric Stripfighter Trina***, and drawing two stories for TOKYOPOP's ***Warcraft: Legends*** anthology series.

CONTRIBUTING PENCILS:

Rocio Zucchi is no stranger to Blizzard and TOKYOPOP. She illustrated the full-length *World of Warcraft: Death Knight,* and inked the story "Crusader's Blood" (*Warcraft: Legends* volume 3). Born in Buenos Aires, Argentina, daughter of an Italian mother and an Argentinian father, she began to draw at a very young age. When she was 13, she met Fernando Heinz Furukawa (her fiancé) who helped her develop her artistic abilities. Rocio has also contributed to *Time: 5* (written by Mauro Mantella, featuring art by Fernando H.F., which will soon be published in the U.S.), *Tantric Stripfighter Trina* (also with Fernando, through TOKYOPOP), the Street Fighter and Darkstalkers Tribute books from Udon Studios, and the webcomic "Heist." She is also a colorist and one of the key members of Altercomics Studios.

INKS:

Walter Gustavo Gomez was born in Buenos Aires in 1979 and became interested in a career in art as a child thanks to TV shows like *Robotech*. After studying sequential art independently, he published his first comic in 1998. Since 2007, he has been a key member of Altercomics Studios, contributing to *Cats on My Head* and *Time 5*. He pencilled a manga story for the nu metal band P.O.D., and he also worked on the manga *Spirit Dancer*. He recently contributed to a number of *Warcraft* and *StarCraft* books for TOKYOPOP, as well as *Tantric Stripfighter Trina*.

CONTRIBUTING INKS:

Fernando Melek (chapters 2,5) was born in 1978 in Tandil, Argentina. He began his professional artistic career in 2004, and has since worked as an illustrator, penciler, colorist and toner in the fields of comics, web comics, covers, calendar illustration, character design, and more. Fernando Melek works for local, national and international publishers. He works well by himself and plays well with others. He's recently contributed to several of TOKYOPOP's *Warcraft* manga.

Gabriel Luque (chapter 1) is a professor of Visual Arts. He self-published the comic *Asesino 55* (Assassin 55) in 2000. In 2003 he created *Japonés en viñetas* (Japanese in Mangaland) for Norma Editorial in Spain, followed by *Japonés en viñetas cuaderno de ejercios 1* (Work Book 1) in 2005. Both books have been reprinted in multiple languages. In 2007, his 100-page manga *Operacion Towertank* was published in Argentina by Editorial Ivrea. He has collaborated as an inker on multiple TOKYOPOP *Warcraft* and *StarCraft* manga.

ASSISTANT INKS:

Gaston Zubeldia (chapters 4,5)

Leandro Rizzo (chapter 4)

Rocio Zucchi (chapter 3)

TONES:

Gonzalo Duarte was born in Buenos Aires in 1986. In 2003, he studied comic illustration at E.A.H. (Argentine School of Comics) under Professor Mariano Navarro, and digital coloring for comics under Professor Hernan Cabrera in 2006. Since 2007 he has been working as a digital colorist, on works such as *Triad* from ECV Press, *Gangland Avalon* from Visionary Comics, and *Primordial Man* from Altercomics Studios. As a toner, he has contributed to several books in TOKYOPOP's *Warcraft* and *StarCraft* lines.

Thanks to Altercomics Studios for contributing such fine artists to *StarCraft: Ghost Academy!*
Check out more of their work at www.altercomics.com.ar.

WORLD OF WARCRAFT

DEATH KNIGHT

PREVIEW

TOKYOPOP and BLIZZARD ENTERTAINMENT proudly present a whole new class of Warcraft manga: *Death Knight!* Written by Dan Jolley (*Warcraft: Legends*) and drawn by Rocio Zucchi, this heartrending epic will give Warcraft fans new insight into the death knight class!

In *World of Warcraft: Wrath of the Lich King,* Thassarian is a renegade death knight, one of the few of his kind to be free of the Lich King's control. Although Thassarian has turned his incredible powers against his former master, he remains feared and despised by most of his Alliance allies. Countless players have aided Thassarian in-game as he battles against the Lich King's agents in Northrend, but few fans know the details of his former life. *Death Knight* is Thassarian's story, a tale that reveals the origins, motivations, and darkest secrets of Warcraft's newest incarnation of death knights.

In the following preview, Thassarian and countless other loyal Lordaeron soldiers have answered Prince Arthas' call to arms to battle the scourge in Northrend. After fighting countless scourge, Thassarian and the battle weary soldiers have been ordered to return to Lordaeron...

World of Warcraft: Death Knight is available in stores now!

TURN THE PAGE FOR AN EXCLUSIVE PREVIEW!

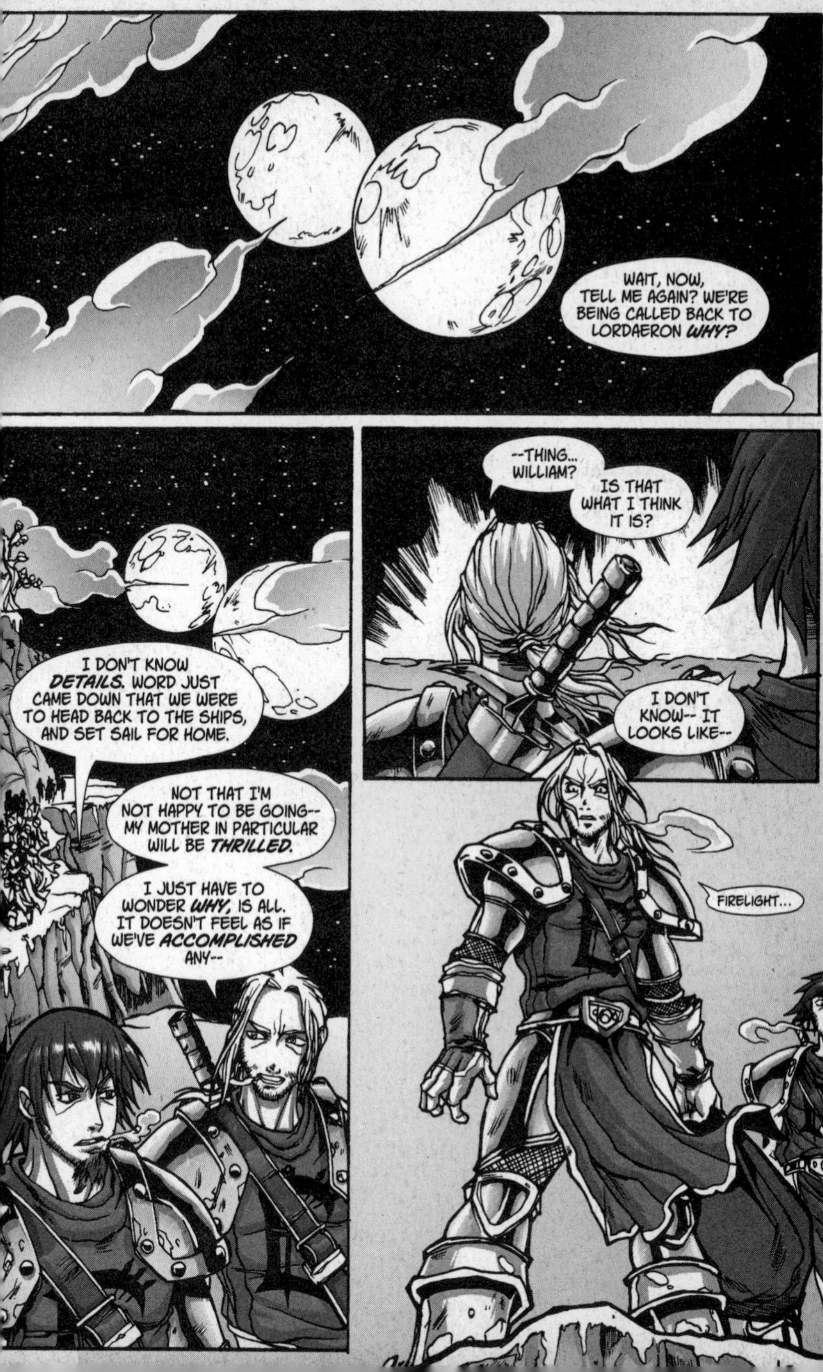
WAIT, NOW, TELL ME AGAIN? WE'RE BEING CALLED BACK TO LORDAERON WHY?
I DON'T KNOW DETAILS. WORD JUST CAME DOWN THAT WE WERE TO HEAD BACK TO THE SHIPS, AND SET SAIL FOR HOME.
NOT THAT I'M NOT HAPPY TO BE GOING-- MY MOTHER IN PARTICULAR WILL BE THRILLED.
I JUST HAVE TO WONDER WHY, IS ALL. IT DOESN'T FEEL AS IF WE'VE ACCOMPLISHED ANY--
--THING... WILLIAM?
IS THAT WHAT I THINK IT IS?
I DON'T KNOW-- IT LOOKS LIKE--
FIRELIGHT...

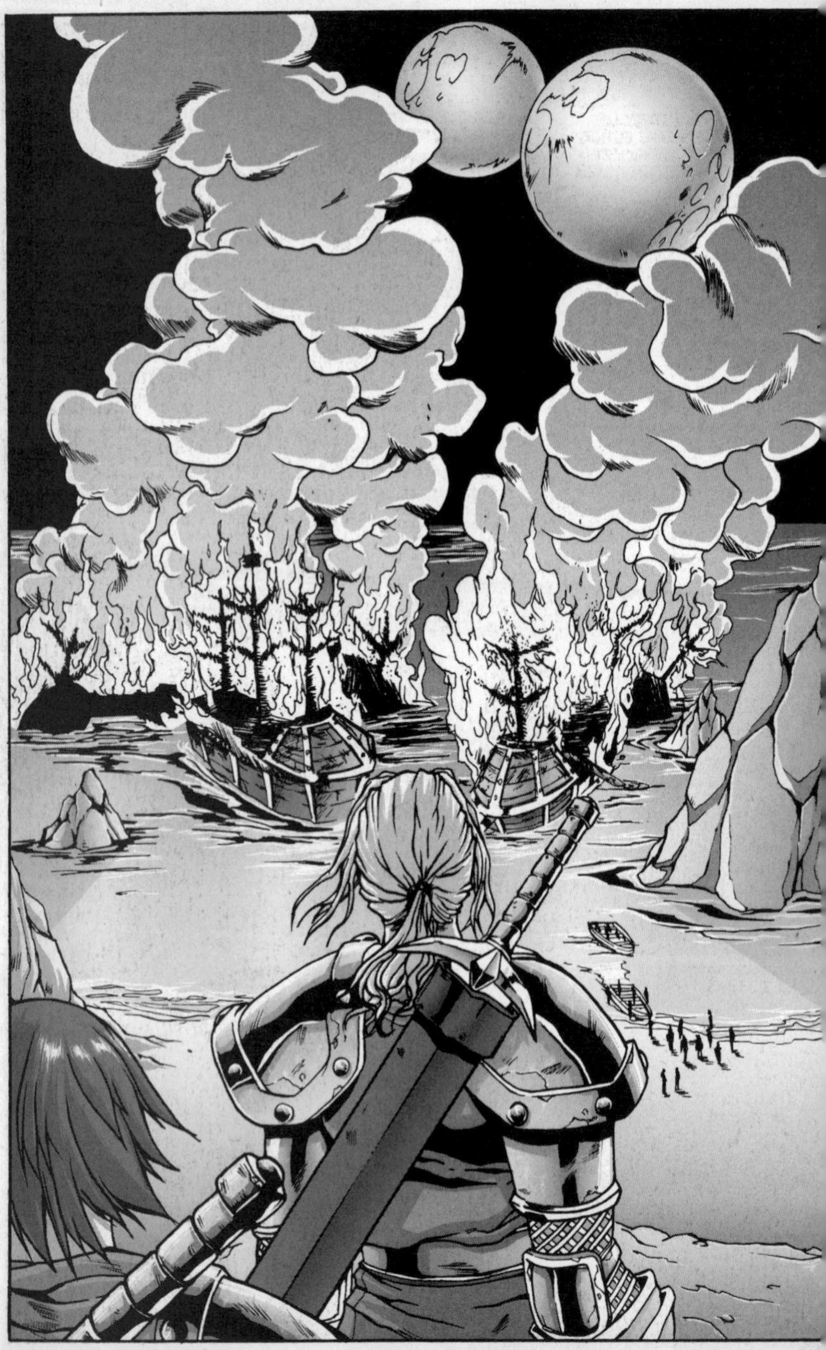

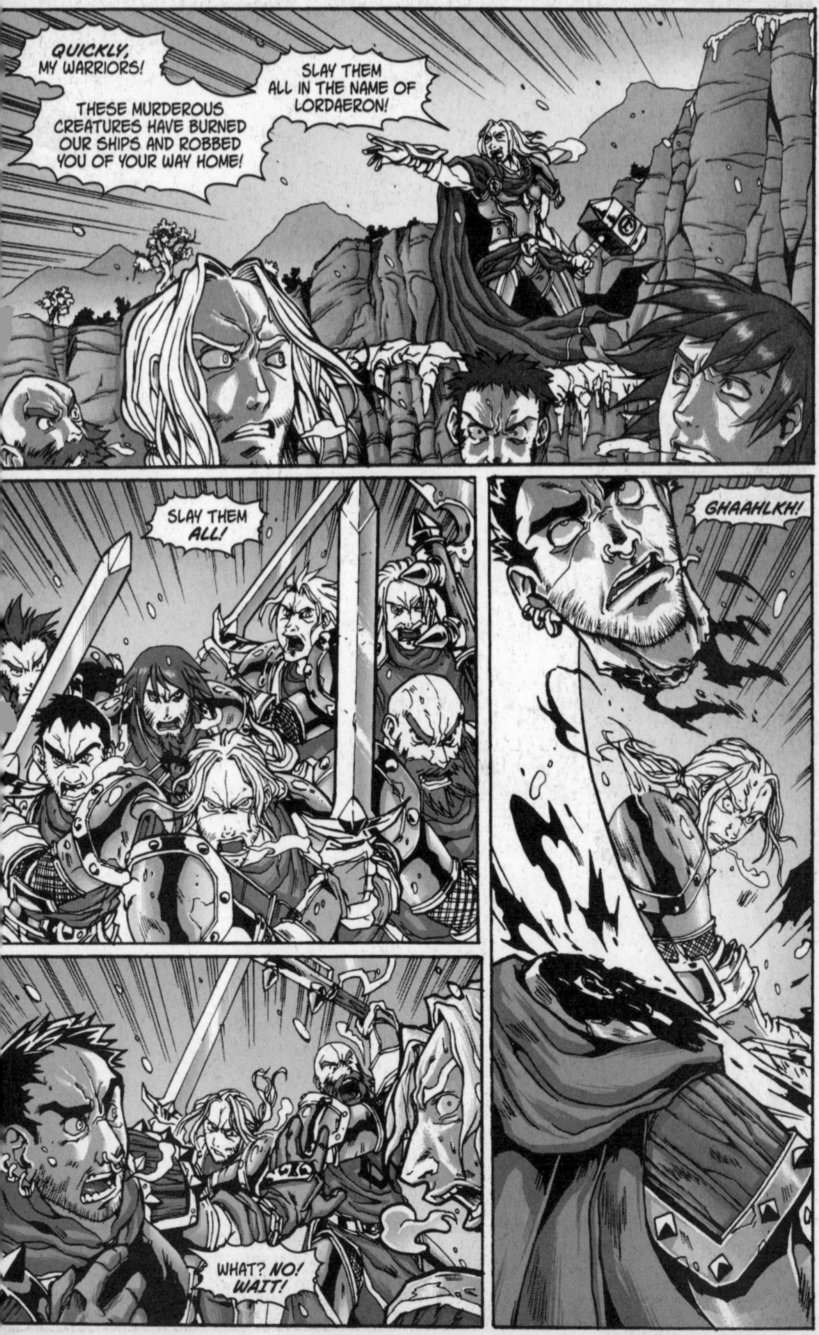
QUICKLY, MY WARRIORS!
THESE MURDEROUS CREATURES HAVE BURNED OUR SHIPS AND ROBBED YOU OF YOUR WAY HOME!
SLAY THEM ALL IN THE NAME OF LORDAERON!
SLAY THEM ALL!
GHAAHLKH!
WHAT? NO! WAIT!

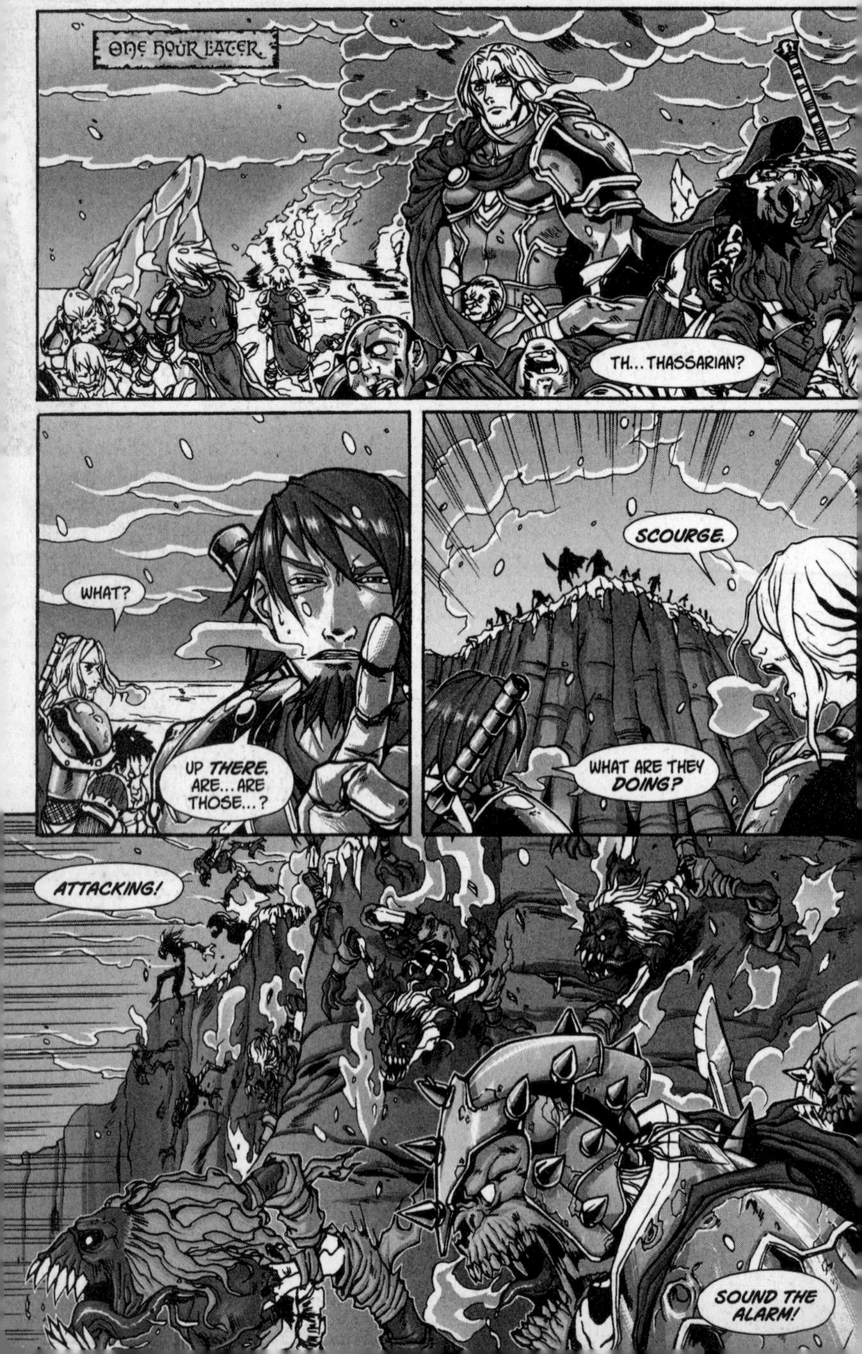
ONE HOUR LATER.
TH... THASSARIAN?
WHAT?
UP THERE. ARE... ARE THOSE...?
SCOURGE.
WHAT ARE THEY DOING?
ATTACKING!
SOUND THE ALARM!

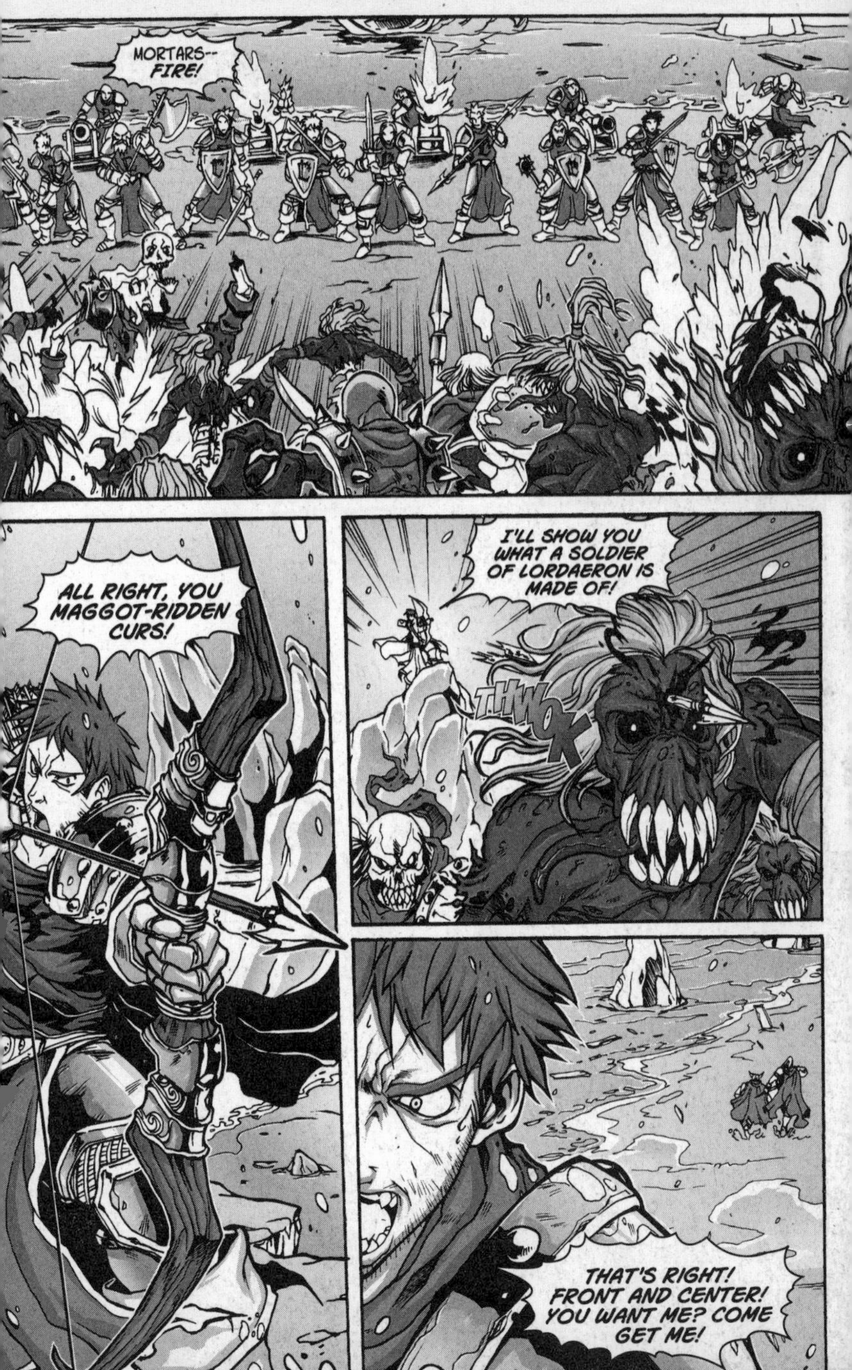
MORTARS-- FIRE!
ALL RIGHT, YOU MAGGOT-RIDDEN CURS!
I'LL SHOW YOU WHAT A SOLDIER OF LORDAERON IS MADE OF!
THWOK
THAT'S RIGHT! FRONT AND CENTER! YOU WANT ME? COME GET ME!

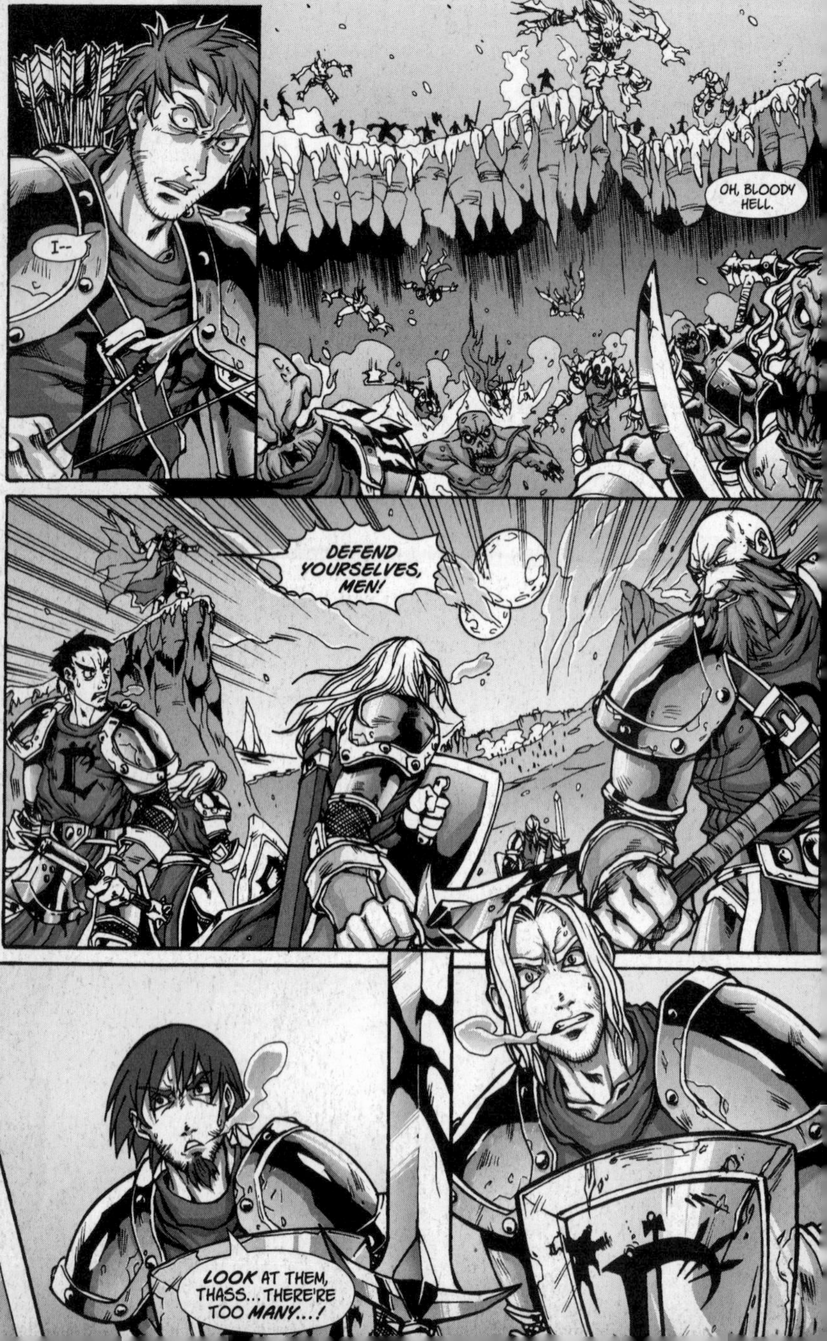
I--
OH, BLOODY HELL.
DEFEND YOURSELVES, MEN!
LOOK AT THEM, THASS... THERE'RE TOO MANY...!

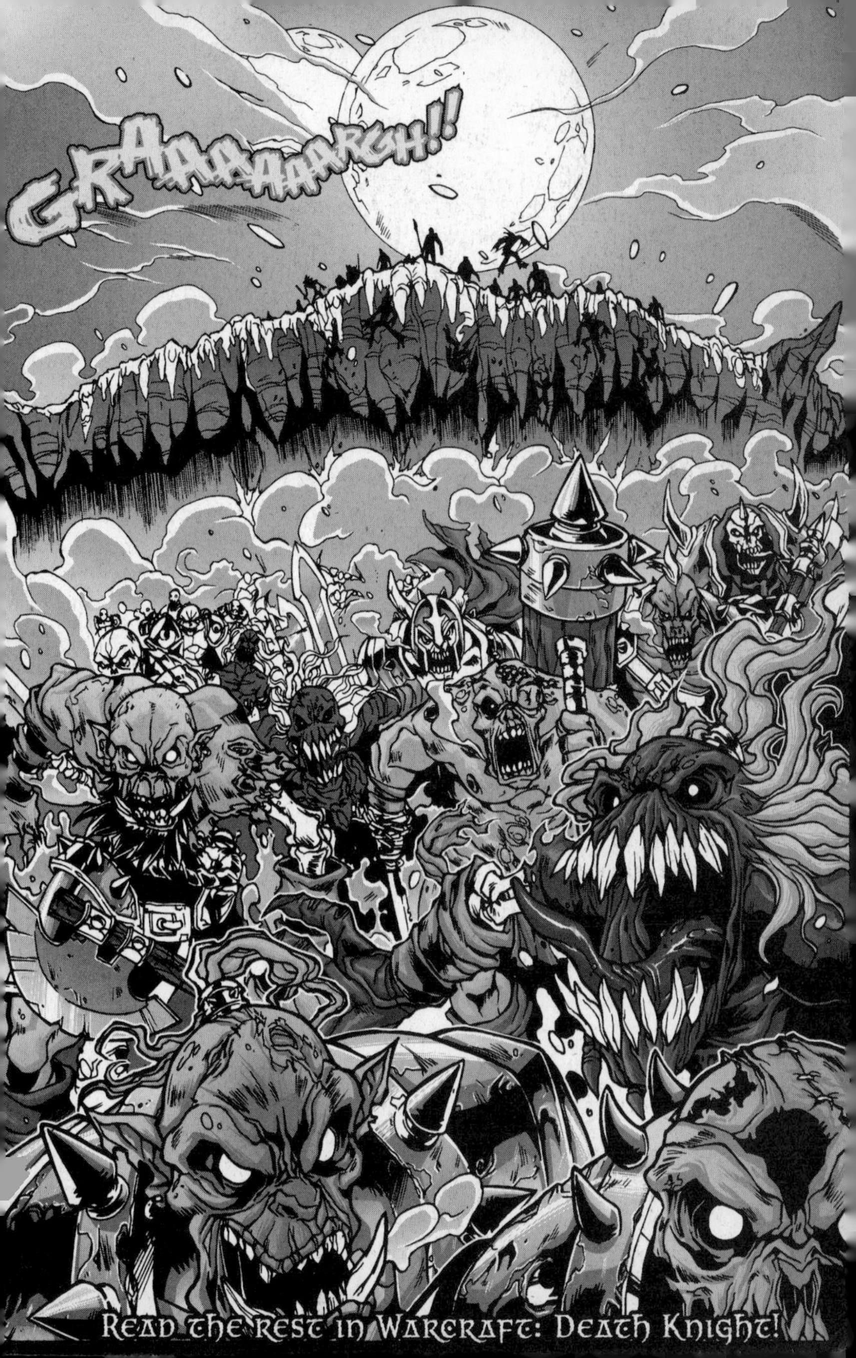
GRAAAAAARGH!!
Read the rest in Warcraft: Death Knight!

Legends Forged Daily

WORLD of WARCRAFT

THE ADVENTURE GAME

Grab your sword, ready your spells, and set off for
adventure in the World of Warcraft! Vanquish diabolical
monsters (as well as your fellow heroes) through intrigue
and in open battle!

Play one of four unique characters, each with their own
abilities and style of play. Ultimately, only one hero can
be the best – will it be you?

FANTASY
FLIGHT
GAMES

LICENSED
BLIZZARD
PRODUCT